Peace Journalism, War
and Conflict Resolution

PETER LANG
New York • Washington, D.C./Baltimore • Bern
Frankfurt • Berlin • Brussels • Vienna • Oxford

Peace Journalism, War *and* Conflict Resolution

EDITED BY
Richard Lance Keeble, John Tulloch, Florian Zollmann

PETER LANG
New York • Washington, D.C./Baltimore • Bern
Frankfurt • Berlin • Brussels • Vienna • Oxford

Library of Congress Cataloging-in-Publication Data

Peace journalism, war and conflict resolution /
edited by Richard Lance Keeble, John Tulloch, Florian Zollmann.
p. cm.
Includes bibliographical references and index.
1. War—Press coverage. 2. Social conflict—Press coverage.
3. Peace—Press coverage. 4. Journalism—Political aspects.
5. Journalistic ethics. 6. Mass media and peace.
I. Keeble, Richard. II. Tulloch, John. III. Zollman, Florian.
PN4784.W37P45   070.44'930366--dc22   2009045810
ISBN 978-1-4331-0725-2 (hardcover)
ISBN 978-1-4331-0726-9 (paperback)

Bibliographic information published by **Die Deutsche Nationalbibliothek.**
Die Deutsche Nationalbibliothek lists this publication in the "Deutsche
Nationalbibliografie"; detailed bibliographic data is available
on the Internet at http://dnb.d-nb.de/.

The paper in this book meets the guidelines for permanence and durability
of the Committee on Production Guidelines for Book Longevity
of the Council of Library Resources.

© 2010 Peter Lang Publishing, Inc., New York
29 Broadway, 18th floor, New York, NY 10006
www.peterlang.com

Printed in the United States of America

Contents

Section 2. Peace (or conflict sensitive) journalism: Theory and practice in an international context

Section 3. Peace journalism's critique: transforming the mainstream

Foreword

JOHN PILGER

War and mayhem happen; peace is utopian. Many journalists believe such an assumption immutable. I did. But the more I investigated causes, the clearer it became that so-called mainstream journalism was committed almost exclusively to the interests of power, not people. There is no conspiracy; since the demise of the great crusading editors, such as John Delane, Edward Smith Hall and Hugh Cudlipp, and the rise of corporate "professional journalism", the media has become the managerial arm of the established order, no matter its preferred disguise as a "fourth estate" and honourable exceptions. Turn the pages of any major newspaper, watch or listen to the evening broadcast news, and be assured that news and opinion come from the top, however circuitous, almost never from the bottom.

In his chapter in the following collection, "Normalising the unthinkable: The media's role in mass killing", David Edwards relates one of his now famous exchanges on medialens.org with Helen Boaden, the BBC's director of news. "To deal first with your suggestion that it is factually incorrect to say that an aim of the British and American coalition [in Iraq] was to bring democracy and human rights," she wrote, "this was, indeed, one of the stated aims before and at the start of the Iraq war and I attach a number of quotes at the bottom of this reply."

Whereupon Boaden supplied, as Edwards describes, "no less than 2,700 words filling six pages of A4 paper of quotations from George Bush and Tony Blair".

I can think of no other admission as demonstrable of a war propaganda role. To Boaden, the proven lies of Bush and Blair, to borrow from Harold Pinter, did not happen even when they were happening; they did not matter; they were of no concern. That her rationale was apparently unconscious merely confirmed rapacious power's grip on media orthodoxy. The war journalism she defended is, in principle, pretty much that of the *Sun*; only the presentation is different.

This happens at a time when British parliamentary democracy has been appropriated by reinvigorated militarism: witness the refusal of MPs to vote on the invasion of Iraq and the standing ovation they gave the warlord Blair when he departed the House of Commons. This is an historic shift, with the main parties now pursuing almost identical foreign as well as domestic policies. The media's role is to present the fiction of difference and democracy and the bloody invasion of countries as "humanitarian" enterprises, acts of altruism whose victims are "us". Mark the manipulative TV images of the flag-wrapped coffins of 18-year-old soldiers being borne through a Wiltshire high street, accompanied by commentary about "Britain's resolve to see this through". In fact, the majority of Britons oppose the current wars, just as a majority regarded Blair as a liar. The journalism of people speaks for this disenfranchised majority.

Looking back, this "peace journalism" has a remarkable if unacknowledged record. During the twentieth century's longest war, in Vietnam, the mainstream media promoted, at best, the myth of America's aggression as an honourable "blunder" that became a "quagmire". This allowed Ronald Reagan to renew the same "noble cause", as he called it, in Central America. The target, once again, was an impoverished nation without resources, Nicaragua, whose threat, like Vietnam, was in trying to establish a model of development different from that of the corrupt colonial dictatorships backed by Washington.

I reported Reagan's wars from Nicaragua, El Salvador and the United States. War journalism so framed the mainstream coverage in the US that liberal newspapers, such as *The New York Times* and the *Washington Post*, actually debated whether or not the Sandinistas by their proximity somewhere south of the border represented a "threat". Truthful or peace journalism countered this by exposing the "secret" and bloody campaign by the CIA to subvert the government in Managua and to make war on the populations of El Salvador and Guatemala via armed and bribed proxies.

Are the wars in Afghanistan and Iraq different? Yes, but there are haunting similarities. Read again Helen Boaden's response to David Edwards and you have an echo of Reagan's "noble cause" of "bringing democracy to others less fortunate". And yet Reagan was responsible not only for the killing of countless thousands throughout Latin America but also for the creation of a force of mujihadeen, who drove the Soviet Union out of Afghanistan and whose drug lords were as far from democracy's embrace as it was possible to be. War journalism made them into heroes. Truthful or peace journalism traced Reagan's war to an inevitable "blow-back", which happened on 11 September 2001.

Today, liberal war journalism promotes the myth of Barack Obama, whose siren call of "change" ensures the status quo and muffles the opponents of war. "From Europe to the Pacific," said Obama in May 2009, "we've been the nation that has shut down torture cha---mbers and replaced tyranny with the rule of law." As William Blum has documented, since 1945, the United States has overthrown fifty governments, including democracies, and crushed some 30 liberation movements, and set up torture chambers from Egypt to Guatemala. War journalism reports what power says it does; peace journalism reports what it does.

This anthology of essays from those who study peace journalism in the international academy is a landmark work. Led by the pioneers of Lincoln University, it challenges war journalism's right to occupy the mainstream, suggesting that those who propagate the profanities of war, no matter their euphemisms, ought to occupy the craft's and humanity's margins until they are finally made redundant.

Introduction: Why peace journalism matters

RICHARD LANCE KEEBLE, JOHN TULLOCH AND
FLORIAN ZOLLMANN

According to the most recent authoritative source, the Stockholm International Peace Research Institute's annual report for 2008, world military spending by 2007 had reached $1.2 trillion.[1] This represented a 6 per cent increase in real terms over the previous year and a 45 per cent increase over the ten-year period since 1998. The United States, responsible for around 80 per cent of the increase in 2005, accounts for some 45 per cent of the world total, distantly followed by the United Kingdom, China, France and Japan each with 4 to 5 per cent of the world share.

American military spending for 2009 was expected to account for 44.4 per cent of federal budget funds ($1,066 billion), with the annual intelligence budget amounting to around $30 billion (Woodward 2004). At the same time, just $284 billion (11.8 per cent) was being directed at projects to eliminate poverty and $52 billion (just 2.2 per cent) to education and jobs.

In the UK, almost 13 million people live in poverty: that's one in five of the population, according to the charity Oxfam.[2] Yet the latest Ministry of Defence figures show around £32 billion is spent annually on the military. Planned expenditure on military equipment alone over the next 30 years stands at £235 billion – with £2.5 billion wasted every year on outdated projects (Norton-Taylor 2009).[3] As the environmental activist and journalist George Monbiot commented, the Department for International Development could be funded twice over just from the MoD's budget for capital charges and depreciation (£9.6 billion) (Monbiot 2009). Globally almost 1 billion people are estimated to be living in poverty (Rizvi 2008).

The United Nations defines "major wars" as military conflicts involving at least 1,000 battlefield casualties each year. In mid-2009, there were at least eight major wars under way, with as many as two dozen "lesser" conflicts ongoing.[4] At the same time, millions of people around the world are confronting abuses of human rights, environmental degradation, violence and repression with courage, imagination and non-violent resistance (see Carter, Clark and Randle 2006).

These are bald, impersonal statistics – but they highlight the wider, political and social context in which this book appears. Indeed, in a world where the priorities of governments appear so misguided in the face of such glaring disparities of wealth (both material and cultural) and privilege and potential environmental catastrophe, are there any more pressing issues than those that surround war and peace – and the media coverage of them?

The emergence of the notion of peace journalism

And yet, while the study of wars and the media coverage of conflict – which we might term war journalism – has been well advanced within the academy for many years, the study of peace journalism has emerged only recently. During the 1970s, peace researchers, activists and academics began to develop the premises underlying the notion of peace journalism (Shinar and Kempf 2007: 9). But the seminal theoretical study was conducted by Johan Galtung (see Lynch 1998: 44), one of the founders of the academic subject of Peace Studies, who essentially contrasted the elements of what he described as "peace/conflict journalism" with those of "war/violence journalism" (in other words, the dominant mode of covering conflict in the mainstream media).

Thus peace journalism "gave a voice to all parties", focused on the invisible effects of violence (trauma and glory, damage to social structures), aimed to "expose untruths on all sides", was "people-oriented", gave "a voice to the voiceless" and was solution-oriented. On the other hand, war journalism dehumanised the enemy, focused on only the visible effects of the violence, was propaganda-oriented, elite-focused and victory-oriented, and tended to concentrate on institutions (the "controlled society").

From these beginnings, a considerable body of work examining the actual or potential role of the media in promoting conflict resolution rather than war and violence has emerged (see Ross 2007). Amongst these, one of the most important was Jake Lynch and Annabel McGoldrick's *Peace journalism* (2005). Significantly many of the contributors to this text refer to it. Lynch and McGoldrick suggest peace journalism is when:

> ... editors and reporters make choices – of what stories to report and about how to report them – that create opportunities for society at large to consider and value non-violent responses to conflict. Moreover it:
>
> - uses the insights of conflict analysis and transformation to update the concepts of balance, fairness and accuracy in reporting;
> - provides a new route map tracing the connections between journalists, their sources, the stories they cover and the consequences of their journalism – the ethics of journalistic intervention;
> - builds an awareness of non-violence and creativity into the practical job of every-day editing and reporting (ibid: 5).

In addition, they offer a 17-point plan for practising peace journalism (ibid: 28–31) which includes:

- Avoid concentrating always on what divides parties, on the differences between what each say they want. Instead, try asking questions which may reveal areas of common ground.
- Avoid focusing exclusively on the suffering, fears and grievances of only one party ... Instead, treat as equally newsworthy the suffering, fears and grievances of all parties.
- Avoid "victimising" language like "devastated", "defenceless", "pathetic", "tragedy" which only tells us what has been done to and could be done for a group of people by others. This is disempowering and limits the options for change. Instead, report on what has been done and could be done by the people.
- Avoid focusing exclusively on the human rights abuses, misdemeanours and wrongdoings of only one side. Instead, try to name all wrong-doers and treat allegations made by all parties in a conflict equally seriously.

Dov Shinar and Wilhelm Kempf's *Peace journalism: The state of the art* (2007) is important for drawing together some of the major writings on the field. In a concluding chapter, Dov Shinar (ibid: 199–210) suggests that peace journalism does not necessarily mean "good news"; rather it is conceived as "a fairer way to cover conflict, relative to the usual coverage and suggests possibilities to improve professional attitudes and performance; strengthen human, moral and ethical values in the media; widen scholarly and professional media horizons and provide better public service by the media" (ibid: 200).

Shifting the focus

Peace journalism, war and conflict resolution now builds on the theoretical and methodological foundations within these seminal texts but expands the focus to new and significant fields. The first section of the book features an eclectic and contrasting range of approaches, often marginalised in both the mainstream and alternative media debates.

Clifford G. Christians is considered the world's leading authority on communication ethics and in his opening chapter draws on the insights of philosophical anthropology with its stress on the "relational self" (as opposed the liberal "individualistic self") and of social philosophy with its stress on dialogic communication (rather than monologic transmission between discrete individuals) to promote a notion of peace communication. Christians' emphasis on spirituality also highlights an essential role of communication as uncovering the significance in life. "It recognises that our important threat is not physical survival but the uncanny. The ultimate menace occurs when lingual systems start disintegrating."

Debating Herman and Chomsky's propaganda model

One of the major inspirations for peace movement media activists worldwide has been the writings of the American maverick intellectual Noam Chomsky – and in particular those he drew up with his colleague Edward Herman on the propaganda model (PM) (see Herman and Chomsky 1988). Accordingly, the mainstream media are seen as operating primarily as propaganda instruments of dominant economic, political, social, cultural and military interests. Chris Atton (2003: 27), in exploring the ethics of the alternative media, suggests that the works of Chomsky (and Edward Said) are constantly cited in alternative media as the seminal demystifiers of corporate media notions of "objectivity".

Here Oliver Boyd Barrett acknowledges that the PM is useful for showing how the corporate media produce a supply of news and views that fits comfortably within the limits acceptable to power elites. At the same Boyd Barrett joins with Robert A Hackett (2007: 75–96) in criticising the PM for saying little about the mechanisms of propaganda in the text itself. But he is more concerned here to critique the PM for prioritising a *systemic* explanation of media performance, thus downgrading the question of *agency*. In particular, Boyd-Barrett, argues that it is impossible to ignore the links between corporate journalists and the intelligence services and other arms of the "secret state" when analysing the coverage of war and peace. Focusing on three case studies – of William Laurence, Judith Miller and Michael Gordon – he concludes:

> Unless the significance of these operations are factored centrally into peace journalism theory and media theory more generally, Western scholars may be doomed to a pluralist "deficit" model of the press, one that assumes that if only there was some tinkering here and there then the press could at last fully serve its purported roles of watchdog, fourth estate and public sphere.

Richard Lance Keeble similarly critiques peace journalism theory that emphasises professional responses arguing that journalism is best seen as *political* practice. According to Keeble "a dominant strand in PJ theory focuses too closely on the notion of journalism as a privileged, professional activity and fails to take into account the critical intellectual tradition which locates professions historically and politically, seeing them as essentially occupational groupings with a legal monopoly of social and economic opportunities in the marketplace, underwritten by the state".

He joins John Hartley (2008) in calling for a radical transformation of journalism theory. We need to move away from the concept of the audience as a passive consumer of a professional product to seeing the audience as producers of their own (written or visual) media. This leads Keeble to highlight the peace journalism of the alternative media both historically and globally and to extend the definition of "journalist" beyond the ranks of the professionals to radical media activists, intellectuals and human rights campaigners.

In his chapter, Jake Lynch synthesises critically a range of propaganda theories (e.g Ellul 1965; Luostarinen 1994; Nohrstedt and Ottosen 2000), focusing in particular on the reporting of the Nato attacks on Kosovo of 1999 and the US/UK invasion of Iraq in 2003. He draws, in particular, on Marianne Perez's exploration (2006) of George Lakoff's theory (2004) that two competing frames govern the conduct of US politics: the "nurturant parent" and the "strict father". Lynch concludes that the logic of peace journalism is "to adumbrate a strategy covering both structure and agency to increase the plenitude of cues and clues for readers and audiences to form their own negotiated or oppositional readings of appeals to support collective violence of one kind or another".

Peace journalism theory and practice in an international context

The second section examines peace journalism theory and practice in an international context. Jake Lynch and Annabel McGoldrick propose a strikingly original transnational research exercise to identify psychological responses, firstly to examples of war journalism – and then to these same reports adjusted to peace journalism framings. The aim, they say, would be to identify thresholds at which war journalism can be confidently pronounced harmful to its consumers, and peace journalism, psychologically beneficial, thereby directly informing the global standard.

Agneta Söderberg Jacobson draws on her experience in the Kvinna till Kvinna Foundation in lobbying rank and file journalists and editors in Sweden to adopt the principles of peace journalism. In addition, the foundation works with women's groups in many conflict-ridden countries – such as in the Balkans, South Caucasus and the Middle East. The promotion of women – both as journalists and subjects of journalism – has to be at the heart of peace journalism, she argues. Even the dominant peace journalism model fails to incorporate adequately a gender perspective. Jacobson thus proposes the addition of the opposing factors of gender blindness and gender awareness to Lynch and McGoldrick's model of the contrasting aspects of war journalism and peace journalism (2005: 6). Making the gender analysis more explicit "would surely make the model more attractive to women journalists and to feminists in general (including men)".

Valerie Alia, in her chapter, explores the ways in which Indigenous peoples around the globe are engaged in a collaborative project that is forging new ways of communicating, and new ways of preventing, mediating and resolving conflicts. In particular, she examines developments in Australia, Greenland, Canada, the United States and Japan. Alia writes of the "guerrilla" or "outlaw" roots of much of Indigenous journalism and she notes, optimistically, that the media guerrillas and outlaws are increasingly coming aboveground and publicising their views and work to an ever-growing global audience.

In contrast to Alia's focus on Indigenous peoples, Florian Zollmann next spotlights the journalism of the American independent journalist Dahr Jamail. Initially reporting from Iraq as a blogger and travel writer, Jamail's distinctive journalism was rapidly recognised and published by various independent and mainstream news organisations. Concentrating on the US attacks on Fallujah, Iraq, in November 2004, Zollmann compares Jamail's reporting with the corporate media's coverage. And through a close textual analysis, he argues that Jamail encapsulates the principles of peace journalism as outlined by Lynch and McGoldrick in their seminal text (op cit). For instance, Jamail focuses on causes, outcomes and the aftermath of the conflict and reveals the effects of violence as well as the suffering of ordinary people. The experiences and views of ordinary Iraqis caught up in the appalling violence of the occupation lie at the heart of Jamail's reporting. Statements by government officials and the military are weighed against these personal testimonies and, contrary to mainstream media practices, do not make up the major frameworks for journalistic understanding. Moreover, unlike embedded reporters, Jamail does not concentrate on the strategic progress of what is labeled as "warfare". Instead, he documents the progressive destructiveness of what could rather be described as "high-tech barbarism".

On the potential of web-based activism

Shifting the focus to India, television producer and academic Pratap Rughani reflects on his own photographic representation of atrocity, drawing on Susan Sontag's critique of Holocaust photography as in general "re-victimising the victim". Rughani also highlights the potential of web-based activism in the digital age and how this historical moment can throw up new opportunities for marginalised peoples.

Continuing the theme of web-based witnessing, Donald Matheson and Stuart Allan next assess a range of ways in which war journalism is being rearticulated by social networks such as YouTube and Flickr, personal media such as blogs and Twitter, social sites such as Facebook and virtual worlds such as Second Life, as well as networks enabled over cell phones. Their case studies look at the Mumbai attacks of 26 November 2008, the Greek street protests in December 2008, the Israeli assault on Gaza in the same month and the Sri Lanka government's final push against the Tamil Tiger rebels in late 2008 and early 2009. In the process Matheson and Allan show how individualised media often intersect with professional and mass media in significant ways as the recording of conflict moves to the level of the interpersonal. As a result, the familiar "culture of distance" engendered by Western journalism's mediation of witnessing is thrown into sharp relief, with the stress on the suffering – as well as the aspirations for peace – of many of those caught-up in the atrocity resonating in social media sites.

Two journalists next outline their very different ways of promoting peace journalism. First Jean Lee C. Patindol draws on her experience of building up a peace journalists' network in the Philippines. Because the very notion of "peace" is controversial in her country (often being associated, for instance, with leftist/ communist groups) journalists there often find the notion of "peace journalism" confusing – and thus it is abandoned in favour of "conflict-sensitive reporting" (as promoted by Ross Howard, 2003).

In contrast, the author, journalist and political activist Milan Rai directs his spotlight on the London-based *Peace News*, which he jointly edits. After outlining its history and placing it firmly within the tradition of the alternative, radical, dissenting press of the early part of the 19th century, Rai argues that his journal captures many of the principles of peace journalism (see Lynch and McGoldrick op cit). For instance, it illuminates "issues of structural and cultural violence, as they bear upon the lives of people in a conflict arena, as part of the explanation for violence"; it frames "conflicts as consisting of many parties, pursuing many goals"; makes "peace initiatives and images of solutions more visible, whoever suggests them"; and aims to equip citizens "to distinguish between stated positions, and real goals, when judging whether particular forms of intervention are necessary or desirable" (op cit 28–31). Making the peace initiatives of the Afghan Taliban and of the Iranian government "more visible" were particular priorities in *Peace News* in late 2009.

But Rai also writes that "*Peace News* has functioned in many ways outside the framework of Lynch-McGoldrick-style peace journalism". For instance, *PN* has not always obeyed the injunction to look at "how shared problems and issues are leading to consequences that all the parties say they never intended", rather than assigning blame. In many conflict situations, *Peace News* has found it appropriate, and indeed necessary, to "assign blame", and to identify (and criticise) the hidden objectives that lie behind the rhetoric of "unintended consequences".

Sociologist Sarah Maltby adds a completely new dimension to the debate over peace and conflict journalism, examining the ways in which the military have used local radio in the Balkans and Afghanistan during peace building and conflict resolution operations. She argues that these activities (while they cannot be considered as "peace journalism") are positioned in terms resonant with some of the key principles of peace journalism, namely: a commitment to providing a voice to the voiceless; a promotion of peace through open dialogue and an orientation to solution. Moreover, Maltby argues that the military's self proclaimed orientation to "peace" in radio stations such as Oksigen and Rana FM raises some interesting questions about the use of discourses of peace and empowerment to legitimate military practices which, at times, appear to be culturally naïve.

Critiquing (and transforming) the mainstream

The final section carries a series of case studies which build on the major strand of peace journalism theory and practice – critiquing mainstream news values and myths of "balance" and "objectivity". Susan Dente Ross and Sevda Alankus, in examining the press coverage of the 2008 election of a new president in the (Greek) Republic of Cyprus and the subsequent bilateral initiatives towards settlement of "the Cyprus problem", examine the way in which the corporate media's obsession with national histories perpetuates the primacy of national identity and the status quo in opposition to those "outside" its borders.

Marlis Prinzing, in contrast, outlines, critically, an ambitious project in which journalists and communication researchers in Germany are not simply critiquing the mainstream but supplying radio, magazines, newspapers, authors and the designers of school curricular materials with features and photographic essays inspired by peace journalism theories.

In a detailed historical, textual analysis, John Tulloch examines the corporate media's reporting of conscientious objectors at the start of the Second World War. Conscientious objectors (COs) – not all of whom, of course, were pacifists – were then four times more numerous than during World War One and thus, while they were marginalised in the media, they could not be entirely ignored. Often they were represented as pantomime eccentrics or shirkers. Focusing, in particular, on the mass-selling *Daily Mirror*, Tulloch concludes that loud trumpeting of human rights in leader columns, intertwined with jeering sarcasm in the letters page, was probably the best deal COs were likely to get.

Academic and activist James Winter, David Edwards, of the media monitoring group Media Lens (www.medialens.org), and Stephan Russ-Mohl, of the European Journalism Observatory (www.ejo.ch) all analyse aspects of the "war journalism" of the corporate media in Canada, the UK and US. James Winter focuses on the cultural and medial representation of Canada's role as part of Western imperialism: "Since the Vietnam War, Canadians have taken great delight in ridiculing US foreign policy, with an air of smugness and self-satisfaction," he writes. "Imagine the surprise, then, as Canadians found themselves up to their necks in the service of imperialism." Winter reveals that contrary to the "altruistic imagery" of benevolence, Canada's foreign policy has been fuelled by military-industrial interests complicit with US imperialism.

The major part of Winter's text discusses coverage of the recent war in Afghanistan by the *Toronto Star*, the largest and most "progressive" newspaper in Canada. According to Winter, this detailed case study "reveals the way in which Canada's mainstream media justify and promote the war, selling it to Canadians on behalf of the government, war-profiteers and the military". Winter concludes that "like their American counterparts, the mainstream Canadian media have adopted the role of stenographers to power, and cheerleaders for the war team".

Relying on Herman and Chomsky's propaganda model, David Edwards and David Cromwell, of Media Lens, have produced hundreds of pages of evidence on the media's crucial role in promoting wars. And through their engagement with journalists, they have been able to pressure mainstream media organisations to alter their standards. In this text, David Edwards explores the limited "spectrum" of media debate (including the BBC) in a range of case studies focusing on Western human rights abuses: "The unthinkable is normalised as a result of the media presenting Western actions within a highly supportive ideological framework," he writes. While US/UK foreign policy and interventions are presented as benign and with peaceful purposes, the media neglects to discuss credible evidence suggesting "British and American mass killing".

Edwards, for instance, focuses on the media coverage of a *Lancet* report in 2006 which suggested the US/UK Iraq invasion of 2003 had led to 655,000 excess deaths. In particular, the media discredited the study by suggesting that it was based on a "dodgy methodology". This was in contrast to research on "the death toll in Congo" which used the same methodological design: "Even though the estimates of death in Congo surprised experienced observers of the conflict, the media reported the figures without concerns about the validity of either the numbers or the methodology," Edwards says.

Stephan Russ-Mohl discusses recent research about US coverage of terrorism, the 2003 Iraq war and subsequent US/Coalition-occupation from the perspective of an "economic theory of journalism". He shows how "mediatised" wars tend to become the subject of one or even several issue-attention cycles – with "an upturn, a turnaround, and a downturn phase" of coverage. Russ-Mohl's economic perspective suggests that shrinking resources of media organisations and an increase in PR and government spin led to a decline in the quality and truthfulness of the mass media.

Peace and pedagogy

Finally, Pakistani journalist and leading media educationist Rukhsana Aslam highlights the way in which a peace journalism curriculum in higher education can both serve to critique dominant values and routines – and provide graduates who will hopefully help in the transformation of the mainstream and the development of alternative, progressive media.

The future

Peace journalism speaks with many voices in this collection. In assembling it, our belief has been that, if the movement for peace/conflict sensitive journalism is to develop, it must draw from an eclectic range of critical perspectives – and be global in ambition. Give the strength of the opposing forces in journalism, such an enterprise is bound to have a flavour of the quixotic, a conversation within the belly of the monstrous war machine. To withstand these forces, we believe that the movement must be intellectually rigorous, courageous, imaginative, life-affirmative – and open to diversity. We welcome further discussion and thought on the themes explored within this book, and will be happy to convey your feedback to any of the contributors. Over to you!.

- Our contact details: Richard Lance Keeble – rkeeble@lincoln.ac.uk; John Tulloch – jtulloch@lincoln.ac.uk; Florian Zollmann – fzollmann@lincoln.ac.uk.

Notes

1   See http//www.globalissues.org/article/75/world-military-spending for these details, accessed on 1 May 2009.
2   See http://www.oxfam.org.uk/resources/ukpoverty/downloads/ukpp_key_facts.pdf, accessed on 11 September 2009.
3   Even so, mainstream newspapers carry regular reports of defence companies and the military calling for extra funding. For instance, see Webb, Tim (2009) Defence firms call for more spending, *Guardian*, 2 September.
4   See http://www.globalsecurity.org/military/world/war/index.html, accessed on 14 September 2009.

References

Atton, Chris (2003) Ethical issues in alternative media, *Ethical Space: The International Journal of Communication Ethics*, Vol. 1, No. 1 pp 26–31

Carter, April, Clark, Howard and Randle, Michael (2006) *People power and protest: A bibliography on nonviolent action*, London: Housmans

Ellul, Jacques (1965) *Propaganda – the formation of men's attitudes*, New York: Knopf

Hartley, John (2008) Journalism as a human right: The cultural approach to journalism, Loffelholz, Martin and Weaver, David (eds) *Global journalism research: Theories, methods, findings, future*, Oxford: Blackwell pp 39–51

Herman, Edward and Chomsky, Noam (1988) *Manufacturing consent: The political economy of the mass media*, New York: Pantheon Books [reissued 1994, London: Vintage Books]

Howard, Ross (2004) *Conflict-sensitive journalism: A handbook*, Denmark: International Media Support (IMS) and Institute for Media, Policy and Civil Society (IMPACS)

Lakoff, George (2004) *Don't think of an elephant! Know your values and frame the debate*, White River Junction, Vermont: Chelsea Green Publishing

Luostarinen, Heikki (1994) *Sergeants of the mind: news management and journalistic counter-strategies in military conflicts*, Helsinki: Hanki ja Jaa Oy

Lynch, Jake (1998) *The peace journalism option*, Taplow: Conflict and Peace Forums

Lynch, Jake and McGoldrick (2005) *Peace journalism*, Stroud: Hawthorn Press

Monbiot, George (2009) Any real climate effort will hurt. So start with the easy bits. Like war toys, *Guardian*, 23 June

Nohrstedt, Stig A and Ottosen, Rune (2000) Studying the media Gulf war, Nohrstedt, Stig A and Ottosen, Rune (eds), *Journalism and the new world order*, Nordicom, Gothenburg

Norton-Taylor, Richard (2009) Brown accused of suppressing report on spiralling arms costs, *Guardian*, 13 August

Ottosen, Rune (2007) Emphasizing images in peace journalism: A case study from Norway's biggest newspaper, Shinar, Dov and Kempf, Wilhelm (eds) *Peace journalism: The state of the art*, Berlin, Regener pp 111–35

Perez, Marianne (2006) Moving mainstream media towards a culture of peace. Unpublished thesis at European University Center for Peace Studies at Stadtschlaining/Burg, Austria

Rizvi, Haider (2008) Global poverty figures revised upward, OneWorld US, 28 August. Available online at http://us.oneworld.net/article/357172-global-poverty-figures-revised-upward, accessed on 11 September 2009

Ross, Susan Dente (2007) (De)Constructing conflict: A focused review of war and peace journalism, Shinar, Dov and Kempf, Wilhelm (eds) *Peace journalism: The state of the art*, Berlin, Regener pp 53–74

Shinar, Dov and Kempf, Wilhelm (eds) *Peace journalism: The state of the art*, Berlin, Regener

Woodward, Bob (2004) *Plan of attack*, London: Simon and Schuster/Pocket Books

SECTION 1. PEACE JOURNALISM: NEW THEORETICAL POSITIONS

1

Non-violence in philosophical and media ethics[1]

CLIFFORD G. CHRISTIANS

Non-violence is an ethical principle grounded in the sacredness of human life. Mahatma Gandhi and Martin Luther King developed it beyond a political strategy into a philosophy of life. For the pre-eminent theorist of dialogic communication, Emmanuel Levinas, the Self-Other relation makes peace normative. When the Other's face appears, the infinite is revealed and I am commanded not to kill (Levinas 1981). Along with *dharma* (higher truth), *ahimsa* (non-violence) forms the basis of the Hindu worldview. In communalistic and indigenous cultures, care for the weak and vulnerable (children, the sick and elderly), and sharing material resources are a matter of course. Death and violence at the World Trade Center, suicide bombings in the Middle East, and killing of the innocent in Afghanistan and Iraq cut to our deepest being. Along with the public's revulsion against physical abuse at home, our consternation over brutal crimes and savage wars are a glimmer of hope reflecting the validity of this principle.

Out of non-violence, we articulate ethical theories about not harming the innocent as an obligation that is cosmic and irrespective of our roles or ethnic origin. When peace is an ethical imperative, it is not reduced to the politics of war but is a fundamental way to understand the sacredness of life intrinsic to our humanness. The principle of non-violence promotes a discourse of peaceful coexistence in community life rather than a focus on peace-making between inter-governmental bodies. Flickers of peace are emerging on our media ethics agenda, but only glimmers compared to major struggles with truth, human dignity and social justice. Johan Galtung has developed and applied the principle systematically through peace journalism concerned not simply with the standards of war reporting, but positive peace – the creative, nonviolent resolution of all cultural, social and political conflicts (e.g. 2000, 2004). As with Galtung, Jake Lynch recognises that military coverage as a media event feeds the very violence it reports and, therefore, has developed the theory and practice of peace initiatives and conflict resolution on the ground (e.g. Lynch and McGoldrick 2005; Lynch 2008). Within this work by media academics and professionals, the broad task remains of bringing the concept of non-violence to intellectual maturity. This chapter seeks to advance that project by giving the non-violence principle theoretical justification.

My perspective on peace and communication is philosophical anthropology.[2] For my framework, I identify the characteristics common and unique to human beings. The status of philosophical anthropology is controversial within the classical philosophical disciplines at present, that is, epistemology, metaphysics, and ethics. Its agenda has been taken over by the philosophy of mind or eclipsed by analytical philosophy in North America. Therefore, while working out the necessary and sufficient conditions of the human species, my overall argument is more broadly ontological.

Social contract theory

For properly justifying non-violence philosophically, the elephant in the room is social contract theory. In coming to grips with the nature of the human in our establishing non-violence as an ethical principle, we must identify the alternatives to social contract as the dominant paradigm.

In social contract theory, a person's moral and political obligations are dependent on a contract or agreement among a society's members. In its modern terms, social contractualism is given its first full exposition and defence in the moral and political theory of Thomas Hobbes (1588–1679). After Hobbes, John Locke (1632–1704) and Jean-Jacques Rousseau (1712–1778) are the best known proponents of this enormously influential theory, in fact, one of the most dominant theories within moral and political philosophy throughout the history of the modern West. In the twentieth century, the social contract tradition gained further momentum as a result of John Rawls' Kantian version.[3] In fact, Virginia Held has argued that "contemporary Western society is in the grip of contractual thinking" (1993). Contractual models have, certainly, come to inform a vast variety of relations and interactions among persons.

However, despite its longevity, prominence and sophisticated defenders, a number of philosophers have questioned the very nature of the person at the heart of contract theory (Pateman 1988). The one who engages in contracts is a Robinson Crusoe, represented by the Hobbesian man, Locke's autonomous self, Rousseau's noble savage, and Rawls' abstract person in the original position. The liberal individual is purported to be universal – raceless, classless and gender neutral – and is taken to represent a generalised model of humanity above cultural differences. But many political thinkers have argued that when we investigate carefully the characteristics of the liberal self, we find not a universal human being, but a historically located, specific type of individual (cf. http://www.iep.utm.edu/s/soc-cont.htm). Macpherson (1973), for example, has concluded that the Hobbesian person is actually a bourgeois man typical of early modern Europe. Feminists have also made it obvious that persons at the heart of the liberal social contract are gendered masculine (e.g. DiStefano 1991). Hobbes' conception of the liberal self, which established the dominant modern conception of the person in Western contract theory, is explicitly masculine. It is radically atomistic and solitary, not owing any of its qualities to anyone else. This model of masculinity, therefore, cannot legitimately claim to be a general representation of all persons. Moreover, such liberal individuals enter into the social contract as a means by which to maximise their own individually considered interests.

For media education and practice committed to the principle of non-violence, the first and radical step is to move beyond contract definitions of the self. When the public is understood in contract terms, aggression and defensiveness are typically considered the natural state of affairs.

Dialogic theory

In terms of a credible ethics of non-violence, philosophical anthropology with its focus on the human, insists that the liberal self be exorcised and replaced by the relational self instead. A shorthand version for peace and communication argues that a dialogic model ought to be substituted for monologic transmission between discrete individuals. In fact, the argument here is stronger – for non-violence to be legitimate intellectually and possible practically, dialogic social philosophy is the only defensible normative communal theory at present. Daryl Koehn (1998), as one example, supports the emphasis in feminist ethics on a relational rather than individualistic self and insists on an empathic instead of a legalistic approach to community life. In the process she argues for a dialogic ethics that makes feminist ethics more credible. A normative dialogic paradigm is a decisive alternative to social contract and a fruitful framework for an ethics of non-violence in an age of globalisation and multiculturalism.

According to the dialogic perspective, *homo sapiens* is the one living species constituted by language; therefore, humans are fundamentally cultural beings. As creators, distributors and users of culture, humans live in a world of their own making. Rather than one-dimensional definitions of the human species as *homo faber, homo economicus* or *animale rationale*, the cultural character of our human-ness illustrates both our dialogic composition as a species and the relationship of human beings and the media. In traditional epistemology, all acts are monologic, though actions may be coordinated with others. However, when the lingual inter-pretation of ourselves and our experience constitutes who we are, human action is dialogic. Our experience is then understood largely in terms of rhythm with other non-individuated actors. Humans are dialogic agents within a language community.

Therefore, all moral matters must be seen in communal terms. A self exists only within "webs of interlocution" and all self-interpretation implicitly or explic-itly "acknowledges the necessarily social origin of any and all of their conceptions of the good and so of themselves" (Mulhall and Swift 1996: 112). Like feminist ethics, dialogic ethics does not think of morality as an impersonal action-guiding code for an individual, but rather as a shared process of discovery and interpreta-tion in which members of a community continually refine their positions in light of what others have said and done. The most defensible ethical stance is one of continuing thoughtfulness (Koehn op cit: 156–161).

Rather than patch up liberal individualism, the dialogic paradigm enables us to start over intellectually and thereby establish a more credible humanness for understanding non-violence and acting peacefully. As a substitute for individual autonomy, Taylor (1994: 32, 34, 36) summarises the social bondedness of dialogic theory as follows:

> We become full human agents, capable of understanding ourselves and hence of defining our identity, through...rich modes of expression we learn through exchange with others. My discovering my own identity doesn't mean that I work it out in isolation, but that I negotiate it through dialogue, partly overt, partly internal, with others. My own identity crucially depends on my dialogical relations with others...In the culture of authenticity, relationships are seen as the key loci of self discovery and self affirmation.

The dialogic lineage of Martin Buber (1965), Paulo Freire (1970, 1973) and Emmanuel Levinas insists on emancipatory struggles and transformative action. Together they make a normative commitment to the dialogic unequivocal. In Freire's (1970) perspective, only through dialogue do we fulfil our ontological and historical vocation of becoming fully human. Under conditions of oppression, through dialogic communication we can gain a critical consciousness as an instrument of liberation (Freire 1973). For Buber, restoring the dialogic ought to be our primary aim as humankind (op cit: 209–24). Buber's philosophy of communication is not content with empirical claims regarding socially produced selves or lingual assertions about symbolic constructions. He speaks prophetically that only as I-Thouness prospers will the I-It modality recede (Buber 1958). Levinas's interaction between the self and the Other makes peace normative; non-violence in his theory is not only a political strategy, but a public philosophy (1981). Together they enable us to endorse dialogue as the apex of normative communication theories and the most appropriate framework for the ethics of non-violence.

Spiritual dimension of the human

In focusing relentlessly on the nature of the human, philosophical anthropology rejects the mainstream's contractual self and validates dialogic communication as the only appropriate framework for the ethics of non-violence. And in concentrating on the relational human in dialogicism, its spiritual dimension becomes *sine qua non*. Buber and Levinas are typically connected to Judaism and Freire's Catholicism is well known. But philosophical anthropology works even more deeply and persistently so that spirituality becomes intrinsic and inescapable. In enhancing rather than suppressing the spiritual dimension, a thicker understanding of humans-as-relational emerges, and a normative strategy is made transparent for acting on the ethics of non-violence. Not only is the liberal self reductionistic, but its secular context prevents it from seeing humans in holistic terms. Therefore, a spacious framework is unveiled by including spirituality within philosophical anthropology rather than adhering to the conceptual boundaries of an epistemology and metaphysics that excludes it.

Spirituality refers to an inherent aspect of everyday life, that perennial propensity of human beings for ultimate meaning. This term defines those sacred times and spaces so engrained in human community that history becomes an empty shell if viewed without it, and our categories blurred if we fail to appreciate spirituality's irrepressible character.

This is not an appeal to a theology of communication or to theological ethics. From St. Augustine in the 5th century to Stanley Hauerwas (see http://stanleyhauerwas. blogspot.com/) today, work in theological ethics is imperative reading. But the argument here is not for a series of formal, scholastic theologies. Even where theologians appear in the argument or elaboration, they serve as springboards to more wide-ranging explanations. Philosophical anthropology with a spiritual inflection does not mean we just write about God or use official theological categories.

Nor is spirituality and non-violence identical to communication and religion. Obviously spirituality comes into its own through institutional religion, and several of the world's major religious traditions enter the analysis here – Jewish, Buddhist, Catholic, Protestant, Animistic, Muslim, Russian Orthodox and so forth. Yet the appeal in spirituality is not basically to organised religions. Religions are filled with distortions; they typically lust after certitude and present dogmatisms in the name of truth. Such accusations the world's religions can meet themselves. Spirituality emphasises another dimension – the religious. The concern of philosophical anthropology, in coming to grips with the relational human, is not formalised dogma, but the quality of experience called "spiritual". In that sense, participation in this analysis of spirituality is welcomed out of concern for peace studies, regardless of whether an explicit theological tradition is held or not. For non-violence to be at home in media ethics, the spiritual dimension of human life will need to be taken seriously.

Spirituality rejects the naïvete that the religious realm can be isolated and established independently. One of the human species' most intriguing problems is why something exists and not nothing, why we find ourselves living on a tiny particle of the vast universe in a minute fragment of time. Our intrinsic spirituality motivates religious life and thought to answer that. Thus the contention here that the religious dimension is still the best form for exploring the human predicament. What are typically dismissed as archaic spiritual values are not limited to a primitive state, but are preoccupations which emerge in those unending struggles across history for freedom and purpose.

In the same way that spirituality brings history into presence, a thematic idea within it might be labelled openness or creativity. While organised religions are normally castigated for being narrow, stifling, and bigoted, the spiritual domain actually means releasing creativity, opening our perception of reality. Spirituality cries out for a polyphonic, multi-dimensional world that prevents both sterility and cacophony.

The most dramatic kind of openness in spirituality, of course, is openness toward the transcendent. Spirituality by definition entails the higher and deeper and more ultimate realities beyond the immanent. In Buber's language it is God, in Paul Tillich (for instance, 1959) a non-symbolic ground of being, in the Russian Orthodox tradition the Primordial principle, and in the New Testament grace. While social contract democracy tends to support a bland, demythologised form of scientifically acceptable religion, the spirituality of everyday life finds the non-empirical not only meaningful but necessary.

In important ways, therefore, spirituality can be defined as humans thrusting out beyond their embodiments and the limited social order under which they live. Spirituality is, then, the human attempt to reach unconstrained reality and the ultimate sphere, or in Rudolf Otto's (1950) terms, "the numinous". Again, this press towards transcendence is neither new nor passé. The assumption is that human beings have a transcendent dimension which if not encouraged to develop properly will steal through the back door in bizarre and destructive ways. Secular culture thus lives dangerously by shutting out transcendent meaning. In so arguing, spirituality not only enhances philosophical anthropology, but adds an important dimension to contemporary discussions of communication and culture. It insists on the need for a centre, an ultimate focus to curb arbitrariness in human relations. At the least, it encourages journalists to take religious language and rituals seriously as arenas where ultimate matters are given existential significance.

Thus spirituality makes the world of meaning absolutely essential for our well-being as humans – and encourages our working that out in highly practical ways as Freire does. Spirituality opens an imaginative journey into the secrets and mysteries of human meaning. Culture is thus considered an historically transmitted pattern of meanings embodied in symbols, and meaning is the fundamental ingredient in human cultures. For spirituality, communication describes the process of creating meanings. Communication is seen as the human attempt to uncover significance in life. It recognises that our important threat is not physical survival but the uncanny. The ultimate menace occurs when lingual systems start disintegrating. We are connected to the history of the human race and to human communities through the realisation that ritual and symbolism are not extraneous to social processes, but intrinsic to humankind as a species.

Social contract has reduced human experience and handles openness awkwardly. The contemporary mind as a whole finds it difficult to grasp the subtlety of our multi-roled, multi-formed existence. Secularisation continues to shape us decisively, yet a revolutionary transformation of consciousness is always held out as a hope by the tradition of spirituality represented here. Its various iterations anticipate the release of the creative, an upsurge of liberating energy, a freeing of people from suffering and dulling restraints. Making spirituality prominent brings all symbolic creations – including song, poetry, drama, metaphor, and worship – into our study of media phenomena.

Above all, the spiritual/religious/numinous is committed to the sacred character of human speech. Spirituality has a sacramental concern for the communication process rooted in its oral-aural form. Already in the ancient world humans understood the powerful force of words in shaping reality. In the tradition Paulo Freire represents, for example, people are assigned the responsibility of naming as a sign of their partnership with God in forming the creation. Those for whom the spiritual is phosphorescent, stand in awe of oral language. Language is spirit, being, reality – a powerful force of creative energy. Words are understood to produce events, not just describe private thoughts. The spirit of Hebrew poetry in Buber's mysticism sees life as essentially personal throughout – the human and divine, and natural reality too. Spokenness across history warrants our hearing still today. While the relationship between abusive speech and violent behaviour is a complicated one, from a spirituality perspective only the language of non-violence is morally acceptable in human relationships.

Spirituality adds to dialogic theory by challenging us to maintain the mystical quality of language. Where do we find the Bubers now among communication theorists and media practitioners, those who revere dialogue as the primary vehicle for relational living and a personalist world? Where are we committed to protecting the sacramental quality of natural language which the Creator bestowed upon it? Spirituality forces us to consider whether we have any longer a profound appreciation for frail human speech as sacred for all human beings everywhere in that it can divide or reconcile, destroy or build up, enslave or set free. Out of the violence and turmoil in the Middle East, for example, are the inspiring stories of Jews and Muslims working together on water projects in Palestine, and teaching their children each other's religion – proving once again that language can empower the moral imagination toward peace.

Holistic humans

Insisting on the spiritual dimension of our humanness enables us to define relational beings holistic. Humans are spiritual embryos, endowed with mystical power that needs to be cultivated by non-violence. In a holistic view of the human species, there is an unseen power that leads the world's creatures in a harmonious way. In Taoism its name is Tian. With humans as whole beings created by nature, the focus is on nurturing and awakening our basic humanity, that is our whole inner being.

Humans are understood to be an indivisible whole, a vital organic unity with multi-sided moral, mental and physical capacities. The body, mind and heart are indivisibly linked and developed in concert with one another. Even deeper than political strategies toward peace is the profound educational need to touch our inner being in order to awaken the higher elements. This is a way of knowing that is non-conceptual or pre-conceptual, one in which the inner powers that reside within us are released. Educators committed to holistic humans cultivate a harmonious spirituality that exists and need not be imposed. Human beings in these terms are elevated to their highest and noblest by the very spirit being nurtured (Huang 2007: 1–5).

Life is understood as a journey of releasing the sacred power residing within life itself. Human beings are not simply biological or psychological entities but spiritual beings seeking expression within the physical and cultural world. In these terms, an ethics of non-violence is primarily activated through a special kind of education. Pedagogy provides an atmosphere in which our inner energy is liberated through a natural internal unfolding. It means, further, that human beings must become inwardly certain that they belong to a supersensible world of soul and spirit that always surrounds them while animating them. Thus education is not an instructional system but an art of awakening what is actually there within the human being. Rather than ignore the spiritual dimension, an ideal education enriches the soul and awakens the unity of our whole being – body, mind, and spirit. In other words, education has to activate a sense of the sacred and the interconnectedness of life, and ultimately expose us to the larger vision of what it means to be a human being inhabiting the cosmos (cf. Huang 2007).

Rather than a Taliban-style indoctrination imposed from without, authentic awakening centres on our inner life and only through such quickening can non-violence flourish. Critical thinking is essential to education in general and to journalism education under consideration here, but being mindful is to bring soul into our lives. Compassion is to see our connectedness to others. Educational goals cannot be centred too narrowly on intellectual development or behaviour control that ignores human growth in holistic terms. When we are harmonious within our selves, we are able to see the whole picture of one's being in relation with others and our connection to the universe. Harmony within spreads to compassion for others and oneness with the eternal.

Taoism

The spiritual dimension of the holistic human is stated in different ways and from different cultural perspectives, but with the same meaning. The Protestant theologian H. Richard Niebuhr turned Christian love ethics into a definition of the person as *The responsible self* (1963). The Dalai Lama's best-selling book, *Ethics for a new millennium* (1999), is written for all though it is intensely spiritual in character. Karol Wojtyla (better known as Pope John Paul II) explicates horizontal love (human-to-human) and vertical love (divine-to-human and human-to-divine) as a trained philosopher speaking to the human race, not as official teaching for the Roman Catholic Church (1981).

As an extended illustration, one way to describe the spiritual dimension of the human is through Taoism.[4] The spirit of Taoism is to recognise a mysterious power in nature, and to pursue the harmonious state of being united with nature (cf. Gunaratne 2005, esp. Chs 1 and 5). It is particularly applicable to the ethics of non-violence because of its origins in the 4th century BC. It was created as a philosophical system when China was occupied by countries that constantly fought against each other to become the dominant authority. Taoists in that era explored what was driving the conflicts and violence, and how human beings were to live in such a society. Lao Tzu and Chuang Tzu are two major figures in developing and advocating it. Lao Tzu's *Tao Te Ching* (2005) is the origin of Taoism and Chuang Tzu's biography, *Chuang Tzu* (1964), presents it poetically.

In terms of Lao Tzu, "Tao cannot be heard, cannot be seen, cannot be told, and should not be named". For him, Tao is a formless mysticism that gives life to all creation and is itself inexhaustible. The Chinese character pronounced as Tao contains two parts – a head (actually an "eye in a head") and a walking foot meaning "to go". Together they mean "the way" (both physically and philosophically/metaphorically) or "the path or road" (Lao Tzu op cit: xiv). Lin Yutang interprets it as truth (Lao Tzu et al 1948: 5). Tao is an energy that guides human action. Tao is within a Self and gradually evolves in the Self when humans embody it. When humans are merged with the Tao, they are at one with nature, both one's "innermost nature and the force of nature we experience everywhere" (Lao Tzu op cit: xv). In this sense "all human actions become as spontaneous and mindless as those of the natural world" (Chuang Tzu op cit: 6).

Chang Tzu's philosophy is about freedom – in his words freeing ourselves from the world (ibid). Thus from Taoism's perspective, the essential point in holistic education is nurturing our inner nature while respecting the mystical power of natural reality. The basic question is how can we live harmoniously in the midst of social orders and values that tend to make human beings soulless objects? Chuang Tzu contends that humans suffer because they have no freedom. We lack freedom because we are attached to material goods, to feelings, knowledge and religions. Our fears and suffering come from our attachments which themselves result from our own web of values. However, anything we believe we own, such as reputation, wealth, and power can be changed when our value system is altered. What we believe we own is merely attachment which has no eternity, and brings no peace, that is, harmony of heart.

Chuang Tzu emphasises that we tune in to the harmony and balance within our own Self and the larger world, rather than live according to a value system that at its best recognises merely part of a human being's significance to the whole universe. When freed from attachment to the external, we are at peace with others, society, the world, and the universe. We neither struggle for good things nor are bothered by what others consider bad things. We refuse to recognise death as any less desirable than life. Living in an era of constant war over power, wealth and territory, Lao Tzu and Chuang Tzu advocate forsaking the value system that twists people's behaviour and intentions and disturbs the harmony within our humanness.

Taoism pursues a society that operates without hurting the harmony within its people and the harmony within nature. Holistic educators promote a form of teaching and learning that retains our inner nature and recognises everyone's uniqueness. Taoism advocates our pursuit of the spiritual life in the midst of the dominant voices touting efficiency, structure and management. It turns people's eyes to the state of life, being at one with the world, in a hope of making the world a better place physically and spiritually. Given the emphasis on the general morality in this chapter, if both media practitioners and the public as a whole were educated in these holistic terms, the ethics of non-violence would flourish (cf. Huang op cit).

Golden rule

Philosophical anthropology that takes spirituality seriously provides us a vocabulary for and definition of the holistic human. The seeds of such holism are already in dialogical humans-in-relation. But spirituality makes holistic humans explicit and transparent. In addition to articulating a human being who thinks and acts non-violently, the spiritual domain gives us a normative strategy for living peacefully – the golden rule (cf. Kang 2006).

From a religious perspective, almost all discussion of the ethics of non-violence refers to the golden rule as a guide for morally appropriate action. Hans Küng is one prominent scholar who emphasises the golden rule as the core of religious ethics. He has concluded, as have many others, that all the great religions require observance of something like: "Do to others as you would have them do to you." This is a norm that is not just hypothetical and conditional, but is categorical, apodictic and unconditional. Küng is correct in saying that it is fully practicable in the face of the extremely complex situations in which individuals or groups most often act (Küng 1993: 58–59; 1996: 23–24; 1997: 96–97, 225, 229, 232). Its secret is avoiding a list of prohibited acts and providing a way to think about behaving toward others.

Küng assumes that the golden rule is so clear and intuitive that we feel no need to ask what it really means. In that sense, acting toward others as we wish others to act toward us is a pre-theoretical given. The rule of reciprocity between others and myself seems unarguable, intuitive, the natural way to live harmoniously in the human world. At least a commitment to the golden rule does not require shared ethical theory; we can generally agree about its importance for non-violence but disagree in our theorising over capital punishment, warfare and euthanasia (cf. Kang 2006). But, as Lindberg (2007) observes, its brevity and simplicity obscure its radical implications. In his words, it proceeds from the assumption of human dignity – we regard others as basically like ourselves. Thus when followed it produces a "community of goodwill".

In his understanding of the golden rule, Confucius states it, on the one hand, in a negative form in the *Analects*: "Do not do unto others what you would not desire others to do unto yourself" (1979: 5.12, 12.2, 15.24). But it is also positive (ibid: 6.30): "Erect others the way you would desire yourself to be erected and let others get there the way you would desire yourself to get there." *The Analects* teach throughout that we should not concern ourselves with acknowledgement from others but worry about failing to acknowledge them (1.1, 1.16, 14.30, 15.19).

For Confucius, I should not study in order to show others, but study for the cultivation of myself (14.24). I should cultivate myself, first of all, in order to serve the other's peace (14.42). "Collecting" my scattered mind and heart, "keeping" and "nourishing" it by means of reading and concentration are the way of Confucian self-cultivation, developed by the Song philosophers in the 12th century. In the Confucian tradition, the effectiveness of the golden rule depends on the degree of my self-cultivation (cf. Kang op cit). The emphasis does not focus exclusively on the reciprocal relation between myself and the other, but includes my moral cultivation. The whole programme of Confucianism is concentrated on moral cultivation in the individual, family, social, national and transnational levels by different stages (from childhood to adult) and by different means (book learning, method of concentration, keeping rituals and so on). In its best forms, Confucianism contributes to the moral education of persons in a concrete community, while being global in scope.

As Young Ahn Kang (ibid) concludes, from the perspective of religious moral-ity, the golden rule when understood generally as a rule of reciprocity can function effectively, if not as a moral principle, then at least as a moral procedure and as an expression of common moral wisdom of almost all humanity.[5] The agencies of civil society can participate in teaching and promoting the golden rule as a path of non-violence both in local communities and global organisations with regard to the problems facing the contemporary world – poverty, malnutrition, war, the loss of cultural identity, and so on. For an ethics of non-violence, there is no reason not to make use of this common rule among peoples, nations, and for multinational cooperation in order to build a world in which cultural diversities are respected and shared. Media organisations as social institutions can resonate with it also as their ethical standard for public affairs reporting.

Conclusion

Rooted in the sacredness of life as a universal value, non-violence is an obvious ethical principle. In order to establish its legitimacy as a moral norm, I have cho-sen philosophical anthropology as the most suitable framework, rather than epis-temology, metaphysics or metaethics. This intellectual strategy validates dialogic relations as the appropriate communications theory in contrast to those appeals to peace and peace-making rooted in social contract theory and its liberal self.

Philosophical anthropology, while orienting us in the right direction toward the nature of the human, is likewise relentless in refusing to allow us to turn elsewhere to secondary questions. While totalising our concentration on human-ness, it leads us into this intellectual space toward the religious dimension. While the spiritual dimension of our humanity is signalled by humans-in-relation, that presumption needs to be made visible and articulate for an ethics of non-violence to be adequately rich and comprehensive. Spirituality, rather than theological ethics or religion, leads to a richer definition of the human as holistic beings and to the golden rule as a normative guide for implementing non-violent action. Religions are often contradictory to peace. Spirituality allows us to think and act beneath institutional structures, including religious organisations, and in so doing we lay the groundwork for revolutionising them.

Peace journalism faces a heavy agenda, described in breadth and depth throughout this book. A semiotics of news reporting from around the world of conflict and war needs to continue unabated.[6] Hard work on epistemology is required of media scholars and professionals. As Seow Ting Lee puts it: "If peace journalism [is] to succeed, journalists must assess their notions of hard news, objectivity, and traditional news values" (2009: 207). Peace journalism is typically understood as an innovation in mainstream newsgathering – along with developmental and public journalism. If these three, and perhaps others, offer new paradigms for reporting, a detailed comparative analysis is needed of their histories, demographics, achievements and structure.[7]

In addition to this demanding agenda – and one could argue, our first order of business – peace journalism must transform its philosophy of the human. Rather than presuming the liberal/contractual self, the foundation of new thinking is holistic humanness where community is ontologically and axiologically prior to persons. When we start intellectually with humans-in-relation, the golden rule becomes a credible normative standard for both the general morality and professional journalism ethics in this contentious age.

Notes

1   An earlier version of this chapter was published as Non-violence in philosophical and religious ethics, *Javnost: The Public*, Vol. 14, No. 4 (2007) pp 5–18.
2   Philosophical anthropology is broadly understood as the philosophical examination of human nature, or more precisely, the necessary and sufficient conditions of being a human being. But it does not presuppose an essentialist human essence of some sort. It has been part of the European philosophical landscape for the past century and a half, emerging as a main interest of post-Hegelian philosophers from Feuerbach (1804–1872) and Marx (1818–1883) to Nietzsche (1844–1890) and Wilhelm Dilthey (1833–1911).
3   For a history and critique of contract theory, see Nussbaum 2006, Ch. 1.
4   This section on Taoism and holistic education is dependent on Huang 2007.
5   For intellectually informed discussion of the golden rule, see Battles 1996.
6   As an illustration of the work accomplished to date and still needed, detailed case studies of violent conflict across the globe are included in Dayton and Kriesberg (2009).
7   For important work on the media's comparative organisational structures, see for example, Hackett and Zhao (2005). Keeble (2008) opens another comparative trajectory, that of alternative media as compared to mainstream journalism.

References

Battles, Jeffrey (1996) *The golden rule,* New York: Oxford University Press

Buber, Martin (1958) *I and thou* (trans. Smith, R.G.), New York: Scribner's, second edition

Buber, Martin (1965) *Between man and man* (trans. Kaufman, W.), New York: Macmillan pp 209–24

Chuang Tzu (1964) *Chuang Tzu: Basic writings* (trans. Watson, B.), New York: Columbia University Press

Confucius (1979) *The Analects* (trans. Lau, D.C.), Harmondsworth: Penguin

Dali Lama (1999) *Ethics for the new millennium,* New York: Riverhead Press

Dayton, Bruce W. and Kriesberg, Louis (2009) *Conflict transformation and peacebuilding: Moving from violence to sustainable peace,* London: Routledge

DiStefano, Christine (1991) *Configurations of masculinity: A feminist perspective on modern political theory,* Ithaca, NY: Cornell University Press

Freire, Paulo (1970) *Pedagogy of the oppressed,* New York: Seabury

Freire, Paulo (1973) *Education for critical consciousness,* New York: Seabury

Galtung, Johan (2000) *Conflict transformation by peaceful means: A participants' and trainers' manual,* Geneva: UNDP

Galtung, Johan (2004) *Transcend and transform: An introduction to conflict work (peace by peaceful means),* London: Pluto Press

Gunaratne, Shelton A. (2005) *The Dao of the press: A humanocentric theory.* Cresskill, NJ: Hampton Press

Hackett, Robert and Zhao, Yuezhi (eds) (2005) *Democratizing global media,* Lanham, MD: Rowman and Littlefield

Held, Virginia (1993) *Feminist morality: Transforming culture, society, and politics,* Chicago: University of Chicago Press

Huang, Wanju (2007) *Historical articulations of holistic education.* Unpublished manuscript, College of Education, University of Illinois-Urbana

Kang, Young Ahn (2006) Global ethics and a common morality, *Philosophia reformata,* Vol. 71 pp 79–95

Keeble, Richard (2008) *On the importance of peace journalism,* UKWatch.net. Available online at http://www.fifth-estate-online.co.uk/comment/peacejournalism.html, accessed on 1 May 2009

Koehn, Daryl (1998) *Rethinking feminist ethics: Care, trust and empathy,* New York: Routledge

Küng, Hans (1993) *Global responsibility: In search of a new world ethics,* New York: Continuum

Küng, Hans (1996) *Yes to a global ethics,* New York: Continuum

Küng, Hans (1997) *A global ethics for a global politics and economics,* New York: Oxford University Press

Lao Tzu (2005) *Tao Te Ching* (trans. Hamill, S.), Boston, MA: Shambhala Publications

Lao Tzu, Lin, Y. and Chuang Tzu (1948) *The wisdom of Laotse* (trans. Lin, Y.), New York: the Modern Library

Lee, Seow Ting (2009) Peace journalism, *The handbook of mass media ethics,* Wilkins, Lee and Christians, Clifford (eds), New York: Routledge pp 258–75

Levinas, Emmanuel (1981) *Ethics and infinity* (trans. Cohen, R. A.), Pittsburgh, PA: Duquesne University Press

Lindberg, Tod (2007) *The political teachings of Jesus,* New York: HarperCollins

Lynch, Jake (2008) *Debates in peace journalism,* Sydney: University of Sydney Press

Lynch, Jake and McGoldrick, Annabel (2005) *Peace journalism,* Stroud, Hawthorn Press

Macpherson, C. B. (1973) *Democratic theory: Essays in retrieval,* Oxford: Clarendon Press

Mulhall, Stephen and Swift, Adam (1996) *Liberals and communitarians,* Oxford: Blackwell, second edition

Niebuhr, H. Richard (1963) *The responsible self,* New York: Harper and Row

Nussbaum, Martha (2006) *The frontiers of justice: Disability, nationality, species membership,* Cambridge, MA: Harvard University Press

Otto, Rudolf (1950) *The idea of the holy,* London: Oxford University Press, second edition

Pateman, Carole (1988) *The sexual contract,* Stanford, CA: Stanford University Press

Taylor, Charles et al (1994) *Multiculturalism: Examining the politics of recognition,* Princeton, NJ: Princeton University Press

Tillich, Paul (1959) *Theology and culture,* Oxford: Oxford University Press

Wojtyla, Karol (1981) *Love and responsibility* (trans. Willetts, H. T.), New York: Farrar Straus Giroux, revised edition

2

Recovering agency for the propaganda model: The implications for reporting war and peace

OLIVER BOYD-BARRETT

Herman, Chomsky and media sociology

Herman and Chomsky's *Manufacturing consent* (1988) proposes that news is shaped by five production filters. These include business interests of media corporations; dependence on advertising for substantial proportions of revenue; professional routines, including excessive reliance on official sources; fear of "flak" (punishment that aggrieved news sources visit on journalists or their employers); and ideological consensus between powerful sources, media owners and journalists. In the 1980s, the consensus was defined by anti-communism. It might be rearticulated today as an uncritical acceptance of global corporate capitalism as natural and positive. This propaganda model (PM) produces a supply of news and views that fits comfortably within the limits acceptable to power elites. For many sociologists, PM is as unremarkable as it is controversial for many practising journalists.

The scholarship of Gramsci (1971), Wolfsfeld (1996) and Bennett et al. (2007) suggests that PM is most evident when consensus between major centres of power in society is strong. Bennett et al's "indexing theory" posits that journalists peg the relative salience they attribute to different sources according to their perceptions of how much authority and credibility these sources appear to enjoy within the power elite. This is a refined extension of Herman and Chomsky's claim that journalistic routines set high store on official or "authoritative" sources. At times of elite dissensus, on the other hand, media may have more room for manoeuvre between competing elite claims.

Herman and Chomsky's preoccupation was to explain how a supposedly independent, critical press could have failed to dissect the rationales that US

administrations from Kennedy through Johnson and Nixon proffered for engagement in Vietnam during the 1960s and 1970s. Journalist-friendly accounts of press
coverage of Vietnam celebrated the courage of the Saigon press corps, while the
administration and Pentagon blamed the press for "losing the war". Herman and
Chomsky argued that press criticism of the war was slow to develop, focused on
minor issues of conduct and process, and avoided the key issue, namely by what
right was the US in Vietnam at all? The challenge, then, is to explain the seeming
incapacity of mainstream media to critically engage (and, I would add, *in timely
fashion*) with the state's pretexts for war. PM provides such an explanation.

But PM has two major flaws. Ironically, it has little to say about the mechanisms of propaganda in the text itself. For that, we must turn to the contributions
of rhetoricians, content and textual analysts and to the "framing" theories of Robert
Entman (2004). Secondly, Herman and Chomsky took pains to present PM as a
systemic explanation that did not require intentionality. PM, therefore, evades or
downgrades the question of *agency*, to which this chapter is mainly addressed and
which is crucial in any analysis of the corporate media's coverage of war and peace.
Robert Hackett (2006) has proposed that Shoemaker and Reese's "hierarchy of
influences" approach and Bourdieu's notion of journalism as a "field" are friendlier
than PM to considerations of "agency", and I do not disagree. My focus, however,
is the culpability of agents in a journalism of "complicity". Lynch and McGoldrick
(2005), by contrast, look to systems theory and the feedback loop for their model
of journalism while proposing a Derrida-style deconstructionist approach for its
reform. But in pushing *agency* off-stage, their approach cannot show why, how or
in what circumstances deconstructionism would be acceptable to the mainstream.

Herman and Chomsky sub-titled their work a "political economy of the mass
media". This tradition rejected the positivist methodology that had characterised
the study of "media effects" over several decades, with remarkable inconclusiveness.
Many such studies dealt with the impact on individuals of representations of violence in television and movies. Political economists regarded this approach, rooted
in the methods of psychology and social psychology, as flawed and a distraction
from more important issues. Positivism channelled public anxiety about media to
the level of the individual media product and the individual consumer, in keeping
with a prevailing Western ideology of individualism. It ignored the links between
media and other sources of power in society, seemingly disinterested in the concrete *institutional, situational* and *commercial* realities of media corporations. It had
little to say about the assimilation of mainstream media into advanced capitalism
as tools of a system of mass consumption, their purpose to help manufacture
individual "need" and "desire" (Barber 2007). This positivist study of media effects

evolved in a direction opposed to the insights, in the 1940s, of Horkheimer and Adorno (2002), who had passionately critiqued the seductive blandness of mediated popular culture and the inability of positivism to fully expose its commercial underpinnings and their implications.

Political economists, in company with sociologists of organisation and occupation, fell prey to the "science trap" – an unreasonable belief that scholarly credibility depends on its ability to deliver empirically established generalisations about a social system or sub-system. In the case of journalism or entertainment, application of scientific method seemed self-evidently virtuous and revealing when pitted against self-promotional autobiographies of journalists (lauding the dramatic, exotic and unusual), and celebrities (celebrating individual talent, creativity, beauty and fun), that hitherto constituted society's principal sources of media understanding. In their place, science-based scholarship offered rich insight into the institutional structures in which front-of-camera performers were embedded, the business principles that underwrote their performances, and the industrial continuities that emerged upon careful observation of the effervescent public face of the communications economy.

Progress beyond self-promotional accounts entailed the risk of losing a sense of "agency". This was the critical linkage – celebrated in the works of the young Karl Marx (1973), the mature Max Weber (1962) and an ageing Jean-Paul Sartre (2003), and rediscovered and articulated in the 1980s-1990s scholarship of sociologist Anthony Giddens (1991) – between the world into which human beings are born, that conditions their opportunities and predispositions to action, and the world on which human beings must, by mere virtue of their existence, act, and whose actions and imprints, with varying degrees of intentionality, exert change. While political economy also struggles to trace the connections between media content and its underlying political-economic determinants, the attribution of culpability to the general level of system arguably invokes generalised, ineffective or misdirected approaches to social change. This is in contrast to a bottom-up, contextually responsive approach that begins with exposure and correction of specific instances of individual or institutional failing and is more likely to induce actual change and enhanced understanding of the change process.

War propaganda and CIA penetration of the media

Any analysis of the coverage of war and peace has to take into account the covert intelligence penetration of the corporate media. In Boyd-Barrett (2004) I noted that Herman and Chomsky, writing in the late 1980s, did not address the 1970s revelations of the Church and Pike Committees (Senate Select Committee on Intelligence Activities; House Select Committee on Intelligence, respectively). These documented extensive, covert CIA penetration of media. The CIA had published hundreds of books, many of them dis-informational, owned dozens of newspapers and magazines worldwide, employed hundreds of US and other journalists. Almost every US news organisation had been penetrated, usually with the cooperation of top ownership or management – themselves sometimes on the CIA payroll. I argued that such intelligence penetration of the media had survived and grown. In Britain, Keeble (2004) collated copious evidence of such penetration by MI6. Its purpose, according to a former assistant editor of the *Observer,* David Leigh, (2000) ranged from the planting of disinformation, through use of the press as cover, to access to pre-publication information.

At stake here is not intelligence penetration specifically but the complicity of journalism with the state's war aims, in both their formal and covert manifestations. David Miller (2005), for example, reported a Spinwatch investigation showing how journalists working for the Services Sound and Vision Corporation, funded by the UK Ministry of Defence, were commissioned to supply reports to the BBC which used these as genuine news. Barstow (2008) chronicled how, before the US invasion of Iraq in 2003, the Pentagon nurtured retired generals as "expert" consultants to television networks. The generals benefited from access to top sources and expense-free travel that they sometimes used in association with work for defence companies to whom they were also consultants. Television networks seemed incurious about the practice, even though their use of such sources dated back at least to the first Gulf War (Kellner 1992). A former CNN chief news executive acknowledged in 2003 that CNN allowed the Pentagon to vet its military analysts.

William Laurence's double act – working for *The Times* and the government

In the next part of this chapter I examine three cases to illustrate the phenomenon (crucial to any formulation of peace journalism theory) of media complicity with war aims. The first is historical. The William Laurence story has been recounted by the Goodmans (2005) and George Roeder (1997: 93). Laurence, a *New York Times* reporter, won a 1946 Pulitzer for his coverage of the 1945 US atomic bombing of Japan. While on *The Times*'s payroll he was also on that of the US government.

He wrote military press releases and statements for President Harry S. Truman and Secretary of War Henry L. Stimson.

Laurence was recruited as a science reporter in the 1930s and wrote many articles in support of atomic power. In the spring of 1945, he attended a secret meeting at his newspaper's Times Square headquarters with General Leslie Groves, director of the Manhattan Project, Arthur Sulzberger, publisher of *The Times*, and the editor-in-chief. The paper acquiesced with Groves's request that Laurence be a paid publicist for the Manhattan Project while continuing to work for *The Times*. Other reporters were unaware of this arrangement. From 1943 the army had understood the radiation effects of atomic bombs, but the task fell to Laurence to explain to the public that the damage they inflicted was attributable solely to their blast power, and that allegations of radiation were nothing more than Japanese propaganda – disinformation that remained current for several years. His role, in effect, was to soften the horror of weapons of mass destruction (WMD).

Judith Miller – spreading fear of WMD

Judith Miller's role in the US invasion of Iraq in 2003, by contrast, was to excite fear of WMD, in the service of deep-level strategic aims. I shall defer to the summary judgement of Alexander Cockburn (2003):

> We don't have full 20/20 hindsight yet, but we do know for certain that all the sensational disclosures in Miller's major stories between late 2001 and early summer, 2003, promoted disingenuous lies. There were no secret biolabs under Saddam's palaces; no nuclear factories across Iraq secretly working at fill tilt. A huge percentage of what Miller wrote was garbage, garbage that powered the Bush administration's propaganda drive towards invasion. What does that make Miller? She was a witting cheer-leader for war. She knew what she was doing. And what does Miller's performance make *The New York Times*?

It is unlikely that senior *Times* management were unaware of what Miller was doing. The evidence rests in the front page stories by-lined by Miller, sometimes co-authored with Michael Gordon, based primarily on anonymous sources. They strengthened the administration's allegations that Iraq had an arsenal of WMD (a concept that bundles together very different weapons with greatly varying destructive capabilities). Administration members, notably Vice-President Dick Cheney, quoted *Times*'s stories in support of their policies (Moyers 2007).

Miller subsequently revealed that Ahmed Chalabi was her key informant, saying that he "provided most of the front page exclusives on WMD to our paper"

(Moore 2004). Chalabi was a dubious source. As a leading figure of the Iraqi National Congress (INC), an umbrella Iraqi opposition group funded by the likes of the Rendon Group and the CIA (SourceWatch 2005), Chalabi had a personal stake in the invasion. He was supported by the Pentagon and the Vice-President as the likely leader to succeed Hussein. These promoted INC intelligence even against contrary evidence from the CIA. Former senior CIA official Vincent Fannistraro declared that the INC's "intelligence isn't reliable at all". He continued:

> Much of it is propaganda. Much of it is telling the Defense Department what they want to hear. And much of it is used to support Chalabi's own presidential ambitions. They make no distinction between intelligence and propaganda, using alleged informants and defectors who say what Chalabi wants them to say, [creating] cooked information that goes right into presidential and vice-presidential speeches (Dreyfuss, December 2002).

Chalabi's reliability was undermined by other aspects of his personal history. In 1992, he was tried in his absence and sentenced by a Jordanian court to 22 years' jail on 31 charges of embezzlement, theft, misuse of depositor funds and currency speculation (Leigh and Whitaker 2003).

The "evidence" that Chalabi filtered to Miller rested on even more dubious sources (Cockburn op cit). One was Khidir Hamza, whose allegation of a continuing nuclear weapons programme under Hussein was based on his 22 years of experience with the Iraqi Atomic Energy Commission. However, he had been dismissed from the programme in 1987 for stealing air conditioning units from the building assigned to his project (Khadduri 2002). He was not regarded by the CIA as a knowledgeable or trustworthy source for claims that Iraq continued to have a viable nuclear weapons programme after the US invasion of 1991 and that only half of it had been destroyed by the Gulf War. Documents provided by Hamza to *The Sunday Times* (UK) were examined by the International Atomic Energy Commission which declared them to be false.

There were many alternative, senior sources for critical assessments of Chalabi or Hamza, but these were routinely ignored or marginalised by Miller, as by the mainstream media generally. After the invasion, Miller was "embedded" with the MET Apha unit, charged with finding WMD in Iraq. During this time, she alleged, falsely – her source proved wholly unreliable – that the unit had found WMD. Howard Kurtz, of the *Washington Post* (25 June 2003) reported that more than six military officers described Miller as acting like a middleman between the Army unit with which she was embedded and the Iraqi National Congress leader, Ahmed Chalabi. When, in April 2003, Miller wrote a letter objecting to an Army commander's order to withdraw the unit from the field, she said this would be a "waste" of time, threatened she would write about it unfavourably in *The Times* and took up the matter with a two-star general, upon which the pullback order was (temporarily) dropped.

Post-invasion reassessments, including public apologies issued by both *The New York Times's* editor and its ombudsman, 2003–04, suggested that senior editors could not control Miller (*New York Magazine*, 7 June 2004). This is implausible, since they could have spiked her stories, had others rewrite them, or given them lower profile. That she may have had a special friendship with the publisher, Arthur Sulzberger, whose ancestor had brokered the Laurence deal in 1945, is not an excuse but an indictment. Miller's peers found her difficult: The *Washington Post* (Kurtz 2005) reported that in 2000, *Times* reporter Craig Pyes refused to "work further on this project with Judy Miller . . . I do not trust her work, her judgement, or her conduct. She is an advocate, and her actions threaten the integrity of the enterprise, and of everyone who works with her . . . She has turned in a draft of a story of a collective enterprise that is little more than dictation from government sources over several days, filled with unproven assumptions and factual inaccuracies . . . (and) tried to stampede it into the paper".

While in jail for 85 days by order of special prosecutor Patrick Fitzgerald in 2005, ostensibly for "protecting her sources", Miller was lionised by elements in the media during the trial of Lewis "Scooter" Libby, Vice-President Cheney's former chief of staff. This raised fresh concerns about Miller's propaganda role in the US invasion of Iraq (FAIR 2005). When assigned as an embed to a unit charged with the search for WMD in Iraq, it emerged, Miller enjoyed a level of security clearance from the US Department of Defense unprecedented for a journalist, such that she was not even at liberty to talk about what she knew to her bosses, colleagues or readers. The assumption that her motive for going to jail was to "protect" Libby was undermined by Libby's defence team, who claimed that Libby had already "excused" Miller of any such obligation the year previously. Miller responded that she needed assurance that this waiver had not been coerced (Schmidt and Vandehei 2005).

If her motive was to protect Libby, then she risked protecting someone charged and later sentenced for the crime of disclosing the identity of a CIA agent, Valerie Plame, who happened to have a special clandestine role countering the proliferation of nuclear weapons (Isikoff and Corn 2006). Miller had not published the information about Plame but had refused to appear before a federal grand jury when she was believed to possess evidence relevant to the leak inquiry. The "outing" of Plame completed a campaign to discredit her husband, Joseph Wilson, the US diplomat who exposed the White House's adoption of fabricated evidence of Iraqi attempts to secure "yellow cake" from Niger. Was Miller bargaining with Fitzgerald to be allowed to testify only on matters related to Libby, and not on other conversations that she may have had with other members of the White House? In any case, her evidence suggested she was prepared to deceive her readers, since she had agreed she would identify Libby as a "former Hill staffer" rather than as a then current member of the administration (Johnson 2005).

The larger question in the Miller case is the culpability of her employer. Given Miller's reporting failures had required public *mea culpa*s in *The Times*'s own pages, and their proximity to the very public dismissal in May 2003 of a junior, African American reporter, Jayson Blair, on the grounds of plagiarism and fabrication (Shafer 2003), it is surprising that the paper continued to protect her. Blair's transgressions arguably paled in comparison to Miller's contribution to a public deception that lied a country into war. This lie was at the cost, according to a 2006 *Lancet* estimate (relegated by *The Times* to its back page), of up to 655,000 Iraqi deaths in excess of those that would have otherwise occurred (Burnham et al 2006), and the deaths of more than 3,000 US service personnel and contractors by spring 2007, and a charge to the US taxpayer of more $3 trillion (Stiglitz and Bilmes 2008).

Before the Libby trial, *The Times*, in December 2005, had exposed illegal NSA domestic spying. Domestic spying flouts the Foreign Intelligence Surveillance Act, and the Fourth Amendment to the US Constitution. The paper had sat on this for a year, even though it could have published before the 2004 presidential elections. *The Times*'s editor-in-chief, Bill Keller, (Grey 2006) excused the year-long delay on the grounds that publishing would "put lives at risk". He did not explain whose lives would have been risked, nor factor into his equation the lives already lost and were continuing to be lost in Iraq. He spoke instead of a conversation he had had with President Bush when Bush threatened that *The Times* "would be held accountable" if it published the story (a good example, perhaps, of Herman and Chomsky's "fear of flak" factor). Two months earlier Keller claimed the story had been delayed because top Bush administration officials assured him that the NSA programme was legal (ibid).

Notwithstanding the WMD scandal, and the misgivings of Barbara Crossette, a former *Times* UN bureau chief, *The Times* allowed Miller to report on the "alleged oil-for-food" scandal whose purpose was to smear the UN secretary general and the UN itself (FAIR 2005). Although she was implicated in the trial of Lewis Libby, *Times* reporters in the Washington bureau (Martin 2007) were blocked from publishing stories on Libby and the leak investigation, and management sought to shield Miller and her contacts in the Bush administration. Veteran *Times* Washington correspondent Todd Purdum was quoted as saying that many news staff were "troubled and puzzled by Judy's seeming ability to operate outside of conventional reporting channels and managerial controls". Only following the Libby trial and Miller's testimony did *The Times* finally break from Miller, negotiating a severance package whose details the newspaper did not make public. One might infer at this point that the paper had learned its lesson and that similar risks would never again be countenanced. In the wake of its public *mea culpas* published in 2003/2004, *The Times* revamped its policies governing the use of anonymous sources.

Michael Gordon and the misreporting of Iran

Yet, as the administration began to beat the drums of war once more, positioning the public for a possible invasion of Iran in 2006 and 2007, here again, under the byline of Michael Gordon (co-author of some of the Miller stories in 2002 and 2003), on 29 January 2007, was more of the same: a front page story based almost wholly on anonymous Pentagon sources, preparing the way for reports of an anonymous Pentagon-arranged press briefing the following day, alleging the supply by Iran of explosive weapons to Iraqi insurgents (see critique by Greg Mitchell, editor, *Editor and Publisher*, 2007).

Similar reports were aired by CBS, ABC and NBC. On this occasion, some elements of the mainstream resisted, notably the *Los Angeles Times*, which rubbished the *Times's* story. The *LAT* had found little to support US accusations. It noted that reporters in Iraq with US troops had not seen "extensive signs of Iranian involvement" (see FAIR 2007). The *LAT* talked to military analysts who questioned whether Iran would even need to provide such weapons, since the technology to make them was simple and widely known in the Middle East. While later press reports talked of the discovery of bomb factories in Baghdad, some reporters wryly observed that the US had left enough of Hussein's arsenals undefended in 2003 for there to be sufficient supply of weapons from that source to arm all parties to the conflict. Academic specialist Juan Cole was quoted by FAIR as saying that "99 per cent of all attacks on US troops occur in Sunni Arab areas and are carried out by Ba'athist or Sunni fundamentalist guerrilla groups, receiving funding from US ally Saudi Arabia and other Gulf monarchies" (see Cole 2007).

Times guidelines required the newspaper should only use anonymous sources when there is a compelling rationale as to why they are considered authoritative, why they have asked for anonymity and why the newspaper cannot print alternative, sourced information that it considers reliable and newsworthy. In this instance, given the record of both the administration and the Pentagon throughout the period 2003–2006, these conditions were not met. As *Editor and Publisher* (Mitchell op cit) noted, Gordon never explained why his sources had demanded confidentiality and did not attempt to convince his reader of his sources' reliability. The story was discounted within days by a leading military source, General Peter Pace, chair of the Joint Chiefs of Staff, who indicated that he was not aware of strong evidence linking Iran's government to the explosives. The Pentagon's propaganda machine was subsequently ratcheted up. Two absences in Gordon's coverage, and that of most other media that covered US claims of Iranian support to Iraqi insurgents (and the temporary capture by Iran, in April, of a group of British marines, in waters that the British claimed were international and that Iran claimed were Iranian) were references to the continual supply of mainstream stories (buried in inside pages) of US covert operations in Iran to provoke disharmony among different Iranian ethnic groups (see Hersh 2005) and the US capture (and possible torture) of Iranian diplomats in Iraq.

Allegations in late January 2007 of Iranian weapons supply to Iraqi insurgents offered a more immediate pretext for war than long-unfolding administration claims that Iran's development of nuclear power for what Iran said were peaceful purposes was, in fact, military. A front page story by Bill Spindle in the *Wall Street Journal* on 20 February 2007, followed by an inside story in *The New York Times* later that month, referenced several factors including ageing oil fields and soaring domestic energy use, that might exhaust Iran's oil exports within a decade. Named sources for this lengthy report were few, but included Mehdi Varzi, a former Iranian diplomat and national oil company official. The desire to avoid an export squeeze, therefore, was a plausible reason why Iran might need nuclear energy, and the report mentioned other Middle Eastern countries, including Egypt and Saudi Arabia, that were also investigating nuclear energy programmes. The story was covered also by an Associated Press report printed in the *International Herald Tribune (IHT)* on 17 February, quoting Iran's top leader Ayatollah Ali Khamenei as saying that the country's oil and gas reserves would dry up eventually.

A possible depletion of Iranian oil supply, consistent with "peak oil" predictions that the world has entered a period of decline in oil availability and production, had implications for the veracity of US claims that Iran sought military nuclear capability, claims that also appeared to exaggerate the speed of any such development. There was little reference back to 1970, when Tehran, (following the CIA's toppling of democratically elected Mossadegh in 1953) still languished under the tyranny of pro-Western despot, Shah Mohammed Reza. The United States and Europe had approved the building of 20 nuclear power plants across Iran and provided it with nuclear technology. The urgent need at this point was for a spate of investigative stories to test the notion of civilian nuclear power as a response to declining oil production. Such stories were nowhere in evidence, their absence a further signal that the US press had been bankrupted as a credible servant of the public sphere. Despite the story's appearance in the *Wall Street Journal* it had little to no impact on other media, and rarely entered into the text of continuing stories about the "threat" of an Iranian nuclear bomb.

'As though' reporting of the Iranian nuclear 'threat'

Continuing Western media emphasis through 2007 on the Iranian nuclear "threat" represented a form of what I have elsewhere (Boyd Barrett 2007) called "as though" reporting. This takes the form of reporting or framing an event *as though* it could be read without reference to alternative angles, often available in other media, which undermine the significance and/or credibility of the primary frame. The development of nuclear energy in Iran was reported *as though* readers could not possibly have had access to alternative accounts that stressed the decline in Iranian oil production when, in point of fact, and as the *Wall Street Journal* report testified, many would have done. The long-standing continuity of this Western journalistic practice, which I argue positions audiences as innocents or idiots, is difficult to explain without invoking a degree of complicity by media with government elites.

"As though" reporting was a defining characteristic of the Miller reports which, with the aid of her newspaper's hierarchy, proclaimed the virtual certainty of the existence of WMD in Iraq. Mainstream media coverage generally did not question whether, even assuming there *were* such weapons, this posed a threat to the US, or to its regional ally, Israel, whose nuclear arsenals were far more substantial than anything Iraq could have mustered. Nor did they provide sufficient justification for invasion as opposed to alternative approaches to resolving the (manufactured) conflict. They did not speculate as to the connections between the administration's thirst for an invasion 2003 in the wake of the Bush policy of pre-emptive warfare and global spectrum dominance, conveniently enunciated in the summer of 2002 – and the secret meeting of oil industry executives, convened by Vice-President Dick Cheney soon after the Bush regime came to power in 2001, during whose deliberations Iraq was a significant item on the agenda, and whose attendees were provided with detailed maps of Iraqi oilfields

(Judicial Watch 2003; Milbank and Blum 2005). Nor was mention made of the speed, following 9/11, with which Cheney and Rumsfeld promoted dubious talk of links between the 9/11 hijackers and Saddam Hussein (North 2006) (evidence we now know to have been extracted by torture), nor of the administration's continuing failure, even lack of interest in, pursuing the alleged culprit for 9/11, Osama Bin Laden (Gellman and Ricks 2002).

Nor did the Miller stories quote informed sources such as ex-marine Scott Ritter, once a member of the UN arms inspection team in Iraq, who discounted the possibility of nuclear WMD and argued that any chemical or biological weapons still left in Iraq had long ago deteriorated and lost their lethal power (Ritter 2003; 2004). Nor was there appropriate concern that the then head of UN weapons inspectors, Hans Blix, and the head of the International Atomic Energy Agency, Mohamed El Baradei, both refuted claims about Iraqi WMD and told the UN Security Council before the invasion that they had found no evidence of such weapons or weapons programmes (Richelson 2004).

"As though" framing was evident in outright deceptions involved in exaggerating the significance of the development of an Iranian nuclear facility, and in the failure of the mainstream media to reconcile claims from the administration that the development had military intent with occasional but recurrent back-of-the-newspaper stories about the stated intentions of the Iranian regime (like Saddam Hussein of Iraq before it) to switch its oil trade from dollars to Euros (UPI 2006). Other elements missing or downplayed in this context included:

- the US capture of Iranian personnel in Iraq;
- the alleged torture of an Iranian diplomat by US forces in Iraq (AFP 2006; Symonds 2007);
- on-going destabilisation tactics by covert US forces deep inside Iran (Hersh op cit; Alexandranova and Kane 2007);
- the enormous nuclear arsenals available to both the US and to Israel (Center for Defense Information 2003);
- evidence and assertions, relating to US complicity in the fomenting of ethnic warfare in Iraq (Whitney 2007), as in the suspicious circumstances surrounding the bombing of the Golden Dome Mosque in Samarra (entirely predictable if the secret government of the US wished to prevent an overwhelmingly Shi'ite Iran from increasing its regional stature in collaboration with a Shi'ite dominated Iraq);
- and obfuscation about Iran's quasi-functioning democracy (the jury is still out, as I write, on the circumstances of the 2009 election) – subject,

of course, to an overriding religious veto, in a manner not dissimilar to that in which US democracy is subject to overriding influences of corporate and plutocratic elites, and the military-industrial complex, so feared by President Eisenhower in his farewell speech to the nation in 1961 (Eisenhower 1961), or in which US elections are routinely characterised by all manner of abuses, including doctored electronics or insufficient supply of voting machines (Harris 2004).

Fear-mongering in 2007 over presumed Iranian *planning* for military nuclear capability acquired more substance in 2009 with the full disclosure by Iran, allegedly in response to a US intelligence discovery, of a hitherto secret but small Iran uranium enrichment facility at Qom (whether suitable for military purposes was disputed), and complaints by the Director General of the UN International Atomic Energy Agency that Iran was uncooperative in providing it with information. The events of 2009, however, do not justify press complicity with an anti-Iran campaign in 2007. Indeed, US intelligence reports published in 2007 (seemingly ignored by the Administration) concluded that Iran had ceased planning for military nuclear capability in 2003 (see Cowell and Sanger 2009).

Conclusion

In this chapter I have exemplified as one of the weaknesses of PM its neglect of the significance of the direct manipulation and subversion of the press by intelligence and other agencies of the "secret government". Unless the significance of these operations is factored centrally into peace journalism theory and media theory more generally, Western scholars may be doomed to a pluralist "deficit" model of the press, one that assumes that if only there was some tinkering here and there then the press could at last fully serve its purported roles of watchdog, fourth estate and public sphere.

Unraveling evidence of the secret government manipulation of media, however, posits a more profound relationship than scholars generally acknowledge between the press and the plutocratic, corporate and security forces whose influences shape, if not determine, the functioning of modern democracies.

Bibliography

Agence France Presse (2006) Iraq protests US capture of Iranian officials, Yahoo! News Asia, 25 December. Available online at http://asia.news.yahoo.com, accessed on *12 November 2008*

Alexandrovna, Larisa and Kane, Muriel (2007) Escalation of US Iran military planning part of six-year administration push, Raw Story, 23 January. Available online at http://www.rawstory.com, accessed on 11 November 2008

Associated Press (2007) Iran's top leader: Oil, gas reserves will dry up, Tehran needs to produce nuclear fuel, *International Herald Tribune*, 17 February

Barber, Benjamin R. (2007) *Consumed: How markets corrupt children, infantilize adults, and swallow citizens whole*, New York: W. W. Norton

Barstow, David (2008) Behind TV analysts: Pentagon's hidden hand, *New York Times*, 20 April

Bennett, Lance, Lawrence, Regina and Livingston, Steven (2007) *When the press fails*. Chicago: University of Chicago Press

Boyd-Barrett, Oliver (2004) Understanding: The second casualty, Allan, Stuart and Zelizer, Barbie (eds) *Reporting war: Journalism in wartime*, London: Routledge pp 25–42

Boyd-Barrett, Oliver (2007) Positioning the news audience as idiot, Maltby, Sarah and Keeble, Richard (eds) *Communicating war: Memory, media and military*, Bury St Edmunds, Arima pp 90–102

Burnham, Gilbert, Lafta, Riyadh, Doocy, Shannon and Roberts Les (2006*)* Mortality after the 2003 invasion of Iraq: a cross-sectional cluster sample survey, *Lancet,* 14 October

Center for Defense Information (2003) The world's nuclear arsenals, April 28. Available online at http://www.cdi.org, accessed on 12 November 2008

Cockburn, Alexander (2003) Judy Miller's War, *Counterpunc*h, 18 August. Available online at http//www.counterpunch.org, accessed on 12 November 2008

Cole, Juan (2007) The danger of Bush's anti-Iran fatwa, Salon.com. 30 January. Available online at http://www.salon.com, accessed on 14 November 2008

Cowell, David and Sanger, David E. (2009) Iran censured over nuclear program by UN watchdog, 27 November. Avaiblable online at http://www.nytimes.com/2009/11/28/world/28nuke.html?_r=1&ref=global-home, accessed on 28 November 2009

Donnelly, Thomas (Principal author) (2000) *Rebuilding America's defenses: Strategy, forces and resources for a new century – A report of the Project for the New American Century.* Available online at http://www.newamericancentury.org/RebuildingAmericasDefenses.pdf, accessed on 14 November 2008

Dreyfuss, Robert (2002) The Pentagon muzzles the CIA: Devising bad intelligence to promote bad policy, *American Prospect*. Available online at http://www.prospect.org, accessed on 14 November 2008

Eisenhower, Dwight. (1961) Eisenhower's farewell address to the nation, Information Clearing House, 17 January. Available online at http://www.informationclearing-house.info, accessed on 5 January 2006

Entman Robert M. (2004) *Projections of power: Framing news, public opinion, and US foreign policy*, Chicago: University of Chicago Press

FAIR (Fairness in Accuracy and Reporting) (2005) Miller's tale: Can the report – or *The*

New York Times – be trusted? CommonDreams, 21 October. Available online at http// www.commondreams.org, accessed on 1 December 2007

FAIR (Fairness in Accuracy and Reporting) (2007) Media advisory: *NYT*, networks offer scant criticism on Iran claims, FAIR, 2 February. Available online at http://www.fair. org, accessed on 1 December 2007

Gellman, Barton and Ricks, Thomas E. (2002) US concludes Bin Laden escaped at Tora Bora fight: Failure to send troops in pursuit termed major error, *Washington Post*, 17 April p. A01

Giddens, Anthony (1991) *Modernity and self-identity: Self and society in the Late Modern Age*, Cambridge: Polity Press

Goodman, Amy (2005) Hiroshima cover-up: Stripping the War Department's *Times* man of his Pulitzer, Democracy Now! 5 August. Available online at http://www. democracynow.org, accessed on 14 November 2008

Gramsci, Antonio (2007) *Prison notebooks*, Volume 3. New York: Columbia University Press

Grey, Barry (2006) *New York Times* editor touts role of establishment press in "war on terror", World Socialist Web Site. Available online at http://www.wsws.org, accessed on 14 November 2008

Hackett, Robert (2006) Is peace journalism possible? Three frameworks for assessing structure and agency in news media, *Conflict and Communication Online*, Vol. 5, No. 2. Available online at http://www.cco.regener-online.de/2006_2/pdf/hackett.pdf, accessed on 14 November 2008

Harris, Bev (2004) *Block box voting: Ballot tampering in the 21st century*, Renton, WA: Talion Publishing

Herman, Edward and Chomsky, Noam (1988) *Manufacturing consent: The political economy of the mass media*, New York: Pantheon

Hersh, Seymour (2005) US conducting covert operations in Iran for possible military strike. Interview with Amy Goodman, Democracy Now! 18 January. Available online at http://www.democracynow.org, accessed on 15 November 2008

Horkheimer, Max and Adorno, Theodore (2002) *Dialectic of enlightenment* (*Cultural memory in the present*), Stanford: Stanford University Press

House Select Committee on Intelligence (1975) *US intelligence agencies and activities: Intelligence costs*, Pike Committee, Washington, DC: GPO

Isikoff, Michael and Corn, David (2006) *Hubris: The inside story of spin, scandal and the selling of the Iraq war*, New York: Three Rivers Press

Johnson, Larry, C. (2005) The big lie about Valerie Plame, TPM Café, 13 July. Available online at http://www.tpmcafe.com, accessed on 30 July 2005

Joint Command, Control and Information Warfare School, Joint Forces Staff College (2002) *Information operations: The hard reality of soft power*, Joint Publication. Available online at http://www.iwar.org.uk/iwar/, accessed on 8 June 2009

Judicial Watch (2003) Cheney energy task force documents feature map of Iraqi oilfields,

Project Censored: The news that didn't make the news, 17 July. Available online at http://www.projectcensored.org, accessed on 4 June 2009

Keeble, Richard (2004) Information warfare in an age of hyper-militarism, Allan, Stuart and Zelizer, Barbie (eds) *Reporting war: Journalism in wartime*, London: Routledge pp 43–58

Kellner, Douglas (1992) *The Persian Gulf TV war*, Boulder/San Francisco/Oxford: Westview Press

Khadduri, Imad (2002) Former Iraqi nuclear scientist speaks out, Redress, 10 June. Available online at http://www.redress.btinternet.co.uk/ikhadduri.htm, accessed on 15 November 2008

Kurtz, Howard (2003) Embedded reporter's role in army unit's actions questioned by military, *Washington Post*, 25 June p. C01

Kurtz, Howard (2005) Reporter, *Times*, criticized for missteps, *Washington Post*, 7 October p. A02

Leigh, David (2000) Britain's security services and journalists: The secret story, *British Journalism Review*, Vol. 11, No.2 pp 21–26

Leigh, David and Whitaker, Brian (2003) Financial scandal claims hang over leader in waiting, *Guardian*, 14 April

Lynch, Jack and McGoldrick, Annabel (2005) *Peace journalism*. Stroud, Gloucestershire: Hawthorn Press

Martin, Patrick (2007) The Libby perjury trial and the Washington media establishment, World Socialist Web Site, 3 February. Available online at http://www.wsws.org, accessed on 3 February 2007

Marx, Karl (1973, orig. 1858) *Grundrisse*, London: Penguin

Milbank, Dana and Blum, Justin (2005) Document says oil chiefs met with Cheney Task Force, *Washington Post*, 16 November p. A01

Miller, David (2004) The domination effect, *Guardian*, 8 January. Available online at http://www.guardian.co.uk/world/2004/jan/08/usa.iraqandthemedia, accessed on 14 November 2008

Miller, David (2005) Did the BBC broadcast fake news reports? Counterpunch, 14 March. Available online at http://www.counterpunch.org/miller03142005.html, accessed on 14 November 2008

Mitchell, Greg (2007) Gordon of *NYT* criticized for using unnamed sources on Iran story, returns with more of same, *Editor and Publisher*, 15 February

Moore, James (2004) How Chalabi and the White House held the front page, *Guardian*, 29 May

Moyers, Bill (Executive Editor) (1987) *The secret government: The constitution in crisis*, PBS documentary, February 14. Available online at http://video.google.com/videoplay?docid=3505348655137118430, accessed on 8 June, 2009

Moyers, Bill (2007) Buying the war, *PBS Special*, 26 April: http://www.pbs.org/moyers/

journal/btw/watch.html, accessed on 8 June 2009

North, David (2006) Five years since 9/11: A political balance sheet, Part II, World Socialist Web Site, 12 September. Available online at http://www.wsws.org, accessed on 12 September 2006

Norton-Taylor, Richard, with Lloyd, Mark (1995) *Truth is a difficult concept*, London: Fourth Estate

Richelson, Jeffrey (2004, February 11) Iraq and Weapons of Mass Destruction, *National Security Archive electronic briefing book No. 80*, 11 February. Available online at http://www.gwu.edu, accessed on 14 November 2008

Ritter, Scott (2003) *Frontier justice: Weapons of Mass Destruction and the Bushwhacking of America*, New York: Context Books

Ritter, Scott (2004) The inspection process was rigged to create uncertainty over WMD to bolster the US and the UK's case for war, *Independent*, 10 October

Roeder, George Jr. (1997) Making things visible: Learning from the censors, Hein, Laura and Selden, Mark (eds) *Living with the bomb: American and Japanese cultural conflicts in the nuclear age*, Armonk, NY: M.E. Sharpe

Sartre, Jean-Paul (2003) *The philosophy of Jean-Paul Sartre*, New York: Vintage

Senate Select Committee on Intelligence Activities (Church Committee) (2007, orig. 1975) *Alleged assassination plots involving foreign leaders: Interim report of the select committee to study governmental operations with respect to intelligence activities*, Ipswich, MA: the Mary Ferrell Foundation. Available online at http://www.maryferrell.org/wiki/index. php/Post-Watergate_Intelligence_Investigations, accessed on 14 November 2008

Schmidt, Susan and Vandehei, Jim (2005) *NY Times* reporter released from jail, *Washington Post*, 30 September p. A01

Shafer, Jack (2003) The Jayson Blair project: How did he bamboozle *The New York Times?* Slate, 8 May. Available online at http://www.slate.com, accessed on 14 November 2008

SourceWatch (2005) The rise and fall of Ahmed Chalabi, SourceWatch: A Project of the Center for Media and Democracy, 25 May. Available online at http//www. sourcewatch.org, accessed on 14 November 2008

Spindle, Bill (2007) Crude reality: Soaring energy use puts oil squeeze on Iran, *Wall Street Journal*, 20 February p. A1

Stiglitz, Joseph and Bilmes, Linda (2008) *The $3 trillion war*, New York: W.W. Norton and Co.

Symonds, Peter (2007) Iranian diplomat accuses US of detention and torture, *World Socialist Web Site*, 11 April. Available online at http://wsws.org, accessed on 11 April 2007

UPI (2006) Iran to require oil payments in Euros, United Press International, 15 May. Available online at http://www.upi.com/energy, accessed on 14 November, 2008

Weber, Max (1962) *Basic concepts in sociology by Max Weber* (trans. Secher, H. P.), New York: the Citadel Press

Whitney, Mike (2007) Information warfare, psy-ops and the power of myth, Center for Research on Globalization, 14 February. Available online at http//www.globalresearch. ca, accessed on 14 February 2007

Wolfsfeld, Gadi (1997) *Media and political conflict: News from the Middle East*, Cambridge: Cambridge University Press

3

Peace journalism as political practice: A new, radical look at the theory

RICHARD LANCE KEEBLE

Let's begin, unusually, by considering three contrasting paintings to help highlight the crucial role of the media in radical, progressive movements. In 1872, the French impressionist Pierre-August Renoir painted fellow artist Edgar Degas relaxing: reading alone, his face close up to the text. This is the image of the solitary bourgeois male consuming the new professionalised newspaper in isolation but clearly with pleasure. Aesthetic concerns predominate.

Then there's Lyonel Feininger's *Newspaper readers* of 1916 (which fetched a mere £3.5m at Christie's in 2004). Its vibrant colours and flowing shapes convey brilliantly a real excitement and pleasure in newspaper consumption. But the figures are like you and me: racing about – their heads are down, intently reading, far too busy consuming the newspapers (significantly blank) far too superficially – and the readers are separate from each other. Significantly, too, they are all travelling in the same direction (to their right, our left!). Amongst all the bustle and individuality of the consuming public there is still an amazing conformism. Interestingly Feininger, an American who became a newspaper cartoonist and illustrator in Germany before concentrating on painting, moved through despair and loneliness to joy and delight during the painting of the piece in 1916.[1]

Finally there's Tina Modotti's 1929 photograph entitled *Campesinos reading El Machete* which radically confronts the feelings of alienation at the heart of our first paintings. It shows peasants with their wonderfully large sombreros, huddled around a copy of the revolutionary newspaper (see Noble 2000). Here the newspaper's central position within the composition is so symbolically powerful: the newspaper is shown educating workers and peasants and inspiring them to revolutionary deeds. And symbolically, too, the reading of the newspaper is a group activity. Politics merges with aesthetics with the photograph, so typical of Modotti's work in general. It's all so beautifully composed: the newspaper, angular and centrally positioned; contrasting with the beautifully round and elegant hats in the corners. And on all of it the sun, hope, shines. The photograph celebrates (without sentimentalising) the tradition of radical journalism committed to progressive social change which has been too often marginalised – and which I am both highlighting and theorising here.

Peace journalism as 'revolutionary' political practice

Jake Lynch and Annabel McGoldrick, in their seminal text on *Peace journalism* (2005) rightly highlight the corporate media's over-reliance on elite source and its focus on events rather than process. Building on the critiques of dominant news values by Galtung and Ruge (1965) and Galtung (1998), they also point out how journalists' "objectivity" conventions ultimately serve to marginalise voices calling for peace, restraint and dialogue. Lynch and McGoldrick even suggest that the peace journalism approach brings us "to the point of a journalistic revolution". And yet they fail to carry this "revolutionary" point to its logical conclusion.

They are not alone. The dominant strand in peace journalism theory focuses on the possibilities for transforming professional routines. Dov Shinar and Wilhelm Kempf, in their seminal *Peace journalism: The state of the art* (2007) draw together some of the leading theorists in the field – virtually all concentrate on professional issues, only occasionally acknowledging any "alternative" outlet. Susan Dente Ross, for instance (ibid: 53–74) ends an extraordinarily detailed and exhaustive review of the PJ literature with a passing reference to "independent, self-critical media" (such as www.IndyMedia.org) and an emphasis on the "norms of professional ethics and objectivity" (ibid: 74). She calls for a "journalism of symbolic rapprochement" involving a transformation of "the images of the self and the others" to end intractable, essentialist, cultural conflicts. But no "revolutionary" changes are needed. She concludes that "peace journalism does not involve any radical departure from contemporary journalism practice. Rather peace journalism requires numerous subtle and cumulative shifts in seeing, thinking, sourcing, narrating and financing the news".

In the final chapter, Dov Shinar (2007: 199–210) outlines the conclusions of a two-year project by the peace journalism group of the Toda Institute for Global Peace and Policy Research. His priorities are largely professional. Listing "four promises of peace journalism", his first is "professional improvement". Peace journalism, he says, "might change the seemingly inherent contradiction between the nature of peace stories and the professional demands of journalists" (ibid: 201). His fourth promise is to widen "scholarly and professional media horizons" away from "functionalism, hard core Marxism and technological determinism".

Thus a dominant strand in PJ theory focuses too closely on the notion of journalism as a privileged, professional activity and fails to take into account the critical intellectual tradition which locates professions historically and politically, seeing them as essentially occupational groupings with a legal monopoly of social and economic opportunities in the marketplace, underwritten by the state. Parkin (1979) and Collins (1990) stress the notion of social closure according to which occupations seek to regulate market conditions in their favour restricting access to a limited group of eligible professionals. Thus, the class origins of leading journalists in the UK still remain remarkably restricted. Research published by an all-party panel chaired by the former cabinet minister Alan Milburn in July 2009 showed that while only 7 per cent of the population attended privately-funded, independent schools some 54 per cent of top journalists did so (Wintour 2009).[2]

Such a notion of closure can also help explain the ideologies of professionalism and "objectivity" which largely exclude alternative, campaigning, social media even from the definition of "journalism". Althusser (1969) saw professions as part of the ideological state apparatus – crucial to the formation of bourgeois hegemony while Ivan Illich (1973) described the professions as "a form of imperialism" operating in modern societies as repressive mechanisms undermining democracy. Liberal theorists such as Mike Saks (1998; 2003) acknowledge the role in professionalisation of such factors as the development of ethical codes of practice, the setting up of education programmes – but they also stress that a certain degree of individual autonomy operates within the professions.

The *Independent*: Not so independent

In keeping with their stress on professional media, Lynch and McGoldrick (op cit: 205) offer the London-based *Independent* as one of the best examples of peace journalism. While the newspaper carries the outstanding reports of veteran reporters Robert Fisk (see Keeble 2009) and Patrick Cockburn, critical research suggests that, in many respects, the *Independent* reproduces many of the dominant news values of Fleet Street. A study by Florian Zollmann, for instance (2007), found that in its coverage of the US assault on the Iraqi city of Fallujah in 2004, the *Independent*, like the Rupert Murdoch-owned red-top tabloid, the *Sun*, failed to highlight the extent to which the attacks contravened the Geneva Conventions governing the conduct of war.

My own research into media coverage of US/UK militarism since 1990 (e.g. 1997, 1999, 2000 and 2004) suggests that the *Independent* largely reproduced dominant, pro-war attitudes over this period. During the US/UK attacks on Iraq in 1991 (when some 250,000 Iraqi soldiers are estimated to have been slaughtered), the Nato "humanitarian" assault on Serbia in 1999 and the invasion of Afghanistan in 2001, the *Independent* closely followed the pro-war consensus on Fleet Street. The *Independent* was critical of the 2003 invasion of Iraq: yet, with the 2 million strong anti-war March in London on 15 February just before the launch of Operation Iraqi Freedom (see Tempest 2003), it could be argued that this was a strategic and financial (rather than a moral and political) decision to exploit a massive mood amongst the public.

Peter Wilby, former editor of the *New Statesman* and the *Independent on Sunday*, defined the stance of the *Independent* during the late 1980s as "Thatcherism with a human face". Later on the editorial line remained "pro-market and generally pro-foreign intervention but compassionate towards the poor (in a vague sort of way) and leftish on social issues such as race, crime and smacking. Its position, in many respects, anticipated Blairism" (Wilby 2008). This is hardly a line to be associated with peace journalism.

Moreover, the *Independent* is too closely tied in to the dominant structures of economic and political power and so can hardly be expected promote consistently values and strategies that radically challenge the *status quo* – such as peace journalism. As David Edwards and David Cromwell point out (2009: 201–4), the chair of Independent News and Media Plc, the multinational company that publishes the *Independent*s is the Irish billionaire Sir Anthony O'Reilly. He earns £15 million a year in salary and dividends. His wife, the Greek shipping heiress Chryss Goulandris, has a fortune estimated at $442 million. INM has interests in Australia, India, Ireland, New Zealand, South Africa and the UK, publishing more than 200 newspapers and magazines with a combined weekly circulation of over 32 million copies.

Peace journalism as a form of political practice: Working within the mainstream

Peace journalism theory can provide a useful critique of the corporate media's promotion of militarism. But it is too elitist in its definition of journalism. And too utopian in its suggestion that improvements in professional routines and reforms in journalism training can bring about significant changes.

Change will, in fact, only come if based on a radical political analysis of the media and society. This will incorporate an awareness of the possibilities of journalistic activities both within and outside the corporate media and as part of a broader political project to democratise the media and society in general (Hackett and Carroll 2006). The strategy will also ultimately involve a radical broadening of the definition of journalism to include intellectuals, campaigners and citizens – all of them articulating their ideas within the dominant and alternative, global public spheres.

Peace journalism theory should not exclude activities within the mainstream. Its closeness to dominant economic, cultural and ideological forces means that the mainstream largely functions to promote the interests of the military/industrial/political complex (Keeble 1997: 24–6). Yet within advanced capitalist economies, currently suffering acute downturns from the global credit crunch (which to a large extent stems from the over-resourcing of US/UK military adventurism), the contradictions and complexities of corporate media have provided certain spaces for the progressive journalism of such excellent writers in the US, UK, France and India as John Langdon-Davies (1897–1971), Martha Gellhorn (1908–1998); George Orwell (1903–1950), I. F. Stone (1907–1989), James Cameron (1911–1985), Albert Camus (1913–1960), Phillip Knightley (born 1929), Seymour Hersh (1937), Susan George (1939), John Pilger (1939), Barbara Ehrenreich (1941), Peter Wilby (1944), Arundhati Roy (1960), George Monbiot (1963) and Naomi Klein (1970). Many of these combine an involvement in the corporate media with regular contributions to the "alternative", campaigning media (see Keeble 2009).

Theorising from a radical, alternative perspective, Robert Hackett usefully suggests that one broad strategy for the way ahead for peace journalism is to reform journalism from within. Herman and Chomsky's model (1988: 2) stresses the role of the corporate media in forming a single propaganda system in which "money and power are able to filter out the news fit to print, marginalise dissent and allow the government and dominant private interests to get their message across to the public". But Hackett argues that this model fails to explore adequately "the openings for oppositional interventions within and against the propaganda system" (op cit: 79) and "does little to identify the scope and conditions under which newsworkers could exercise the kind of choices called for by PJ".

Hackett therefore draws on the "hierarchy of influences" model of Shoemaker and Reese (1996) and Bourdieu's analysis of the media as a relatively autonomous institutional sphere (1998) to theorise the activities of newsworkers within the corporate media to promote peace journalism. Shoemaker and Reese identify five layers of influence within the media field – firstly the media workers themselves with their professionally related roles and ethics; secondly the daily work routines within the newsroom; next, the organisational imperatives of profit oriented, hierarchically structured media institutions; next, the extra-media influences such as governments, market structures and technology; and finally ideology (see Hackett 2007: 80–1). Bourdieu, on the other hand, while suggesting that journalism is a distinct field with its own ethos, also acknowledges that individual journalists are "active and creative agents". Thus Hackett concludes that the hierarchy and field models both suggest some degree of agency for newsworkers. "There is indeed a necessary role for dedicated journalists to take the lead" (ibid: 93).

The historical role of the alternative media – from the French Revolution to Iran today

Significantly Hackett acknowledges the limitations of journalists operating within the mainstream. "Ultimately, it seems probable that in Western corporate media, at least, journalists have neither sufficient incentives nor autonomy *vis-a-vis* their employers to transform the way news is done without support from powerful external allies" (ibid). Clearly, the crucial role of the non-corporate media in the development of peace journalism – and more broadly on the formation of an alternative peace and democratic culture – needs to be acknowledged. Historically, the alternative media have helped provide the basis on which an alternative, global public sphere (and an alternative peace culture) has been built. To take just a few examples: John Hartley has highlighted the centrality of journalists such as Robespierre, Marat, Danton, Hébert to the French Revolution of the 1790s (1996; see also Chapman 2008). Again, in the first half of the 19th century in the UK a massively popular radical, unstamped (and hence illegal) press played a crucial role in the campaign for trade union rights and social and political reforms (Black 2001; Conboy 2004; Curran and Seaton 2004). Later on many feminists and suffragettes (such as Sylvia Pankhurst: see Davis 1999) were both radical journalists and political agitators.

Informal underground communication networks and the role of newspapers such as the *Sowetan* were crucial in the anti-apartheid struggle in South Africa in the 1970s and 1980s (Downing 2005: 150–3). Jonathan Neale (2001: 122–30), in his seminal study of the Vietnam War, identified around 300 anti-war newspapers in the armed services during the course of the conflict. For instance, a small group of Trotskyists were behind *Vietnam GI*, a newspaper produced in Chicago with a print run of 15,000 and a mailing list of 3,000 in Vietnam. At Fort Bragg, a chapter of GIs United Against the War put out *Bragg Briefs*. Seymour Hersh's exposure of the My Lai massacre of March 1968, (when US soldiers slaughtered up to 500 men, women and children) was first published by the alternative news agency, Despatch News Service (see Knightley 1982: 259–60).

From 1963 to 1983, the Bolivian miners' radio stations highlighted the rights of workers. In Poland during the 1980s alternative publications of the Polish Roman Catholic Church and the samizdat publications of the Solidarity movement played crucial roles in the movement against the Soviet-backed government of the day (Atton 2009: 269).

In Nicaragua during the 1980s and 1990s the Movement of Popular Correspondents produced reports by non-professional, voluntary reporters from poor rural area that were published in regional and national newspapers – and they helped inspire revolutionary education and political activities. In the 1990s, the Revolutionary Association of Women of Afghanistan bravely reported on the abuse and execution of women under the Taliban producing audio cassettes, videos, a website and a magazine (ibid). This century we have seen the use made of websites by reformist movements in Burma and more recently (with Twitter, Flickr, Facebook and YouTube) in Iran (Kirkpatrick 2009; Garton Ash 2009). Similarly, in Peru, in 2009, Indigenous activists used Twitter and YouTube to highlight human rights abuses as more than 50,000 Amazonians demonstrated and went on strike in protest over US-Peru trade laws which threatened to open up ancestral territories to exploitation by multinational companies (Schnieter 2009).

Don't hate the media – be the media: The crucial role of the alternative media

Today, the internet and the blogosphere provide enormous opportunities for the development of peace journalism ideals – and a global peace culture. Stuart Allan (2006: 7) celebrates the bloggers and the "extraordinary contribution made by ordinary citizens offering their first hand reports, digital photographs, camcorder video footage, mobile telephone snapshots or audio clips". A great deal of this "citizen journalism" (while challenging the professional monopoly of the journalistic field) actually feeds into mainstream media routines and thus reinforces the dominant news value system (Hass 2005). The internet and blogosphere only become interesting when they serve to challenge the mainstream as crucial elements in progressive social and political movements.

Much of the theorising on peace journalism sees it as an aspiration –focusing too much on the journalist as professional producer. But we need to follow John Hartley in making a radical transformation of journalism theory. We need to move away from the concept of the audience as a passive consumer of a professional product to seeing the audience as producers of their own (written or visual) media. Hartley even draws on Article 19 of the Universal Declaration of Human Rights which he suggests proclaims the radical utopian-liberal idea that everyone has the right not only to seek and receive but to "impart" (in other words communicate) information and ideas (Hartley 2008: 42).

> The UN Declaration of journalism as a human right is aspirational; a challenge to action, not a description of facts. It represents an ideal type of liberal demo-cratic politics. If it is to mean anything in practice it needs to be championed, extended, used and defended (ibid).

For Hartley the UDHR in effect throws up enormous challenges to journalists, journalism educators and theorists. For if everyone is a journalist then how can journalism be professed? "Journalism has transferred from a modern expert system to contemporary open innovation – from 'one-to-many' to 'many to many' communication." Let us see how this redefinition of journalism can incorporate many different forms of media activity into the alternative public sphere.

The role of radical alternative journalists

Firstly, there is the role of radical journalists. George Orwell (1903–1950) is best known as the author of *Animal Farm* (1945) and *Nineteen Eighty-Four* (1949) but he was also a distinguished progressive journalist who concentrated most of his writing on obscure, alternative journals of the Left – such as *Controversy, New Leader, Left Forum, Left News, Polemic, Progressive, Politics and Letters*. From 1943 to 1947 he was literary editor of the leftist journal, *Tribune*, and through writing his regular "As I Please" column, instinctively developed a close relation-ship with his audience. This relationship was crucial to the flowering of Orwell's journalistic imagination. While he realised mainstream journalism was basically propaganda for wealthy newspaper proprietors, at *Tribune* he was engaging in the crucial political debate with people who mattered to him. They were an authen-tic audience compared with what Stuart Allan (2004: 85) called the "implied reader or imagined community of readers" of the mainstream media (Keeble 2001, 2007).

Today, in the UK, the *Morning Star* (www. morningstaronline.co.uk) significantly carries the logo under its masthead: "For peace and socialism". As the newspaper of the Communist Party of Britain, it is not a pacifist journal, but historically, movements seeking the resolution of conflicts by peaceful means have forged strategic alliances where appropriate with non-pacifist groups. So the mention of the *Morning Star* in the context of peace journalism may be controversial – but it is legitimate.

Its issue of 8–9 August 2009 is typical. A news item, ignored by the corporate media, reports the launch of a campaign by the International Trade Union Confederation and Mayors for Peace calling for the abolition of all nuclear weapons by 2020 (see www.itc-csi.org/peace). A full-page, colour photo-feature focuses on democratic struggles around the world, so one shows a woman offering prayers as she releases lanterns on the Motoyasu River opposite the Atomic Bomb Dome in Hiroshima, Japan, on the anniversary of the US atomic bomb attack. Another shows workers occupying the factory of the wind turbine manufacturers, Vestas, on the Isle of Wight, waving to supporters in the street.

A feature by the campaigning journalist John Pilger reviews some texts (ideal for holiday reading) for anyone wanting to understand US imperialism (such as Joseph Heller's *Catch-22*, Kurt Vonnegut's *Slaughterhouse five* and Harold Pinter's collected prose, poetry and political pieces). And to help the peace and radical movement organise, it provides a wonderfully eclectic "progressive website listing" and a list of radical events around the country (such as a seminar on Afghanistan, Pakistan and the "war on terror", organised by Leeds Coalition Against the War).

In the United States, Alexander Cockburn and Jeffery St Clair produce Counterpunch, an alternative investigative website (www.counterpunch.org). Out of their writings come many publications. There's also the excellent *Middle East Report* (www.merip.org), the *Nation* (www.thenation.com), *Mother Jones* (www.motherjones.com), *Z Magazine* (www.zcommunications.org/zmag), *In These Times* (www.inthesetimes.com); in Chennai, India, *Frontline* (www.frontlineonnet.com); in London there's the investigative www.corporatewatch.org. Coldtype.net in the UK brings together many of the writings by radical journalists, campaigners and academics (such as Felicity Arbuthnot and William Blum). Dahr Jamail is a freelance journalist reporting regularly from a critical peace perspective on the Middle East (seewww.dahrjamailiraq.com: see Chapter 8) while Democracy Now! is an alternative US radio station (with allied website and podcasts) run by Amy Goodman, overtly committed to peace journalism.

Chris Atton (2002: 19–25) argues that alternative media such as these often draw inspiration from Chomsky's critique of the corporate myths of "balance" and "objectivity" (1989) and stresses, instead, their explicitly partisan character. Moreover, they seek "to invert the hierarchy of access" to the news by explicitly foregrounding the viewpoints of "ordinary" people (activists, protestors, local residents), citizens whose visibility in the mainstream media tends to be obscured by the presence of elite groups and individuals (Atton 2002: 20).

The role of radical intellectuals

Then there's the role of radical intellectuals such as the American historian Tom Engelhardt (www.tomdispatch.com). Other radical intellectuals prominent in the blogosphere have included the late Edward Said, Noam Chomsky, Norman Solomon, James Winter, Mark Curtis and the recently deceased African intellectual campaigner and journalist Tajudeen Abdul-Raheem. In the UK, academics David Edwards and David Cromwell edit the radical media monitoring site www.medialens.org which monitors the mainstream media from a radical Chomskyite/Buddhist perspective and in support of the global peace movement. Professor David Miller and William Dinan are part of the collective running www.spin-watch.org which critiques the PR industry from a radical, peace perspective.

The role of research centres

Some research centres play important roles in the formation of an alternative global public sphere. For instance, http://globalresearch.ca is the website of the Centre for Research and Globalisation, an independent research and media group based in Montreal. It carries excellent articles by Michel Chussodovsky, Professor of Economics at the University of Ottawa. Special subjects on the site include US war agenda, crimes against humanity, militarisation and WMD, poverty and social inequality, media disinformation and intelligence. There is also the website produced by the London-based Institute of Islamic Political Thought (www.ii-pt.com).

Political activists doubling as media activists

Political activists often double as media activists. Take for instance IndyMedia (www.indymedia.org). It emerged during the "battle of Seattle" in 1999 when thousands of people took to the streets to protest against the World Trade Organisation and the impact of global free trade relations – and were met by armoured riot police. Violent clashes erupted with many injuries on both sides. In response 400 volunteers, rallying under the motto "Don't hate the media: be the media", created a site and a daily news sheet, the *Blind Spot*, which spelled out news of the demonstration from the perspective of the protestors. The site incorporated news, photographs, audio and video footage – and received 1.5 million hits in its first week. Today there are more than 150 independent media centres in around 45 countries over six continents. Their mission statement says:

> The Independent Media Centre is a network of collectively run media outlets for the creation of radical, accurate, and passionate tellings of the truth. We work out of a love and inspiration for people who continue to work for a better world, despite corporate media's distortions and unwillingness to cover the efforts to free humanity.

In the UK, *Peace News* (for non-violent revolution), edited by author and political activist Milan Rai and Emily Johns, comes as both a hard copy magazine and a lively website (www.peacenews.info) combining analysis, cultural reviews and news of the extraordinarily brave acts of peace movement campaigners internationally (see Chapter 12). As its website stresses, it is "written and produced by and for activists, campaigners and radical academics from all over the world". Not only does their content differ radically from the mainstream. In their collaborative, non-hierarchical structures and sourcing techniques alternative media operations challenge the conventions of mainstream organisational routines. (Atton 2002: 22–5) describes the alternative journalism of the British video magazine *Undercurrents* and Indymedia as "native reporting". "Both privilege a journalism politicised through subjective testimony, through the subjects being represented by themselves."

Members of Fit Watch, a protest group opposed to police forward intelligence teams (Fits), the units that monitor demonstrations and meetings, similarly combine political and media activism in their "sousveillance" – the latest buzzword for taking videos and photographs of police activities and then uploading them on to the web (Lewis and Vallée 2009; Coatman 2009). They are part of a growing international media activist, protest movement. In Palestine, for instance, B'Tselem, the Israeli human rights group, gave video cameras to 160 citizens in the West Bank and Gaza and their shocking footage of abuses by Israeli settlers and troops was broadcast on the country's television as well as internationally (McCarthy 2009).

'Citizen journalists'

Citizens and campaigners in the UK and US who upload images of police surveillance or brutality on to YouTube or citizens who report on opposition movements via blogs, Twitter and websites in authoritarian societies such as China, Burma, Iran and Egypt can similarly be considered participants in the alternative media sphere. Commenting on the role of citizen blogs during the 2003 Iraq invasion, Stuart Allan stresses (2006: 111):

> ... these emergent forms of journalism have the capacity to bring to bear alternative perspectives, contexts and ideological diversity to war reporting, providing users with the means to connect with distant voices otherwise being marginalised, if not silenced altogether, from across the globe.

And for Atton (2009: 268), participatory, amateur media production contests the concentration of institutional and professional media power "and challenges the media monopoly on producing symbolic forms".

Peace movement and human rights organisations

Peace movement and international human rights organisations also produce excellent campaigning sites which can be viewed as forms of activist journalism. For instance, http://ipb.org is the site of the International Peace Bureau founded in 1891 and Nobel Peace Prize winner in 1910. It currently has 282 member organisations in 70 countries. Or there is the Campaign for the Abolition of War (http://www.abolishwar.org.uk). Formed in 2001 following the Hague Appeal for Peace in 1999, its founder president was Professor Sir Joseph Rotblat FRS, Nobel Peace Prize Laureate; while its founder chair was Bruce Kent. They work closely with the International Peace Bureau in Geneva for an end to arms sales, economic justice, a more equitable United Nations, political rights for persecuted minorities, a world peace force (instead of gunboat democracy), conflict prevention and education for peace in schools, colleges and the media.

The organisation, Reprieve (www.reprieve.org.uk), campaigns on behalf of those often unlawfully detained by the US and UK in the "war on terror" and its director Clive Stafford Smith writes regular pieces for the "quality" press and the leftist *New Statesman* magazine, highlighting cases of abuse. For instance, on 10 August 2009, he wrote in the *Guardian* of three cases of government cover-ups. In the first, the government was refusing to hand over to the High Court details about the horrific torture of Binyam Mohamed (in Morocco and at the notorious US detention facility at Guantánamo Bay, Cuba) on the grounds that it would endanger future intelligence co-operation with the Americans. In the second case, after the government admitted that two men had been taken for torture ("rendered" in the jargon) via the Indian Ocean island of Diego Garcia, they were still refusing Reprieve's requests for their names. And the final case involved cover-ups over Britain's complicity in the renditions of prisoners from Iraq to abuse in Afghanistan (Stafford Smith 2009). In the US, the American Civil Liberties Union (see www.aclu.org) has consistently campaigned to expose the human rights abuses which have accompanied the "war on terror" and produced a important series of reports on the issue.[3]

Beyond 'alternative utopianism': The Iranian Revolution of 1979

Let us next consider dominant notions of conflict which are closely tied to professional ideologies; how they obscure the importance historically of nonviolent strategies – and the implications of the accompanying political analysis for journalistic practice. Kate Coyer rightly warns of "alternative utopianism" (2005). Indeed, there is a danger of exaggerating the peaceful and democratic possibilities of the alternative and web-based media – particularly since, as Colin Sparks stresses (2005), the internet globally still remains an elite medium. Yet, historically, nonviolent people's protests are not mere utopian aspirations – they have achieved many remarkable successes The Iranian revolution of 1979 provides a perfect example. In that year, the Shah of Iran, who ruled over one of the most oppressive and murderous regimes of the last century, was removed from power following a remarkable campaign of non-violent civil disobedience.

As Kurt Schock comments in his analysis of nonviolent resistance movements (2005: 2): "The lifeblood of the shah's regime was drained by mass civil disobedience." On 16 January 1979 the Shah was forced to flee to Egypt while on 1 February, Khomeini, cheered on by crowds of five million, returned from exile. Two armed guerrilla movements in Iran, the Fedayeen and the Mujahhadin, had been ineffective in challenging the state. The shah was toppled by an unarmed insurrection in which ordinary citizens engaged in methods of nonviolent action such as protests, demonstrations, strikes, boycott and civil disobedience. "Moreover, Khomeini encouraged non-violent discipline and urged people to treat soldiers as brothers rather than as enemies. Soldiers who deserted from the military were treated as heroes and carried atop people's shoulders in mass marches" (ibid).

Countering the myth of revolutionary violence

All this completely contradicts dominant public, academic and corporate media conceptions about revolutions and radical social, protest movements. Generally they are perceived as inevitably violent.[4] Yet the evidence suggests that the Iranian revolution, in fact, was part of an extraordinary trend in which authoritarian regimes have been most seriously challenged by nonviolent, unarmed resistance movements.

For instance, there were unarmed, "people power" insurrections against:

- the military juntas in Bolivia in the late 1970s;
- the Duvalier regime in Haiti and Nimiery regime in Sudan in 1985;
- the regime of President Marcos in the Philippines in 1986;
- the regime of Philippine President Joseph Estrada in 2001 (known as EDSA II: the Second People Power Revolution).

In addition there were pro-democracy movements in:

- Chile, South Africa and South Korea in the 1980s
- Bangladesh, Nepal, Mali, Madagascar and Thailand between 1989 and 1993
- Indonesia between 1997–98 and in Nigeria between 1998–99.

The hegemony of the Soviet Union in Eastern Europe, the Caucasus and Central Asia was also dislodged largely through nonviolent resistance movements, beginning with the Solidarity movement in Poland in the 1980s. Between 1989 and 1991 most communist regimes from East Germany to Mongolia were toppled by unarmed insurrections. Moreover, from 2000 to 2006, organised civilian populations successfully employed nonviolent strategies including boycotts, strikes and protests to challenge authoritarian regime and exact political concessions in Serbia (2000), Madagascar (2002), Georgia (2003) and Ukraine (2004–5), Lebanon (2005), Kyrgyzstan (2005) and Nepal (2006) (see Stephan and Chenoweth 2008: 7–8). Even after the left-leaning Honduran President Manuel Zelaya was removed in a coup in July 2009 the masses responded non-violently to the military repression organising strikes, marches and closing down television and radio stations in protest (Milne 2009).

In a major analysis covering the years 1900 to 2006, Stephan and Chenoweth show that major nonviolent campaigns have achieved success in 53 per cent of cases compared to 26 per cent for violent resistance campaigns. They focus, in particular, on East Timor's struggle for independence, 1988–99, the "people power" movement that ousted Philippine dictator Ferdinand Marcos in 1986 and the failed, mass non-violent resistance movement against the Burma dictatorship in 1988. According to Stephan and Chenoweth there are two main reasons for the success of non-violent resistance: firstly a campaign's commitment to nonviolence enhances its domestic and international legitimacy encouraging more broad-based commitment to the resistance which translates into increased pressure on the target. Secondly, while regimes can easily justify counter-attacks against violent resisters, violence against nonviolent groups is likely to backfire against the regime. They conclude:

> Our findings challenge the conventional wisdom that violent resistance against conventionally superior adversaries is the most effective way for resistance groups to achieve policy goals. Instead, we assert that nonviolent resistance is a forceful alternative to political violence that can pose effective challenges to democratic and nondemocratic opponents and at times can do so more effectively than violent resistance (ibid: 9).

The overall picture is still very complex. People power movements also suffered defeats in several countries over this period: in El Salvador, Niger, Palestine, Pakistan, Burma, Tibet, China, Kenya and East Timor. At the same time, armed guerrilla movements also achieved successes: the Taliban in Afghanistan in the mid-1990s. Marxist-Leninist-Maoist inspired armed revolutionary groups continue with the Sendero Luminoso (Shining Path) in Peru, the Revolutionary Armed Forces of Colombia, the New People's Army in the Philippines, the Maoist rebels in Nepal, the Tamil Tigers in Sri Lanka, the fighters of Hamas in Palestine and Hezbollah in Lebanon.

But it can be concluded that in the late 20th century armed guerrilla insurgencies declined while non-violent strategies for challenging regimes increased. The role of the media in these insurrections has yet to be properly researched. Yet journalists clearly have the responsibility to promote the voices of those engaged in nonviolent direct action to their proper place within the historical record.[5]

Conclusion: The right of all to journalism

In short, I'm calling for a radical political re-theorising of journalism and more specifically peace journalism. Corporate media globally has long been challenged by alternative forms. But the emergence of internet-based media has highlighted the need to acknowledge the right of all (and not just the members of a professionalised, privileged and largely white, male elite) to communicate in the main or alternative public spheres. To re-write Karl Marx: Go for it journalists – you have nothing to lose but your professional chains.

Out of my theory – which views journalism as essentially *political* practice – emerges a political strategy for change. As Richard Falk argues, if peace journalism is to become more than an argument at the outer margins of political debate, it has to become a *political* project on the agenda of global reform (2008: ix). But this strategy is not based on "alternative utopianism". In fact, the record of "people power" movements (marginalised in the media) over recent decades suggests that the nonviolent political option is more likely to succeed than violence. Whether the peace journalism option succeeds remains to be seen.

Notes

1   See http://cartoons.osu.edu/FEININGER/index.html, accessed 5 August 2009.
2   The same report also showed that 75 per cent of judges, 70 per cent of finance direc-
    tors, 45 per cent of top civil servants and 32 per cent of MPs were privately educated
    (see Wintour op cit). A report in 2006 by the Sutton Trust found a similar domination
    by public school graduates of the top journalistic jobs in the UK. See http://www.
    pressgazette.co.uk/story.asp?storycode=34562&encCode=8896956351BC8106713J
    TBS737226611, accessed on 14 September 2009.
3   For instance, in August 2009, a federal judge upheld an appeal from the ACLU for
    the release of a long-suppressed report by the CIA's inspector general which suggested
    that the agency threatened a captured al-Qaida leader with a power drill and pistol in
    a mock execution (Beaumont 2009).
4   Gandhi's struggle for independence in India and Martin Luther King's civil rights
    campaigns in the US are the exceptions, as Veronique Dudouet points out (2008: 2).
5   A detailed bibliography, regularly update by April Carter, Howard Clark and Michael
    Randle, on people power and protest since 1945 can be accessed at http://www.civil-
    resistance.info/bibliography.

References

Allan, Stuart (2004) *News culture*, Maidenhead: Open University Press, second edition
Allan, Stuart (2006) *Online news: Journalism and the internet*, Maidenhead: Open
    University Press
Althusser, Louis (1969) *For Marx*, London: Penguin
Atton, Chris (2002) *Alternative media*, London: Sage

Atton, Chris (2009) Alternative and citizen journalism, Wahl-Jorgensen, Karin and Hanitzsch, Thomas (eds) *The handbook of journalism studies*, New York, Abingdon, Oxon: Routledge pp 265–78

Beaumont, Peter (2009) CIA "threatened al-Qaida leader with mock execution", *Observer*, 23 August

Black, Jeremy (2001) *The English press 1621–1861*, Stroud, Gloucestershire: Sutton Publishing

Bourdieu, Pierre (1998) *On television*, London: Pluto Press

Chapman, Jane (2008) Republican citizenship, ethics and the French Revolutionary press, Keeble, Richard (ed.) *Communication ethics now*, Leicester: Troubador pp 131–41

Chomsky, Noam (1989) *Necessary illusions: Thought control in democratic societies*, London: Pluto Press

Coatman, Clare (2009) Watching the watchers, *Red Pepper*, June/July pp 18–9

Collins, Richard (1990) Market closure and the conflict theory of professions, Burrage, Michael and Torstendahl, Rolf (eds) *Professions in theory and history: Rethinking the study of professions*, London, Newbury Park and New Delhi: Sage pp 24–42

Conboy, Martin (2004) *Journalism: A critical history*, London: Sage

Coyer, Kate (2005) If it leads it bleeds: The participatory newsmaking of the Independent Media Centre, de Jong, Wilma, Shaw, Martin and Stammers, Neil (eds) *Global activism, global media*, London: Pluto Press pp 165–77

Curran, James and Seaton, Jean (2004) *Power without responsibility: The press, broadcasting and new media in Britain*, London: Routledge, seventh edition

Edwards, David and Cromwell, David (2009) *Newspeak in the 21st century*, London: Pluto

Davis, Mary (1999) *Sylvia Pankhurst: A life in radical politics*, London: Pluto

Downing, John (2005) Activist media, civil society and social movements, de Jong, Wilma, Shaw, Martin and Stammers, Neil (eds) *Global activism, global media*, London: Pluto Press pp 149–64

Dudouet, Véronique (2008) *Nonviolent resistance and conflict transformation in power asymmetries*. Available online at www.berghof-handbook.net, accessed on 1 May 2009

Falk, Richard (2008) Foreword, Lynch, Jake (2008) *Debates in peace journalism*, Sydney: Sydney University Press pp v–xix

Galtung, Johan (1998) High road – low road: Charting the course for peace journalism, *Track Two*, Vol. 7, No. 4, Centre for Conflict Resolution, South Africa. Available online at http://ccrweb.ccr.uct.ac.za/archive/two/7_4/p07_highroad_lowroad.html, accessed on 7 April 2009

Galtung, Johan and Ruge, Mari Holmboe (1965) The structure of foreign news, *Journal of International Peace Research*, Vol. 1 pp 64–90 [reprinted in Tumber, Howard (ed.) (1999) *News: A reader*, Oxford: Oxford University Press pp 21–31]

Garton Ash, Timothy (2009) Twitter counts more than armouries in this new politics of people power, *Guardian*, 18 June

Hackett, Robert A. (2007) Is peace journalism possible? Shinar, Dove and Kempf, Wilhelm (eds) (2007) *Peace journalism: The state of the art*, Berlin: Regener pp 75–94

Hackett, Robert A. and Carroll, William K (2006) *Remaking media: The struggle to democratise public communication*, New York, Abingdon, Oxon: Routledge

Hartley, John (1996) *Popular reality: Journalism, modernity, popular culture*, London and New York: Arnold

Hartley, John (2008) Journalism as a human right: The cultural approach to journalism, Loffelholz, M and Weaver, D. (eds) *Global journalism research: Theories, methods, findings, future*, Oxford: Blackwell pp 39–51

Hass, Tanni (2005) From "public journalism" to the "public's journalism"? Rhetoric and reality in the discourse on weblogs, *Journalism Studies*, Vol. 6, No. 3 pp 387–96

Herman, Edward S. and Chomsky, Noam (1988) *Manufacturing consent: The political economy of the mass media*, New York: Pantheon Books

Illich, Ivan (1973) The professions as a form of imperialism, *New Society*, 13 September

Keeble, Richard (1997) *Secret state, silent press: New Militarism, the Gulf and the modern image of warfare*, Luton: John Libbey

Keeble, Richard (1999) A Balkan birthday for Nato, *British Journalism Review*, Vol. 10, No. 2 pp 16–20

Keeble, Richard (2000) New Militarism and the manufacture of warfare, Hammond, Philip and Herman, Edward S. (eds) *Degraded capability: The media and the Kosovo crisis*, London, Pluto Press pp 59–59

Keeble, Richard (2001) Orwell as war correspondent: A reassessment, *Journalism Studies*, Vol. 2, No. 3 pp 393–406

Keeble, Richard (2004) *Information warfare in an age of hyper-militarism*, Allan, Stuart and Zeliger, Barbie (eds), Reporting war, London: Routledge pp 43–58

Keeble, Richard (2007) (eds) The lasting in the ephemeral: Assessing George Orwell's As I Please columns, Keeble, Richard and Wheeler, Sharon (eds) *The journalistic imagination: Literary journalists from Defoe to Capote and Carter*, Abingdon: Routledge pp 100–15

Keeble, Richard (2009) War and the journalistic imagination: The reporting of George Orwell and Robert Fisk, *Literary Journalism: Newsletter of the International Association of Literary Journalism Studies*, summer pp 4–8

Kirkpatrick, Marshall (2009) Dear CNN: Please check Twitter for news about Iran, Read Write Web, 13 June. Available online at http://www.readwriteweb.com/archives/dear_cnn_please_check_twitter_for_news_about_iran.php, accessed on 26 August 2009

Knightley, Phillip (1982) *The first casualty: The war correspondent as hero, propagandist and myth maker*, London: Quartet

Lewis, Paul and Vallée, Marc (2009) Police footage reveals treatment of pair who asked for badge number, *Guardian*, 22 June

Lynch, Jake and McGoldrick, Annabel (2005) *Peace journalism*, Stroud: Hawthorn Press

McCarthy, Rory (2009) Cameras for action, *Guardian*, 22 June

Milne, Seamus (2009) The Honduras coup is a sign: The radical tide can be turned, *Guardian*, 13 August

Neale, Jonathan (2001) *The American War: Vietnam 1960–75*, London: Bookmarks

Noble, Andrea (2000) *Tina Modotti: Image, texture, photography*, Albuquerque: University of New Mexico Press

Parkin, Frank (1979) *Marxism and class theory: A bourgeois critique*, London: Tavistock Publications

Ross, Susan Dente (2007) (De-)Constructing conflict: A focused review of war and peace journalism, Shinar, Dove and Kempf, Wilhelm (eds) (2007) *Peace journalism: The state of the art*, Berlin: Regener pp 53–74

Saks, Mike (1998) The wheel turns? Professionalisation and alternative medicine in Britain, *Journal of Interprofessional Care*, Vol. 13, No. 2 pp 129–38

Saks, Mike (2003) *Orthodox and alternative medicine: Politics, professionalization and health care*, London: Sage

Schneiter, Teague (2009) Social media and online technologies for Indigenous rights in Peru, 17 September. Available online at http://hub.witness.org/en/blog/social-media-and-online-technologies-indigenous-rights-peru, accessed on 30 September 2009

Schock, Kurt (2005) *Unarmed insurrections: People power movements in nondemocracies*, Minneapolis and London: University of Minnesota Press

Shinar, Dove (2007) Peace journalism: The state of the art, Shinar, Dove and Kempf, Wilhelm (eds) (2007) *Peace journalism: The state of the art*, Berlin: Regener pp 199–210

Shinar, Dove and Kempf, Wilhelm (eds) (2007) *Peace journalism: The state of the art*, Berlin: Regener

Shoemaker, Pamela J. and Reese, Stephen D. (1996) *Mediating the message: Theories of influences on mass media content*, New York: Longman

Sparks, Colin (2005) Media and the (global) public sphere: An evaluative approach, de Jong, Wilma and Shaw, Martin and Stammers, Neil (eds), *Global activism, global media*, London: Pluto Press pp. 34–49

Stafford Smith, Clive (2009) All talk and no trouser, *Guardian*, 10 August

Stephan, Maria J. and Chenoweth, Erica (2008) Why civil resistance works: The strategic logic of nonviolent conflict, *International Security*, Vol. 33, No. 1 pp 7–44. Available online at http://belfercenter.ksg.harvard.edu/files/IS3301_pp007–044_Stephan_Chenoweth.pdf, accessed on 1 May 2009

Tempest, Matthew (2003) Stopping the war and beyond, *Guardian*, 22 December

Wilby, Peter (2008) It is. Is he? *Guardian*, 14 April

Wintour, Patrick (2009) Britain's closed shop: Damning report on social mobility failings, *Guardian*, 22 July

Zollmann, Florian (2007) Fighting fanatics, killing people: The limits of corporate journalism during the US assault on Fallujah, *Ethical Space: The International Journal of Communication Ethics*, Vol. 4, No. 4 pp 24–35

4

Propaganda, war, peace and the media

JAKE LYNCH

Back in the early 2000s, BBC News 24, the corporation's domestic rolling TV news channel, was at a low ebb. Without its own controller since the inaugural incumbent, Tim Orchard, left, it projected a generally lacklustre image, compounded by suffering a series of conspicuous on-air embarrassments. Worse: these tended to show the BBC in an unflattering light compared with its commercial rival, Sky News.

One was the "David Beckham debacle" in the Soham murder case. Two ten-year-old girls, Holly Wells and Jessica Chapman, went missing from their home in a small town in eastern England in August 2002, both wearing replica soccer shirts as modelled by their hero, the then Manchester United footballer, David Beckham. Some days passed before their bodies were found, and speculation mounted that the England captain would record a video message to the girls, appealing to them to come home in case they had simply wandered off on some misguided adventure.

It so happened that a senior police officer on the case went by the name of Superintendent David Becks – "Becks" being, also, the midfielder's widely known nickname. At one point, Sky displayed a "crawler" across the bottom of their picture, giving the information that there was to be a "Becks statement in half an hour". News 24, frustrated at being repeatedly beaten to break new developments, immediately followed suit. However, in a deliciously characteristic twist, the BBC deemed the use of a nickname to be inappropriate in the context of a solemn event, so they proudly emblazoned on the screen the startling information that David Beckham himself was to make a personal intervention in the story. Sky, of course, had been referring to the other Becks.

Not long afterwards, a spokesman for the US corporation, Dow Chemical, contacted BBC World, News 24's sister channel which takes over the same slot overnight, offering a live interview about an important new development in the campaign for compensation by victims of the Bhopal chemical disaster. Dow took over the company responsible, Union Carbide, in 2001, and had been resisting any claims. The spokesman, however, revealed that Dow was now ready to admit liability and pay out in full. Except, it wasn't, and the interviewee, who spoke from the BBC's Geneva studio, had nothing to do with the company. Anyone could be hoaxed once, perhaps – but the BBC compounded the error by playing a recording of the same interview on air again, an hour later.

Throughout this time came the annual "day of shame" when Sky News would carry off the Royal Television Society award for Best News Channel – a period spanning arguably the biggest single story in the rolling news era, the attacks in the US of 11 September 2001. As an insider – I worked as a reporter and presenter for Sky from 1996 to 2001 and then for the BBC channels for another five years – I witnessed at first hand the sense of corporate contumely at Television Centre, hardening into a (perhaps typically British) determination to try harder, especially when the 2003 invasion of Iraq came on to the agenda. This was going to be "our war": we were not, we resolved, going to be at home to Mr Cock-Up.

It's a roundabout way of explaining a media frame with important implications for at least one element of the propaganda about the war, namely that Iraqis would welcome the US and allied troops as "liberators" from the regime of Saddam Hussein. The key image in cementing this impression in place came with the fall of Saddam Hussein's statue on 9 April 2003. Across the Atlantic, Fox News presenter David Asman told viewers: "If you don't have goose bumps now, you will never have them in your life" and NBC's Tom Brokaw likened the event to "all the statues of Lenin [that] came down all across the Soviet Union".

The journalistic virility test over the fall of Saddam

At the BBC, language was more restrained, but the editorial tension over the coverage boiled down to one simple resolve, ground out through management's gritted teeth: *this-WILL-happen-live-on-the-BBC* – a kind of journalistic virility test that News 24 must pass, if it wanted to survive. The drama took several hours to unfold. First, an American soldier climbed a ladder and covered Hussein's head with the Stars and Stripes, passed from a colleague on the ground. Then, as if suddenly sensitive to the "error", they replaced it with an Iraqi flag instead. A rope was tied around the neck of the huge statue, by which time a number of onlookers had gathered around the plinth, in Baghdad's Firdaus Square. Some of them grabbed the other end and heaved. Eventually, the metal gave way, and Saddam was duly pulled down from his high position – both figuratively, by the invasion, and now literally, at least in effigy.

Throughout this time, the live BBC camera remained trained on the narrowly defined area around the statue itself, in common with others from broadcasters the world over. Programme producers knew they dare not "blink" – cut away for a couple of minutes' sports round-up, say, or a digest of the other main stories that day – for fear of missing the crucial moment. It was the highly competitive nature of the television news business, felt with especial keenness on the BBC newsdesk after the sequence of reverses I have described, that mandated an unblinking glare on that one aspect of the conflict.

Before long, dissenting voices, from outside mainstream media, drew attention to aspects of the wider picture, framed out in the concentration on the statue itself, that did not fit with the story as presented. Far from the swelling crowds that propelled state communism into the dustbin of history, a wide shot of Firdaus Square revealed that the small knot of demonstrators visible in the picture were, in fact, the only ones present. The rest of the area – a vast urban *piazza* – was empty. And, just in case any did try to gain access, a US armoured vehicle was positioned to stop them at the head of each of the four roads giving on to the square itself. A closer look at some of those celebrating the *denouement* revealed remarkable resemblances to bodyguards who had accompanied Ahmed Chalabi, head of the Iraqi National Congress, as he returned from exile in the US days earlier.

This was, in other words, a rent-a-crowd, and John Stauber and Sheldon Rampton follow a trail of evidence, in their book, *Weapons of mass deception*, that the whole event (including the apparent "error" with the flags) was staged: the work, specifically, of a public relations consultant named John W. Rendon, whom they note is "a self-described 'information warrior'" (2003: 5). Rendon characterises his work simply as "using communication to meet . . . corporate policy objectives" (ibid). A key message frame for supporting the war – "we're here to help you" – thus meshed with a key media frame – "don't miss the crucial moment" – to produce a strong and resonant image. A study in content analysis on the coverage by major UK broadcasters of this invasion phase of the conflict found that the BBC was more likely than either of its main two rivals, Sky and ITN, to present Iraqis as "welcoming" the "liberating" troops (Lewis 2003).

Defining propaganda

The episode meets every one of the criteria for defining propaganda, in the influential and carefully constructed formula devised by Jowett and O'Donnell: "The deliberate and systematic attempt to shape perceptions, manipulate cognitions and direct behaviour to achieve a response that furthers the desired intent of the propagandist" (1999: 6).

The concept is distinguished, they say, in "emphasis[ing] purpose" (ibid: 3); propaganda, to *be* propaganda, must be "wilful, intentional and premeditated" (ibid: 7). The story of Saddam's statue shows, however, another aspect of propaganda, and it interrogates the intentionality and directionality inscribed in Jowett and O'Donnell's formula, to resemble more closely what Scheufele (1999), in a historical survey of literature on theories of media effects, calls a "feedback loop" involving message frames, media frames and audience frames, which means it is always already there, by the time a story breaks or develops.

Other writers on propaganda have attempted to dislodge from it the component of intentionality, including Jacques Ellul who regarded it as part and parcel of technologically advanced societies, having "certain identical results" (1965: xv). Propaganda was, in other words, a triumph of form over content, since these results were similar even when the agency for propaganda had quite different intentions, as, for instance, under Communist or Fascist regimes and in liberal democratic political and social formations.

There is an anticipatory trace, here, of Jacques Derrida's concept of logocentrism: the shared characteristic of even apparently antagonistic strands of Western intellectual traditions, in being arranged around a series of binary oppositions, held in place by a "transcendental signifier". It is the *kind* of thinking that propaganda stimulates – the way perceptions and cognitions take shape around it – rather than the specific content, which serves to re-inscribe these hierarchies, making them seem natural and therefore bolstering the position of those occupying the favoured position "on top". News is the ideal vehicle for this because it weaves images and snippets of information into what Gaye Tuchman calls a "web of facticity...To flesh out any one supposed fact, one amasses a host of supposed facts that, when taken together, present themselves as both individually and collectively self-validating" (1978: 86).

Heikki Luostarinen (1994) produced a formalist model of war propaganda that emphasised its three main symptomatic narrative characteristics, rather than the intentionality of its authors. Firstly, referential levels of the narrative are harmonised, so stories about everything from the quotidian events to the mythical references and metaphors apparently "fit in" to the same overarching theme. Pictures from early in the invasion of Iraq, which I remember being avidly seized on in the BBC newsroom and put straight to air, showed US Marines handing out food parcels to a handful of apparently grateful Iraqi civilians in the southern border town of Umm Qasr. It seemed to be a "detail that captured a whole story", even though – as with the apparent popular glee at the pulling-down of the statue – it flatly contradicted the facts on the ground. Years later, I shared a speaking platform in Sydney with Matt Howard, a former Marine and veteran of the campaign, who recalled being directly ordered *not* to hand out spare ration packs because that was "not your job".

Secondly, Luostarinen suggests, war propaganda narratives are based on motivating logic: lessons from the past and why they mandate action now. Publics in the "coalition of the willing" countries were told it was imperative to "strike first to save ourselves", rather than wait, as US National Security Adviser Condoleezza Rice told a television interviewer, "for the smoking gun to be a mushroom cloud". And thirdly, such narratives are rich in polarising references to positive and negative identification and socialisation.

How 'balance' promotes war

I have argued elsewhere (2005) that news coverage showing a dominant strain of war journalism forms a receptive vehicle for such narratives – at least in this last respect – owing to conventions of news that arose, in turn, from the economic and political interests of the media industry, notably the preference in public service broadcasting, exemplified by BBC News, for "balance". The easiest way to produce balanced coverage of a conflict is to construct it as dyadic ("on the one hand, on the other hand"), but this lends itself to the sequence of logic that Johan Galtung has called DMA syndrome, where Dualism leads inexorably to Manicheism – a world divided into good and evil – and the last battle between the two, or Armageddon.

This formalism in defining and apprehending propaganda, emphasising the imbrication of its narrative characteristics with news conventions – "like a mortice and tenon joint in carpentry" as Lynch and McGoldrick say (2005: 4) – has sometimes risked appearing acontextual. The implication of Luostarinen's first symptom of war propaganda might be simply that the one prime predictor of newsworthiness in a potential story is that it is already regarded as a story. Of Johan Galtung and Mari Holmboe Ruge's eight "tuning factors" in *The structure of foreign news* (1965), no fewer than three have to do with this sense of inertia. News "must be *meaningful*, able to be slotted in to pre-existing codes or narratives, to be made sense of when it is received... it must be *consonant* with what is expected... [Another] observation is that a signal that is *already tuned into* is more likely to continue" (see Lynch and Galtung 2010).

Nohrstedt and Ottosen consider the propaganda around the previous US-led invasion of Iraq, in 1991, in the context of globalisation, quoting the "relativisation" theory of Roland Robertson to distinguish this from rival "economistic interpretations" of what globalisation means (2000: 27). "Globalisation as a concept," Robertson says, "refers both to the compression of the world and the intensification of consciousness of the world as a whole" (1992: 8). We are "witness to – and participants in – a massive, twofold process involving the interpenetration of the universalisation of particularism and the particularisation of universalism" (ibid: 100).

Nohrstedt and Ottosen observe that, as we become increasingly aware of cultural differences, since globalisation – notably in the media domain – shrinks the distance between us, "we also have to face the fact that some perspectives are promoted with universalist claims" (op cit: 27). The interpenetration to which Robertson refers can be appreciated, perhaps, as well in television news as in any other discursive practice of globalisation, since the art of journalism is often to convey a larger "truth" through visual metonym, as with the statue or the food parcels.

Humanitarian warfare

Universalist claims are made on behalf of various analytical factors in conflict, some with better credentials than others. The campaign to oust Saddam Hussein's forces from Kuwait won support at the UN Security Council as a response under Chapter VII of the UN Charter to an act of aggression: a clear breach of international law. In order to keep public opinion "on side" in the main US-led countries, various other factors were drawn into the propaganda, but it was underpinned by the perception of a need to restore order and collective security in the international community.

The period between the two campaigns spanned a transition in UN thinking, however, summarised in the landmark Millennium Report, *In larger freedom*, which placed human security at the centre of the organisation's work:

> No shift in the way we think or act can be more critical than this: we must put people at the centre of everything we do... A new concept of security is evolving... a more human-centred approach to security as opposed to the traditional state-centred approach (UN 2000).

To sketch in, briefly, the sequence of connecting events from 1991 to 2003, the successful ejection of Iraqi occupying troops from Kuwait and restoration to power of the country's monarchical rulers was supposed to usher in a "new world order", in which the old Cold War divisions could be set aside, and the international community could police itself by consensus, with the Pentagon as the leader of its enforcement arm. This notion was put back on ice shortly afterwards, however, when US forces withdrew in ignominy from Somalia in 1993, having been drawn into a costly firefight in the so-called "Black Hawk Down incident", otherwise known as the second Battle of Mogadishu.

The failure of UN peacekeeping missions to prevent communal violence and slaughter in both Rwanda (in 1994) and the disintegrating federal state of Yugoslavia (during the 1990s) highlighted important lacunae and complications in the collective security model. Some decisive action, and the wherewithal to resolve upon it, seemed to be required to respond to violence within states, not just between states. So it was that human security and human rights became a *casus belli* in themselves – one that saw the US and allies involved in their next major shooting war, over Kosovo in 1999.

The then UK Prime Minister Tony Blair made an early attempt to contextualise this in terms of international law, declaring, in a speech in Chicago while the bombs were actually falling, in April 1999, that "massive refugee flows caused by oppression" should be viewed as a "threat to international peace and security": the language of Article 42 of the UN Charter in Chapter VII, which permits the authorisation of military action (Blair 1999). But Blair ignored the inconvenient facts. Those fleeing their homes in the province in 1998 had all gone back again by the beginning of the following year. The later and far bigger refugee flows out of Kosovo were triggered first by the onset of Nato's bombing campaign, then again by its cessation, with a net displacement of as many as 200,000 non-ethnic Albanian civilians.

Hence the "shifting war aims" (Lynch and McGoldrick op cit: 104): Blair told the British parliament, on the eve of bombing, that "it will have as its minimum objective to curb continued Serbian repression in Kosovo in order to *avert* a humanitarian disaster". A year later, Blair's defence secretary George Robertson – by now ennobled as Lord Robertson of Port Ellen and elevated to be Secretary General of Nato – was recalling the conflict in a lecture to an American audience: "I went to Kosovo on the first anniversary of Operation Allied Force, Nato's air campaign to end and *reverse* the ethnic cleansing of the Albanian community."

The campaign enjoyed strong initial public support in the US and allied countries, largely through appeals to humanitarian instincts: despite, rather than because of, hard-headed arguments over international law and facts on the ground. It could not, ultimately, be presented as a restoration of law and order because it entailed siding with a plucky band of rebels, the Kosovo Liberation Army, against a sovereign state. And it had political personnel to match. Whereas, in Operation Desert Storm of 1991, George Herbert Walker Bush, patriarch of the American power elite, was joined by fellow conservatives, John "Back to Basics" Major and Helmut Kohl, the "father" of German reunification, now the spokespersons-in-chief were a bunch of baby boomers representing the "progressive" side of politics: Bill Clinton, Tony Blair and, in Germany, even the leader of the Green Party, foreign minister Joschka Fischer.

US foreign policy and the 'nurturant parent' frame

Marianne Perez, in an unpublished, but important piece of research titled *Moving mainstream media towards a culture of peace* (2006), considers, in a peace journalism context, George Lakoff's theory that two competing frames govern the conduct of US politics: the "nurturant parent" and the "strict father". The former, Lakoff says, stems from a belief that "the world is basically good and can be made better, and it is our responsibility to work towards that"; whereas the latter operates on a basic understanding of the world as "dangerous and difficult". In foreign policy, therefore, the nurturant parent frame mandates "cooperation to extend [our] values to the world", while the strict father sees it as an instrument to "maintain sovereignty and impose moral authority while seeking self-interest" (2004).

Perez maps these distinctions on to what she suggests is an analogous binary opposition supplied by Johan Galtung's notion of competing peace and security discourses. She concludes:

> The peace discourse and nurturant parent frame share similar values. Notably, they both believe that positive change is within our power; that there are alternatives to violence; that empathy is a key component of human relations; and that all are equal. These maxims imply that people should be engaged in the world and that cooperation and dialogue can be fruitful. What holds true for individuals also applies to groups, nations, and states because the latter are simply agglomerations of individuals (op cit: 20).

With Operation Allied Force of 1999, however, the nurturant parent frame had been co-opted to supporting a course of violence. The US was bombing out of a sense of empathy. What could be loosely defined as the "international peace and humanitarian community" was split down the middle by this development. The campaign coincided with plans by activists for a gathering in the Netherlands to mark the centenary of the 1899 Hague Convention, which committed signatory states to "obviate, as far as possible, recourse to force in the relations between States", in order to "ensure the pacific settlement of international differences". A hundred years on, the conference bore the grand title of the Hague Appeal for Peace, but, such were the divisions over Kosovo, it earned the nickname, the Vague Appeal for Peace.

Perez makes a carefully reasoned case for the US Department of Defense to be matched by a specially created Department of Peace, the better to institutionalise the nurturant parent frame in responding to international conflicts: a particularisation of the universal, and a universalisation of the particular. And yet, in the governments of Germany and the UK, while they did not have a formally appointed Minister of Peace, the nearest equivalent in each cabinet came out in support of the war. The aforementioned Fischer was joined, in the trenches, so to speak, by Britain's international development secretary and darling of the Labour Left, Clare "Bomber" Short, who earned herself the soubriquet with her apparent ardour for pounding Yugoslavia into submission in 1999. (Perez raises, but does not resolve, the question of how a Minister of Peace would fit into notions of collective cabinet responsibility.)

The point is, evoking *either* the strict father *or* the nurturant parent frame – or both – could now lead to war. War by the US and allies is, post-Kosovo, a floating signifier. Hence, the final, decisive turn in Blair's successful battle for public and parliamentary approval of Britain's participation in the invasion of Iraq in 2003 came when the difficulty and danger of leaving Saddam Hussein in possession of "weapons of mass destruction" shifted to the moral responsibility to spread "our values", overthrowing a repressive regime and replacing it with democracy. Message frames, media frames and audience frames joined to produce a dominant reading in favour of war.

This sense of drift in the symbolic realm was matched by a disconnection of war from its connotation of "purpose", its intentionality, or perhaps directionality, in the intransitive domain of the referent, as well. Ismael Hossein-Zadeh takes issue with the most popular oppositional reading of the invasion, summarised in the slogan familiar from posters stuck on to thousands of bus stops and mailboxes: "No blood for oil." Instead, he argues for the primacy of the military-industrial complex (or "empire", as he puts it), requiring ongoing combat – whatever the stated pretext – to survive. War is not fought instrumentally but as an end in itself:

> Actual shooting wars are needed not only for the expansion but for the survival of this empire. Arms industries need occasional wars not only to draw down their stockpiles of armaments, and make room for more production, but also to display the "wonders" of what they produce: the "shock and awe"-inducing properties of their products and the "laser-guided, surgical operations" of their smart weapons (2006: 19).

Postmodern warfare

Philip Hammond considers these developments in light of the postmodern "death of the subject...a profound doubt about political agency" (2007: 8), although he also complains that theorists of the postmodern were too ready to detect the impossibility of political agency when they were really looking at the weakness of the Left at particular historical moment. Hammond himself suggests that international politics in general, and war in particular, can be seen as "postmodern in that the era of the modern nation-state has passed...since the end of the Cold War" (ibid: 14).

The military adventures in the period since the fall of the Berlin Wall have, Hammond argues, symptomised a restless search for "a sense of purpose and meaning...powerful Western states have used interventions in other people's wars to offset their own crisis of meaning" (ibid: 15 and 24). He quotes the observation, made after the ignominious US withdrawal from Somalia, by Colin Powell, then Chairman of the US Joint Chiefs of Staff, that the American public would put up with casualties in war if they believed the sacrifice was worth it. Alan Kay finds that public approval for the US use of force can reach "consensus levels" if six "screens" are passed, including the presence of allies to share risks and costs but also the apparent pursuit of a "visionary objective" (2000). Hammond identifies "humanitarian spectacle" as the correlative of this political condition, both feeding it and feeding off it:

> American military muscle was thus to be given new meaning in the post-Cold War era, no longer as a guarantor of the West's freedoms against the menace of communism but as the steel fist inside a humanitarian velvet glove (op cit: 38).

The picture, then, is not, or not only, of military resources being coolly deployed by a single controlling agency to attain carefully fixed strategic objectives, but rather one of general and undifferentiated momentum towards organised violence, built in to the political configuration of the United States in particular, as now the sole superpower. All this violence requires propaganda narratives to justify its use to the American and other publics and, moreover, is promiscuous in its opportunistic appropriation and assimilation of images and concepts connoting purpose and meaning.

I have argued elsewhere that parties to conflict "play to a gallery the media have created" (2009a). The intensification in what Nohrstedt and Ottosen call "medialisation" (op cit: 15) – not only of war, but of everyday life – demands the provision of war propaganda just as the "hard" components of the military-industrial complex require constant, ongoing combat if their returns of "shareholder value" are to meet the expectations of globalised capital markets. Arms companies and TV companies alike continue to prosper in the age of what Gore Vidal called "perpetual war for perpetual peace" (2002), as the theatre of operations formerly known as Afghanistan morphs, under President Obama, into "Af-Pak" and stretches for decades ahead. The share prices of the so-called "four horsemen" – the big four US arms companies, Boeing, Raytheon, General Electric and Northrop Grumman, fell steeply in the early months of the new presidency, but its first defence budget saw a recovery in which they abruptly switched trajectory, to outperform the stock market as a whole (Lynch 2009b).

Cascading activation

Robert Entman is the author of what can be read as a last, gallant attempt to recover and restore a sense of unified controlling agency to the provision and promulgation of war propaganda, with his model of "cascading activation" in the strange case of the missing Saudis (2003). This explains, Entman says,

> how interpretive frames activate and spread from the top level of a stratified sys-
> tem (the White House) to the network of non-administration elites, and on to
> news organisations, their texts, and the public – and how interpretations feed
> back from lower to higher levels.

Entman examines the "frame contest" over the attribution of blame in the 9/11 attacks, and the apparent paradox that, while it quickly became known that 15 of the 19 hijackers were Saudis, it was Afghanistan, not Saudi Arabia, that found itself in the cross-hairs for retribution. Rejecting "complacent views of America's free press", he presents a model in which "influence" cascades down a series of steps with the Administration at the top and the public at the bottom. Media are on the third step of five, below "other elites" such as Congress members and staffers, ex-officials and experts but above the news frames that journalism produces, whose efficacy in shaping perceptions and cognitions in the community at large can then be measured in opinion polls.

Agreeable as it is to be in the company of Entman's acute insights and lucid prose, this formula implies a directionality that takes too little account of the nature of the relationship between corporate America in general, and corporate media in particular, and the realities of Washington politics. On canvases broad and narrow, media were and are actively seeking to influence political and policy decision-making all the time, and often highly successful in doing it. Danny Schechter, in his 2005 film – called, like the Rampton and Stauber book, *Weapons of mass deception* (see www.wmdthefilm.com) – observes that, just as Colin Powell, by now promoted to Secretary of State, was presenting evidence from intelligence agencies about Iraq's weapons, at the United Nations, so media companies were lobbying his son, Michael Powell, chairman of the Federal Communications Commission (FCC), to relax still further the rules on cross-media ownership.

"There was a question raised," Schechter says, in an in-vision commentary. "Did the FCC agree to waive the rules if the media companies agreed to wave the flag?" Jeff Chester, director of the Center for Digital Democracy, tells Schechter: "You don't go in and report critically on an administration that you hope will give you billions and billions of dollars in new policies." One of the networks hoping to benefit from the rule changes in prospect, NBC, is owned by General Electric, which, as well as being a major defence contractor, was also one of the biggest donors to the Bush campaign.

Increasing influence of corporate PR over the news agenda

The dots are joined through such phenomena as the increasing influence of corporate PR over the news agenda, and the proliferation, as on-air pundits, of representatives of corporate-funded think-tanks, typically promulgating various military stratagems or technologies. The well-founded claim by the American Enterprise Institute to have conceived and effectively promoted the idea of a 2008 "troop surge" in Iraq, through well-timed media contributions including an influential column in the *Washington Post*, is a case in point. As Herman and Chomsky say:

> The same underlying power sources that own the media, and fund them as advertisers, that serve as primary definers of the news, and that produce flak and proper-thinking experts, also play a key role in fixing basic principles and the dominant ideologies (2002: xi).

In a larger context, the distinction between the US Administration – of any stripe, but especially under the younger Bush – as the supposed originator of framing hegemony in Entman's model, and the US corporate sector, becomes more difficult to sustain, the more closely the relationships are examined. One who did peer into them, the investigative journalist Greg Palast, titled his book, on the business-fuelled rise of the neo-conservatives, *The best democracy money can buy* (2003), chronicling how corporations not only lobbied for the adoption of policies favourable to their interests, but were actually entrusted with devising and implementing the means by which Bush was elected in the first place, including the manipulation of voter rolls in swing states. Saudi Arabia was never going to be the fall guy for 9/11 because of the pre-existing web of entanglements between the Kingdom and the upper reaches of the business and political elites of both the US and the UK, as Craig Unger argues in *House of Bush, House of Saud* (2007), showing "the secret relationship between the world's two most powerful dynasties".

Conclusion: The logic of peace journalism

Proliferating feedback loops are present at all levels, all the time; an elaboration of Entman's model, perhaps, multiplying and dividing strokes and lines, rather than an argument to discard it altogether. The situation has never been better described than by Michel Foucault in *The history of sexuality*, in a passage which is, therefore, worth quoting at length:

> There is no power that is exercised without a series of aims and objectives. But this does not mean that it results from the choice or decision of an individual subject; let us not look for the headquarters that presides over its rationality; neither the caste which governs, nor the groups which control the state apparatus, nor those who make the most important economic decisions direct the entire network of power that functions in a society (and makes *it* function); the rationality of power is characterised by tactics that are often quite explicit at the restricted level where they are inscribed (the local cynicism of power), tactics which, becoming connected to one another, attracting and propagating one another, but finding their base and condition of support elsewhere, end by forming comprehensive systems: the logic is perfectly clear, the aims decipherable, and yet it is often the case that no-one is there to have invented them, and few who can be said to have formulated them (1978: 95).

We are immersed in war propaganda; our media relations, our very medialised existence perhaps, are saturated in it, its subjectivity de-centred and dispersed. It is always already there. "Where there is power, there is resistance," Foucault goes on to say, but "this resistance is never in a position of exteriority in relation to power" (ibid). If we want to take issue with power relations in the media domain, it is in that domain that we must work. That is the logic of peace journalism, and it forms the underpinning for the attempt, in the following chapter, to adumbrate a strategy covering both structure and agency to increase the plenitude of cues and clues for readers and audiences to form their own negotiated or oppositional readings of appeals to support collective violence of one kind or another.

References

Blair, Tony (1999) Doctrine of the international community, 24 April. Available online at http://www.number10.gov.uk/Page1297, accessed on 29 June 2009

Ellul, Jacques (1965) *Propaganda – the formation of men's attitudes*, New York: Knopf

Entman, Robert M. (2003) Cascading activation: Contesting the White House's frame after 9/11, *Political Communication*, Vol. 20, No.4 pp 415–32

Foucault, Michel (1978) *The history of sexuality* (trans. Hurley, Robert), London: Penguin

Galtung, Johan and Ruge, Mari (1965) The structure of foreign news: The presentation of the Congo, Cuba and Cyprus crises in four Norwegian newspapers, *Journal of International Peace Research*, Vol. 1 pp 64–91

Hammond, Philip (2007) *Media, war and post-modernity*, Oxon: Routledge

Herman, Edward and Chomsky, Noam (2002) *Manufacturing consent: The political economy of the mass media*, New York: Pantheon

Hossein-Zadeh, Ismael (2006) *The political economy of US militarism*, London: Palgrave Macmillan

Jowett, Garth S. and O'Donnell, Victoria (1999) *Power and persuasion*, London: Sage

Kay, Alan (2000) When Americans favor the use of force, *International Journal of Public Opinion Research*, Vol, 12, No. 2 pp. 182–90

Lakoff, George (2004) *Don't think of an elephant! Know your values and frame the debate*, White River Junction, Vermont: Chelsea Green Publishing

Lewis, Justin (2003) Biased Broadcasting Corporation, *Guardian*, 4 July

Luostarinen, Heikki (1994) *Sergeants of the mind: news management and journalistic counter-strategies in military conflicts*, Helsinki: Hanki ja Jaa Oy

Lynch, Jake (2009a) What is peace journalism?, Transcend Media Service website, 13 November

Lynch, Jake (2009b) Coalition of the Unwilling: The phenomenology and political economy of US militarism, Blanchard, Lynda-ann and Chan, Leah (eds) *Ending war, building peace*, Sydney: Sydney University Press

Lynch, Jake and McGoldrick, Annabel (2005) *Peace journalism*, Stroud: Hawthorn Press

Lynch, Jake and Galtung, Johan (2010) *Reporting conflict: New directions in peace journalism*, Brisbane: Queensland University Press (in press)

Nohrstedt, Stig A and Ottosen, Rune (2000) Studying the media Gulf war, Nohrstedt, Stig A and Ottosen, Rune (eds), *Journalism and the new world order*, Gothenburg: Nordicom.

Palast, Greg (2003) *The best democracy money can buy*, New York: Plume

Perez, Marianne (2006) Moving mainstream media towards a culture of peace. Unpublished thesis at European University Center for Peace Studies at Stadtschlaining/Burg, Austria

Rampton, Sheldon and Stauber, John (2003) *Weapons of mass deception: The uses of propaganda in Bush's war on Iraq*, New York: Tarcher/Penguin

Robertson, Roland (1992) *Globalisation: Social theory and global culture*, London: Sage

Scheufele, Dietram A. (1999) Framing as a theory of media effects, *Journal of Communication*, Vol. 49, No. 1 pp 103–22

Tuchman, Gaye (1978) *Making news: A study in the construction of reality*, New York: Free Press

UN (2000) *Millennium report: We, the peoples*. Available online at http://www.un.org/millennium/sg/report/, accessed on 29 July 2009

Unger, Craig (2007) *House of Bush, House of Saud*, New York: Gibson Square Books, revised edition

Vidal, Gore (2002) *Perpetual war for perpetual peace*, New York: Thunder's Mouth Press/Nation Books

SECTION 2. PEACE (OR CONFLICT SENSITIVE) JOURNALISM: THEORY AND PRACTICE IN AN INTERNATIONAL CONTEXT

5

A global standard for reporting conflict and peace

JAKE LYNCH AND ANNABEL MCGOLDRICK

Newspaper journalism has never had as many readers as in 2009. Newspaper journalism is in crisis. Spot the contradiction – or actually, there is no contradiction. Most of those poring over stories from such world-renowned mastheads as the London *Guardian*, *The New York Times* or *Le Monde* are doing so on screen, not on paper. The UK newspaper market, for instance, now has ABCe ratings from the Audit Bureau of Circulation, with the top titles each recording almost 20 million "unique users" per month. The trouble is, a third, at best, are calculated to be in the UK, and the rest are regarded, by advertisers, as worthless.

Hence the crisis; talked about, as ever, and construed as a "global problem", because it is felt as keenly as anywhere in the United States, with such venerable publications as the *Seattle Post-Intelligencer*, the *Philadelphia Inquirer* and the *Boston Globe* struggling to produce swollen profits to pay off debts from leveraged buyouts and takeovers, at the same time as competing with proliferating new media sources and platforms.

Internet journalism, pessimists say, will never sustain the in-depth investigations and authoritative feature writing of its newspaper forebear, because the nature of the medium is such as to emphasise short attention-spans and frequent updates. Readers can so easily browse on elsewhere, after all; and how much information can be fitted on to the single screen of an iPhone? Similar concerns are manifest over television journalism, now increasingly skewed to the demands of 24-hour rolling news, with its constant deadlines and urge to oversell any minor development in a running story.

It's the latest challenge to boosterism by exponents of the "information society" and its supposedly benign, even revolutionary effects in bringing the world's population together into a "global village" of shared values and assumptions. The first iterations of this view came a decade or so ago with the considerable support of then US Vice-President Al Gore, who, it was said, once claimed to have personally invented the internet. The real quote was slightly different, though it speaks volumes about the way the vainglorious Gore was perceived that the exaggerated version was so widely accepted. He actually told CNN's Wolf Blitzer that, while in office, he "took the initiative in creating the internet", meaning that he was responsible for legislation to enable its growth and spread (CNN 1999).

The 1991 "Gore Bill" set up the National Information Infrastructure, which Gore referred to, in an influential turn of phrase, as the "information superhighway". In a popularising essay for *Scientific American* magazine, the then Senator looked forward to its potential:

> Rather than holding back, the US should lead by building the information infrastructure, essential if all Americans are to gain access to this transforming technology...high speed networks must be built that tie together millions of computers, providing capabilities that we cannot even imagine (Gore 1991: 150–2).

At the same time, critics were complaining that the rosy Gore perspective was reproducing some notorious aspects of the discredited "modernisation" school of development theory, summarised a generation earlier by one of its prominent exponents, Daniel Lerner:

> The new technology, diffused as mass media, has transformed social organization...by "mobilising the periphery" of previously inert populations for relatively vigorous participation in the policy process. A whole new array of "audiences" has been created, everywhere, to interact with the new technologies. Out of this has grown, everywhere, the demand for "open societies". The historical Western pattern whereby cash customers became media consumers and then political participants (voters) is being re-enacted on a world scale (1973: 543).

Cees Hamelink was one who observed that many on the periphery had remained un-mobilised, and that the rapidly growing influence of the new Information and Communication Technologies (ICTs) risked marginalising them all over again:

> The extent of telecommunication grids is very limited in most of the developing countries. There are 1 billion telephones in the world and the 48 least developed countries have some 1.5 million of them. Some 15 per cent of the world's

population has access to over 70 per cent of the world's telephone lines. More than 50 per cent of the world's people have never made a phone call. The costs of providing adequate telecom infrastructures are considerable and cannot be met by national budgets alone (1998).

Reliance on commercial mechanisms to implement technology transfer risked reproducing these inequalities within countries, as well as between them, Hamelink wrote; a warning that has only grown in salience in the past decade, with ever faster and more costly cable connections now available to improve internet connectivity. What the unconnected masses in poor countries have in common with the scattered internet newspaper readers of the rich world is that neither group can be aggregated into a market; that is to say, there are not enough of them, with enough money, in one place, for advertisers to pay for media to reach them.

As former professional reporters, the present authors tend to be "on guard" against too-ready assumptions that journalism, *per se*, is a "good thing", and that those cut off from its benison must therefore be in a deprived condition. However, as Kaarle Nordenstreng (2001) reminds us, key instruments of global governance prescribe communication rights, notably the twin Articles 19 of the Universal Declaration of Human Rights of 1948 and the International Covenant on Civil and Political Rights, drafted twenty years later. Clause 2 of the ICCPR states:

> Everyone shall have the right to freedom of expression; this right shall include freedom to seek, receive and impart information and ideas of all kinds, regardless of frontiers, either orally, in writing or in print, in the form of art, or through any other media of his [sic] choice.

Advocates for communication rights typically map this formula on to some or other variant of the concept named by Amartya Sen as the "capabilities model". Sen defines freedom as "individual agency, which is qualified and constrained by the social, political and economic opportunities available to us" (1999: 1); that is, it is of limited use or value to prescribe our notional rights if they cannot be attained in practice. Neither, Nordenstreng argues, should they be seen as an end in their own right, but rather in the context of the post-war settlement, which was geared towards building peace, both between and within states. He quotes from the 1980 MacBride Report, *Many voices, one world*, commissioned by UNESCO to examine problems in the world information and communication order:

> The primary function of the media is always to inform the public of significant facts, however unpleasant or disturbing they may be. At times of tension, the news consists largely of military moves and statements by political leaders

which gives rise to anxiety. But it should not be impossible to reconcile full and truthful reporting with a presentation which reminds readers of the possibility – indeed the necessity – of peaceful solutions to disputes.

The implication, then, of prescribing communication rights, as the world community decided to do, not once but twice, is that their attainment by as many people as possible should be seen as a potential contribution to peace. The "information society" concept has revived and strengthened concerns about widening inequalities in attaining communication rights and the increased (in relative terms) marginalisation of people who cannot be aggregated into commercially viable markets. This, indeed, risks extending the distance between their actual and potential life prospects, thereby constituting a form of violence in itself, on the definition by Johan Galtung (1969) which has strongly influenced the concept of positive peace, now accepted by the UN as an indispensable part of its mission. If journalism, in this context, is a good thing, but one that cannot be sustained or delivered satisfactorily by markets, there is both a need and a justification for non-market mechanisms to be applied.

Hamelink's own prescription is for "a substantial allocation of public funding for the costs of accessing and using ICTs, and a massive effort in human resource training for the mastery of ICT-related skills", the better to deliver on "people-centred ideals . . . [such as] human security, autonomy and equality" (Hamelink op cit). Majid Tehranian took up the challenge of the MacBride Report directly, with its call for a New World Information and Communication Order, or NWICO, and proposed a UN Media Development Bank to support and sustain peace journalism as a "system of global media ethics". Such a venture could be funded, Tehranian argued, by a small tax on the use of global commons – the electromagnetic spectrum and the geo-stationary orbit – by media corporations (see Tehranian 2002).

These suggestions raise an important question: if public money is to be made available to support beneficial journalistic enterprise, as a supplement to commercial funding, who will discriminate between worthy and unworthy recipients, and on what basis? It is in this context that a global standard for reporting conflict is conceived, on the basis of peace journalism (PJ), and here introduced.

A global standard for reporting conflict

Journalism is a form of public communication distinctive in being driven chiefly by "internal goals" (Hanitzsch 2007). Journalists aim to do "good journalism", by reference to news values such as fairness, in their own terms, and accuracy. PJ is derived, ultimately, from the insight first offered in *The structure of foreign news* (Galtung and Ruge 1965), that news content is governed by representational conventions, producing discernible patterns of inclusion and omission. Dominant conflict reporting patterns emphasise official sources over "people sources"; event over process, and violence over peace. They construct conflicts as a "tug-of-war" (Lynch and McGoldrick 2005: 8) between two parties contesting a single goal.

News needs remedial measures to "give peace a chance" because these conventions predispose it to a form of war journalism, which is neither fair nor accurate. Hence, PJ, a set of "choices – of what stories to report, and how to report them – that create opportunities for society at large to consider and to value non-violent responses to conflict" (ibid: 6). The external goal of peace is added *instrumentally*, to deliver more successfully on internal goals of fairness and accuracy.

At the same time, research evidence suggests that reports adjusted to exhibit framing characteristics analogous to distinctions in the peace journalism model ("escalation" and "de-escalation") elicit measurable differentials in cognitive responses (Kempf 2007). Separate evidence indicates that exposure to television news, undifferentiated into war journalism and peace journalism, is a psychological stressor, leaving subjects frightened, depressed and anxious, with lasting effects (Szabo and Hopkinson 2007). In a further study, Serlin found that a group of Vietnam war veterans, diagnosed with Post-Traumatic Stress Disorder, experienced a worsening of symptoms while watching US television coverage of war in Iraq – not by sheer exposure to disturbing images but because "political spin" and "arbitrary realities" exacerbated their sense of the meaninglessness of death (Serlin 2006: 148). It was context, in other words, rather than the images themselves, which triggered the effect.

McGoldrick showed interview subjects two versions of the same story, a TV report of a bombing in Jerusalem (from Lynch and McGoldrick 2004) – one war journalism, the other peace journalism. Subjects found the first "liable to lead to a sense of disconnection or 'switching off' ", whereas the second was "replete with opportunities to 'connect' with the story, even learn something new … [it was] refreshing and – in a word used by nine out of the 11 interviewees – balanced" (2008: 91).

War journalism, orientated towards official sources, is prey to propaganda, defined as attempts to "shape perceptions, manipulate cognitions and direct behaviour" (Jowett and O'Donnell 1999: 6), since "in the nature of public relations, most authority figures issue a high quotient of imprecise and self-serving declarations" (Bagdikian 2000: 176). Indeed, news offers a suitable target because, as Tuchman puts it, "the acceptance of representational conventions as facticity makes reality vulnerable to manipulation" (1978: 109). It is a discourse which, in Hall's terms, "naturalise[s] representation to the point where you cannot see that anyone produced it" (1997: 21), thus offering to fix the meaning of key concepts in ambiguous causal scenarios such as social conflict. News consumers are, McGoldrick avers, "disturbed because [they] are drawn into a conspiracy of meaning-making" (op cit: 96).

PJ, by contrast, "draws attention to vantage points from which to inspect dominant discourses on the outside" (Lynch 2008a: 151), prompting and equipping readers and audiences to form what Hall (1980) calls "negotiated" readings. In this, it is analogous to therapy, whose "job is to *un*fix meaning", McGoldrick says (op cit: 96), "the core of so many approaches like Gestalt, and Cognitive Behavioural Therapy". So PJ represents a way of making news less potentially harmful to the psychological health of its consumers.

Most news comes from corporate sources, and media corporations have grown in size and influence to become some of the world's biggest, with, in many cases, a regional or global reach. There is a case for *preferring* PJ, both as a contribution to fairness and accuracy and as a means to minimise psychological harm to consumers. It can therefore be proposed as the basis for a global standard in news about conflict, as an aspirational target for editors and reporters and a form of consumer protection, to be adopted and implemented at an organisational level. By devising and calling for it to be implemented in the context of NWICO, the take-up of such an idea could also benefit from what Hackett and Zhao call the "positive legacy in civil society mobilization to articulate a democratic alternative vision at the World Summit on the Information Society" (2005: 17).

An important emerging research paradigm has already seen PJ operationalised as the basis for generating comparative data on conflict reporting in different media from different countries, notably by nine authors whose articles are collected in a special edition of *Peace and Policy*, the journal of the Toda Institute for Peace and Policy Research, which sponsored the work (Ross et al 2008). Such methods, combined with and augmented by investigations of differentials in the psychological impact of exposure to news about conflict framed as war journalism and PJ respectively, could calibrate the reporting of news about conflict to mesh with quality assurance criteria which form the basis of ISO9001: 2008, the latest version of the globally recognised standard for quality management and delivery of products and services from the International

Standardisation Organisation, administered by national accreditation bodies in each member state.

The PJ concept was first developed by Johan Galtung as the "policy implications" (Lynch and Galtung 2010) of *The structure of foreign news*. Galtung later adumbrated, in table form, the characteristics of war journalism and PJ respectively (in Lynch and McGoldrick 2005: 6). From this model, evaluative criteria were developed for content analysis, in Lynch (2004 and 2006) and Lee and Maslog (2005) and Lee, Maslog and Kim (2006). Between them, these studies yielded data comparing different media in the same country, and selected media from different countries. A study of UK press reporting of the "Iran nuclear crisis", in 2005 (Lynch 2006) used critical discourse analysis to produce five coding criteria arising out of a single aspect of the Galtung table – in which PJ constructs conflicts as taking place in "open space, open time [with] causes and exits anywhere" – and then applied them to 211 reports in 12 publications. The studies by Lee et al apply more primary distinctions between the two, to compare news from six Asian countries and produce a comparative PJ "quotient".

The countries in these studies show a considerable diversity of media systems and conflict dynamics, so the *Daily News*, the leading government-supporting paper in Sri Lanka (a country beset by a major insurgency, in a very different phase when these data were collected) appears alongside the *Jakarta Post*, a liberal, pro-reform publication in Indonesia (a country embarked on a sometimes uneasy, but fundamentally successful transition to democracy). The two states are, furthermore, separated by 56 places in the world press freedom rankings compiled by Reporters Without Borders (see www.rdf.org), but the comparison has proven useful, being widely cited in subsequent research. To allow for diversity between the "mediascapes" of different countries, Shinar proposed five outline headings for the collection of comparative data. PJ can be recognised as:

- exploring backgrounds and contexts of conflict formation, and presenting causes and options on every side so as to portray conflict in realistic terms, transparent to the audience;
- giving voice to the views of all rival parties;
- offering creative ideas for conflict resolution, development, peacemaking and peacekeeping;
- exposing lies, cover-up attempts and culprits on all sides, and revealing excesses committed by, and suffering inflicted on, peoples of all parties;

- paying attention to peace stories and post-war developments (2007: 200).

At the same time, several researchers investigated the feasibility of journalists actually doing peace journalism, particularly in view of the relationship between structure and agency as factors governing the content of news reports. Hackett (2006) compared three theoretical frameworks to conceptualise the scope for journalistic agency, to be addressed by exhortatory or pedagogical initiatives. Critiques of news practices by senior journalists, such as, in the US, Fallows (1997) and, in the UK, Lloyd (2004) often call for such desiderata as those listed by Shinar, above, as means of delivering fair and accurate reporting. Both are explicit, however, that this is not an area suitable for remedial action by legislation from governments.

The idea for a global standard is conceived, therefore, as a potential contribution to what Hackett and Schroeder call an "enabling environment for the practices of PJ" (2008: 29), while avoiding calls for legislation and top-down governmental regulation. The value and potential traction of such a standard will depend, to some extent, on its acceptability to journalists and, as Hackett and Carroll remark, journalists can become allies for media reform "if they develop connections (ideological and/or personal) with social movements... [or] if their professional status and ideals are blatantly violated" (2006: 201). Such alliances would be foreclosed if proposals from social movements for remedies to the violation of journalistic ideals involved more legislation. Instead, a global standard would hand the initiative to agencies committed to properly informed consumer choice and protection, including statutory agencies, which operate at arm's length from government, but also a far greater number of private and civil society groups.

In research on reception of news about conflict, the significance of the Kempf study, quoted above, is to establish that distinctions in the war journalism/peace journalism model are ideational, leading to measurable differentials in cognitive response. The Szabo and Hopkinson data – gathered from questionnaires – are significant in suggesting that exposure to news *per se* can be a psychological stressor, among otherwise healthy subjects; one whose effects require "a directed psychological intervention such as progressive relaxation" to "buffer" the impact (op cit: 57). Serlin's work with Vietnam war veterans diagnosed with PTSD suggests the stress is caused by contextual factors rather than, say, the mere fact of witnessing scenes of death and destruction – which, in most mainstream Western news media, are sanitised, anyway. McGoldrick (op cit) pulls these threads together, suggesting, in simple terms, that war journalism is bad for us, and more PJ would be better for us.

Adaptations of the peace journalism model

As researchers have applied the original PJ model, it has undergone some important adaptations. Data collected for comparative studies could be derived from applying criteria divided into "active" and "passive" PJ indicators, following Lynch's innovation in analysing the reporting of the "war on terrorism" in the Philippines, in Filipino and international media respectively (Lynch 2008c). Active indicators are: "iteration and exploration of backgrounds and contexts; provision of cues to form negotiated and/or oppositional readings of war propaganda; and coverage of suggestions and initiatives for peace, from whatever quarter" (ibid.: 100). Any attempt to produce a PJ "quotient" for robust comparison would have to devise ways to allot different weightings to active and passive indicators – typically, the avoidance of certain linguistic forms – to produce more "realistic" overall scores.

The other main adaptation of the PJ model concerns its claim to be regarded as preferable journalism in that it provides more accurate representations of conflict. "Accurate" because a conflict has three components – the "ABC" of attitude, behaviour and contradiction (Galtung, 2000: 14), where A and B are merely the visible symptoms of C, which is what the conflict is "about". News conventions emphasise the surface at the expense of the underlying reality, the contradiction, which makes the resulting representation inaccurate. PJ, a deliberate remedial strategy to iterate backgrounds and contexts, is more accurate. Shinar's third PJ heading also concerns accuracy. The peace researcher, John Paul Lederach, reflects:

> I have not experienced any situation of conflict...where there have not been people who had a vision for peace...Far too often, however, these same people are overlooked and disempowered either because they do not represent "official" power (1997: 94).

Those wielding official power are journalists' prime sources, so the resulting representations of conflict are therefore less "peaceful" than is warranted. To connect with visions and creative ideas for peace, emanating from beyond these sources, therefore makes PJ more accurate.

Some of the claims of PJ, then, are realist, in the sense of fidelity to "[a] reality [that] exists independently of our knowledge of it" (Danermark et al 2002: 17). Lynch has characterised it (2007) as a form of critical realism, based on the attenuated proposition that "[whilst] this knowledge is always fallible, all knowledge is not *equally* fallible" (ibid.). Implicit in the Galtung schema is a theory of representation in which reality can be *mis*represented by the action of being fitted into distorting structures, or codes, at the point of production. Latterly, theories of meaning-making have been de-centred, notably in Hall's concept that no act of representation is complete until it has been received, or decoded, and that – far from there being one reality, with its own clear meaning which is then re-presented, in more or less faithful form – representation itself is "constitutive" of the reality (1997: 8).

In Galtung's table, PJ was "truth-orientated" while war journalism was "propaganda-orientated". In light of Hall, it has been adapted (notably in Lynch 2008c) so PJ is that which abounds in cues and resources for readers and audiences to "negotiate" their own readings, unfixing the meaning of self-serving definitions and representations. This formulation draws on Roeh and Cohen's notion of "open" and "closed" television news (1992), itself inspired by such primary texts as Barthes (1975). (Similarly, the first of Shinar's headings allows for a plurality of backgrounds and contexts rather than implying that there is one "correct" version.) In this sense, if no other, PJ can be seen as fairer and more useful, when measured against public service undertakings of the kind inscribed in guidelines for broadcasters, typified by the BBC's formula: "equipping audiences to form their own views".

Conceptual frameworks for testing cognitive and psychological effects of exposure to news are derived from theories of media effects and can best be described as a supple variant of "social constructivism" (Scheufele 1999: 105). It must gauge strong effects, to pick up variations attributable to different forms of encoding – "framing images of reality... in a predictable and patterned way" (McQuail 1987: 331) – whilst also allowing for what Gamson and Modigliani call the "feedback loop" between journalism and its audiences: "media discourse is part of the process by which individuals construct meaning, and public opinion is part of the process by which journalists... develop and crystallize meaning in public discourse" (1989: 2). Any meaningful research into this process would require in-depth interviews in which subjects are conceived as active participants in meaning-making, at what Hall (1980) calls "the moment of decoding".

The point of trying to build the findings into the structure of an international standard is that the International Standardisation Organisation formula for quality assurance is conceived as a management approach, calling for implementation across all systems and procedures in a subscribing firm. The project design, therefore, draws on theories of structure and agency and their respective and combined influence on the content of news reports, notably Shoemaker and Reese's "hierarchy of influences" model. Newsroom routines, for converting raw material (information) garnered from suppliers (sources) and delivering it to customers (audiences and advertisers) lead to standardised and recurring patterns of content (1996: 109).

This effect is compounded by the organisational imperatives of media institutions, in which profit orientation and hierarchical structures generally ensure content is shaped in accordance with ownership interests. These, Lynch and McGoldrick have argued, are more difficult to define – and therefore more negotiable – than is commonly assumed (2005: 200). And if PJ is to be adopted by news organisations – even if not known by that name – then it can and must emanate from the level of management, as well as commending itself to individual journalists. Keeble bemoans the "dominant journalistic culture" which "stresses the importance of technical skills" over a "reflective, analytical, ethical approach" (2009: 2). Clearly, a "whole-organisation" approach will be needed if such an entrenched culture is to be effectively challenged.

It remains a valid exercise, in principle, to compare media between countries because "most of what we consume as media is still national in origin and orientation" (McNair 2006: 8); a pattern which, Nossek finds, still prevails "even after the accelerated technological development of the 1990s" (2004: 343). Moreover, the bodies responsible for administering international standards are usually national in scope. At the same time, media would have to be compared within each country, in order to demonstrate what is already possible – addressing, implicitly, Hanitzsch's objection that "a peaceful culture is a *precondition* of PJ, rather than its outcome" (2007: 7) – while the transnational comparisons would demonstrate what could be possible.

Research design: How would it work?

A story that includes material satisfying criteria under each of Shinar's five headings could be allotted one "point". One that includes all five would score five points. So each individual story would be "marked" initially out of five. Following Lee, Maslog and Kim (2006), three indicators of "passive" PJ could then be added, for the avoidance of: emotive language; "labeling" of conflict parties as good and bad, and partisan reporting. To recognise the lesser importance of these indicators, compared with the main framing characteristics, each could be allocated the score of 0.5, to be added to, or subtracted from, the initial score. "Scores" for each media outlet, and for each country, could then be expressed as mean averages.

Unlike previous studies, which have compared coverage of particular conflict stories in different media outputs, this research would have to examine the reporting of conflict, broadly defined, in any arena and any section of the newspaper or programme, since the object is to investigate the feasibility of deriving systems and procedures suitable for across-the-board implementation at an organisational level. The process of "filling in" Shinar's headings would have to apply coding criteria sufficiently fine-grained to pick up ideational distinctions in particular stories and contexts, while maintaining the same basic categories to enable meaningful comparisons.

Testing psychological responses, to generate data comparing the consequences of exposure to the two forms of journalism, would require two distinct and complementary procedures. In one, a large number of participants – a group of several dozen students, say – would watch an evening news bulletin, with the same script for both presenter and reporters as was actually broadcast, only re-presented and re-voiced by other local journalists. They would be asked to record their responses in questionnaires, drawing on inventories and scales to measure mood disturbance (Grove and Prapavessis 1992); state anxiety (Spielberger, Gorsuch and Lushene 1970) and positive/negative affect (Gauvin and Szabo 1992).

A separate group of about the same number would watch a second version of the bulletin, covering the same stories, at roughly the same length for each item, presented and voiced by the same journalists. This time, the scripts and material for the stories would be adjusted to PJ framings. The same questionnaire would then be applied to the participants in this second group, to generate a comparison between the psychological impact of exposure to television news as it is, and as it could be with more PJ.

In a second procedure, a smaller group would be selected to yield a reflective and socially engaged sample (as in McGoldrick op cit), and interviewed in depth about their cognitive and psychological responses, to the examples shown and to news in general. Some of these (Group 1) would have to be shown the "normal" television bulletin; some the adjusted PJ version (Group 2) and some (Group 3) each in turn. The "controls" – Groups 1 and 2 – are necessary to address the objection McGoldrick herself anticipates:

> By showing the second, PJ version I alerted participants to the constructedness of the first...by the time subjects were responding to the second version, they knew there *were* two versions, and this itself clearly has an effect on their process of decoding (ibid: 96).

Following Janesick (2000), triangulation would then be used to refine inter-view protocols as data collection progresses. Data would be analysed using

Interpretative Phenomenological Analysis (IPA) to interpret meanings embedded in the texts thus produced, applying a hermeneutical, rather than discourse analytical method:

> Discourse analysis regards verbal reports as behaviours in their own right, which should be the focus of functional analysis. IPA, by contrast, is concerned with cognitions, that is understanding what the particular respondent thinks or believes about the topic under discussion (Smith, Jarman, and Osborn 1999)).

Conclusion: Identifying war journalism as 'harmful', peace journalism as 'psychologically beneficial'

These are the basic components of an experimental design to devise and apply a global standard for the reporting of conflict, but researchers carrying out such a project would also have to construct, through independent research and reference to appropriate scholarly literatures, a model for identifying meaningful correspondences, in themes and sub-themes, and generating valid comparisons, between data gathered in different countries. The aim would be to identify thresholds at which war journalism can be confidently pronounced harmful to its consumers, and peace journalism, psychologically beneficial: thereby directly informing the global standard.

In terms of public understanding, the credentials of PJ – based, as it is, on insights from rigorous scholarly research on conflict and peace – to be considered as *good* journalism, make it an important means for media to fulfil their public service role, as set out in such documents as the Ethical Code of the Media, Entertainment and Arts Alliance and the Editorial Policies of the Australian Broadcasting Corporation, and many other similar statements around the world.

"Report and interpret honestly, striving for accuracy, fairness and disclosure of all essential facts," the former begins. "Do not suppress relevant available facts, or give distorting emphasis." The PJ concept is based on acknowledging the conventionality of news, which leads to patterns of omission and distortion. It calls for "a policy of seeking out important stories, and important bits of stories, which would otherwise slip out of the news, and devis[ing] ways to put them back in" (Lynch 2008a: 4) – an echo of provisions in the ABC document, which calls for journalists to achieve the mandatory goal of "balance" by presenting "a wide range of perspectives", and to be "enterprising in perceiving, pursuing and presenting issues which affect society and the individual". "The corporation is also required to be innovative," it continues. "The ABC seeks to be a pace-setter in community discussion."

Initiatives designed to engender more PJ can, therefore, be construed as contributions to public understanding of the wider world and to the vitality of community discussion. And, in offering a basis on which to discriminate in favour of news that is good for us, on both social and psychological criteria, it can inform and strengthen arguments for extra-market funding for journalism to enable its benefits to be spread to those caught in the penumbra of the dazzling information society of the 21st Century.

- The research by Jake Lynch and Annabel McGoldrick on a Global Standard for Reporting Conflict is supported under the Australian Research Council's Linkage Projects funding scheme (No. LP0991223) in partnership with the International Federation of Journalists and Act for Peace.

References

Bagdikian, Ben H. (200) *The media monopoly*, Boston, Mass.: Beacon Press

Barthes, Roland (1975) *The pleasure of the text* (trans. Miller, Richard), New York: Hill and Wang

CNN (1999) Transcript: the Vice President on CNN's *Late Edition*. Available online at http://edition.cnn.com/ALLPOLITICS/stories/1999/03/09/president.2000/transcript.gore/, accessed on July 20, 2009

Danermark, Berth, Ekstrom, Mats, Jakobsen, Liselotte and Karlsson, Jan (2002) *Explaining society*, Oxford: Routledge

Fallows, James (1997) *Breaking the news*, New York: Vintage Books

Galtung, Johan (1969) Violence, peace and peace research, *Journal of Peace Research*, Vol. 6, No. 3, pp 167–191

Galtung, Johan (1998) High road, low road, *Track Two*, Vol. 7, No. 4, Centre for Conflict Resolution, South Africa

Galtung, Johan (2000) *Conflict transformation by peaceful means – a participants' and trainers' manual*, Geneva: UNDP

Galtung, Johan, and Ruge, Mari Holmboe (1965) Structure of foreign news, *Essays in Peace Research*, Ejlers: Copenhagen pp 118–51

Gamson, William A. and Modigliani, Andre (1989) Media discourse and public opinion on nuclear power: a constructionist approach, *American Journal of Sociology*, Vol. 95 pp 1–37

Gauvin, Lise and Szabo, Attila (1992) Application of the experience sampling method to the study of the effects of exercise withdrawal on well-being, *Journal of Sport and Exercise Psychology*, Vol. 14 pp 361–74

Gore, Albert (1991) Infrastructure for the global village, *Scientific American*, September

Grove, Robert J. and Prapavessis, Harold (1992) Preliminary evidence for the reliability and validity of an abbreviated profile of mood states, *International Journal of Sport Psychology*, Vol. 23 pp 93–109

Hackett, Robert A. and Zhao,Yuezhi (2005) Media globalization, media democratization, Hackett, Robert A and Zhao,Yuezhi (eds), *Democratizing global media: One world, many struggles*, Lanham: Rowman and Littlefield pp 1–36

Hackett, Robert A. (2006) Is PJ possible?, *Conflict and Communication Online*, Vol. 5, No. 2. Available online at www.cco.regenner-online.de. Available online at http://www.cco.regener-online.de/2006_2/pdf/hackett.pdf, accessed on 29 June 2009

Hackett, Robert A. and Carroll, William K. (2006) *Remaking media*, Oxford: Routledge

Hackett, Robert A and Schroeder, Birgitta (2008) Does anybody practise peace journalism? *Peace and Policy*, Vol. 13 pp 26–46

Hall, Stuart (1980) Encoding/decoding, Hall, Stuart et al (eds), *Culture, media, language*, London: Hutchinson pp 128–38

Hall, Stuart (1997) *Representation and the media*, Media Education Foundation documentary. Transcript available online at http://www.mediaed.org/cgi-bin/commerce.cgi?preadd=action&key=409, accessed on 29 June 20009

Hamelink, Cees (1998) The digital advance: more than half the world's population have never made a phone call. Will ICTs assure us change? *Viewpoint*, United Nations Research Institute for Social Development, 1 June

Hanitzsch, Thomas (2007) Situating PJ in journalism studies, *Conflict and Communication Online*, Vol. 6, No. 2. Available online at http://www.cco.regener-online.de/2007_2/pdf/hanitzsch.pdf, accessed on 29 June 2009

Janesick , Valerie J. (2000) The choreography of qualitative research design', Denzin, N.K and Lincoln, Y.S. (eds) *The handbook of qualitative research*, London: Sage

Jowett, Garth S and O'Donnell, Victoria (1999) *Power and persuasion*, London: Sage

Keeble, Richard (2009) *Ethics for journalists*, Oxford: Routledge, second edition

Kempf, Wilhelm (2007) Two experiments focusing on de-escalation oriented coverage of post-war conflicts, Shinar, Dov and Kempf, Wilhelm (eds) *Peace Journalism: The state of the art*, Berlin: Regener pp 136–57

Lederach, John Paul (1997) *Building peace: Sustainable reconciliation in divided societies*, Washington DC: United States Institute of Peace Press

Lee, Seow and Maslog, Cris (2005) War or peace journalism in Asian newspapers, *Journal of Communication*, Vol. 55, No. 2 pp. 311–29

Lee, Seow, Maslog, Cris and Kim, H. S. (2006) Asian conflicts and the Iraq war – a comparative framing analysis, *International Communications Gazette*, Vol. 68, No. 5–6 pp 499–518

Lerner, Daniel (1973) Notes on communication and the nation state', *Public Opinion Quarterly*, Vol. 37, No. 4, winter pp 543–4

Lloyd, John (2004) *What the media are doing to our politics*, London: Constable

Lynch, Jake (2004) Reporting the world: An ethical challenge to international news, Caparini, M. (ed.) *Media in security and governance*, Baden-Baden: Geneva Centre for the Democratic Control of Armed Forces pp 97–118

Lynch, Jake (2006) What's so great about peace journalism? *Global Media Journal,* Mediterranean Edition, Vol. 1, No. 1 pp 74–87. Available online at http://globalmedia. emu.edu.tr/spring2006/7.%20Jake%20Lynch%20Whats%20so%20great%20 about2.pdf, accessed on 1 January 2007

Lynch, Jake (2007) A course in pace journalism, Conflict and Communication Online, Vol. 6, No. 1. Available online at http://cco.regener-online.de

Lynch, Jake (2008a) *Debates in peace journalism*, Sydney: Sydney University Press

Lynch, Jake (2008b) Peace journalism and its discontents, Kempf, Wilhelm (ed.) *The peace journalism controversy*, Berlin: Regener pp 83–103

Lynch, Jake (2008c) Active and passive peace journalism, *Peace and Policy*, Vol. 13 pp 99–113

Lynch, Jake and Galtung, Johan (2010) *Reporting conflict: New directions in peace journalism*, Brisbane: Queensland University Press (in press).

Lynch, Jake and McGoldrick, Annabel (2004) *News from the Holy Land* (video), Stroud: Hawthorn Press

Lynch, Jake and McGoldrick, Annabel (2005) *Peace journalism*, Stroud: Hawthorn Press

McGoldrick, Annabel (2008) Psychological effects of war journalism and peace journalism, *Peace and Policy*, Vol. 13 pp 86–98

McNair, Brian (2006) *Cultural chaos – journalism, news and power in a globalised world*, Oxford: Routledge

McQuail, Denis (1987) *Mass communication theory: An introduction*, Thousand Oaks, CA: Sage, second edition

Nordenstreng, Kaarle (2001) Something to be done: transnational media monitoring, *Transnational Broadcasting Studies Journal*, Spring edition. Available online at http:// www.tbsjournal.com/Archives/Spring01/nordenstreng.html, accessed 20 July 2009

Nossek, Hillel (2004) Our news and their news, *Journalism*, Vol. 5 pp 343–68

Roeh, Itzhak and Cohen, Akiba A. (1992) One of the bloodiest days: A comparative analysis of open and closed television news, *Journal of Communication*, Vol. 42, No. 2 pp 42–55

Ross, Susan Dente et al. (2008) Peace journalism in times of war, *Peace and Policy*, Vol. 13, Toda Institute for Peace and Policy Research

Scheufele, Dietram A. (1999) Framing as a theory of media effects, *Journal of Communication*, Vol. 49, No. 1 pp 103–22

Sen, Amartya (1999) *Development as freedom*, Oxford: Oxford University Press

Serlin, Ilene A. (2006) Psychological effects of the virtual media coverage of the Iraq war, Kimmel, R. and Stout, C.E. (eds) *Collateral damage: Psychological consequences of America's war on terrorism*, Westport, CT: Praeger pp 145–63

Shinar, Dov (2007) Peace journalism: The state of the art, Shinar, Dov and Kempf, Wilhelm (eds) *Peace journalism – state of the art*, Berlin: Regener pp 199–210

Shoemaker, Pamela and Reese, Stephen (1996) *Mediating the message*, White Plains, NY: Longman

Smith, Jonathan A., Jarman, Maria, and Osborn, Michael (1999) Doing Interpretative Phenomenological Analysis, Murray, M. and Chamberlain, K. (eds) *Qualitative health psychology*, London: Sage

Spielberger, Charles D., Gorsuch, Richard L. and Lushene, Robert E. (1970) *Manual for the state-trait anxiety inventory: Self-evaluation questionnaire*. Palo Alto, CA: Consulting Psychologists Press

Szabo, Attila and Hopkinson, Katey (2007) Negative psychological effects of watching the news in the television, *International Journal of Behavioral Medicine*, Vol. 14, No. 2 pp 47–62

Tehranian, Majid (2002) Peace journalism: negotiating global media ethics, *Harvard Journal of Press/Politics*, Vol. 7, No. 2 pp 58–83

Tuchman, Gaye (1978) *Making news: A study in the construction of reality*, New York: Free Press

6

When peace journalism and feminist theory join forces: A Swedish case study

AGNETA SÖDERBERG JACOBSON

The faces of the young Palestinian women follow me attentively. Peace journalism is something new for Niba, Rashma, Hajad and the other women in the group. War journalism, on the other hand, is all too familiar to them. When I describe the features of so-called "war journalism" – the black and white dualism, the fixation on physical violence, men with power filling up the pages, the lack of context and background – they cry out in recognition: "That's exactly what our media are like!" As newly qualified journalists, they are struggling to adapt to reality. The news media in Palestine are, to a high degree, a part of the conflict. All media belong to one political faction or another and the freedom of movement for individual journalists is very limited.

The women in the group are attracted to ideas of peace journalism. They acknowledge the ideas and say that they would like to work with such standards, but they do not believe it is possible in Palestine. We use one full day to monitor the local news media.[1] The number of women represented is extremely low, only the news in Arabic on the Al Jazeera television network[2] features any women. And the examples of war journalism pile up.

Someone in the group admits that they did not expect it to be that bad. But how can you change the standards of journalism in an occupied territory where the political struggle is placed above all else? Maybe it's possible to make some small changes; one woman's voice instead of a man's on a "hard" issue, some information on social issues could be added, and a little more background folded in. The discussion continues...[3]

Since launching in 1993, the Kvinna till Kvinna Foundation has been involved with issues relating to how women are affected by war and armed conflict. From the beginning, it was clear to us that the media tend to focus on women's vulnerability in wars and conflicts, but that they rarely report on strong women working to promote peace and human rights. We found that women in particular, and civil society as a whole, are clearly marginalised in conflict reporting.

Women not valued as news

The Kvinna till Kvinna Foundation's partners in conflict-ridden countries in the Balkans, the Middle East and the South Caucasus all tell the same story. It is extremely difficult for them to make themselves heard in the media, and to get the media interested in what they say and do – and especially how they influence the society in which they live – because what women do is not valued as news. Some women are even attacked in the media for their political work in support of women's rights, peace and reconciliation.

It was against this background that Kvinna till Kvinna launched the project "The image of women in the media". Its purpose was to influence the media to become more gender- and conflict-sensitive in their coverage. In our work, we found the concept of peace journalism[4] to be a helpful practical and analytical tool. Drawing from our own experience and the peace journalism model, we started scrutinising the news media more systematically from a gender and peace journalism perspective.

In 2004, Kvinna till Kvinna participated in a global media monitoring study, coordinated by the World Association of Christian Communication. Organisations from 70 countries analysed different forms of news media during one day.[5] The analysis of the material showed that 79 per cent of the news subjects[6] in the global news flow were men, 21 per cent were women. The study covered many important parameters concerning gender representation in the media, but was unfortunately missing one important category – conflict reporting. Relying on our observations over the years, we assumed that the gender imbalance in this specific category was even more distorted.

We knew from experience how little interest the Swedish media displayed in meeting representatives from our partner organisations when they visited the country. In November 2007, a group of women from our partner organisations in the Middle East came to Sweden on a study trip. At that point, we had twelve women from Iraq, Jordan, Syria, Egypt and Lebanon in Stockholm, each willing to be interviewed about the wars going on in their region. One Iraqi woman from Basra had witnessed how women had been brutally beaten and killed in her home town. We invited the media to come and meet the group: one journalist came, a trainee from Swedish Television, who later explained that he had not produced a story because "the material was not interesting enough". The story speaks for itself – women's experiences are not regarded as newsworthy unless their story has already been picked up by a major international media organisation.

Frustrated and angry at the situation, we decided it was time to monitor the gender-imbalance in conflict reporting in the Swedish news media. During two weeks at the beginning of 2008, the Kvinna till Kvinna Foundation's media group[7] made a study of the conflict reporting in all major Swedish news providers.[8] We counted the number of women and men appearing as news subjects. We looked at the various roles given to men and women. Were they representatives of the parties in conflict, or of civil society, or were they independent experts? Did they themselves speak, or were they presented through voice-over? Were they named or were they anonymous? We also monitored the extent to which peaceful conflict resolution was taken up and whether the underlying cause of a conflict was included in the reporting.

Some of our findings

So what were the major findings of our study? Firstly, even though both men and women participate in conflicts and are affected by them, women receive only 15 per cent of media conflict coverage. Correspondingly, 85 per cent of the news subjects were men. In the visual material illustrating conflict coverage, men appear in 75 per cent of the images and women in 25 per cent.

Secondly, of the total news subjects, a large majority were official sources and only a few were representatives of civil society. Individuals from civil society appear rarely as news subjects. Representatives of peace groups, human rights groups and humanitarian groups appeared in as few as four of the total news items (262 pieces). The parties featured in the reports were chiefly officials and adversarial factions. When NGO representatives were featured it was generally in the coverage by journalists reporting on location.

Thirdly, experts who were interviewed were mainly men. Of the experts used in the coverage, 11 per cent were women and 89 per cent were men. The particular media players monitored in the study used experts in one third of their news items. Most experts were official sources. We also looked at how the conflicts were explained and found that the background of the conflict was focused on in about 46 per cent of the news items. However, on closer inspection, it was clear that the background information consisted mainly of event and incident reports rather than explanations of the underlying causes of conflicts.

The monitoring methodology

A few words about the monitoring methodology. A check was carried out to ensure that there would be no major events taking place during the period that could impact on foreign news reporting. The selection of media players represented an equal distribution between radio, television and print media. The emphasis was on daily reporting, and no local media were included. Two evening newspapers and a weekly news magazine were also monitored – but their coverage of conflicts was too fragmented and sparse, rendering it difficult to analyse. There were a total of 262 news items about conflicts during the analysis period.

The observations were analysed using a matrix consisting of 70 quantitative questions. Eight people were engaged to conduct the analysis, all of them with extensive media backgrounds. A pilot survey was conducted before the main survey, testing the questions on a small selection of media, to check validity and reliability. Over the course of the monitoring, the group constantly discussed cases in which uncertainty arose as to the categories. A certain bias in the reporting is impossible to avoid completely. The findings of the monitoring, however, are clear enough to provide plenty of room for a margin of error. The results of the monitoring all point in the same direction: Women and civil society are not regarded as newsworthy, and journalists' interest in covering peaceful conflict resolution is limited.

The media players we studied were not overjoyed by the results we presented. It was obvious they did not appreciate the embarrassing figures on gender imbalance in their conflict reporting. However, as it turned out, our study made headlines on the primary newscast of Swedish public service radio. The story was also picked up by other media players and became the subject of several editorials in major Swedish newspapers. The results of the study also led to lively discussions in the blogosphere.

The findings of the study were presented at a seminar in May 2008 at the Department of Journalism, Media and Communication, at Stockholm University. Four representatives of management staff and one reporter from major Swedish media groups took part in a debate on the quality of Sweden's news media's coverage of war and armed conflicts. The discussion quickly became heated; the panellists could not accept their responsibility to keep a balance in reporting when it comes to gender and official/civil sources.

How the media's 'logic' excludes women's voices

The media directors argued that the imbalance was justifiable in that it reflected the actual distribution of power in society. Several of them maintained that the primary task of the media is to shine a critical light on power. None of them seemed to want to acknowledge the professional code whereby the task of the journalist is to report on society's many aspects and to give all parties in a conflict a voice. The realisation that the organisations of civil society are a key source in the business of shining a critical light on power (and that they are watchdogs in themselves) was also notably absent.

One comment from Karl Viktor Olsson, foreign affairs editor at the Swedish central news agency Tidningarnas Telegrambyrå (TT), clearly shows how the prevailing power structures in society rule news production:

> In order to deliver up-to-the-minute news coverage, we have to speak to the people who make the decisions, and they are usually men. It is not the journalists' job to change society, and the fact that the inequality of our world is reflected in our reporting does not bother me.

Swedish researcher Ylva Brune has studied the coverage of human rights (including women's rights) in the Swedish media. Not surprisingly, she has found that the media reflect the *de facto* discrimination of groups in society generally. She states: "There seems to be a mechanism of media logic at work here: the media reflect society's power structure, not its composition" (Brune 2007: 7).

Voice in their own right

This bias in media coverage is synonymous with the white, male, Western hegemony that has been ruling the world for centuries. The simple fact that women constitute more than half of the world's population but feature in just 21 per cent of the global news media coverage[9] is alarming. Yet most media consumers hardly notice this imbalance; we are so used to this gender bias that it has become a more or less accepted representation of reality.

The fact that the gender imbalance is even more accentuated in conflict reporting is not surprising. War, armed conflicts and security policy have always been male domains where women's voices have been neglected and even ridiculed. The traditional division of labour designates women to take pride in civil and domestic life, whereas men receive recognition for executing official and military power. One might think that such gender stereotypes are finally about to subside, at least in the Western hemisphere, yet it would seem that they still hold true in the world of media.

Another aspect of gender representation in conflict reporting is that women are more frequently portrayed as victims. It is true that modern warfare does target women, and civilians in general, to a greater extent than ever before[10], and, of course, it is extremely important to report on all different forms of violence that women are subjected to. However, setting the media's focus exclusively on the vulnerability of women, at the expense of giving them space and a voice in their own right, could contribute to even further exploitation.

During the wars in the former Yugoslavia (and in Rwanda) in the 1990s, the media increasingly drew attention to women's vulnerability. Indeed, it was thanks to the international media that it became generally known that rape was being systematically used as a method of war. It was right, and important, that these war crimes be brought to light. Media coverage was part of the reason the international community, in the founding statute of the permanent International Criminal Court in the Hague, included the use of rape as a method of war as a crime subject to sanction by the court.

However, the attention surrounding these war crimes had several negative aspects. The greatest problem was that coverage of women's vulnerability often caused further exploitation of women who had suffered traumatic experiences. The media hounded rape victims for interviews. Another problem was the fact that the image of women as victims became prevalent. Subsequently, those women who were active in peace-building (and warmongering) received very little coverage.

When women in active roles as breadwinners, activists – and soldiers – are relegated to the background, the picture becomes distorted. When women are presented almost exclusively as victims it becomes easy to forget that women are also protagonists who influence, and are influenced by, conflict outcomes. The ability of women to make themselves heard in society on the same terms as men is in itself a critical factor in societal development. A society in which women's voices (or women as a group) are marginalised is not a democracy in the fullest sense of the word. If we believe that the connection between democracy and sustainable peace is valid, we cannot ignore the fact that gender equality is a key precondition of sustainable peace.

Ignored and ridiculed

Women's rights activists are often subjected to "master suppression techniques"[11] – such as marginalisation, or being ignored and ridiculed – by the media. Some are also attacked for their political work in support of women's rights, peace and reconciliation (Barry: 2008).[12] Unlike male activists, female activists find that whatever they are accused of is presented as being linked to their gender. They can be hung out to dry by the media, accused of being immoral, promiscuous, prostituted and homosexual.

In Serbia, for example, the organisation Women in Black, which promotes peace and Kosovo's independence, has been accused in the media of conducting prostitution and of being lesbian. The ultimate case of misogyny propagated by the media occurred before the Rwandan genocide, when hate campaigns carried on in the media against a particular ethnic group often focused on women. One of the first victims of the genocide was the prime minister, Agathe Uwiringiyimana, the first woman to hold the post. In the year before the genocide, she was often portrayed in propaganda and politically extremist literature as promiscuous and as a threat to the nation.

The concept of master suppression techniques was originally formulated to analyse how power is exerted in society by the (male) elite, but it can be successfully applied to gender relations in the media. (Söderberg Jacobson 2006). Women are made invisible when they receive less coverage than men in the media. The fact that women are seldom portrayed as actors is also an act of marginalisation.

Heaping blame and putting to shame

There is a prevailing trend in modern society that requires women to dress and behave in a sexually attractive manner. Yet when they do so, it can happen that they are portrayed as, or accused of, being provocative. Typical instances of media vilification of women can be found in their style of reporting on rape cases and other crimes perpetrated against women. In many of these circumstances the media focus disproportionately on the victim's alleged sexual behaviour.

Moreover, when the media publish images of women's bodies, more or less naked and often nameless, women become objects. Such a choice of image may be justifiable in a few cases, but it is most often done out of routine and ignorance. An article on trafficking in human beings is not illustrated with men sitting in a bar, for example, but rather with a woman posing in a sex club.

Ridiculing or belittling of an individual or a group can occur in many different situations. When women's legitimate authority and leadership, including their technical expertise, are neglected or ignored their voices are removed from public conversation and political discourse. To focus on the physical features of a person instead of their professional competence is another means of belittling, as is constant commenting on the outer appearance of women and girls and how they dress.

A typical example of how women are belittled in the media can be found in *Dagens Nyheter*, the largest selling Swedish morning newspaper, of 7 January 2006. In a long article entitled "Women in white seize power", about Ellen Johnson Sirleaf, at that time a candidate for the presidency of Liberia, a great deal of attention is paid to her dress sense. However, the article makes no mention of the fact that Johnson Sirleaf has been a minister in a previous government, has worked for both the World Bank and the United Nations, and has even been sentenced to jail for political reasons. On the contrary, readers are informed that she is publicly called "Mama Ellen" and the question is raised as to whether her popularity among the people and her charisma will be enough to solve Liberia's enormous problems. One could reasonably ask oneself why the author of the article chooses to ignore Johnson Sirleaf's political worthiness and, instead, seems intent on portraying her as a political novice.

This situation is exacerbated by the disproportionately low representation of women as figures of authority by the media. When women do make the news, they more often than not do so, not as figures of authority, but as symbols of glamour and beauty, or as vulnerable victims. When women's voices and experiences are omitted from and by the media it is appropriate to talk about gender-based censorship (Callamard 2006). The Gender Media Monitoring Report of 2005 and other studies, such as our own, show that censorship can be the handmaiden of gender-based power, discrimination and inequality and further, that this type of censorship might actually be exercised in and by the media. Several media organisations and advocacy groups have highlighted the responsibility of the media to work actively against gender discrimination. The organisation Article 19[13] states that:

> public service broadcasters should be obliged by law to take positive steps in order to fight against discrimination and intolerance, including gender based, while other media organisations, media enterprises and media workers have a moral and social obligation to do so.

And in a booklet promoting gender balance in the media, published in 2009 by the International Federation of Journalists (see www.ifj.org), the organisation acknowledges that:

> fair gender portrayal is a professional and ethical aspiration, similar to respect for accuracy, fairness and honesty. Journalism has its roots in the fight for decency, progress and rights for all.

Lack of gender perspective – even within the peace journalism model

Gender analysis is an inevitable means for action in the struggle to improve conflict reporting, (and, of course, journalism in general). All too often, a gender perspective is missing in the self-reflective analysis within the media business itself, especially when it comes to foreign news and conflict reporting. Peace journalism is no exception. When Kvinna till Kvinna became aware of peace journalism we saw similarities between its analysis and conclusions and our own work. However, on closer study, we discovered a critical difference: there was no articulated gender perspective in the model. Despite an obvious overlap between peace journalism and feminist perspectives on news media there were no references to any common analysis of power structures or society as a whole.

Feminists and the women's movement have been talking for a long time about gender imbalance in the media and how this connects with peace and sustainable development. Back in 1995, the World Conference on Women in Beijing affirmed that the media is one of the most important areas to focus on in order to achieve gender equality in the world. The conflict analyses offered by peace journalism and the women's movement share the same fundamental principles – that all of the parties in a conflict must be heard, and that members of civil society should be given greater opportunities for input in conflict reporting.

That all parties must be given a chance to be heard is a basic rule of journalism. However what or who the parties are is a matter open for interpretation. Even if women, the elderly and children are not considered permanent active combatants, they are clearly participants in a conflict. Allowing these parties to be heard creates a broader perspective on the conflict. During wars and conflicts, it is the women who are largely responsible for day-to-day survival and are engaged in the civil society. It is also common for women to instigate peace initiatives that transgress borders, such as in the Israel-Palestine conflict. This is largely because women see possibilities due to their experiences in conflicts, which may differ from men's experiences. However, these initiatives seldom receive attention in the media.

Feminist theory and peace journalism

Another aspect of peace journalism that harmonises with feminist theory is its emphasis on structural problems. This becomes clear when it comes to violence.

Where conventional conflict reporting automatically addresses the apex of the "violence triangle" – so called "direct violence" – peace journalism emphasises the base, that is, the context and underlying arguments of the conflict. In terms of this focus, factors such as poverty, the distribution of natural resources and gender inequality become vital explanations of violence, more than reprisals or hate between ethnic or religious groups.

All in all, the arguments above indicate that new elements ought to be added to Lynch and McGoldrick's model of the contrasting aspects of war journalism and peace journalism (2005: 6). By adding one pair of opposing factors, gender blindness and gender awareness, the model will become more comprehensive and better suited to reflect the reality of the issues.

The new gender agenda: Lynch and McGoldrick's war journalism/peace journalism model modified to incorporate gender blindness/gender awareness

War journalism:	Peace Journalism:
War/violence	Peace/conflict
Propaganda	'Truth'
Elite	People
Victory	Solution
Event over process	Process over event
Direct violence	Culture and structural violence
Closed space and time	Open in space and time
Gender blindness	Gender awareness

One counterargument to this addition could be that the gender dimension is already implicitly present in the original model, as a sub-dimension of the factors "elite" versus "people". Mainstream news media tend to focus on the elite, where women traditionally are scarcely represented. Peace journalism on the other hand, aims to relocate the interest towards people, or rather towards the civil society, where female participants abound.

So far so good, but I would argue that a more explicit gender analysis would be of benefit to the peace journalism model as such. It would surely make the model more attractive to women journalists and to feminists in general (including men). Moreover, gender theory has become an integrated part of most academic fields and is hard to ignore in the process of gaining credibility in the academic world.

How patriarchal norms are built into news making

In a recent article, Jake Lynch contributes to the discussion with an interesting analysis of how patriarchal norms and structures are built into mainstream news making[14]. Drawing from Johan Galtung's "gatekeeper theory", he explains how prevailing news values, and the news industry in general, are constructed out of vertical thinking. Deeply rooted binary oppositions, such as "men over women", make hierarchical patriarchal structures seem natural. Editors, journalists and media consumers, tend to accept the prevailing power distribution and refrain from critical thinking.

Feminist theory is in itself an important tool to encourage thinking "out of the box" – the equivalent to critical thinking and the very essence of peace journalism. Not to say that feminism in itself never gets stuck in its own box, but as long as patriarchal norms continue to reign there will be a need for feminist analysis. Feminist theory, along with other radical theories that question the status quo, have the capacity to inspire creativity. Within the non-violence tradition creativity holds a unique position. Martin Luther King once said that violence was "the antithesis of creativity" (Lynch and McGoldrick op cit). Creativity, in the sense of finding and suggesting new ways of looking at the situation at hand, is crucial for effective non-violent interventions. According to Johan Galtung's alternative formula for peace, there can be no (positive) peace without adding a certain amount of creativity (ibid: 17).

Peace = non-violence + creativity (= peace journalism)[15]

Consequently the critical and creative aspect of feminist theory fits perfectly with the ideas of peace journalism. Jake Lynch's article can be read as an invitation to women activists and feminists to join in the movement to change the prevailing standards of conflict reporting, and, by extension, the media industry as a whole. He notes that patriarchy has often been seen as an impediment to peace, and ends his article:

> The cause of peace has often been seen as overlapping with the struggle against patriarchy, itself a form of cultural and structural violence in many forms. These are struggles that should be seen as overlapping in the media domain as well.

Do women make better peace journalists?

In this context it is also important to acknowledge that women are not always agents for good. In terms of conflict reporting, we need to recognise that women participate in battles and are also decision-makers during wars and conflicts. To ensure a just and comprehensive representation of conflicts, it is also important to show women who deviate from the norm of the "good woman". Women are not "good" to any greater extent than men.

Johan Galtung has suggested that women would make better peace journalists. Jake Lynch also elaborates this perception in his article. In a psychological study by Annabel McGoldrick, war journalism and peace journalism reports were played to interview subjects to gauge different audience responses. Jake Lynch read the war journalism reports while Annabel McGoldrick read the peace journalism reports (McGoldrick 2008). Much of the content was the same, but the words and tone in which they were delivered differed. The woman, Annabel McGoldrick, was found by almost everyone who watched the reports to be easier to listen to. Jake Lynch goes on to ask:

> Her voice is emphasising empathy and understanding, both qualities suitable for peace journalism. Is it, therefore, a "woman's voice", and is peace journalism better carried out by women than by men?

One might wonder if a switch in the traditional gender roles would have affected the results? What if the woman delivered the war journalism report? Would that change the perceptions of the interview subjects? And, interestingly, what tone of voice would a male journalist have used when presenting a peace journalism report? The larger point is: What do we gain from applying a gender aspect to the practice of peace journalism? Would it attract more practitioners? Would it ultimately help to bring about a better gender balance in conflict reporting? I do not think so. It seems more likely that such thinking will steer peace journalism into biologism and squeeze it into the rut of "soft issues" – that is, it will become earmarked for women – possibly scaring off male journalists in the process.

The issue itself incorporates the key feminist question of when and to what extent is it relevant to distinguish between men and women. How can we describe women as victims, and refer to their vulnerability, without further establishing or strengthening patriarchal thinking and norms? It might be that in many cultures, women typically have to become competent in a broader range of different discourses than men and this could possibly make them more likely to take up peace journalism.

However, the Kvinna till Kvinna survey gives no clear evidence that gender affects reporting. Such thoughts were articulated, however, by a few of the media managers we interviewed. This focuses particularly on the fact that women choose less conventional subjects when they get the chance to do jobs of substantial length. It is also clear that women are often involved in different types of projects involving communication for development (for instance, community radio stations).

The question is whether we should focus on gender differences. A better starting point for peace journalism would be to assume that both genders are capable of seeing beyond journalistic conventions. It would surely make the theory more attractive to male as well as female journalists. A productive approach for peace journalism would be to focus on and analyse the media logic that results in men and women being reflected so differently in conflict coverage (as well as in news reporting generally).

One of our international guests at the seminar where we presented our media study, Inna Michaeli, of the Israeli organisation, Women's Coalition for Peace, articulated succinctly how the media's Catch 22 regarding gender could be resolved: "You (the media) choose sides – you choose the side of power, which marginalises us. You say there are no women in key positions – but if you talk to us we will become important."

Conclusion: A project in progress

For Kvinna till Kvinna the work with women's media rights has just begun. So far we have mainly been focusing on lobbying journalists and editors in Sweden. We believe it is now time to take our work with peace journalism one step further. We have long talked about the possibility of using the concept to help strengthen our partner organisations in the regions where we are working. On a number of occasions we have presented the peace journalism concept to our partners – and have received very positive responses. According to their comments, peace journalism would be a useful tool to help them better understand the media and learn about, and start using, media activism.

One important issue for our partner organisations is how to develop effective relations with the media – to get their message through. For a start they have to build relations with media actors and also gain respect among journalists who are covering the conflict in their region. We want to create a common ground, a temporary meeting place, which would transfer the ideas of peace journalism and at the same time help to build relations between the civil society (our partner organisations) and the media.

During the next two or three years, the Kvinna till Kvinna Foundation will arrange regional workshops for our partner organisations focusing on peace journalism. The workshops will cover a number of issues, such as "how peace journalism relates to the media situation in your country" or "how the theories of peace journalism can help you in your lobby work towards your local media".

In addition, local media and civil society actors will be invited to a conference on conflict resolution, organised by the Kvinna till Kvinna Foundation in cooperation with local media organisations. The aim is to create a common platform, as neutral as possible, for media and NGOs to meet and discuss conflicts on a more abstract level. The focus of the conference will be on theories of conflict resolution rather than on the actual conflicts themselves. The conference will be an occasion for the participants of the peace journalism workshops to use newly acquired knowledge and argumentation skills.

To end this phase of the project an international conference will be arranged in Stockholm in 2011. The aim is to gather NGOs, media workers and researchers engaged in issues regarding the relations between gender, media and conflict from all over the world.

Notes

1   The monitoring exercise was conducted on 18 March 2009. It covered five daily newspapers and the Al Jazeera news channel in Arabic. On average, only 6 to 7 per cent of the people in the illustration material (including advertisements) were women.
2   Al Jazeera is a major Arabic television network based in Qatar.
3   Notes from a workshop at Bir Zeit University in Ramallah, in the West Bank (March 2009), in cooperation between Fojo Media Development Institute and the Media Training Centre at Bir Zeit.
4   See www.peacejournalism.org.
5   On 16 May 2005.
6   Definition of news subject: the people who are interviewed, or whom the news is about. See www.whomakesthenews.org.
7   At present the Kvinna till Kvinna Foundation's media group consists of eight professional journalists and researchers.
8   Daily newspapers in the survey: *Dagens Nyheter, Svenska Dagbladet, Sydsvenska Dagbladet*; news on television: *Aktuellt* on SVT (Swedish public service television), Nyheterna TV 4 (commercial-television channel); radio: *Kvart i fem Eko*t on SR (Swedish public service radio); news agency: Tidningarnas Telegrambyrå.
9   See www.whomakesthenews.org.
10   www.unicef.org/graca/women.htm.
11   See www.kilden.forskningsradet.no/c16881/artikkel/vis.html?tid=55475.

12 For further examples see the report Insiste, Persiste, Resiste, Existe – Women Human
    Rights Defenders Security Strategies available from www.kvinnatillkvinna.org.
13 Article 19 is a human rights organisation with a specific mandate and focus on the
    defence and promotion of freedom of expression and freedom of information world-
    wide. See www.article19.org.
14 http://www.transcend.org/tms/article_detail.php?article_id=1154.
15 Definition from Lynch, Jake and McGoldrick, Annabel (2005) *Peace journalism* p. 17.

References

Barry, Jane with Nainar, Vahida (2008) *Women human rights defenders' security strategies*:
    Insiste, Persiste, Resiste, Existe, Canada: the Kvinna till Kvinna Foundation, Frontline
    Protection of Human Rights and Urgent Action Fund. Available online at http://www.
    kvinnatillkvinna.se/article/3005, accessed on 29 June 2009

Brune, Ylva (2007) *Svenska nyhetsmedia och mänskliga rättigheter i Sverige (Human rights
    reporting by Swedish news media) SOU 2007: 102*, Stockholm. Available online at
    http://www.regeringen.se/content/1/c6/09/62/79/355d7eaa.pdf, accessed on 29 June
    2009

Callamard, Agnès (2006) *Gender-based censorship and the news media*, London: Article 19

Lynch, Jake (2009) *Women's business?* 27 April. Available online at www.transcend.org/tms/
    article_detail.php?article_id=1154, accessed on 27 April 2009

Lynch, Jake, and McGoldrick, Annabel. (2005) *Peace journalism*, Stroud: Hawthorn Press

McGoldrick, Annabel (2008) Psychological effects of war journalism and peace journalism,
    Peace and Policy, Vol. 13 pp 86–98

Nafgshbandi, Asa'ad (2009) *Getting the balance right; Gender equality in journalism*,
    Brussels: International Federation of Journalists. Available online at http://unesdoc.
    unesco.org/images/0018/001807/180707e.pdf, accessed on 29 June 2009

Söderberg Jacobson, Agneta (2006) *Reporting on women in war and armed conflict*
    (in Swedish), Johanneshov: the Kvinna till Kvinna Foundation

7

Crossing borders: The global influence of Indigenous media

VALERIE ALIA

Indigenous peoples around the globe are engaged in a collaborative project that is forging new ways of communicating, and new ways of preventing, mediating, and resolving conflicts. The discussion that follows is based on more than twenty years of research in several countries, with a focus on Canada's pivotal, international role in the development of Indigenous media outlets and networks. An important starting-point for my own thinking is Ien Ang's idea of the "progressive transnationalisation of media audiencehood" (Ang 1996: 81). However, I find the designation, "transnationalisation" too restrictive, and have sought to broaden it, to encompass internal colonialism and boundaries between ethnicities and regions. Since 2003, I have called the fluid crossing of boundaries and places – the *inter*nationalisation of Indigenous media audiencehood and media production – the New Media Nation (Alia 2009a; Alia 2003).

Arjun Appadurai (1990: 298–99) uses the term *mediascapes* to describe media environments, representations and dissemination of information and *ethnoscapes* to describe people and their cultural contexts. The absences and inaccuracies of mainstream coverage, and the scarcity of Indigenous journalists, have led Indigenous people to develop their own mediascapes and communication outlets. Using a range of old and new technologies, they are sending information to a rapidly expanding global audience – promoting common interests while maintaining/restoring particular languages and cultures. Radio remains the chosen medium for local communication, transmitted in traditional ways, and via the internet, which has made it possible to bring local broadcasts to a global listener community.

While access is far from universal, it continues to improve, with the help of free-access facilities in libraries and community centres (notably, among Inuit in the Canadian Arctic). The internet has become the primary outlet for broader interactive communication, a forum for discussion and debate, and a tool for global and regional constituency building and cross-border organisation. Locally, nationally, and internationally, Indigenous media have helped to mediate conflicts, as we will see in the discussion (below) of the pivotal role of Mohawk radio stations in Canada's 1990 "Oka Crisis". The New Media Nation is more than a network: it is a force for global socio-political change.

Declarations and apologies: Indigenous peoples on the world stage

In September 2007, the United Nations General Assembly adopted the Declaration on the Rights of Indigenous Peoples. At the time, only four countries voted against the Declaration: Canada, Australia, New Zealand and the United States (Cultural Survival 2007: 5). In early 2009, after a change in government with the election of Kevin Rudd as Prime Minister, Australia reversed its position and signed the Declaration, leaving Canada, New Zealand and the United States the remaining naysayers. In April 2009, Mary Simon, President of Canada's national Inuit association, Inuit Tapiriit Kanatami (ITK), issued a statement via her "President's Blog" on the ITK website, praising Rudd's action and pressing the remaining governments to sign:

> On behalf of Inuit Tapiriit Kanatami, I salute Kevin Rudd, Prime Minister of Australia, for leading his government to their endorsement of the UN Declaration on the rights of Indigenous Peoples last week. With this move by Australia, there are just three countries left who voted against a move that followed more than two decades of debate, negotiations and agreement. As an Inuk [Inuit individual] and a Canadian, I am ashamed that Canada is one of those three dissenting countries (Simon 2009).

Simon highlighted the Declaration's support of the "individual and collective rights of indigenous peoples, as well as their rights to culture, identity, language, employment, health, education and other issues" and its prohibition against discrimination, adding:

> It bewilders me that after so much thoughtful and educated consideration having been dedicated to these issues over a 20 year period, our Canadian government does not see what an esteemed body such as the United Nations does, with its eye on history and the well being of the global population – that the

world's Indigenous peoples have for the most part been marginalised over history, resulting in socio-economic and health conditions that continue to do damage to these populations. I sincerely hope that Canada becomes the next nation, and certainly not the last, to see the light, and right, of this United Nations Declaration (ibid).

Besides supporting the UN human rights programme, Australia's newly-elected Kevin Rudd had campaigned on promises of a long overdue apology for the injustices, physical, and emotional abuse visited on Indigenous children by the residential schools to which they were sent – sometimes pressured, sometimes forced to leave their communities, families, and homes. In 2008, Rudd made good his promise and issued a formal apology. Canada's then Prime Minister, Stephen Harper, had long been unwilling to make such an apology to Indigenous peoples in Canada. After the Australian apology and continuing pressure from Indigenous and non-Indigenous citizens, organisations, and politicians, he finally acceded, and Canada issued its own formal apology for the horrors and traumas of the residential schools to which Indigenous children – First Nations ("Indian") and Inuit ("Eskimo") were sent.

My husband, the historian and journalist, Pete Steffens, and I watched the proceedings in Canada's House of Commons on television from our home in western Canada. The events were broadcast on all of the major media networks. We chose a particularly appropriate one: the Aboriginal Peoples Television Network (http://www.aptn.ca/corporate/) – the network which, since 1999, has broadcast programming produced by and for Indigenous people throughout Canada. Its very existence is a testament to the survival and triumph of Indigenous people over what have often seemed insurmountable odds. APTN is the world leader in a flourishing, and rapidly growing global movement.

The New Media Nation is part of the worldwide explosion of Indigenous news media, information technology, film, video, music, visual and other arts, and the concomitant revival and restoration of Indigenous languages and cultures. It presents (and indeed, has already demonstrated) unprecedented opportunities for networking and peacemaking. Existing outside the control of any particular constituency or nation state, its members are able to network, engage in transcultural and transnational lobbying, and access information that is often inaccessible within individual nation states. The New Media Nation demonstrates James Clifford's thesis that cultural action, "the making and remaking of identities, takes place in the contact zones, along the policed and transgressive intercultural frontiers of nations, peoples, locales" (Clifford 1997: 7). To help understand the context within which the "Nation" can foster media-assisted conflict resolution, let us look briefly at the structural violence theory of Swedish peace researcher, Johan Galtung.

Structural violence theory, Indigenous media and conflict resolution

Johan Galtung identifies two basic kinds of violence, *direct* or *personal*, and *structural*. By *direct violence*, he means the violence between individuals or groups, which results in injury or death. By *structural violence*, he means the harm that comes to people because of a range of societal structures and the behaviours they engender. The effects of direct violence are inarguable and blatant; those of structural violence are sometimes less visible or immediate, and therefore harder to discern and define. Nevertheless, Galtung reminds us that there "is no reason to assume that structural violence amounts to less suffering than personal violence" (Galtung 1980: 7).

Structural violence can be deeply destructive – not only on symbolic, cultural, and psychological levels, but on physical levels as well. Furthermore, it is often the case that structural violence forms a foundation for, or is a cause of, direct violence. Cultural genocide (ethnocide) is a form of structural violence that affects more than individual and collective psyches. Among its consequences are poverty, ill health, and – particularly in Indigenous communities – conflict within communities and with external "authorities", and waves of suicide. In my work in the Canadian Arctic, almost every family I have met has direct experience of suicide.

Indigenous media have long addressed themselves to such problems, and to trying to reform and transform damaging conflicts and structures. In my book, *Media ethics and social change* (2004), I looked at the ways in which media and forms of violence interact. The following diagramme, adapted from that book, takes off from Galtung's theory, and places the two forms of violence as points on a continuum.

Government, societal, and journalistic intervention can affect the nonviolence/violence continuum at any point. Journalists and mass media are omnipresent players in the escalation, or the defusing, of conflicts. Journalistic practice can reside with structural violence by limiting or controlling access to information, by providing inaccurate or damaging information. It can also become direct, as when the (mis)judgments of journalists, politicians and other leaders cause danger and even death.

A model for examining levels of violence (adapted from Alia 2004)				
Nonviolence - - - - - - - - - - Structural Violence - - - - - - - - - - Direct Violence				
Total non-violence; mediation; conflict resolution	Oppressive or repressive structures, formal and informal (legal sanctions and restrictions, etc.) (disempowerment)	Cultural genocide: forced or enforced changes to personal and place names; destruction of identities and languages	Culture-wide and community-wide patterns of suicide; state-sanctioned killings, or 'collateral' deaths resulting from actions and sanctions	War, geno-cide, legally sanctioned execution

Structural violence and media responsibility in Papua New Guinea

A disturbing example of this kind of misjudgment occurred in 2008, when the venerable *New Yorker* magazine published a highly problematic article about Indigenous people in *Papua New Guinea* (PNG), by a well-respected scientist/journalist, Jared Diamond (Diamond 2008). Rhonda Roland Shearer, Michael Kigl, Kritoe Keleba, and Jeffrey Elapa prepared a meticulously researched report detailing the article's indignities and inaccuracies and challenging the author and publisher to correct them.

> If Jared Diamond had changed the names of people and tribes and simply said that he was unsure if the stories he heard were true, Daniel Wemp, his single source for his tale of Papua New Guinea (PNG) tribal revenge, would not be in the danger that Diamond and his publisher, the *New Yorker* maga-zine, placed him in. This crisis was set in motion...on April 21, 2008, with the publication in the *New Yorker* of the Pulitzer Prize-winning author and renowned UCLA scientist's *article*, "Annals of Anthropology: Vengeance Is Ours: What can tribal societies tell us about our need to get even?" (Shearer et al. 2009).

From his conversations with one man who had been his driver on a bird research trip several years earlier, Diamond wove a "tale of two tribes, the Handa and Ombals, and their endless and futile violence based on a relentless 'thirst' for revenge" (ibid). Under the auspices of the Art Science Research Laboratory

(ASRL) she and her husband, Stephen Jay Gould, co-founded, and her Stinky Journalism.com media ethics project, Rhonda Roland Shearer sent a team of PNG-based researchers to the community and region in question. The numerous errors and fabrications that they found are chronicled in the 2009 report, *Jared Diamond's factual collapse: New Yorker mag's Papua New Guinea revenge tale untrue: Tribal members angry, want justice.* It was a classic case of fitting the "research" to the predetermined thesis, which Diamond had publicised as the subject of his next book. The manner and method calls to mind earlier colonial "encounter" stories – based on hearsay and casual tourism, an approach that most social scientists and conscientious journalists abandoned long ago.

Diamond described two Southern Highlands "Nipa" clans, the Handas and the Ombals, engaged in "an endless cycle of violence that had raged for decades" (ibid). When ASRL researcher, Michael Kigl, visited Daniel Wemp's Nipa home in the Southern Highlands, in July 2008, he learned that Wemp "had no idea that he or people he mentioned to Diamond in random stories about tribal warfare back in 2001–2002, would be publicly named, and worse, erroneously linked to heinous crimes". Yet informed consent is a near-universal guiding principle for scientists and journalists alike. For example, the American Anthropological Association (AAA) Code of Ethics calls on researchers to "be open about the purpose(s), potential impacts, and source(s) of support [with]...funders, colleagues, persons studied or providing information, and with relevant parties affected by the research" (AAA 1998).

In one of the most blatant misrepresentations, Diamond recounted a tale of one man's "very public suffering as a wheelchair-bound paralytic", presumably caused by a hired assassin's arrow attack. When the researcher arrived, he discovered the man in question walking and "carrying a large bag of dirt over his shoulder" – no paralysis, no wheelchair. The researcher also found that the two supposedly warring men had never met before the *New Yorker* piece was published. According to the ASRL report, the two men at the centre of the article are misidentified. One, whom Diamond calls a "warrior", "is not a warrior but a former village court peace officer..." Shearer contends that the article is not just sloppy science, but a potential danger to the lives of the featured individuals. "One can easily understand that members of the Handa and Ombal [tribes] are angry they have been labelled killers and rapists of Huli women by Diamond and the *New Yorker* – accusations that spread widely when the article was posted on the Internet – when they were actually victims of the conflict cited!" (ibid). The AAA code states that researchers:

must do everything in their power to ensure that their research does not harm the safety, dignity, or privacy of the people with whom they work, conduct research, or perform other professional activities [and must] actively consult...with the goal of establishing a working relationship that can be beneficial to all parties involved...While anthropologists may gain personally from their work, they must not exploit individuals, groups, animals, or cultural or biological materials. They should recognize their debt to the societies in which they work and their obligation to reciprocate with people studied in appropriate ways (AAA op cit).

Furthermore:

they are not only responsible for the factual content of their statements but also must consider carefully the social and political implications of the information they disseminate [and] must do everything in their power to insure that such information is well understood, properly contextualized, and responsibly utilized (ibid).

Just as journalists and media organisations can contribute to the escalation of conflicts, they can also help to prevent, de-escalate, or mediate them. They cannot always choose the outcomes of their work. But they are sometimes able to play a constructive, proactive role in conflict prevention and resolution. Many of the media outlets and projects created by women, ethnic minorities, Indigenous people(s), and others are consciously, carefully, and conscientiously organised in alternative ways. The people who found and run them work to transform structural violence and seek nonviolent solutions to omnipresent challenges and problems, as in the examples of Indigenous broadcasting that follow.

Journalism and nonviolence: Mediation and conflict resolution in Mohawk territory

Despite the changing technologies that have enabled an array of "new" media, in Indigenous and many other minority communities, radio remains the medium of choice, sometimes narrowcasting, sometimes broadcasting to an ever-widening, internet-driven audience. The communications scholar, Lorna Roth, observes (1993) that radio fosters linguistic, cultural and sometimes physical survival. During the 1990 confrontation between townspeople at Oka, Québec, and the people of the Kanehsatake Mohawk First Nation, radio played a crucial role in providing public information, conflict prevention and conflict resolution.

It started with attempts to expand a golf course onto a sacred Mohawk burial ground. Mohawk resistance, police and military intervention led to a blockade of Kanehsatake. To ensure continuing coverage, two young Mohawk broadcasters, Marie David and Bev Nelson, camped out for four months, in the headquarters of radio station CKHQ, until the crisis ended. During that time, they kept their own community informed of the daily events they witnessed, while also informing a wider national and international audience, and helping to defuse anger and correct misunderstandings caused by mis- and dis-information. As other stations picked up their broadcasts, "the listening audience rapidly grew"; they were interviewed on Canadian and international radio and television, and some of their reports were "sneaked out by a supportive Montreal journalist for rebroadcast" on stations in Montreal, across Canada, and internationally (ibid).

While CKHQ provided the daily, on-the-spot reports, the broadcasters and their community received crucial support from CKRK, the radio station in the neighbouring Mohawk community of Kahnawake. Because Kahnawake was not directly involved in the conflict, it had more freedom to report and distribute information. The prime mover at CKRK was its founder and station manager, Conway Jocks, a brilliant and multi-talented journalist, manager/broadcaster, historian, artist and cartoonist. Jocks had always espoused the value of progressive, constructive talk-back radio; in this case, it became a life-saver. At peak hours, CKRK reached more than 300,000 listeners, building "a public opinion support base for the Mohawk position and acting as a conflict mediator (ibid)."

At the centre was the station's flagship phone-in show, *The Party Line* (ibid). Along with the customary chronicles of daily life, familiar to a community station, listeners were informed about military and police manoeuvres, political negotiations and developments, survival strategies (how to maximise limited food and resources), ways to respond to interviews and field questions from the public, while Band Council members appealed for "calm and sobriety". CKRK kept information flowing and encouraged public discussion, carefully maintaining an atmosphere of quiet normality, while featuring music playlists with "high message value", featuring songs like John Lennon's *Give peace a chance* and *The freedom song* by Frosty, a well-known resident of Kahnawake (ibid).

Conway Jocks considered rumour to be the greatest danger because of its potential for escalating conflict. So he fact-checked with care, and broadcast only what he was able to confirm. That principle differed sharply from the confrontational, incendiary practices familiar to non-Indigenous talk-back shows. *Party Line* was so successful, in attracting audiences and helping to defuse conflict, Jocks extended its normal broadcast hours and brought in an experienced announcer, Nathalie Foote, who had worked for the station before. As Jocks described it, the programme "soon turned into a barricade jumper, the only direct link with the outside world for us inside who were rapidly taking on a fortress mentality" (ibid).

During the summer of 1990, every *Party Line* broadcast opened with a Mohawk prayer, followed by the rules of conduct, which included proscriptions against the use of foul language, and surnames. Sometimes fielding more than a hundred calls an hour, Foote managed to keep her voice soft. She invited callers to share their feelings, even if they included expressions of racism. There were limits, some imposed by Canadian broadcast regulations. However, it was her conviction that even angry and offensive speech deflected the focus from direct and personal harm to safety-valve "venting" and more constructive dialogue. This applied not only to non-Indigenous callers. She invited Mohawk "effigy-burners and rock-throwers" to call in and explain their actions – once again, redirecting violence to talk. She was influenced by Martin Luther King's Gandhian view that "if violence is the language of the inarticulate", the opportunity to speak can provide an outlet for anger and frustration, and can help to diminish physical violence.

The success in defusing tension depended a great deal on the station's policies and the host's considerable skills. When callers made hostile comments, Foote quietly thanked them and hung up. Roth, who had provided radio training at Kanehsatake, was able to hear many of the broadcasts. She said that Nathalie Foote rarely "blew her cool" and managed to maintain diplomacy "through some very tense periods" Most importantly, she found "new ways of using radio...for catharsis and conflict mediation...she developed a technique for diffusing tension – psychotherapeutic radio" (ibid).

The role of CKRK-FM at Kahnawake and the inside-the-barricades CKHQ broadcasts by Marie David and Bev Nelson at Kanehsatake, echoed the earlier experience of Lakota people during the 1973 siege at Wounded Knee in South Dakota, USA. During that crisis, it had also been mainly women who kept the radio station functioning, providing ongoing information and morale-building support. Just as the women at Kanehsatake made the station their temporary home, Lakota women occupied, and where necessary, camped out at their community radio station and kept the broadcasts going under tense and sometimes life-threatening circumstances (Crow Dog and Erdoes 1992).

Mapping the Indigenous media universe

Australia

In Australia, the first exclusively Indigenous station began broadcasting in 1985. Today, it is part of the National Indigenous Media Association of Australia (NIMAA), which has 136 community broadcaster members. Its code of ethics illustrates some of the differences between Indigenous and mainstream media. It asks that journalists respect "confidences... especially secret sacred information" and observe "all tribal, geographical and sacred rights and areas" (NIMAA 2005). Another difference is the dedication, throughout the Indigenous world, to serving remote communities and regions that mainstream media often deem too "insignificant" and unprofitable to bother with. The Remote Indigenous Broadcasting Service (RIBS) broadcasts more than 1,000 hours of Indigenous content a week to about 160 licensed community radio and television stations, while smaller-scale licensed and unlicensed stations continue to extend the service even farther. Some 50 community radio stations broadcast locally produced Indigenous programming in regional and urban areas, with more than 20 radio stations licensed as Indigenous-owned and run, a handful of Indigenous narrowcast radio services and an Indigenous commercial station (Alia 2009b: 46).

Kalaallit Nunaat (Greenland)

In 1979, the Home Rule Act designated *Kalaallit Nunaat* (Greenland) a special cultural community within the Kingdom of Denmark, and the precedent-setting Landsting (Greenland parliament) and Landsstyre (Greenland government) began officially to govern the country (ibid: 47). In 1980 broadcasting was one of the first institutions to come under Home Rule control. Broadcasting in Greenland began in 1925, when the first telegram was sent by wireless. While the first broadcasts were Danish-controlled, *Kalaallit* (Greenlandic Inuit) got involved early on. *Kalaallit Nunaata Radioa* (KNR), the national (public) broadcaster, has both radio and television service. Danmarks Radio (DR, Danish public radio) distributes its newscasts via satellite, supplemented by a few privately owned radio and television stations. KNR emerged in the midst of a cultural revival and much of the music broadcast on its radio outlet is home grown. Kalaallit singer-songwriters were among the first to write and record in their own language, supported by a large and growing public and private recording industry; they have influenced Indigenous musicians worldwide.

The United States

Even in relatively wealthy "first world" countries such as the United States, it is a mistake to assume that people have universal media access. As late as 2007, the Finnish communications scholar, Ritva Levo-Henriksson, found that many Native American communities had poor (or no) access to relevant radio, television or the internet. Some had no electricity; solar power does not work well with television, which does not reach even all of the homes with satellite access. Radio is the most accessible and affordable medium (Levo-Henriksson 2007: 107). This is not just because the people are poor and computers scarce, but because the US has not developed a culture of shared community access comparable to Canada's.

There is a much broader and farther-reaching concern, addressed in Levo-Henriksson's work, which speaks to the issue of conflict prevention and resolution. She observes that different visual codes can affect not only production values and approaches, but people's ability to respectfully communicate with each other. For example, the Hopi ethic that individuals must not look directly at each other directly contradicts non-Indigenous guidelines for conducting television interviews. "The representative of the world 'out there' mostly talks, whereas the representative of the Hopi culture mostly 'listens'" (ibid). Culturally relevant broadcasting was not available on the Hopi Reservation until 2000, when KUYI-FM, the Hopi radio station on First Mesa was launched. Created by the Hopi Radio Project, its aim is to develop "a Hopi-owned, Hopi-run FM public radio station". The station's call letters come from the Hopi word, *kuyi*, meaning "water". As in Canada and elsewhere, Hopi have found a different way of doing radio. The inaugural broadcast began with the words: "You're listening to KUYI" followed by the Hopi crier, Jimmy Lucero, shouting the news in Hopi (ibid: 103).

The most progressive media project in the United States was probably Alaska's Indigenous newspaper, *Tundra Times*. Founded as a lobbying tool of the Alaska Native Brotherhood (ANB) during a prolonged conflict between Indigenous and commercial fisheries, its power was considerable, and its influence soon became international. Its founders were the Tlingit leader, William Paul, and the Seattle-educated artist and Alaska Inupiat leader, Sikvoan Weyahok (Howard Rock). Paul transformed his people's traditional Raven narratives into political rhetoric. Starting from stories of Raven controlling and silencing people, Paul said that Indigenous people must control the media, and re-appropriate "the White man's journalism" (Alia 2009b: 48–9). The *Tundra Times* ceased publication in 1997. During its life-span, the newspaper helped to mediate conflict among Indigenous groups and peoples, and between Indigenous peoples and the government. It nurtured the pan-Indigenous movement that united Aleut, Yup'ik, Inupiat, Athabascan, Tlingit, Haida and Tsimshian peoples. With the newspaper front and centre, the movement's best known and farthest-reaching achievement was the signing of the Alaska Native Claims Settlement Act (ANCSA). The American Indian Radio on Satellite network distribution system (AIROS) operates 24 hours a day using the internet and public radio. The Navajo Nation introduced its new wireless network in 2003.

Canada

In Canada, "new media" were in place almost as soon as they emerged. When I first went to what is now Nunavut in the Canadian Eastern Arctic in the early 1980s, even the smallest Inuit communities received equipment and access and expertise, and Inuit were actively developing websites others uses of the new technologies. Inuktitut fonts were available by the mid-1980s and computers were provided to schools, adult education centres and community centres. Teleconferencing became an important tool for conducting inter and intra-community meetings, legal, medical and social services and government business in a region with challenging weather, distances, terrain, and prohibitive transportation and communication costs. The satellite distribution system had enabled the creation of Television Northern Canada (TVNC), which in 1999 was expanded to become APTN.

With its generally supportive communication policies and APTN, the nationwide Aboriginal Peoples Television Network, Canada remains the leader in Indigenous communications. Although the first Indigenous broadcasts were on Alaskan radio in the 1930s, the United States has done very little to support Indigenous media, over the years. With only about one-seventh the population of the United States, Canada has the overwhelming majority of Indigenous media outlets – several hundred Indigenous radio stations, compared to about 30 in the US; a dozen regional networks, a national radio network, several television production outlets, and APTN. The strength and persistence of Indigenous lobbying and pressure has been a major factor, within the context of Canada's unique history of supporting minority media in general, and Indigenous and northern media in particular.

Inuit beyond borders

Inuit have been major players in the development of Indigenous media in Canada, while internationally, they have created some of the world's most effective and politically astute organisations, notably the Inuit Circumpolar Council (ICC). Indigenous people from many parts of the world regularly attend ICC assemblies as observers, and carry ideas and strategies home. At the ICC assembly I attended in 1989, I met Indigenous Hawaiian, First Nations, and Sámi observers and journalists. Founded in 1977 by the late Eben Hopson of Barrow, Alaska, as the Inuit Circumpolar Conference, the ICC has flourished and grown into a major international non-government organisation representing about 150,000 Inuit of Alaska, Canada, Greenland, and Chukotka (Russia). The organisation holds Consultative Status II at the United Nations. On its website (www.inuitcircumpolar.com), the ICC explains its origin and mandate:

> To thrive in their circumpolar homeland, Inuit had the vision to realize they must speak with a united voice on issues of common concern and combine their energies and talents towards protecting and promoting their way of life.

ICC's international office is housed with the Chair, which rotates every three years; each member country has a national office and a national president (ICC 2006). The ICC issued its global vision from the start, declaring itself to be "under four flags" (Canadian, Greenlandic, US, and Soviet/Russian). During the Cold War, when Siberian people could not leave the Soviet Union, each ICC assembly displayed all four flags, with an empty chair placed in front of the Soviet flag. In 1989, under Gorbachev's leadership, Inuit from Chukotka were permitted to attend the assembly in Sisimiut, Greenland. I was lucky enough to be there for one of the most moving experiences I have known, when Siberians were warmly welcomed, and were finally able to occupy the chairs in front of their country's flag.

Ainu in Japan

Ainu, in Japan, are among the Indigenous people most recently arrived in the new media universe. They have endured a painful history. In 1593, the warlord Toyotomi Hideyoshi handed the rights to the ancestral Ainu homeland on the island of Ezo (now Hokkaido) to the Matsumae clan. In 1869, Japan established the Hokkaido Colonial Office; in 1899, the Meiji government enacted the Hokkaido Former Aborigines Protection Law. Much as "reserves" in Canada and "reservations" in the US herded Indigenous people together and left their lands open to colonial use, Japan appropriated Ainu lands and lives. Ainu received designated tracts of land; their property was placed under government control, and the state took over control of their education. Shigeru Kayano founded the tiny but influential Ainu radio station, FM Pipaushi, in 1997. His son,

Shiro Kayano, chaired the organising committee for the Indigenous People's Summit in Hokkaido, and continues to broadcast on FM Pipaushi. Ainu have begun to expand their networking efforts, and have visited Indigenous media outlets in other countries. In 2008, following the formal apologies to Indigenous peoples of Australia and Canada, the government of Japan finally officially recognized Ainu as Indigenous peoples. (Alia 2009b: 49)

From local to global: Indigenous media networks

According to Linda Tuhiwai Smith, Indigenous peoples have been highly effective in using various kinds of networking to build relationships across cultural, national, and regional borders, and disseminate knowledge and information. Just as Amnesty International and other organisations use worldwide publicity to reveal, challenge, and help prevent imprisonment, torture, disappearances and killings, the globalisation of Indigenous media networks is at once a vehicle for communication and violence-prevention. As Smith puts it: "Networking is a way of making contacts between marginalised communities in the face of non-Indigenous society, which controls most forms of communication" (Smith 1999: 157). Drawing on her own experience as a scholar of Maori descent with international and transnational connections, Smith considers Indigenous peoples' networking a form of resistance, especially in states that commonly practise police surveillance of Indigenous activists and their families. In states such as Guatemala, where Indigenous peoples are especially threatened and sometimes "disappeared", networking can be dangerous (ibid).

The Guatemala Radio Project

The Guatemala Radio Project is one of many local projects with global links which are helping to publicise and protect Indigenous peoples and provide outlets for expression (of both viewpoints and creativity), information, and education. Much as black Africans were the majority in South Africa under apartheid, the Indigenous (mostly Maya) peoples of Guatemala constitute the disempowered (and persecuted) numerical majority. In 1997, peace accords officially ended more than 30 years of civil war in Guatemala, and guaranteed Indigenous people the right to community media. However, that right is still being challenged; Indigenous broad-casters are intimidated and in some cases, their stations are damaged or destroyed. To gain a voice, Indigenous and other minority peoples developed more than a thousand unlicensed stations. In 2005, the NGO, Cultural Survival, organised the Guatemala Radio Project to support and strengthen local stations that were already broadcasting to Maya peoples across the country. The project manages to survive, despite the persistence of government harassment (Cultural Survival 2006: 5).

The launch of World Indigenous Television

In 2008, Maori in Aotearoa (New Zealand) took Indigenous media networking to new heights when they convened the founding conference of the first global Indigenous television network, the World Indigenous Television Broadcasters Network (WITBN: http://www.witbn.org/). Their preliminary announcement proclaimed: "WORLD INDIGENOUS TELEVISION IS HERE!" (Maori Television 2007). The conference theme was "Reclaiming the future". WITBN's interim council included broadcasters from Australia, Canada, Fiji, Ireland, Norway, Scotland, South Africa, Taiwan, and Wales, and the full members of its inaugural council are: APTN (Canada), BBC Alba (Scotland), NRK Sámi Radio (Norway), S4C (Wales), TG4 (Ireland), TITV/PTS (Taiwan), and Maori Television (New Zealand). The first official council meeting took place in 2009, at Karasjok, Norway in Sápmi (the Sámi homeland that crosses northern Finland, Norway, Sweden and Russia), hosted by NRK Sámi Radio. Also in 2009, WITBN launched a scheme for exchanging programmes and news broadcasts among the world's Indigenous television outlets (WITBN 2009).

Conclusions: Outlaws and visionaries: looking back and moving forward

Elsewhere, I have written of the "guerrilla" or "outlaw" roots of much of Indigenous journalism (Alia 2009b). Increasingly, the media guerrillas and outlaws are coming above ground and publicising their views and work to an ever-growing global audience. One of the early visionaries was George Manuel, a leader of the Shuswap (Secwepemc) Neskonlith First Nation in British Columbia, Canada. Frustrated by the limits of local power and communication, and of the policies and politicians of individual nation states, he envisioned an international organisation of Indigenous peoples, whom he called the "Fourth World". While generally credited to Manuel, the term originated in his discussions with Mbuto Milando during Milando's term as first secretary of the Tanzanian High Commission in Canada. Manuel said that people must organise on every front – local, regional, national, and global. To that end, he met with Mbuto Milando and Julius Nyerere in Tanzania and with Maori, Native American, Peruvian, Australian, Sámi and other leaders, and helped to draft the Universal Declaration of the Rights of Indigenous Peoples.

The Inuit broadcaster and political leader, Rosemarie Kuptana, famously compared "the onslaught of southern television and the absence of native television to the neutron bomb, saying: 'Neutron bomb television...destroys the soul of a people but leaves the shell of a people walking around'" (Kuptana 1982). She and George Manuel argue that mainstream communication helps to create and sustain oppression, and that Indigenous peoples need their own media outlets, programming, and networks.

In 1975, George Manuel founded the World Council of Indigenous People. His rallying cry was: "Indigenous peoples must stand together and send their voices beyond national borders, to 'be heard by the world'." (Alia 2009b: 41–2). Today, their voices are heard through an array of media, supported by increasing technological sophistication. Most Indigenous media outlets have their own websites. Blogs are growing, especially where there is more government control and less media freedom. In its most progressive and effective forms, blogging is the new journalism, able to cross geographic, cultural and political borders and help build community, transcending the limits imposed by attitudes, policies, and governments of the regions and countries where they reside. This is only a "taster" of what is happening around the world. The picture changes so rapidly, one is breathless, trying to keep up.

References

AAA (1998) *Code of Ethics of the American Anthropological Association*, American Anthropological Association. Available online at http://www.aaanet.org, accessed on 29 June 2009

Alia, Valerie (2003) Scattered voices, global vision: Indigenous peoples and the "New Media Nation", Karim, K. H. (ed.) *The media of diaspora*, London and New York: Routledge pp 36–50

Alia, Valerie (2004) *Media ethics and social change*, Edinburgh: Edinburgh University Press

Alia, Valerie (2009a) *The new media nation: Indigenous peoples and global communication*, New York and Oxford: Berghahn Books

Alia, Valerie (2009b) Outlaws and citizens: Indigenous people and the "New Media Nation", *International Journal of Media and Cultural Politics*, Vol. 5, Nos 1 and 2 pp 39–54

Ang, Ien (1996) *Living room wars: Rethinking media audiences for a postmodern world*. London: Routledge

Appadurai, Arjun. (1990) Disjuncture and difference in the global cultural economy, *Theory, Culture and Society*, Vol. 7 pp 295–310

Clifford, James (1997) *Routes: Travel and translation in the late twentieth century,* Cambridge, Massachusetts and London: Harvard University Press

Crow Dog, Mary and Erdoes, Richard (1992) *Lakota woman*, New York: Grove Press

Cultural Survival (2006) Promoting indigenous participation in democracy in Guatemala, *Annual Report 2006*, Cultural Survival

Cultural Survival (2007) UN adopts the Declaration on the Rights of Indigenous Peoples, *Cultural Survival Quarterly* Vol.31, No. 3, October pp 4–5

Diamond, Jared (2008) Annals of anthropology: "Vengeance is ours", *New Yorker*, 21 April

Galtung, Johan (1980) *The true worlds: A transnational perspective*, New York: the Free Press

ICC (2006) Inuit Circumpolar Council. Available online at http://www.inuitcircumpolar.com/index.php?ID=1&Lang=En, accessed on 1 May 2009

Kuptana, Rosemarie (1982) *Inuit Broadcasting Corporation presentation to the CRTC on cable tiering and universal pay TV* (speech), Inuit Broadcasting Corporation. Available online at http://www.inuitbroadcasting.ca/, accessed on 1 May 2009

Levo-Henriksson, Ritva (2007) *Media and ethnic identity: Hopi views on media, identity, and communication*, New York and London: Routledge

Maori Television (2007) *Be sure to book in early. This is one Hui you will not want to miss* (flyer). World Indigenous Television Broadcasting Conference, November, unpaginated

NIMAA (2005) Indigenous Media Codes of Ethics (1st draft) in press pack, *NIMAA: The voice of our people*. Fortitude Valley, Queensland, Australia: National Indigenous Media Association of Australia

NITV (2007) Black TV launches on Black Friday, online media release, 13 July. Available online at http://nitv.org.au/, accessed 1 May 2009

Roth, Lorna (1993) Mohawk airwaves and cultural challenges: Some reflections on the politics of recognition and cultural appropriation after the summer of 1990, *Canadian Journal of Communication*, Vol. 18, No. 3 pp 315–31

Shearer, Rhonda Roland, Kigl, Michael, Keleba, Kritoe. and Elapa, Jeffrey (2009) *Jared Diamond's factual collapse: New Yorker mag's Papua New Guinea revenge tale untrue: Tribal members angry, want justice*, Special Report: Media. New York: Stinky Journalism News, Art Science Research Laboratory's Media Ethics Project, 21 April. Available online at http://www.stinkyjournalism.org/latest-journalism-news-updates-149.php

Simon, Mary (2009) Australia endorses the United Nations Declaration on the Rights of Indigenous Peoples, President's Blog, Inuit Tapiriit Kanatami (ITK). Available online at http://www.itk.ca/trackback/550, accessed on 6 April 2009

Smith, Linda Tuhiwai (1999) *Decolonizing methodologies: Research and Indigenous peoples*, London and New York: Zed Books

WITBN (2009) *WITBN Newsletter*, Issue 14, 20 February

8

Iraq and Dahr Jamail: War reporting from a peace perspective

FLORIAN ZOLLMANN

American independent journalist Dahr Jamail has written some of the most comprehensive journalistic first-hand accounts on the US/Coalition-occupation of Iraq. For eight months, throughout four different periods between November 2003 and February 2005, Texas-born Jamail immersed himself in Iraqi society - embedded with the Iraqi people, he explored the occupation of Iraq from an insider's perspective. In between and after these visits, he has reported on Middle Eastern affairs from Lebanon, Syria, Jordan and Turkey as well as within the United States. In January 2009, he returned to Iraq to continue his investigations. While initially reporting from Iraq as a blogger and travel writer, Jamail's distinctive journalism was rapidly recognised and published by various independent and mainstream news organisations. Today, Dahr Jamail is an acclaimed international journalist.[1]

Before travelling to Iraq, Jamail worked as a mountain guide, freelance journalist and social worker in Alaska. In 2003, he decided to go to Iraq because he felt desperate about his government's decision to attack the country and how the US media covered the invasion and occupation. In his book *Beyond the Green Zone* (2007: 3), a collection of his journalism from Iraq, Jamail reflected:

> ...I wondered what I might do to bring the information I found reported in other countries back to the uninformed, horribly misled population of my own country. ...I went to Iraq for personal reasons. I was tormented by the fact that the government of my country illegally invaded and then occupied a country that it had bombed in 1991. Because the government of my country had asphyxiated Iraq with more than a decade's worth of "genocidal" sanctions (in the words of former United Nations Humanitarian Coordinator for Iraq Denis Halliday). The government of my country then told lies, which were

obediently repeated by an unquestioning media in order to justify the invasion and occupation. I felt that I had blood on my hands because the government had been left unchecked.

As this statement indicates, Dahr Jamail's journalism is animated by a deep sense of attachment to those suffering injustices. Furthermore, siding with the victims of Western aggression, and exposing the perpetrators of human suffering and crimes, are key features of Jamail's writings. But what are the distinctive attributes of Dahr Jamail's journalism? How does his war reporting differ from mainstream media coverage? To answer these questions, I will discuss how the corporate press in the US covered the invasion and occupation of Iraq. I will then introduce Dahr Jamail's journalism more generally and analyse his reporting of the second US assault on Fallujah in November 2004.

The following account covers a selection of Jamail's journalism, which consists of numerous articles (as available on his website) and two books.[2] The assault on Fallujah appeared to be an important case to study because it had devastating consequences for the people in the city. Furthermore, most of the journalists stationed in Iraq did not stay in Fallujah during the assault. For journalists not embedded with the military it has been extremely difficult to cover the occupation. As Robert Fisk (2005) writes, "[r]arely, if ever, has a war been covered by reporters in so distant and restricted a way". Fallujah was no exception. Nevertheless, Jamail's writing on Fallujah appeared to differ profoundly from that of the corporate mainstream (see Zollmann 2007) and it seemed important to analyse why that was the case.

Media coverage of the invasion and occupation of Iraq: War journalism

The US/Coalition invasion and occupation of Iraq was carefully propagandised by the US and UK governments. Numerous studies have discussed these efforts and demonstrated that the case for the invasion and occupation of Iraq was built on misinformation, distortion and fear-mongering (e.g. Rampton and Stauber 2003; Miller 2004; Solomon 2005; Edwards and Cromwell 2006; Herman and Chomsky 2008).

Research suggests that the US media provided a limited range of debate consonant with the planning and objectives of the US administration. It failed to investigate the planning and execution of the invasion/occupation of Iraq in an independent fashion (e.g. Boyd-Barrett 2004; Nichols and McChesney 2005; Bennett, Lawrence and Livingston 2007; Friel and Falk 2007; Herman and Chomsky op cit: 291–6).

During the invasion and occupation of Iraq, warfare was covered extensively by embedded journalists with almost unprecedented frontline access (Keeble 2004: 49–50). Because of their closeness to coalition forces, the so-called embeds were heavily criticised for effectively being "in bed" with the military (Lewis et al 2006: 188). According to Lewis et al. (ibid: 195), the embedding system was part of the government/military "public relations model" with the function of creating "*positive* coverage" in accord with official perspectives. Embedded journalists inevitably narrowed down the focus on the progression of war without revealing the hidden enemy and the gruesome details of combat, thus "giving the narrative an almost fictional quality" (ibid: 191). Nevertheless, the study by Lewis et al. (ibid: 188–9), which focused on coverage by British embeds, stressed that embedded reporting did not substantially differ from non-embedded and often provided perspectives that "contradicted official military claims". However, the researchers pointed to a general problem of coverage: the media was as close to the state as usual during wartime (ibid: 197).

A major case of media distortion during the build-up to the invasion and its aftermath was the reporting on Iraq's alleged possession of weapons of mass destruction (WMD). The WMD claim was used by the Bush administration to justify going to war and prominently carried in the US press – without sufficient challenge (for a study on media coverage of the WMD issue see Moeller 2004; also Boyd-Barrett op cit and Herman and Chomsky op cit: 292–4).

The New York Times, for instance, presented the existence of Iraq's WMD's in multiple editorials as fact while ignoring extensive contradicting evidence (Herman and Chomsky op cit: 293; Friel and Falk op cit). Only by June 2003, when the US/ Coalition had already invaded Iraq and established its puppet regime, did some major US mainstream media organisations acknowledge that the Bush administration claims about WMDs were lies. In May 2004, *The New York Times* even apologised to its readers in an editorial for parts of its coverage on the alleged WMDs. But this happened without seriously questioning its news gathering practices which include a steady reliance on news provided by official sources (see Boyd-Barrett op cit).

The WMD case demonstrated how easily the press followed the frames and outright lies provided by government thus supporting its war effort. But more striking was the fact that, even if Iraq had possessed WMDs, the US would not have been entitled to attack the country. As Michael Mandel (2005a) writes

[t]he war in Iraq...constitutes the quintessential war of aggression, falling very far short...of any justification in self-defense or authorization by the Security Council of the United Nations, the only two accepted legal grounds for war in international law.

Accordingly, the number of legal experts who saw the Iraq War as a violation of international law far exceeded the few who depicted the invasion as legal (see Mandel 2005b: 33). Yet significantly, the US press was unable to discuss these issues. For example, *The New York Times* which, as Friel and Falk (op cit: 148) document in an extensive study ignored "international law in its coverage of the US invasion of Iraq". Furthermore, as the authors point out, *The New York Times* did not mention that the Bush administration committed "the supreme international crime" under the international law principles embodied in the Nuremberg precedent" which was mainly instituted by the US to outlaw Nazi-Germany's aggression (ibid: 147–9). Michael Mandel argues that according to this legislation "the whole legal and moral responsibility for death and destruction rested at the invaders" of Iraq while "every casualty was a crime for which the leaders of the attacking coalition were personally criminally liable" (Mandel 2005b: 31).[3]

The findings of two statistical studies, one conducted by the Johns Hopkins School of Public Health (published in the British medical journal, the *Lancet*, in 2006), the other by the British polling organisation Opinion Research Business (published in 2007), indicate that by mid-2007 more than 1 million Iraqis may have been killed as a direct result of the 2003 invasion (McElwee 2008; see also Edwards and Cromwell 2007). According to McElwee (op cit), both studies have been largely neglected in the US media. Remarkably, as McElwee further notes, the Johns Hopkins School uses a cluster survey method which is commonly accepted to quantify birth and death rates during natural and man-made catastrophes. The same design has been used, for instance, to measure civilian deaths in Sudan's Darfur region, where about 200,000 people have been killed in recent years (ibid). McElwee (ibid) writes that "while the Darfur figure has been cited over 1,000 times by major US press outlets [in 2007]...the estimate for Iraq is ignored".

Thus, the media neglected scientific evidence which suggested that Coalition forces might have conducted serious crimes. But a framework that describes massive Iraqi civilian deaths as a result of US/Coalition policies does not fit within the mainstream media's reporting which tended to portray warfare during the invasion as clean, precise and humanitarian (see Keeble op cit: 53–4). Similarly, coverage on the occupation of Iraq rather focused on Sunni/Shi'a animosities and resulting violence without acknowledging that sectarian strife and the high amount of civilian deaths had been a result of US-occupation policies (see Arnove 2007: 114–5).

This brief overview of the coverage of the invasion and occupation of Iraq suggests that mainstream reporting had many features of "war journalism" (see Lynch and McGoldrick 2005: 7): discourses were framed in accord with official narratives whereas important evidence on US government actions, the existence of WMDs, the international law context and the effects of the invasion and occupation (particularly civilian deaths) was largely omitted. The omission of evidence and perspectives, it could be argued, supported the efforts of the US government to invade Iraq and remain in occupation – with terrible consequences for the people of Iraq.

Dahr Jamail: Reporting people

Dahr Jamail's journalism has covered many topics and his practices range from social reportage to investigative journalism and war reporting. His approaches resembles that of the British investigative and campaigning reporter John Pilger and the *Independent*'s veteran foreign correspondent and author, Robert Fisk. According to McLaughlin (2002: 15) the "two principles" of Pilger's journalism are to report the views of those most affected by war (civilians and combatants) and "to reveal the hidden agendas of war". Fisk, he further emphasises, stresses the journalists' need to be aware of the historical background of the conflicts they are reporting (ibid: 15–7).

When reflecting on his journalistic approach, Jamail said he "wanted to report on where the silence was" about "[h]ow are Iraqis getting by, what's their daily life like?" (Dahr Jamail cited in Moss 2008).[4] Moreover, Jamail has been concerned with the deeper factors behind US foreign policy:

> Going into Iraq, I felt it was really important to read up on the history, find out what is the US security strategy, what is US foreign policy. Only then can you understand the facts and the nature of the US's historical involvement in Iraq (cited in ibid).

McLaughlin (op cit: 16) stresses that Fisk depicts "himself as a foreign correspondent, not a war reporter". Jamail could be primarily seen as a foreign correspondent as well because his journalism covers many other areas than war. Generally, the following broad themes could be identified:

- everyday life under occupation;
- the state of public services and living standards;
- civilian deaths;
- long- and short-term US military and political policies;
- US military operations/warfare/"counter-insurgency" strategies and their outcomes;

- emergence and policies of the resistance;
- Iraqi administration policies, reconstruction and aid;
- corporate malfeasance;
- torture and terrorism;
- sectarian and ethnic tensions/violence;
- and soldiery.[5]

However, these themes had probably been covered by many other journalists. So what are the specific and distinct attributes of Jamail's reporting practices? As a result of the 2003-invasion, Iraq was torn apart by war and ethnic hostilities. It had quickly become one of the most dangerous countries in the world. Working under these conditions was extremely risky. Independent journalists had not only to cope with the situation on the ground but had to expect hostilities from US/ Coalition forces: At best, they were treated with suspicion (Keeble op cit: 50) and at worst, they were directly targeted by the military (Curtis 2004: 102). As a result, the majority of journalists stayed safe by covering press conferences or remaining in military company (Fisk op cit).

Despite this, Jamail accepted great dangers in order to work independently. Like a local beat reporter, he covered the streets, neighbourhoods and public service institutions of Iraq. Consequently, his journalism mainly contextualises events from the people's perspective. A striking example of Jamail's journalism was one of his earlier writings, a news report published on his website in January 2004 (Jamail 2004a):

> ...Sadiq Zoman Abrahim, 55 years old, was detained this past August in Kirkuk by US soldiers during a home raid which produced no weapons. He was taken to the police office in Kirkuk, questioned by the Americans there, then transferred to Kirkuk Airport Detention Center. ...
>
> ...the Americans transferred him, comatose, to the hospital in Tikrit. ...
>
> According to the administrative staff at the hospital, the only information provided by the Americans was the incorrect name and a medical report which said Mr. Abrahim had suffered a heart attack. They provided no information as to where he had been picked up, no address and no other personal information.
>
> It is documented by both the hospital and Iraqi Red Crescent in Tikrit (who took the photos of Mr Abrahim), that the Americans dropped the comatose man off with the aforementioned information. ...
>
> The doctors at the hospital in Tikrit, after performing diagnostic tests, informed the family that Mr Abrahim had suffered massive head trauma, electrocution, and other beatings on his arms. An EKG proved that his heart was functioning

perfectly. The family was told that he was in an unrecoverable state and would be in a coma for the rest of his life from the obvious trauma suffered from torture. ...

This horrible situation raises many questions.

If the Americans knew who he was and where he was when they detained him, why did they fail to provide this information to the hospital when Mr Abrahim was dropped off?

Why did the Americans fail to notify the hospital of Mr Abrahim having an accident if there had been one?

How do you explain the massive head trauma, the burns on the bottoms of his feet caused by electrocution and bruises on his arms, if he had only suffered a heart attack as the medical report provided by the Americans states?

The family saw Mr Abrahim in perfect health upon being detained by the Americans. He was in their custody the entire time until dropped off at the hospital in Tikrit.

No firearms, bombs, or other incriminating evidence was ever found by searches conducted in the home of Mr Abrahim upon his detention. His family states that they have no idea why he was detained.

Even if the worst case scenario was true: that Mr Abrahim was an active member of the resistance and/or a high ranking Ba'ath Party member, does this justify being tortured by electrical shock and being bludgeoned into a coma?

Is this not a violation of International Law?

Should not he have been held for a trial to determine whether he was innocent or guilty?

Today Sadiq Zoman Abrahim lies staring at the ceiling, eyes wide open, in Haitha, Iraq.

His family is left sitting with him, with nothing else but unanswered questions from the CPA [Coalition Provisional Authority].

The clear structure of the writing, the use of public and civilian sources, the references to moral and legal contexts, the concern for human suffering and the demand to find out about its perpetrators could be seen as typical features of Jamail's journalism. But it was also significant, being one of the first reports suggesting the US's use of torture in Iraq. The Abu Ghraib scandal, which highlighted appalling torture at a US prison near Baghdad, emerged only four months later. In *Beyond the Green Zone*, Jamail (2007: 80) explained his handling of Zoman's story:

Back at my hotel that night, I emailed editors at many major newspapers in the United States. I managed to send out a total of 150 emails... I urged each editor to send their own reporter to cover this story, adding that there were countless stories like this one waiting to be reported. I didn't feel the need to cover it myself; I just wanted the information to be made public. Having neither a large audience nor having had a piece published in a well-known publication, I felt the best plan would be to just feed the story to some established outlets in the hope of it getting covered. I did not receive a single email or call in response.

In the end, Jamail was only able to publish Zoman's story in the independent internet news-daily, the *New Standard*. The article was further contextualised and included testimonies from the US's 4th Infantry Division, the unit responsible for taking Zoman, which claimed that the military had nothing to do with his injuries (ibid).

The second US assault on Fallujah in November 2004

When reporting on the occupation of Iraq, Jamail's journalism has also focused on the Iraqi resistance movement and its struggles with the occupying powers. These included the coverage on the first and second US assaults on Fallujah. US military forces attacked and devastated Fallujah twice, in April and November 2004, to crush the rebel stronghold which had emerged in the course of 2003. During the first siege, Jamail travelled to Fallujah and produced a first-hand account of the US onslaught (see e.g. Jamail 2004h). Again, in November 2004, Fallujah was stormed by US military forces. Without staying in the city but by using testimony of citizens, refugees, doctors and various organisations Jamail reported on the attack.

Fallujah is located in the Sunni-dominated al-Anbar governorate in the western region of Iraq. The rebel movement had significantly been fuelled by US-military policies which included intimidation, harassment, detention, and killings of civilians. Furthermore, the de-Ba'athification programme, which disempowered the Sunni minority as representatives of the former ruling class, encouraged the Iraqis to revolt. Although mainly consisting of Sunni Arabs, the resistance included numerous tribes, groups and organisations (Allawi 2007: 177–8).

US officials had framed the second US assault on Fallujah as a fight against terrorists and local insurgents. They argued that Abu Musab al-Zarqawi, said to be the top al-Qaeda terrorist in Iraq, resided in the city. In addition, the people of Fallujah, who the US claimed were being intimidated by foreign fighters and local insurgents, needed extra help to prepare them for their upcoming elections (see Filkins and Glanz 2004; Lloyd Parry 2004). During the upcoming "battle" the biggest high-tech army in history applied its firepower on a town where approximately 3,000–4,000 lightly armed insurgents and 50,000 civilians were expected to hide. About 80–90 per cent of Fallujah's total population had fled prior to the attack (Zollmann 2007).

Dahr Jamail: Peace journalism in practice

As the attack on Fallujah ground on, Jamail wrote richer reports by synthesising the testimony provided by different sources. On 8 November 2004, the day the assault officially started, Dahr Jamail (2004b) wrote a report using the statements of residents from Baghdad to encapsulate their views. As indicated above, Jamail was not able to speak with people in Fallujah because the city was sealed off by US forces. Nevertheless, interviews with local people in Baghdad could provide an important perspective for the Western readership:

> ... What Iraqi people are saying could be even more worrying to the occupation forces than the attacks.
>
> "The Fallujans should fight for their city," says Mahmoud Shakir, 80, former commander of the Iraqi police in Baghdad. "They are not terrorists, and there has been no proof of foreign fighters in Fallujah. And if there are Arabs there, they are more accepted than the Americans and coalition forces. In the name of liberty, they must fight." ...
>
> Ibrahim Mikhail who drives his car as a taxi now because he is afraid to join the Iraqi police force believes that if the US military would stay in their bases there would be less violence.
>
> "Why can't the US Army leave our cities," he said. "If their tanks will stay off our streets and the soldiers will stop raiding our homes, people would stop attacking them, especially Fallujans."
>
> US forces say al-Zarqawi is in Fallujah, "but Fallujans and now more people in Baghdad view the Americans as terrorists", he said. ...

It appears that Jamail uses his sources to respond to official claims: they address and indirectly refute General Casey's statements that the resistance consisted of terrorists and foreign fighters led by al-Zarqawi. Furthermore, the text suggests a causal relation between US military actions and resistance attacks. Both arguments were later confirmed (see Khan and Jamail 2005; Zollmann 2007, 2008). Furthermore, evidence suggested that the US was engaged in what Herman and Peterson (2002) describe as "wholesale" terrorism because the military applied indiscriminate force killing a large number of civilians and used military means to intimidate and coerce the people of Fallujah – actions that fall under the US Code definition of terrorism (see ibid).

On 10 November, another article provided further context. Again, Jamail (2004c) used the viewpoints of Iraqis and different political organisations:

> ...The Iraqi Islamic Party, a major Sunni political party, has withdrawn from the Iraqi interim government. "We are protesting the attack on Fallujah and the injustice that is inflicted on the innocent people of the city," said Abd al-Hamid from the party. "We cannot be part of this attack."
>
> Resistance to US forces seems to be rising sharply. "Even if the Americans take the city, they will only anger the rest of Iraq," said Dr Khalid al-Obeidy, professor at Baghdad University. "We have a dummy government who does only what the Americans tell them to do, so this martial law is from the Americans, not from any Iraqi government," he said about the recent institution of martial law.

Jamail's sources incorporated several evaluations which appeared to be accurate. Later developments confirmed that the resistance was not quelled by the assault (see Allawi op cit: 340). Furthermore, the Interim Government set up by the US could, according to US military law, rightly be seen as a "puppet government" which was following US orders (see Boyle 2005). The text suggested tensions within the Iraqi Interim Government, as depicted in the Sunni's withdrawal from the body which consisted of different fractions representing Shia, Kurdish and Sunni groups. The sources selected and their opinions may represent Jamail's own stance. Should he have presented a more balanced view, providing statements by US allies like the Iraqi-Kurds whose militias were part of Coalition forces?

In 2004, different polls revealed that the large majority of Iraqis regarded foreign troops as occupiers and only a tiny minority saw them as liberators (Arnove op cit: 28–9). It seems unlikely that this majority favoured a full-scale military attack against one of their own cities. Furthermore, there was a legal-moral issue: a military attack on a densely populated city could hardly be justified. The Geneva Conventions, which were binding for US/Coalition forces, protected the civilians and their property (Boyle op cit). These facts and the outcomes of the assault may have proven Jamail's stance as right. On 16 November, he presented the following civilian casualty figure (2004d):

> BAGHDAD — At least 800 civilians have been killed during the US military siege of Fallujah, a Red Cross official estimates.
>
> Speaking on condition of anonymity for fear of US military reprisal, a high-ranking official with the Red Cross in Baghdad told IPS that "at least 800 civilians" have been killed in Fallujah so far.

His estimate is based on reports from Red Crescent aid workers stationed around the embattled city, from residents within the city and from refugees, he said.

"Several of our Red Cross workers have just returned from Fallujah since the Americans won't let them into the city," he said. "And they said the people they are tending to in the refugee camps set up in the desert outside the city are telling horrible stories of suffering and death inside Fallujah." ...

The Red Cross official said they had received several reports from refugees that the military had dropped cluster bombs in Fallujah, and used a phosphorous weapon that caused severe burns.

The US military claims to have killed 1,200 "insurgents" in Fallujah. Abdel Khader Janabi, a resistance leader from the city has said that only about 100 among them were fighters.

"Both of them are lying," the Red Cross official said. "While they agree on the 1,200 number, they are both lying about the number of dead fighters." He added that "our estimate of 800 civilians is likely to be too low". ...

The way Jamail contextualises the information demonstrates his commitment to facts: the anonymity of the Red Cross source is revealed and the way the organisation came up with the casualty figure is documented. Furthermore, Jamail neither sides with US/ Coalition nor resistance forces. Rather, he lends credibility to the Red Cross official who dissects different "official" proclamations of casualties. The article also refers to the US's possible use of cluster bombs and phosphor as well as the prevention of Red Cross personnel entering the city – all acts that violate the Geneva Convention.

In further reports, Jamail complemented the picture of the military attack and its effect on the population of Fallujah. The following selection of articles was published in November and December 2004:

... The Iraqi Red Crescent Society states that scores of civilians have died in Fallujah. Thousands of families remain trapped in the city with no source of food, clean water or electricity. They report outbreaks of cholera, as well as children bleeding to death because there are no medical facilities left in the city. ...(Jamail 2004e).

She weeps while telling the story. The abaya (tunic) she wears cannot hide the shaking of her body as waves of grief roll through her. "I cannot get the image out of my mind of her foetus being blown out of her body."

Muna Salim's sister, Artica, was seven months' pregnant when two rockets from US warplanes struck her home in Fallujah on 1 November. "My sister Selma and I only survived because we were staying at our neighbours' house that night," Muna continued, unable to reconcile her survival while eight members of her family perished during the pre-assault bombing of Fallujah that had dragged on for weeks...

Both sisters described a nightmarish existence inside the city where fighters controlled many areas, food and medicine were often in short supply, and the thumping concussions of US bombs had become a daily reality...

"Our situation was like so many in Fallujah," said Selma, continuing, her voice now almost emotionless and matter of fact. The months of living in terror are etched on her face.

"So many people could not leave because they had nowhere to go, and no money" (Jamail 2004f).

Baghdad — Men now seeking refuge in the Baghdad area are telling horrific stories of indiscriminate killings by US forces during the peak of fighting last month in the largely annihilated city of Fallujah. ...

Many refugees tell stories of having witnessed US troops killing already injured people, including former fighters and noncombatants alike (Jamail 2004g).

While the first text (Jamail 2004e) is written in the style of a news report summarising the situation in Fallujah in accord with the information Jamail could obtain from relief organisations, the second article (Jamail 2004f) is structured as a news portrait. It focuses on the terrible story of civilian suffering. Most strikingly, Jamail uses shocking graphic images to highlight the civilians' plight. Such devices are largely neglected by the mainstream media when focusing on US actions but appear regularly in Jamail's texts. The final article (Jamail 2004g) suggests the occurrence of further and extensive war crimes as claimed by different Iraqi refugees featured in the text.

Taken together, it becomes clear that the distinctive feature of Jamail's war reporting is that he primarily reports what he learns from ordinary people. Statements by government officials are weighed against these personal testimonies and, contrary to mainstream media practices, not used as major framework of journalistic understanding. In further contrast to embedded reporters, Jamail does not discuss the strategic progress of what is labelled as "warfare". Instead, he documents the progressive destructiveness of what could rather be described as high-tech barbarism. Hence, Jamail's reporting differs profoundly from the mainstream.

Take, for instance, *The New York Times*, which proclaimed a military success for the assault on 15 November: "Military commanders point to several accomplishments in Falluja. A bastion of resistance has been eliminated, with lower than expected American military and Iraqi civilian casualties" (Schmitt 2004). On 27 April 2005, Dahr Jamail and Jonathan Steele (Steele and Jamail 2005) wrote a comment titled "This is our Guernica". It was published in the British newspaper the *Guardian* and concluded remarkably differently:

In the 1930s the Spanish city of Guernica became a symbol of wanton murder and destruction. In the 1990s Grozny was cruelly flattened by the Russians; it still lies in ruins. This decade's unforgettable monument to brutality and overkill is Fallujah, a text-book case of how not to handle an insurgency, and a reminder that unpopular occupations will always degenerate into desperation and atrocity.

The aftermath

Today, the people of Fallujah are not allowed to return to a normal life. We have to return to Dahr Jamail to hear about their story: "The city remains sealed. Many residents refer to it as a big jail," Jamail and a fellow correspondent wrote (al-Fadhily and Jamail 2008), because they

> must still carry around a US-issued personal biometric ID card which must also be shown any time you enter or exit the city if you are local. Such a card can only be obtained after US military personnel have scanned your retinas and taken your fingerprints (Jamail 2009b).

Since the 2004 assaults there has been very little reconstruction. Furthermore, parts of Fallujah seem to be contaminated. Human rights groups and Fallujah's hospital administration found about 5,900 unknown illness cases in Fallujah in 2006, with the majority being "cancers and abnormalities" (al-Fadhily and Jamail op cit.). These illnesses could have been caused by residues of the US's use of phosphor or other chemical agents. Already in 2005, Dahr Jamail (2005) reported that several refugees had told him about some strange actions by the US military which still controlled much of Fallujah. For instance, in areas where the heaviest fighting had occurred, soldiers were removing and carrying away huge amounts of soil. In other areas, houses and streets were power-blasted with water. "What is the US trying to hide in Fallujah?" asked Dahr Jamail (ibid). As yet, the mainstream media has not investigated the fate of the people of Fallujah.

Conclusion

Martha Gellhorn, the American war reporter, once reflected on her journalism saying she reported "from the ground up, not the other way around" (cited in Pilger 2004: 1). The same could apply to Jamail's approach: he represents the reality experienced by the Iraqi people. Thus, his war reporting counters the mainstream perspective which frames events as defined by state-corporate elites. Furthermore, Jamail reflects on current events in a fashion that bears similarity to what has been identified as "peace journalism" (Lynch and McGoldrick 2005: 6). Jamail's journalism focuses on causes, outcomes and the aftermath of the conflict and reveals the effects of violence as well as the suffering of ordinary people.

The second US assault on Fallujah resembled a massacre: between 4,000–6,000 people may have been killed. The city's compensation commissioner announced that 36,000 of the city's 50,000 homes were destroyed together with 60 schools and 65 mosques and shrines. Independent and foreign media reported numerous violations of the Geneva Conventions suggesting that US military planners and forces may have conducted serious war crimes (see Marqusee 2005; Holmes 2007; Zollmann 2007). Didn't Dahr Jamail's journalism indicate these realities throughout?

David Spark writes that "[i]nvestigative reporting seeks to gather facts which someone wants suppressed. It seeks not just the obvious informants who will be uncontroversial, or economical with the truth, but the less obvious who know about disturbing secrets and are angry or disturbed enough to divulge them" (cited in Nuttall 2006: 206). Moreover, investigative journalism has often been led by public service agendas and inquiries into possible crimes (ibid: 207). I would argue that Jamail's war reporting encapsulates the best features of investigative journalism.

Liberal press theories suggest that the media should operate as a "fourth estate" to give "expression to a richly pluralistic spectrum of information sources", contribute to society as a "system of checks and balances" on the powerful and thus "make democratic control over governing relations possible" (Allan 2004: 47). This study suggests that Jamail's "peace journalism" certainly satisfies these requirements.

Notes

1 See http://dahrjamailiraq.com/, accessed on 2 May 2009; http://www. beyondthegreenzone.org/, accessed on 2 May 2009; Jamail (2007); Moss (2008); Fitzsimmons (2008). Among other organisations Dahr Jamail has written for Inter Press Service, the *Guardian*, Truthout, *Asia Times*, the *New Standard* and *Le Monde Diplomatique*. Jamail's works have also been published in various media such as the *Nation*, the *Independent*, the *Sunday Herald*, *Al-Jazeera*, *Foreign Policy in Focus*, ZNet and TomDispatch.com. His writings have also been translated and published in different countries throughout the world. Dahr Jamail has appeared as a guest on

Democracy Now!, the BBC, Pacifica Radio and NPR. In 2007, Dahr Jamail won the Martha Gellhorn Prize for Journalism (see sources cited above).

2   See Jamail (2007) and (2009).
3   Translation by the author.
4   It might be worth mentioning that Jamail has also written on the conditions of US soldiers in Iraq and their attitudes about occupation and war: see e.g. Jamail (2009a).
5   The themes were identified through a random search in Jamail's published journalism and book, *Beyond the Green Zone: Dispatches from an unembedded journalist in occupied Iraq* (2007).

References

al-Fadhily, Ali and Jamail, Dahr (2008) Iraq: Five years on, Fallujah in tatters, Inter Press Service, 14 April. Available online at http://ipsnews.net/news.asp?idnews=41971, accessed on 10 July 2009

Allan, Stuart (2004) *News culture*, Maidenhead, Berkshire: Open University Press, second edition

Allawi, Ali A. (2007) *The occupation of Iraq: Winning the war, losing the peace*, New Haven and London: Yale University Press

Arnove, Anthony (2007) *Iraq: The logic of withdrawal*, New York: Metropolitan Books

Bennett, W. Lance, Lawrence, Regina G. and Livingston, Steven (2007) *When the press fails: Political power and the news media from Iraq to Katrina*, Chicago: University of Chicago Press

Boyd-Barrett, Oliver (2004) Judith Miller, *The New York Times* and the propaganda model, *Journalism Studies*, Vol. 5, No. 4 pp 435–49

Boyle, Francis A. (2005) Belligerent Occupant, ZNet, 29 December. Available online at http://www.zmag.org/znet/viewArticlePrint/4718, accessed on 2 July 2009

Curtis, Mark (2004) *Unpeople: Britain's secret human rights abuses*, London: Vintage

Edwards, David and Cromwell, David (2006) *Guardians of power: The myth of the liberal media*, London: Pluto Press

Edwards, David and Cromwell, David (2007) The media ignore credible poll revealing 1.2 million violent deaths in Iraq, 18 September. Available online at http://www.medialens.org/alerts/07/070918_the_media_ignore.php, accessed on 20 May 2009

Filkins, Dexter and Glanz, James (2004) All Sides Prepare for American Attack on Fallujah, *New York Times*, 6 November

Fisk, Robert (2005) *The US press in Iraq: Hotel Room Journalism*, Counterpunch, 17 January. Available online at http://www.counterpunch.org/fisk01172005.html, accessed on 20 May 2009

Fitzsimmons, Caitlin (2008) Reporters share Gellhorn prize. Available online at http://www.guardian.co.uk/media/2008/may/19/pressandpublishing.middleeastthemedia, accessed on 2 June 2009

Friel, Howard and Falk, Richard (2007) *The record of the paper: How the* New York Times *misreports US foreign policy*, London: New York

Herman, Edward S. and Peterson, David (2002) The Threat Of Global State Terrorism: Retail vs wholesale Terror, Z Magazine, January

Herman, Edward S. and Chomsky, Noam (2008) *Manufacturing consent: The political economy of the mass media*, New York: Pantheon Books, third edition

Holmes, Jonathan (2007) *Fallujah: Eyewitness testimony from Iraq's besieged city*, London: Constable

Jamail, Dahr (2004a) Detained, bludgeoned and electrocuted into a coma, 7 January. Available online at http://www.informationclearinghouse.info/article5482.htm, accessed on 24 May 2009

Jamail, Dahr (2004b) Resistance over Fallujah builds up in Baghdad, Inter Press Service, 8 November. Available online at http://dahrjamailiraq.com/resistance-over-fallujah-builds-up-in-baghdad, accessed on 25 May 2009

Jamail, Dahr (2004c) US will lose more by "victory", Inter Press Service, 10 November. Available online at http://dahrjamailiraq.com/us-will-lose-more-by-victory, accessed on 25 May 2009

Jamail, Dahr (2004d) 800 Civilians feared dead in Fallujah, Inter Press Service, 16 November. Available online at http://dahrjamailiraq.com/800-civilians-feared-dead-in-Fallujah, accessed on 1 June 2009

Jamail, Dahr (2004e) The Iraqi resistance spreads, Inter Press Service, 16 November. Available online at http://dahrjamailiraq.com/the-iraqi-resistance-spreads, accessed on 1 June 2009

Jamail, Dahr (2004f) Inside Fallujah: One family's diary of terror, *Sunday Herald*, 22 November. Available online at http://dahrjamailiraq.com/inside-fallujah-one-family%E2%80%99s-diary-of-terror, accessed on 1 June 2009

Jamail, Dahr (2004g) Fallujah Refugees Tell of Life and Death in the Kill Zone, *The New Standard*, 3 December. Available online at http://dahrjamailiraq.com/fallujah-refugees-tell-of-life-and-death-in-the-kill-zone, accessed on 1 June 2009

Jamail, Dahr (2004h) Americans slaughtering civilians in Fallujah, Antiwar.com, 13 April. Available online at http://www.antiwar.com/orig/jamail.php?articleid=2303, accessed on 3 June 2009

Jamail, Dahr (2005) What is the US trying to hide in Fallujah? Antiwar.com, 19 January. Available online at http://www.antiwar.com/jamail/?articleid=4470, accessed on 15 June 2009

Jamail, Dahr (2007) *Beyond the Green Zone: Dispatches from an unembedded journalist in occupied Iraq*, Chicago: Haymarket Books

Jamail, Dahr (2009a) *The Will to Resist: Soldiers who refuse to fight in Iraq and Afghanistan*, Chicago: Haymarket Books

Jamail, Dahr (2009b) Iraq's "Teflon Don": The new Fallujah up close and still in ruins, TomDispatch.com, 12 February. Available online at http://www.tomdispatch.com/post/175033, accessed on 12 June 2009

Khan, Omar and Jamail, Dahr (2005) Remembering the first siege of Fallujah: Excerpts from testimony submitted to the World Tribunal on Iraq, ZNet, 14 February. Available online at http://www.zmag.org/content/showarticle.cfm?ItemID=7246, accessed on 21 September 2007

Keeble, Richard (2004) Information warfare in an age of hyper-militarism, *Reporting war: Journalism in wartime*, Allan, Stuart and Zelizer, Barbie (eds), London: Routledge pp 43–58

Lloyd Parry, Richard (2004) Hand over Bigley's killer or face attack, rebel town told, *Times*, 14 October

Lynch, Jake and McGoldrick, Annabel (2005) *Peace journalism*, Stroud, Gloucestershire: Hawthorne Press

Mandel, Michael (2005a) Nuremberg lesson for Iraq war: It's murder, Knight-Ridder Newspapers, 30 August. Available online at http://www.commondreams.org/views05/0830–33.htm, accessed on 12 May 2009

Mandel, Michael (2005b) *Pax Pentagon: Wie die USA der welt den krieg als frieden verkauft*, Frankfurt am Main: Zweitausendeins

Marqusee, Mike (2005) A name that lives in infamy: The destruction of Fallujah was an act of barbarism that ranks alongside My Lai, Guernica and Halabja, Guardian, 10 November. Available online at http://www.guardian.co.uk/world/2005/nov/10/usa.iraq, accessed on 12 December 2008

McElwee, Patrick (2008) A million Iraqi dead? The U.S. press buries the evidence, *Extra!*, January/February. Available online at http://www.fair.org/index.php?page=3321, accessed on 20 May 2009

McLaughlin, Greg (2002) *The war correspondent*, London: Pluto Press

Miller, David (ed.) (2004), *Tell me lies: Propaganda and media distortion in the attack on Iraq*, London: Pluto Press

Moeller, Susan D. (2004) *Media coverage of weapons of mass destruction*, Center for International and Security Studies at Maryland: University of Maryland

Moss, Stephen (2008) "I wanted to report on where the silence was", *Guardian*, 8 May

Nichols, John and McChesney, Robert W. (2005) Tragedy and farce: How the American media sell wars, spin elections, and destroy democracy, New York: New Press

Nuttall, Nick (2006) Investigatice reporting: The times they are a-changin'?, *The newspapers handbook*, Keeble, Richard (ed.) London: Routledge, fourth edition pp 204–18

Pilger, John (2004) *Tell me no lies: Investigative journalism and its triumphs*, London: Jonathan Cape

Rampton, Sheldon and Stauber, John (2003) *Weapons of mass deception: The uses of propaganda in Bush's war on Iraq*, London: Robinson

Schmitt, Eric (2004) A goal is met. What's next?, *New York Times*, 15 November

Solomon, Norman (2005) *War made easy: How presidents and pundits keep spinning us to death*, Hoboken: John Wiley

Steele, Jonathan and Jamail, Dahr (2005) This is our Guernica: Ruined, cordoned Fallujah is emerging as the decade's monument to brutality, Guardian, 27 April

Zollmann, Florian (2007) Fighting fanatics, killing people: The limits of corporate journalism during the US assault on Fallujah, *Ethical Space: The International Journal of Communication Ethics*, Vol. 4, No. 4 pp 24–9

Zollmann, Florian (2008) Warfare as remedy: How the *Independent* framed the first US assault on Fallujah, *Occasional Working Paper Series*, University of Lincoln, UK, Vol. 1, No. 1

9

Are you a vulture? Reflecting on the ethics and aesthetics of atrocity coverage and its aftermath

PRATAP RUGHANI

- *This chapter emerged from a photographic essay 'Remembering Khairlanji' and should be viewed alongside it (with the Plate numbers in text). See the 'photography' tab of www.lotusfilms.co.uk website.*

Introduction

How do journalists, photographers, documentary filmmakers and editors exercise judgements about what kind of images to capture, commission, solicit and publish or broadcast in the aftermath of atrocity? What are the ethical and aesthetic responsibilities that attend documentary work which seeks to witness and record, hand-in-hand with contributors? These issues deliver a third, less discussed question which is the focus of this chapter: what are the intentions and responses of practitioners who file video, photography and words from such extreme situations?

In my documentary film, writing and photographic work such considerations raised their head in different environments: Rwanda, Cambodia, on the edges of Gaza, in Soweto, South Africa, Aushwitz/Birkenau, Aboriginal Australia, Hiroshima and, in the moments discussed here, when photographing in the Indian state of Maharashtra. Typically, there will be some inner discomfort for practitioners to work with in the crucible of locations where terrible events unfold: places where practitioners' judgements span the desire to connect humanely with victims of hatred whilst creating stories and imagery.

To unpack some of this, it may help to clear the way by clarifying what is not being attempted. Discussions of atrocity coverage often flower into passionate debates seeking to locate or refute bias. Decisions that configure what kind of violence is shown can reflect the highly politicised charge of terrible events. Journalists such as Martin Bell have sought to question the universalising claims of news values to reveal their own specificity, for example in his discussion of the "journalism of attachment" (1996).

I am not attempting the essential examination of whether a given conflict is covered "objectively" or the valuable debate of whether people, especially in richer, Western societies, are insulated from fuller engagement with reality by sanitised news values. I focus, rather, on detailed questions of *how* coverage is achieved: in particular, the approaches of visual practitioners (photographers, documentary makers, journalists), especially those who develop abiding connections with their subjects in their coverage of atrocity and have the decency to be troubled by the attempt.

Concentrating on these questions and practitioners' individual responses (my own included) may raise some useful objections. This choice does not seek to dismiss an important critique of the bourgeois emphasis on the individual nor to discount the idea that an author has little control over how meaning is received by audiences as the work circulates. Such objections can be held alongside the individual experience from which stories are fashioned and beg a fuller discussion elsewhere. James Nachtwey, considered by many to be the pre-eminent "frontline" photojournalist, writes:

> No matter how overwhelming an event, what happens to people at ground level happens to them individually, and photography has a unique ability to portray events from their point of view (Nachtwey 2009: 5).

Whichever viewpoints are assumed, it is valuable to ask whether graphic images of suffering, war and atrocity are *necessarily exploitative*. To navigate such a treacherous and valuable phrase, specific practitioners' reflections are examined in order to expose ethical decisions and reach, not a resolution but an engagement with the persistent questions that covering atrocity and its aftermath should pose.

Practitioners' perspectives

Is atrocity coverage *necessarily* exploitative? To know of terrible events is one of the conditions of moving towards a response that could encourage a path away from atrocity as part of the conditions for peace. George Rodger, the much-admired photographer and co-founder of the Magnum Photographic Agency, says of his work at Bergen-Belsen:

> I photographed the dead. I had to. Well, that was something that the world absolutely had to know about and they could only know about it through pictures. So I took the pictures (Rodger 1987).

But *how* do we know what we do about Bergen-Belsen from Rodger's work? Which practitioner choices – of subjects, framing and composition, angle and analysis – enable paths of identification and understanding? Individual stories and images, their context and framing, imply an analysis even if this is only revealed – or betrayed – "against the grain" of their intention. What are often missing from discussions of such work, however, are practitioners' critical perspectives. How practitioners understand their experience can inform and refine the ethical debate, especially when they are faced with extreme events.

A willingness to acknowledge the role of a practitioner's subjectivity can help expose ethical concerns in the detail of uncomfortable and awkward self-questioning. What are the perceived needs of the story compared to the needs of interviewees or subjects of the story, who are the most important people in the documentary process? This is rarely a neat exchange, since the practitioner's work may well highlight tensions between the perceived demands of a story and a subject's sensibility.

However, such an emphasis on self-questioning runs counter to a culture of journalism that prides itself on a naturalised "common-sense" response in exercising news judgements; which prefers to see not a story but "*the* story" as something "self-evident" rather than constructed. This is a delicate area. At the same time, the preoccupation with practitioner subjectivity invites an important critique of how documentary can become over-determined with the playing out of the practitioner's process rather than the reality of another.

I concentrate in what follows on practitioner experiences, but parallel questions are troubling audiences who are now, as Susan Sontag writes, increasingly "spectator[s] of calamites":

> Wars are now also living room sights and sounds. Information about what is happening elsewhere, called "news", features conflict and violence. "If it bleeds it leads" runs the venerable guideline of tabloids and twenty-four-hour headline news shows – to which the response is compassion, or indignation, or titillation, or approval, as each misery heaves into view (Sontag 2003: 18).

Questions of what visual journalism is made from conflict are increasingly relevant to practitioners and audiences alike. In the age of the blog and citizen journalism, a new world of audiences cross a threshold of interactivity to become producers as well as consumers (Beckett 2008) with motives which range (echoing Sontag's responses) from circulating such imagery in "mash-up infotainment" in the blogosphere to creating activist-led story-telling agitating for change.

The role of reflection in research

Anne Aghion is an Emmy-award winning French-American documentary-maker who completed her documentary film trilogy on the Rwandan justice and reconstruction process in 2009, visiting Rwanda more than twenty times across eight years. With her commitment to long-form documentary projects in Rwanda, Aghion argues for the importance of reflection in shaping how work is made and how the vectors of ideas emerge from impulse and interaction with the culture:

> Before I even started to film anything I went to Rwanda on several occasions, for several weeks each time. I needed to find a balance between the filmmaking process, which is a combination of urgency and bullying, and patience – an ability to wait for the events to unfold. I needed to take time, both for my sake and for the sake of those I was trying to understand. Taking time marks the respect that we are able to give the world...
>
> I am slow... I find it far more interesting to reflect on how you live "after" – in reflection on reflection – than to examine the details of survival itself. Crisis is very painful, but what we need to know more about is how to live after the crisis, or in a crisis of a more enduring kind (Aghion 2009: 42).[1]

Donald Schön's seminal exploration of professional life, *The reflective practitioner* (1983), brings reflection to the centre of analysing professional practice emphasised by Aghion. This approach is significantly taken up in journalism studies by Machin and Niblock (2006). Schön makes a key distinction between reflection-in-action and reflection-on-action. Reflection-in-action is discussed as being akin to "thinking on your feet" (Schön op cit: 68) and is interested in practitioners' moments of confusion, puzzlement and surprise. Reflection-on-action includes discussions with colleagues (Machin and Niblock op cit: 45) that can lead to significant developments in professional practice.

Both approaches can help in sifting ethical and aesthetic decisions, revisiting location experience to help inform and refine responses. In my photographic and directing work, I have benefited from thinking about practitioners' choices and their justification. Ambiguous situations mean that there are no foolproof reflexes and there have been difficult judgements for me to make about how to film sequences in a Sudanese refugee camp[2], during the Sierra Leone civil war[3] and in producing a photographic essay following a series of murders in India.

Murder in Khairlanji

My main case study is a sequence of images taken in Khairlanji, a small village in the central Indian state of Maharashtra, India, where a series of murders were planned and carried out to punish a so-called "untouchable" or "Dalit" family for their increasing success. The motive for the murders was the refusal of a Dalit family, the Bhotmanges, to tolerate an attempted land-grab by higher caste Hindus. Such extreme violence was informed by the changing social status of the Bhotmange family, one of a handful of Dalit families whose success in their village of 178 households was evidenced by the new confidence of their eldest daughter Priyanka Bhotmange who topped the class at secondary school, won a local award and was clearly on her way out of the shadows of caste constriction.

It is worth noting that caste discrimination and the practice of "untouchability" were outlawed in the Indian constitution, adopted by the newly independent nation in 1949. The great Dalit leader, Dr B. R. Ambedkar, as India's first law minister, framed the new Indian constitution, but caste discrimination persists and these murders provide evidence of a horrifying extreme of routine prejudice, an abiding disfigurement of Indian society and culture.

Personal experience

To help reflect on and clarify my own intentions and responses, I keep field notes. These are normally private but the following quotes aim to open out a process to see if critical reflection can help crystallise questions of documentary contact. The following notes were made in an intense two-day period in December 2007 when photographing the aftermath of a series of caste-based murders and are based on access negotiated with activists agitating for a trial of the murderers. When researching the story I worked with a local doctor who invited me to his home for tea [see Plate 1, www.lotusfilms.co.uk, photography tab 'Remembering Khairlanji']:

> A local doctor,[4] translating in Marathi for me, suddenly produced photographs, flashing broken and leaking bodies across a laptop that left me grappling – not knowing how to respond – wondering how much to show of "reality" yet honour the memory of people so dehumanised that such violence was possible (Rughani 2007).

> I spent the day with the one surviving family member, Bhyyalal Bhotmange to do some photography with him. He has a bodyguard and needs protection since his living presence has become a rallying point in the fight for a fair trial.

> For some time I hadn't taken the camera out of my bag. I'm waiting until it feels right – is it intrusive? – am I planning some kind of theft? He must expect me to have a camera but I don't want to initiate. As we talk of his loss, part of my mind is clocking light sources and possible angles (ibid).

In those moments I remember twin impulses: seeking empathic connection with Bhayyalal, the sole survivor of this murdered family, at the same time knowing that I needed to leave with publishable material. My eyes engaged his, but part of my mind was already filtering the location for ways to look at him. How do aesthetic considerations play out in such situations? It felt like impertinence to notice how this train of thought had already reached its destination. I thought that seeing the location of the murders was important but was wary of suggesting it.

> I'm relieved that he's suggested going to the village where his family were killed. I feel compelled to see where this happened; to stand with him in this place.

> We arrive in Khairlanji and visit his home where his wife, sons and daughter were assaulted, beaten, sexually abused, murdered and dumped in a neighbouring canal. It was a theatrical series of murders – designed to send the strongest signal to "low caste" people not to challenge high-caste power. I wonder: should I write more of the grisly detail to bring out some of these horrors? When is silence worse? But how to do this without further degrading what's left? (ibid).

This final question continues to circle around me here in London, stalking my memory of Khairlanji. What is the tension between striving to convey the weight and horror of such atrocities on the one hand and the risk of cheapening and sensationalising these events, for example, by the casual distribution of graphic stories and imagery in a commodified culture of "infotainment"?

Ethics and aesthetics

> We pushed back the wooden doors from the field, stepping into the skeletal frame of this terrible place (ibid) [see Plate 2].

I followed Bhayyalal into the family home. Choices about frame sizes and lenses became more and more "automatic". It was a wordless time where my body moved intuitively, trying to be alive to Bhayyalal's emotional "temperature". No words in the sight of the unspeakable. At a muffled distance the rhythm of village life at sunset; bullock carts clattering their return ... picture-book yellow-orange light leaking under Bhayyalal's broken door.

> There are times when the camera is like a telescope – drawing you in to close-up detail, connecting you with the subjects. Other times it's like a fence, separating – numbing (in this sense the camera delivers a kind of anaesthetic). Is this a necessary distance in order to function?
>
> Sometimes these twin moments are alive in the mind, heart and hands simultaneously. Elucidating and pulling away from...
>
> In the few minutes we were allowed in to the house, by the shrine I found myself putting the camera down; wanting to pay respects. Needing to absorb these realities in order to find some kind of photographic response (ibid).

A way of visualising takes shape. For Anne Aghion in Rwanda, an aesthetic evolved which centres on recovering the dignity of victims, developed in partnership with Rwandan cameraman James Kakwerere:

> The more emotional things are, the *less* you want to be framing in close-up. If you do that, it becomes voyeuristic and I don't think it's necessary – we're talking filming at a reasonable distance and you can get the emotion without being close.
>
> What's being said is sometimes so powerful that you don't need to go in tighter (Aghion, in an interview with the author).

Aghion uses mid and wide shots extensively. For her the tight close-up is an invasion: an idea that runs counter to mainstream norms, especially in the US broadcast sector. Andi Gitow, an experienced United Nations television producer in New York and former network news producer at NBC, is also a psychology expert in post-traumatic stress disorder. She says:

> I don't agree with staying wide as a rule. When someone talks I want to see the subtleties, especially what isn't verbalised – responses of their eyes and facial muscles.

> Shot sizes are critical for the network. Anything emotional: go in tight – start mid-shot, go in tighter – the cameraman and I develop signals to just go shoulders up and ease in tightly (Gitow, in an interview with the author).

Both Gitow and Aghion have spent many years producing extended explorations of the aftermath of trauma and reach contrasting conclusions. Aghion's experience has led her to turn away from the journalistic convention of the close-up:

> I know every manipulative trick that's used – to zoom in on someone's pained expression but I don't think the answer is to do that.
>
> Editing is full of music and montages and in the context of that kind of editing you're manipulating people's emotional responses and in the end that takes away the power. This is where a lot of the editorial questions come in – to go in tight is pornographic and exploitative (Aghion, in an interview with the author).

There's a structural difference between directing a camera crew where shot sizes are more often discussed between director and camera person (even if the style is agreed in advance) and the dynamic of being a single person operator, taking still photographs or writing a story. In the still photographic work in Khairlanji, responses emerge unspoken as consciousness responds to the environment, making a series of decisions that move the hands and eye [see Plate 3].

> Sometimes the camera remains a barrier between you and what's inside the frame; this mutual regard is punctuated by the trip of the shutter. Quite how these competing directions unfold depends on many things, not always visible to me in that moment. To stop and think much at the time is hard. You need still to function within a small window of time and yet how one does this depends on what's gone before, the rush of one's life delivering this current moment. Somehow the best thing to do is to let the impact happen and allow it to shape the act of looking (Rughani 2007).

In these moments a wide spectrum of reactions unfurl, from anger to horror, pity to empathy, sorrow and even irrational guilt. A blend of all this and more. Concurrently. Often not fully consciously. Close attention to the cross-currents of emotion and intellect can lead the practitioner towards insistent questioning of individual motive and response – a scintilla of feeling – or eruption of emotion. Although uncomfortable all these may hold clues for the ethics of documentary practice.

> I find I'm holding my throat. Involuntarily. Mr Bhotmange is suddenly in front of me, walking the charred floor.

He's trying to tidy the place up a bit – fix the garden – as though we were expecting someone might drop in for tea. He's trying to tidy the place up – is there a madness to this "normality" given what happened here?

By the end of the day, we've seen many locations where the violence unfolded. Someone asks me what I'm thinking. I must look distracted even though my hands are preoccupied with rhythm of camerawork; checking contrast in the failing light and finding compositions through fractured inner conversation. Shards of ideas. Then the quiet. Just responding. I have the comfort of a purpose here or at least its illusion. I can see Nachtwey in my head, just as he's being asked: "What kind of a vulture are you? Preying on others? Making your shots from the disasters of others?" It's a harsh and tender, precisely aimed and necessary question; one that visitors and viewers should be decently troubled by (Rughani 2007).

Reflecting on these notes now, I am aware of different processes at work on location. Filming can connect and alienate. For Andi Gitow there are moments where she and her team have held back at the last moment when an inner voice compels her:

At what point do you stop an interview? The longer the interview goes on the more their defences are down. But sometimes you have to ask whether you would rather walk away with this compelling TV moment but at the cost of your integrity and most importantly the emotional health of your interviewee? (Gitow, in an interview with the author).

The experience of a stills camera in my hand seemed to echo this, sometimes elucidating and drawing me in [see Plate 4] sometimes distancing and forming a physical barrier between my face and Bhayyalal's. Progress in gathering imagery was, therefore, unpredictable, emerging through the primacy of developing sensitivity to Bhayyalal. This process is no science and relates strongly to empathic resonance, individual history and personal sensibility, in relation to the unique events of that generate story.

Attention to persistent internal and external pressures, however, carries a danger of over-emphasis on the practitioner's view. Photographer-academic Paul Lowe argues that the practitioner's position is difficult because it often bears unreasonable expectations:

Typically the practitioner feels that the event is important and should be witnessed, documented and evidenced. It's especially hard for freelances because you've made a personal decision to go and most people feel that bearing witness has a consequentialist outcome – i.e. the hope that this won't happen again…

But too much is expected of the film or the photograph; soon the debate shifts from the event to the *representation* of the event – the critique – why didn't the photographer intervene rather than why didn't the world intervene?.

It's "shoot the messenger" (Lowe, in an interview with the author).

The "consequentialist" assumption is at the heart of the work of the human rights activist group Witness (www.witness.org). Their slogan encapsulates this emphasis: "See it, film it, change it". Sam Gregory is programme director and draws heavily on video activism and citizen journalism as a way to circulate stories of human rights abuses:

> A report like *Dual injustice*, about a murder in Ciudad Juarez, Mexico, is our ultimate ethical video because it looks at police failings and the systematic murder of women and the use of torture. We then use this individual story to press for policy change (Gregory, in an interview with the author).

A campaigning organisation's position crosses the line from notions of "objective" to "committed" reportage, but the ethics of the use of graphic imagery persists, to be uncovered anew in each situation. Some practitioners (and I've found myself responding in this way) seek a way to gesture towards events more metaphorically [see Plate 5].

> Is symbol and suggestion the key in documentary photography of atrocity? When faced with suffering on a grand or even epic scale, how is it possible to look too directly or even literally at these too-frequent events? It's like trying to look into the sun (Rughani 2007).

The vulture question

In the documentary film *War photographer*, James Nachtwey is asked: "Are you a vulture?" For George Rodger at Bergen-Belsen, the question did not come from an interviewer:

> I'd be talking to somebody, a prisoner there. It actually did happen. Cultured man. He was so happy to be liberated and he'd been a long time in the camp and in the middle of a sentence he suddenly fell down dead ... I actually photographed him. To my absolute horror I found I was getting the dead into photographic compositions to make good pictures and I thought "My God, I'm getting as though this doesn't mean anything to me" and I couldn't accept this – such absolute horror really didn't affect me as much as it should. And so I decided then and there that I was going to quit. I'm not going to take another picture and I just felt it was the end for me. I couldn't take any more (Rodger, speaking in *A life in photography*, 1987).

The question "Are you a vulture?" gestures towards a philosophical hinterland where journalism ethics are linked to broader issues of moral philosophy. Mapping the philosophical positions alone would consume too much space here, but I want briefly acknowledge a defence made by Kevin Carter who won a Pulitzer Prize in 1994 for his picture of a starving Sudanese girl in *The New York Times* (23 March 1993). Asked about taking his shot and leaving (in other words, not helping the girl he photographed, who lies slumped whilst a vulture waits), Carter argued for the position of the journalist as observer.[5]

Luc Bovens identifies contradictory motives among practitioners in conflict zones, evidencing the significant violations of dignity and privacy which are implied in the creation and circulation of graphic imagery. This leaves a trace.

> A morally decent person takes on a certain amount of responsibility for the unforeseen consequences of his actions and does not devote all his energy exculpating himself (Bovens 1998: 208).

Editorial guidelines and practitioner experience

A range of editorial guidelines suggest that a balance is to be struck between the perceived needs of journalists and audiences to be informed and subjects' sensibilities. The BBC's editorial guidelines on *War, terror and emergencies* state:

> We should respect human dignity without sanitising the realities of war. There must be clear editorial justification for the use of very graphic pictures of war or atrocity.[6]

The BBC's statement on *How to deal with a serious incident in a live broadcast* adds that practitioners should:

> ... balance the public interest in full and accurate reporting against the need to be compassionate and to avoid any unjustified infringement of privacy. It is rarely justified to broadcast scenes in which people are dying. It is always important to respect the privacy and dignity of the dead. We should avoid the gratuitous use of close ups of faces and serious injuries or other violent material.[7]

Such guidelines are variously interpreted depending on context, audience, perceived political climate and cultural norms. Greg Dyke, as Director General of the BBC, described how in 2003 Jana Bennett, the BBC's Director of Television deputising for Dyke on holiday, favoured the view that:

> We should include pictures of dead British soldiers in Iraq in a documentary made for BBC Two's *Correspondent* series ... I tended to agree but it wasn't an easy call ... When the BBC's Governors' complaints committee considered the

issue a couple of months later they took the view that we'd made the wrong decision and should not have broadcast the pictures (Dyke 2004: 250–1).

Strong criticism of the broadcast followed from the *Sun* newspaper, backed by families of some of the dead soldiers. The charge of sensationalism and insensitivity from the *Sun*, however, is not applied to coverage of fatalities caused by British military action. Does the *Sun's* concern betray a fear that radical questioning may follow if a fuller picture of war emerges? James Nachtwey argues:

> If everyone could be there just once to see for themselves what white phospho-rous does to the face of a child or what unspeakable pain is caused by the impact of a single bullet or how a jagged piece of shrapnel can rip someone's leg off – if everyone could be there to see for themselves the fear and the grief, just one time, then they would understand that nothing is worth letting things get to the point where that happens to even one person, let alone thousands (Nachtwey op cit).

To conclude with questions

At one end of the scale, perhaps due to bad luck, judgement or moral sensibility, some have been burned by their experience and simply stopped producing stories and images from conflict, feeling that this is the last response open to them. For George Rodger, one corner of his consciousness arrested another. In the Kevin Carter case quoted earlier of the vulture and the child, a sparkling career ended when he committed suicide in July 1994 within a few months of his Pulitzer Prize. Although it is unclear what impact his reflections on these photographs had on him, such extremes highlight the dangers of the territory. Other responses from leading practitioners who continue to work with image and text suggest a close attention to their personal motives and beliefs. James Nachtwey says:

> The worst thing is to feel that as a photographer I am benefiting from someone else's tragedy. This idea haunts me. It's something I have to reckon with every day because I know that if I ever allowed genuine compassion to be overtaken by personal ambition, I will have sold my soul. The only way I can justify my role is to have respect for the other person's predicament. The extent to which I do that is the extent to which I become accepted by the other; and to that extent, I can accept myself (ibid).

Fergal Keane, the Irish writer and broadcaster who was for many years the BBC's correspondent in South Africa, adds:

The key thing to remember ... is that it is possible in the midst of tragedy and sorrow (and we witness a great deal of that) to believe in a kind of hopeful future. Now Rwanda challenged that for me. Edward Behr, who went right through the Second World War, who went through Algeria, Congo and Vietnam, he managed to hold on to a fundamental optimism about human beings and I still do. You'd go mad if you took the other route.[8]

How possible is it to emerge from these situations and piece together stories and images that do not further damage the dignity of people who have been violated? Here are some key questions that could provide necessary guidance, distilled from field notes and research:

- Am I clear enough about my own intentions and motives and the motives of those who may seek to be featured? What do victims of atrocity want others to know?
- What impact might involvement with the project have on the subjects featured?
- Can the representation and framing of subjects help subjects recover their dignity?
- How aware am I of the sensitivities of subjects and audience?
- What are my instincts telling me?
- Is there a way to do more than trade in misery and inhumanity? Are there even moments of renewal or empowerment?

I have tried to open out something of my own attempts to reflect on experience in order to ask what kind of working methods can practitioners live with? This is not to attempt a definition, as responses will differ for each practitioner and audience. I'm interested rather in staying open to being troubled by ethical challenges of such questions as they reconfigure through the experience of filming and photographing in the aftermath of trauma and atrocity. Through that process, attending to doubt and uncertainty, images and sentences surface as stories. The moments of shock that force them into consciousness and into the culture of media continue to trouble me – productively, I hope [see Plate 6].

Notes

1   All Aghion quotes from research interview in New York on 29 August 2009, except this one.

2   *Glass houses* (2004), the British Council, directed by Pratap Rughani, Lotus Films Productions.
3   *New model army* (2001) Channel 4, directed by Roger Mills and Pratap Rughani, Umbrella Films Productions.
4   The doctor is well-regarded as a reliable source but is not named here as he has been threatened.
5   http://africanhistory.about.com/b/2006/04/12/the-journalist-the-vulture-and-the-child.htm, accessed on 11 September 2009.
6   http://www.bbc.co.uk/guidelines/editorialguidelines/edguide/war/editorialprinci.shtml, accessed on 31 August 2009.
7   http://www.bbc.co.uk/guidelines/editorialguidelines/advice/liveoutput/howtodeal-withas.shtml, accessed on 31 August 2009.
8   See http://www.penguin.co.uk/static/rguides/uk/keane_inter.html, accessed on 20 September 2009.

References

Aghion, Anne (2009) Living together again, in Rwanda, Wagner, Aleksandra (ed.) *Considering forgiveness*, New York: Vera List Center for Art and Politics pp 142–9

Beckett, Charlie (2008) *Supermedia : saving journalism so it can save the world*, Malden, MA: Wiley

Bell, Martin (1996) *In harm's way*, London: Penguin

Bovens, Luc (1998) Moral luck, photojournalism and pornography, *The Journal of Value Inquiry*, Vol. 32: pp 205–17

Dyke, Greg (2004) *Inside story*, London: HarperCollins

Keane, Fergal. interviewed by Penguin. Available online at http://www.penguin.co.uk/static/rguides/uk/keane_inter.html, accessed on 20 July 2009

Machin, David and Niblock, Sarah (2006) *News production: Theory and practice*, London: Routledge

Nachtwey, James (2009) Introduction, *Humanity in war, Frontline photography since 1860*, Geneva: ICRC Publications

Rodger, George (1994) *Humanity and inhumanity: The photographic journey of George Rodger*, text by Bruce Bernard, London: Phaidon

Rughani, Pratap (2007) Field notes, Khairlanji, India, unpublished

Schön, Donald A. (1983) *The reflective practitioner: How professionals think in action*, London: Basic Books

Sontag, Susan (2003) *Regarding the pain of others*, New York: Picador

Films

George Rodger: A Life in Photography (1987), directed by Noel Chanan, London: the Photographers Gallery, VHS

War photographer (2002), directed by Christian Frei, Christian Frei Film Productions, DVD

Unpublished interviews

Agihon, Anne, independent documentary film-maker

Beckett, Charlie, Director POLIS, journalism and society think-tank based at the London School of Economics

Gitow, Andi, Senior Producer, UN, News and Media Division, New York

Gregory, Sam, Programme Director, Witness

Lowe, Paul, Course Director, MA Photojournalism, London College of Communication, University of Arts, London.

Poeuv, Socheata, CEO, Khmer Legacies

Page, Shepherd, Freelance documentary maker, BBC TV Training, BBC Elstree

Sutherland, Patrick, Reader in Photography, London College of Communication

Acknowledgement

The author thanks Mr Bhayyalal Bhotmange, whose willingness to re-visit the remains of his family home left some necessary documentary struggles to reflect on, and to Susan Sontag, whose brilliant insights and humane responses frame a challenge to anyone proposing to make new work from the suffering of others.

10

Social networks and the reporting of conflict

DONALD MATHESON AND STUART ALLAN

Introduction

Over the past decade, many individuals caught up in conflicts have sought to bear witness – whether civilians in Belgrade waiting for NATO bombs to fall, US soldiers in Iraq with personal digital cameras, or humanitarian workers in Somalia – through eyewitness accounts shared via digital media networks. While few of them may have self-identified as journalists *per se*, their voices have embodied powerful claims to provide honest testimony of the horrors of war's impact on everyday life, as well as richly perceptive – if deeply subjective – interpretation of its conduct. In claiming the right to be heard, whether through blogs, photographs, videos or tweets, their vital contributions have recast the status of the professional war correspondent.

Many scholars watching these developments highlight the potential of networked media to change the priorities of news organisations; not least, as Coleman (2005: 277) puts it, to "lower the threshold of entry to the global debate for traditionally unheard or marginalised voices, particularly from poorer parts of the world which are too often represented by others". Terzis and Smeets (2008) suggest these media may help to transcend geo-political barriers created by national media systems, thereby boosting the efforts of moderate voices to redefine the nature of ongoing conflicts. In exploring the evolving nature of what peace journalism researchers call "war journalism" (see Galtung 1998), however, many questions arise about the extent to which the familiar forms of "us" and "them" dichotomies typically prevailing in Western news reports can be transgressed, let alone dismantled. The picture is also a rapidly evolving one, with emergent forms, practices and epistemologies only gradually beginning to consolidate, and even then often in surprising ways.

Accordingly, we take a case study approach here, discussing four conflicts that flared up in late 2008. Our primary aim is to identify and assess a range of ways in which war journalism is being rearticulated by social networks, including content-sharing websites such as YouTube and Flickr, personal media such as blogs and the micro-blogging platform Twitter, social sites such as Facebook and virtual worlds such as Second Life, as well as networks enabled over cell phones.[1] Turning to the first of our case studies, we see that it was during the tragic events in Mumbai in November 2008 that the journalistic potential of social networking was suddenly made dramatically apparent in a crisis. Even before news of the attacks had begun to appear in the electronic media, Twitter was providing eyewitness accounts from users describing what was happening.

Social media 'come of age' during India's '9/11'

Widely dubbed as "India's 9/11", the attacks – evidently perpetrated by ten members of a Pakistan-based militant organisation – began to unfold in Mumbai on the evening of 26 November 2008. Several different sites were targeted, including the city's main train station, Chhatrapati Shivaji Terminus (CST), where commuters were shot indiscriminately; Nariman House, associated with the Jewish Chabad Luvavich movement, where 13 hostages were taken (five of whom were murdered); the Trident-Oberoi Hotel, where 30 people were killed; and the Taj Mahal Palace Hotel, where most of the casualties took place as the assailants moved from floor to floor in a killing spree. In total, at least 172 people died, and more than 300 others were injured, over a 60-hour siege that transfixed horrified news audiences around the globe.

During the crisis, the highly sensationalised news coverage provided by the Indian news media – what critics called the "TV terror" of the 24-hour news channels – was widely condemned for reporting "exclusives" which more often than not proved to be wildly inaccurate rumours (Pepper 2008; Sonwalkar 2009; Thussu 2009). Attracting much more positive attention, however, was the surprising role played by ordinary citizens in gathering information, with the micro-blogging service Twitter regularly singled out for praise as a vital source for real-time citizen news. Examples of messages or "tweets" (posts being limited to 140 characters), some of which were cited in various news reports, included the following:

One terrorist has jumped from Nariman house building to Chabad house – group of police commandos have arrived on scene (anonymous, #mumbai channel).

Special anti-hijacking group called Rangers entering Nariman House, at least 80 commandos (scorpfromhell).

Hospital update. Shots still being fired. Also Metro cinema next door (mumbaiattack).

Blood needed at JJ hospital (aeropolowoman).

Facinating. CNN is filling airtime; #mumbai channel is full of tidbits posted by witnesses (yelvington).

At least 80 dead, 250 injured. American and British targeted (ArtVega).

Tagging posts with the hashtag #mumbai made them easily searchable for other users to find. Saad Khan (2008), at the Green and White blog, described a "tweets frenzy" where "minute-by-minute updates about the location of the blasts/skirmishes, positions of the security forces, location of the journalists and safe passages for stranded commuters", amongst other topics, were shared. While agreed details were in short supply, there was little doubt that users gained a keen sense that news was breaking in "real time" in an extraordinarily dynamic, interactive environment.

Concerns over 're-tweeting'

Despite the steady stream of messages, very few of the individuals behind them were actually eyewitnesses on the scene. Some bloggers, angered by the "ripple effect" of inaccurate, unfounded – or simply outdated – claims being "re-tweeted" (re-distributed), challenged the notion that Twitter deserved recognition as a news source. Posting in the early hours of the events was Tom on TomsTechBlog.com, for example, who wrote:

> The facts ARE THE NEWS. Nothing else is relevant. In fact, the noise that Twitter generates in situations like these is downright cruel and dangerous.
>
> Let me give you the perfect example of what I mean.
>
> If you watch Twitter you'll see people reporting an attack at the Marriot Hotel [sic] in Mumbai. The problem is there was NO ATTACK on the Marriot. The Ramada hotel next door was attacked by several gun men but nothing's happened at the Marriot.
>
> Now imagine, if you're someone who has family or friends at the Marriot right now. You'd be scared out of your mind over information that's completely false.

I'm sorry but it really makes me angry. What you have here are people who simply don't care if they get the news right. They're turning the most dire of situations into entertainment by using Twitter to "be involved in the story". They throw their little tweets out not caring who they scare half to death and then brag about how great Twitter is for "beating the mainstream media at reporting the news" (TomsTechBlog.com 2008).

In the hours following the early reports, the majority of tweets were either relaying secondary observations taken from mainstream news reports, correcting previous messages, or offering links to online sources for fresh perspectives. Examples of the latter were links to sites such as Google map, which documented the location of the attacks, as well as Wikipedia and Mahalo, which constantly updated known details. Videos in the dozens were being uploaded to YouTube, while Flickr displayed users' photographs ("Vinu" posting particularly grisly images).

Sites such as Metblogs Mumbai, GroundReport, Global Voices, NowPublic, Poynter.org, and iReport.com, amongst countless others, were busy aggregating citizen reports. Meanwhile major news organisations were moving swiftly to gather insights. In addition to using tweets as source statements, several news organisations endeavoured to interview users for exclusive insights. Reuters drew upon blogging posts, such as one from Dina Mehta's blog ("I've been tweeting almost all night, too, from Mumbai. Upset and angry and bereft"), to supplement its coverage (cited in Lee 2008). *The New York Times*, via its blog The Lede, asked its readers in the city to email photographs or to insert a written description of events in the "comment field" on its webpage.

How the BBC made use of the new social media

In the case of BBC News Online, the site's running account supplemented information provided by the Corporation's correspondents with details from news agencies, Indian media reports, official statements, blog posts, emails, and Twitter messages – "taking care to source each of these things", as Steve Herrmann (2008), editor of BBC News Interactive, explained. In his words:

As for the Twitter messages we were monitoring, most did not add a great amount of detail to what we knew of events, but among other things they did give a strong sense of what people connected in some way with the story were thinking and seeing. "Appalled at the foolishness of the curious onlookers who are disrupting the NSG operations," wrote one. "Our soldiers are brave but I feel we could have done better," said another. There was assessment, reaction and comment there and in blogs. One blogger's stream of photos on photosharing site Flickr was widely linked to, including by us. All this helped to build up a rapidly evolving picture of a confusing situation (ibid).

Despite these advantages, however, Herrmann and others were aware of the risks associated with using material when its veracity could not be independently verified. One instance of false reporting, repeatedly circulated on Twitter, claimed that the Indian government was alarmed by what was happening on the social network. Fearful that the information being shared from eyewitnesses on the scene was proving to be useful to the attackers, government officials – it was alleged – were urging Twitter users to cease their efforts, while also looking to block Twitter's access to the country itself. On the BBC's Mumbai live event page, it was reported:

1108 Indian government asks for live Twitter updates from Mumbai to cease immediately. "ALL LIVE UPDATES – PLEASE STOP TWEETING about #Mumbai police and military operations," a tweet says.

The BBC was widely criticised by some commentators for reporting a claim which was later revealed to be untrue. Speaking with the benefit of hindsight, Herrmann acknowledged that the BBC should have checked first or at least noted that it had no independent confirmation. Yet he also pointed out that the BBC did not use the material in its own news stories, only on the Mumbai live event page, and defended the principle of the BBC sharing what it knew as quickly as possible, even before facts had been fully checked. In the case of the live event page, users perhaps gained insight into a developing story while also having to accept some responsibility for assessing the quality – and reliability – of the information being processed. "The truth is," he wrote, "we're still finding out how best to process and relay such information in a fast-moving account like this" (ibid).

Whether or not a "paradigm shift" was being ushered in by social networking was a matter of debate amongst some commentators, but there seemed little doubt that the events represented some sort of transitional moment. Twitter, in particular, won plaudits for capturing the rawness of the tragedy in reportorial terms. "Last night," Claudine Beaumont of the *Daily Telegraph* pointed out, "the social web came of age" (*Daily Telegraph*, 27 November 2008). Stephanie Busari (2008) of CNN agreed: "It was the day social media appeared to come of age and signalled itself as a news-gathering force to be reckoned with."

This was not to deny its limitations as a trustworthy news source – serious criticisms having surfaced about inaccuracies and rumours being circulated in addition to the examples cited above – but rather to acknowledge the potential of social networking for first-hand crisis news, and thereby an important dimension to digital war reporting. "It was Twitter's moment," wrote Brian Caulfield and Naazneen Karmali (2008) in Forbes.com, the service having been transformed from one specialising in "distributing short, personal updates to tight networks of friends and acquaintances into a way for people around the world to tune into personal, real-time accounts of the attacks".

Mediating the Greek street protests 2008

The contributions of individuals to mediating events in conflict situations is not always readily assimilable to the normative ideals of journalism. In Greece, when street protests broke out in December 2008, social media relayed the young protestors' outrage, thereby helping to give shape to the articulation – and co-ordination – of dissent.

"Rebellion is deeply embedded in the Greek psyche. The students and school children who are now laying siege to police stations and trying to bring down the government are undergoing a rite of passage," the BBC's Malcolm Brabant (2008) reported. "They may be the iPod generation, but they are the inheritors of a tradition that goes back centuries," he added, before turning to describe the "current wave of violence" testing the limits of social stability. Brabant, like other journalists on the scene, was struggling to make sense of events which defied easy explanation.

Most news accounts agreed that the spark that ignited the student protest was the shooting of a 15-year-old student, Alexandros Grigoropoulos, by a police officer – for no apparent reason – on the evening of 6 December 2008 in the centre of Athens. The incident received extensive coverage and "near-universal condemnation" (Gemenis 2008) in the Greek media. Where accounts differed was at the level of context; that is, when presenting the details necessary to enable distant audiences to understand the nature of the ensuing crisis, as well as its larger significance. Brabant's references to the "Greek psyche" as having a predisposition to rebellion were one way to explain the forces involved; another was to frame events historically, where previous examples of police brutality were held to be suggestive of a larger pattern over recent decades. Still another strategy, however, revolved around the gathering of insights being generated via social networks amongst the protestors themselves.

Social networking sites lead the way

Internet and social networking sites, the latter including Facebook, MySpace and Twitter, proved to be playing a pivotal role in mobilising protestor collaboration in real-time. Television commentator Pavlos Tsimas (2008) described that he received an email about the developing protest within 80 minutes of the shooting, yet found nothing about the events on television that night or in most of the next day's newspapers. Paul Haven (2008) reported for AP that several Greek web sites emerged as key information sources on clashes, planned demonstrations and police activity. Twitter – via tags such as #griots – relayed reports of the protests, as well as information for protestors to help co-ordinate their efforts, such as details about where to meet, what to do, and how best to protect themselves. Blog postings and photographs uploaded to Flickr recorded the violent turmoil – along with links to a YouTube video which appeared to contradict police claims.

Here it quickly became apparent not only that the shooting needed to be situated in relation to protracted civil unrest in Greek public life, but that the protestors themselves did not form a single, monolithic group. The majority of those involved were students, primarily from secondary schools, engaged (peacefully, in the main) in marches and rallies. A second, smaller element, was composed of groups of "anarchists" (or "*koukouloforoi*" – "the hooded ones") intent on seizing the moment to articulate dissent in any way possible – which included torching cars and smashing shop-fronts. Not surprisingly, the actions of the latter figured prominently in news reports. "Without a doubt," Alexis S (2008), a "peaceful protestor from Thessaloniki" observed, "such coverage focused on the most sensational, frightening, collective and dramatic cases of the countless incidents that took place in Greece's major cities since Saturday night."

For journalists looking beyond sweeping claims about "the iPod generation", it was important to connect with young people to better understand what they were feeling, and why. Traditional news media, Andrew Lam (2008) noted, "were trying to play catch up in a world full of Twitterers and bloggers", a challenge made worse by the need to "filter real news from pseudo news" under intense time pressure. Social network sites proved to be especially valuable resources in this regard. In addition to providing live reports, personal accounts, photographs and videos (most in English, if not in Greek), they afforded journalists a different level of connection. This level was described by the *Economist* as being indicative of a "new era of networked protest":

> A tribute to the slain teenager—a clip of photos with music from a popular rock
> band—appeared on YouTube, the video-sharing site, shortly after his death; more

than 160,000 people have seen it. A similar tribute group on Facebook has attracted more than 130,000 members, generating thousands of messages and offering links to more than 1,900 related items: images of the protests, cartoons and leaflets.

A memorial was erected in Second Life, a popular virtual environment, giving its users a glimpse of real-life material from the riots. Many other online techniques—such as maps detailing police deployments and routes of the demonstrations—came of age in Athens. And as thousands of photos and videos hit non-Greek blogs and forums, small protests were triggered in many European cities, including Istanbul [and] Madrid. Some 32 people were arrested in Copenhagen (*Economist* 2008).

The 'rise of a new global phenomenon'

For Evgeny Morozov (2008), the networked protest in Greece provided a "glimpse of what the transnational networked public sphere might look like" and, as such, signalled the rise of a new global phenomenon. Readily acknowledging that the internet had helped to make protest actions more effective in the past, he nonetheless believed that what happened in this case was:

> probably the first time that an issue of mostly local importance has triggered solidarity protests across the whole continent, some of them led by the Greek diaspora, but many of them led by disaffected youth who were sympathetic of the movement's causes.

In journalistic terms, the crisis provided evidence that every citizen could be a front-line correspondent, a prospect which called into question the viability of the mainstream news media – not least their capacity to set the news agenda. New media – ranging from established blogs and forums to "radicalised" Facebook pages – "directed the flow of information" in the larger "struggle for meaning", Maria Komninos and Vassilis Vamvakas (2009) argued. This left the major news organisations, especially the commercial television channels, "obliged to report on and to follow, basically, the information originating in the internet".

Bearing witness to the cost of war: Social media during the Israeli assault on Gaza

The political struggle to contain publicly raised voices of protest, and therefore allow the violent suppression of threats to power and security, was in evidence, in brutally explicit form, only weeks later when the Israeli Defence Force (IDF) invaded the Palestinian territory of Gaza. In this latest turn of the long-running conflict, control over images and civilian accounts of the effects of the violence was a crucial element of Israeli strategy, in which web-based media proved critical.

Certain iconic images recur in accounts of the plight of the Palestinian people. Among the more recent of these is video footage, taken by France 2 cameraman Talal Abu Rahma, of 12-year-old Mohammed al Dura, dying in crossfire between Israeli and Palestinian forces in Gaza in 2000, as his father fruitlessly tried to shield him. It was this kind of powerful imagery of the civilian cost of war that the Israeli military sought to restrict when it launched its two-week air and ground attack on the Palestinian territory of Gaza on 27 December 2008. With very few exceptions (Al Jazeera had six staff already in Gaza City) news teams were kept out of the war zone, ostensibly for safety reasons, despite an Israeli Supreme Court ruling allowing them in. Strategists in Israeli newspapers talked of the relatively clear window that the IDF now had to act without too much international pressure, as long as "blunders" were kept to a minimum (*Jerusalem Post*, 30 December 2008). By the end of two weeks, more than 1,400 Palestinians, among them at least 300 children under 17 years of age, had died, with 5,000 more wounded (IFFCG 2009).

The *Independent's* Middle East correspondent Robert Fisk (2009) described the Israeli use of an "old Soviet tactic" from Afghanistan, namely clearing the country of reporters so it could wage brutal war unhindered. Yet images and stories did emerge during the fighting that attested to the ordeal of those within the besieged city. Local stringers, now commonly used by overseas news organisations in conflict areas where access is difficult or expensive (Hamilton and Jenner 2004), provided footage and news reports. In addition, despite the lack of electricity and erratic phone networks, humanitarian workers and a limited number of locals gave "a small window into the suffering of Gaza's civilian population" through blogs, email and other web-based media (Fitzgerald 2009).

The *Guardian*, for example, quoted from a podcast interview at Mideastyouth.com with a young teacher, Ramzy; particularly his criticism, delivered in a flat, tired voice on the second day of war, of both Hamas and Israel: "We are the big losers here, the Palestinian people, not Hamas or Israel. If the attacks continue, more civilians will lose their lives and these civilians are dying for nothing" (cited in Percival 2008). Al Jazeera republished entries from the blog of Oxfam researcher and Gaza resident Mohammed Ali, including the following:

Today, I left my neighbourhood for the first time since this waking nightmare started. As my wife and I said goodbye, I knew that we were both thinking the same thing, that this could be the last time we ever see one another. As I closed the door behind me, I heard my child sobbing uncontrollably. Just as I headed out, I heard that the Israeli government had announced a three-hour lull in fighting. I wondered what they thought we could do in three hours; banks are closed and the Israeli government is restricting money coming into Gaza, shops are shut or their shelves empty, people now have to queue for up to six hours just for a loaf of bread...or nothing...(Ali 2009).

Individualised and professional media intersect

Individualised media were beginning to intersect with professional and mass media in significant ways. To some extent, then, aspects of the recording of the conflict moved to the plane of the interpersonal. Here individual voices were heard, speaking from the position of the civilian, aid worker or peace activist caught up in the violence, and speaking of their own personal experiences and emotions. Prominent among their concerns were basic human needs, such as obtaining gas to make a hot meal or to know that loved ones were safe, perspectives often lost in the more dramatic news coverage of death, grieving and political finger-pointing. In Gaza, where entrenched poverty, lack of basic infrastructure and restrictions imposed on mobility contribute to the political crisis, these voices – although inevitably those of the wealthier, better educated with access to computers – provided some important context for those outside the region to be able to relate to those living under siege. The familiar "culture of distance" (Williams 1982) engendered by Western journalism's mediation of witnessing was thrown into sharp relief, with the emphatic suffering – as well as the aspirations for peace – of many of those caught-up in the atrocity resonating in social media sites.

The voices of Gazans, Israelis and those further afield available on the internet were rarely simply seeking to be heard and understood, however. More often they were seeking to influence public perceptions. A disappointed Alan Abbey of the Poynter Institute contrasted the independent observation on Twitter during the Mumbai attacks with the "heated rhetoric from non-Gazans and international observers" and Israeli tweeting that was "more ideological than reportorial" (Abbey 2008). Masouras (2009) described a global peace movement at work online:

that uses Flickr to share photos from demonstrations, Twitter to republish reports and argue heatedly, and collaborative portals and blogs to collate reports, as it petitions the slothful international community to enact a ceasefire and react to the developing humanitarian crisis.

Thus the line between reporting and political action was often thoroughly blurred. One conservative US website, pjtv.com, sent Samuel J. Wurzelbacher, the "Joe the plumber" of John McCain's 2008 presidential campaign, to Sderot in Israel to "correct" the bias of mainstream media reporting. This "ordinary Joe", who argued on his arrival that the media "have no business" in war zones, was widely criticised by journalists for his limited and fixed opinions about the justice of the Israeli case for war (see Trager 2009). Yet his supporters valued precisely his ordinariness: "the lack of fancy training would make him more trustworthy in my eyes," commented one web user (Bruce NV comment in ibid.). As *The New York Times* public editor Clark Hoyt (2009) observed, there were significant numbers of readers for whom the "truth of war" was not to be found in carefully balanced accounts of Hamas's and the IDF's claims and counter-claims. Making sense of the conflict for them involved articulating their outrage – alternatively directed at Hamas or Israel – in the register of their own lifeworlds.

Also participating in this online articulation of public opinion were governments. The Israelis, in particular, used the web to bypass mainstream media, one commentator observed, in efforts to shore up local and US public support for the war (Monck 2009). Monck quoted Israeli spokesman Major Avital Leibovich describing the blogosphere and new media as "another war zone. We have to be relevant there". Video taken by IDF camera crews within Gaza and from drones flying overhead were posted on YouTube – attracting a million views over the next six months; about 50 US bloggers were contacted regularly during the fighting, with the apparent aim of encouraging supportive commentary; a press conference for non-journalists was held by the Israeli ambassador to the US on Twitter (ibid).

Baratz (2009) pointed out that the apparent transparency of the Israeli state in providing raw material about its campaign, allowing individuals to feel like journalists, was more apparent than real. Indeed, the propaganda machine of the state was now, she noted, "in our social nooks online". Overall, there can be no doubt that the Israeli state was successful in reducing the imagery available to audiences in Israel and in the US, and therefore relieving political and diplomatic pressure to halt the attacks. In doing so, and thereby propelling the social web to greater prominence as a platform where accounts of civilian suffering could be shared, it perhaps also contributed to a further polarisation of opinion on the Palestine-Israel conflict. Journalism, as a relatively neutral space, was "missing in action" to use Monck's (op cit) phrase, effectively replaced by claim and counter-claim by impassioned citizens.

War without witnesses in Sri Lanka

The Sri Lanka government, John Pilger (2009) suggested, learned from the IDF experience in banning all but a few local reporters, when it launched its final push against the separatist Tamil Tigers in late 2008. And here again the internet became a site where the attempt to bear witness became difficult to distinguish from partisan argument.

As the 20-year-long war between the Sri Lankan state and the Liberation Tigers of Tamil Eelam (LTTE) came to a close in late 2008 to early 2009, a very large population of civilians – perhaps as many as 200,000 people – was caught between the warring forces. British newspapers estimated that 15,000–20,000 people died in the last four months of fighting, yet the outside world – or indeed the Sri Lankan public – heard little. This was, as Canadian politician Michael Ignatieff noted, a "war without witnesses" (cited in Bell 2009). It was near impossible for overseas news organisations, humanitarian groups or foreign governments, barred even from northern Sri Lankan towns or refugee camps outside the zone of operations, to substantiate accusations that the LTTE was using civilians as human shields and shooting those who sought to escape its last tiny territory of Mullivaikal, or that the Sri Lankan Army was bombing those same trapped civilians and executing surrendering soldiers. In the months after the LTTE's destruction, few foreign reporters or aid workers were allowed into the government-run camps for internally displaced people, and those who managed to get near them heard stories that people talking to the media risked being killed (Walsh 2009).

In this vacuum of reporting from news organisations, the internet played a pivotal role in providing information and images. Yet, given the context of atrocious civil war (in which both the LTTE and the Sri Lankan government have been accused of using terror and of gross abuses of human rights), and the long-running propaganda war between the two sides, information and discussion online appeared rarely able to shift beyond accusation, distrust and fixed positions. A well-organised effort by members of the Sri Lankan Tamil diaspora, many of them refugees from the conflict, had led to television stations and websites in the West (often in European languages) which provided news for Sri Lankans overseas and also sought to challenge a Western media indifferent to their suffering and political aspirations.

Some of these media outlets had strong links to the Tamil Tigers – Euro TV and Tamil Television Network were, indeed, closed down by European governments under anti-terrorism laws in 2007–8. Foremost among these, and not closed down, was the online news service, Tamilnet.com, whose editor Dharmeratnam Sivaram had overseen, until his assassination in 2005, the training of a network of local teachers, government clerks and other correspondents in reporting techniques and the use of computers, modems and digital cameras, as well as the formation of a network of translators and editors across North America, Europe and Australia (Whitaker 2004). Whitaker quotes Dharmeratnam describing this service as making "ironic use" of the conventions of news, in the sense that it mimicked neutral western media to serve its nationalist ends (ibid: 486). In response to the significant presence of supporters of Tamil independence online, the Sri Lankan government launched its own online media effort, running images from the battlefield, government statements and supportive international media stories on its Defence Ministry site, making it one of the country's most popular websites (Hull 2009).

How online media highlighted civilian casualties

It was these online media which, in the conflict's final stages, provided powerful but highly partial accounts of events of the war and civilian casualties. A former LTTE member, Nirmala Rajisingam (2009), wrote that "the blood-splattered images and messages have inundated cyberspace: via Facebook and YouTube and other cyberspace outlets, via a torrent of emails, the drenching claim is simple, direct and frightening: genocide". Tamil expatriates, deeply concerned about the fate of relatives caught up in the fighting or in refugee camps, exchanged accounts of atrocity and fed them to wider media. A Tamil living in Canada, Arul Siva, commented:

> When families are getting killed, sitting at home and watching sitcoms is no longer a norm. Rather, constantly talking about each other's family's plight and how we can save their lives is the daily discussion (cited in Taylor 2009).

It was through one such network, which calls itself War without Witness, that video statements recorded of doctors working in a school converted into a makeshift hospital in Mullivaikal were released to world media, providing first-hand testimony of the bombing of civilians, including one by a Dr. Shanmugarajah relating the killing of 47 staff, patients and relatives:

Both the patients and their helpers were sleeping next to each other in tarpaulin sheets. We didn't have the facility of a safe bunker. The artillery hit directly on the hospital and caused this damage. When the shell hit, all people were running to save their lives...it was chaos...it is difficult for me to ask other staff to stay and work (translated; cited in Chamberlain 2009).

These accounts, filtered through the diaspora and the Tamil Tigers' supporters, were clearly at the same time desperately needed witness statements and the rebels' last weapon to buy international support for a ceasefire as they faced annihilation. No witness statement circulating online was ever merely that; all too easily their claims were dismissed as propaganda by those opposed to the Tigers (see *Sunday Observer* 2009).

In this severely contracted civil society, the rise of citizen journalism in the country's richer south (particularly following the dramatic attention given in the West to the idea of "citizen journalism" after the 2004 Indian Ocean tsunami) has been a significant development (Gunawardene 2008; Allan and Thorsen 2009). Many of the blogs that have emerged avoid politics, but prominent among initiatives which have tackled difficult subjects is a network of sites set up by Colombo-based writer Sanjana Hattotuwa. These include Groundviews, a tri-lingual website mostly peopled by academics, journalists, and aid workers, and Vikalpa, a YouTube channel that ranked amongst the site's 100 most popular channels in May 2009. The guidelines for contributors to Groundviews encourage submissions from a citizen's perspective that are:

1. pithy and provocative;
2. bear witness to the denial of justice, human rights and gross ceasefire violations;
3. essentially humanises and critiques conflict and peace through alternative cultural, social, economic and political perspectives.[2]

Citizen media 'helping the country towards peace'

The sites, as their critics point out, are dominated by political discussion among certain Colombo intellectuals and have been known to censor some political views (see debate on Sepia Mutiny 2008), but they also profile the perspectives and experiences of a wider range of individuals. Among those was the appeal by a teenager, Aruni Pradeepika, calling for help in bringing back her father who had been abducted from his fields by LTTE soldiers in August 2007, and a series of video essays on Vikalpa about the future of Sri Lankan Tamil self-government. Hattotuwa (2007) claims that such citizen media:

> can help move the country towards peace. Through web-based technologies, even citizens in Sri Lanka who have been effectively cut out of mainstream media – bursting, as it is, with the propaganda of political elites – have found new ways of expressing themselves, their concerns, their aspirations and their ideas for resolving conflict.

However, the use of social media for political ends remains constrained. Gunawardene (op cit) records incidents where individuals who have filmed public events on their cell phones have been harassed by the police, who accused them of threatening public security. "One citizen who passed on such footage to an independent TV channel was later vilified as a 'traitor'," he wrote. In the context of Sri Lanka's "war on terror", as the government termed its campaign, the potential of individual voices to humanise or to bear witness should not be overstated.

Conclusions: Social media rewriting the protocols of war reporting

Social networks, as this chapter has sought to demonstrate, are rapidly rewriting the principles and protocols of war and conflict reporting. Judged by traditional criteria of Western news journalism, collaborative approaches to news gathering offer compelling forms of engagement and immediacy, but they are also prone to inaccuracy, with key "facts" lacking verification or corroboration. The latter difficulties are sometimes compounded, in turn, by the implication of the networks in the violence itself. The echo chambers to prejudice and rumour provided by some of the tweeting from Mumbai or by "Joe the plumber" in Sderot are cautionary.

Yet the wide availability of the technologies of the internet and the cell phone, and the importance of these in so many people's daily lives, mean that when political violence occurs, these media will be part of the story. In some situations, such as Gaza or Sri Lanka, social networks fill silences created by censorship and suppression. In addition, the ways they are used by individuals to make connections across diasporas, to mobilise support and to build complex global public spaces outside those established by news organisations and states, open up distinctive forms of communication which journalism cannot afford to ignore. Scholars of peace journalism, too, are confronted by a need to be able to account for this phenomenon in the exploration of the conditions for journalism that extends beyond elite voices and dramatic coverage from battle zones.

At times the citizen dispatches relayed in these spaces, especially when amplified by news organisations, revealed their potential to narrow the distance that otherwise allows distant publics to ignore their plight (see also Matheson and Allan 2009). The voices of Greek students, for example, were heard in their grief and anger, propelling their demands for change beyond the televisual iconography of rioting. The impromptu efforts of individuals and groups to formalise the sometimes inchoate imperatives of networked media figure prominently here, such as the Sri Lankan Groundviews, with an explicit ethos to cross boundaries, as well as the institutionalisation of the likes of Twitter within the repertoire of news reporting.

The connections formed and the distinctive kinds of publicness enabled here cannot be underestimated as a political force. There is some cause for optimism that the re-distribution of communicative power fostered by digital technologies will contribute to a broadening of global public spheres. At the same time, however, much work remains to be done to dislodge the prevailing frames of "us and them" permeating so much of Western war and conflict reporting. In each of the four cases discussed above, the spectre of militarised states exploiting security threats as a rationale for policing the boundaries of public discussion and debate loomed large.

Notes

1 These largely interpersonal media dominate the internet – by traffic, they are rivalled only by search engines and online auction sites – and are a significant part of everyday life for many people in both the global north and south. The International Telecommunication Union estimated in March 2009 that there were 4.1 billion cell phone subscriptions globally, alongside 1.5 billion people with internet access (ITU 2009). Like any new media, while they have no intrinsic orientation towards either peace-making or war-mongering, social network media have the potential to disrupt existing relations of power in opening up communication that had hitherto been constrained (see Curran 2002: 65). Whether cell phones are instrumental in political organisation, such as during the "EDSA II" (the Second People Power Revolution which overthrew Philippine President Joseph Estrada) protests in Manila in 2001, is hotly debated (see Rafael 2003), but the contribution they have made to news gathering has been at times startling.

2 http://www.groundviews.org/submission-guidelines/.

References

Abbey, Alan (2008) Gaza battles on Twitter, blogs, Poynter Online, 30 December. Available online at http://www.poynter.org/column.asp?id=31&aid=156317, accessed on 24 June 2009

Ali, Mohammed (2009) Gaza: We are slowly being suffocated, Oxfam News Blog, 8 January. Available online at http://www.oxfam.org.uk/applications/blogs/pressoffice/?p=3003, accessed on 24 June 2009

Allan, Stuart and Thorsen, Einar (eds) (2009) *Citizen Journalism: Global perspectives*. New York: Peter Lang

Baratz, Maya (2009) Twitter, YouTube among the new propaganda tools of the battle in Gaza, VentureBeat, 5 January. Available online at http://venturebeat.com/2009/01/05/twitter-youtube-among-the-new-propaganda-tools-of-the-battle-in-gaza, accessed on 25 June 2009

Bell, Stewart (2009) Sri Lanka waging a war without witnesses, *National Post*, 7 May. Available online at http://www.nationalpost.com/news/story.html?id=1570574, accessed on 24 June 2009

Brabant, Malcolm (2008) Rebellion deeply embedded in Greece, BBC News Online, 9 December. Available online at http://news.bbc.co.uk/1/hi/world/europe/7771628.stm, accessed on 24 June 2009

Busari, Stephanie (2008) Tweeting the terror: How social media reacted to Mumbai, CNN, 27 November. Available online at http://www.cnn.com/2008/WORLD/asiapcf/11/27/mumbai.twitter/, accessed on 24 June 2009

Caulfield, Brian and Karmali, Naazneen (2008) Mumbai: Twitter's moment, Forbes.com, 28 November. Available online at http://www.forbes.com/2008/11/28/mumbai-twitter-sms-tech-internet-cx_bc_kn_1128mumbai.html, accessed on 10 August 2009

Chamberlain, Gethin (2009) Makeshift Sri Lanka hospital is shelled, taking 47 lives, GuardianUnlimited, 12 May. Available online at http://www.guardian.co.uk/world/2009/may/12/sri-lanka-hospital-shelling-tamil-tigers, accessed on 1 June 2009

Coleman, Stephen (2005) Blogs and the new politics of listening, *Political Quarterly,* Vol. 76, No. 2 pp 272–80

Curran, James (2002) *Media and power,* London: Routledge

Economist (2008) Rioters of the world unite, *Economist,* 18 December

Fisk, Robert (2009) Keeping out the cameras and reporters simply doesn't work, *Independent,* 5 January

Fitzgerald, Mary (2009) On the front lines of Gaza's war 2.0, *Irish Times,* 10 January

Galtung, Johan (1998) High road, low road: Charting the way for peace journalism. *Track Two,* Vol. 7, No. 4

Gemenis, Kostas (2008) Greece in turmoil: riots and politics, openDemocracy, 10 December. Available online at http://www.opendemocracy.net/article/greece-in-turmoil-riots-and-politics, accessed on 24 June 2009

Gunawardene, Nalaka (2008) When citizens turn on journalists, *AsiaMedia*, 29 February. Available online at http://www.asiamedia.ucla.edu/article.asp?parentid=88214, accessed on 24 June 2009

Hamilton, John M. and Jenner, Eric (2004) Redefining foreign correspondence, *Journalism*, Vol. 5, No. 3 pp 301–21

Hattotuwa, Sanjana (2007) The promise of citizen journalism. openDemocracy, 22 January. Available online at http://www.opendemocracy.net/terrorism/articles/srilanka220107, accessed on 24 June 2009

Haven, Paul (2008) Greek-inspired protests spread across Europe, Associated Press Worldstream, 12 December

Herrmann, Steve (2008) Mumbai, Twitter and live updates, BBC News Online, 4 December. Available online at http://www.bbc.co.uk/blogs/theeditors/2008/12/theres_been_discussion_see_eg.html, accessed on 24 June 2009

Hoyt, Clark (2009) Standing between enemies, *New York Times*, 11 January

Hull, C. Bryson (2009) Q+A: Sri Lanka's propaganda war, Reuters, 14 May. Available online at http://uk.reuters.com/article/idUKTRE54D2Z220090514, accessed on 23 June 2009

IFFCG (2009) *No safe place*. Report by the Independent Fact Finding Committee on Gaza presented to the League of Arab States, 30 April. Available online at http://www.pchr-gaza.org/files/PressR/English/2008/Report%20full.pdf, accessed on 24 June 2009

ITU (2009) The digital divide and the MDGs, International Telecommunication Union Newsroom, 16 June. Available online at http://www.itu.int/newsroom/media-kit/story9.html, accessed on 30 June 2009

Khan, Saad (2008) Twitter cause a little controversy after Mumbai attacks: What about Pakistan? Green and White, 27 November. Available online at http://greenwhite.org/2008/11/27/twitter-cause-a-little-controversy-after-mumbai-attacks-what-about-pakistan/, accessed on 10 August 2009

Komninos, Maria and Vamvakas, Vassilis (2009) The role of new media in "the December 2008 revolt" in Greece, *Encyclopedia of social movement media*, Downing, John (ed.) London: Sage

Lam, Andrew (2008) Letter from Athens, New America Media, 16 December

Lee, Melanie (2008) Blogs feed information frenzy on Mumbai attacks, Reuters, 27 November. Available online at http://www.reuters.com/article/technologyNews/idUSTRE4AQ2Q020081127, accessed on 24 June 2009

Masouras, Asteris (2009) Twittering away: The social media and the war in Gaza, New Europe, 12 January. Available online at http://www.neurope.eu/articles/91859.php, accessed on 24 June 2009

Matheson, Donald and Allan, Stuart (2009) *Digital war reporting*, Cambridge: Polity

Monck, Adrian (2009) War 2.0: Israel's post-journalism campaign in Gaza, Adrianmonck.com, 7 January. Available online at http://adrianmonck.com/2009/01/war-20-israels-postjournalism-campaign-gaza/, accessed on 26 June 2009

Morozov, Evgeny (2008) The Alternative's alternative, openDemocracy, 29 December. Available online at http://www.opendemocracy.net/article/email/the-alternatives-alternative, accessed on 24 June 2009

Pepper, Daniel (2008) India's media blasted for sensational Mumbai coverage, *Christian Science Monitor*, 24 December. Available online at http://www.csmonitor.com/2008/1224/p01s01-wosc.html, accessed on 24 June 2009

Percival, Jenny (2008) Podcasting from the Gaza strip, *Guardian* News Blog, 28 December. Available online at http://www.guardian.co.uk/news/blog/2008/dec/28/gaza-attacks-podcasting-ramzy, accessed on 27 June 2009

Pilger, John (2009) Distant voices, desperate lives, *New Statesman*, 14 May. Available online at http://www.newstatesman.com/asia/2009/05/sri-lanka-pilger-british-tamil, accessed 10 August 2009

Rafael, Vicente L. (2003) The cell phone and the crowd: Messianic politics in the contemporary Philippines, *Public Culture*, Vol. 15, No. 3 pp 399–425

Rajisingam, Nirmala (2009) The Tamil diaspora: Solidarities and realities, openDemocracy, 17 April. Available online at http://www.opendemocracy.net/article/the-tamil-diaspora-solidarities-and-realities, accessed on 24 June 2009

S, Alexis (2008) Eye witness from Thessaloniki, openDemocracy, 12 December. Available online at http://www.opendemocracy.net/blog/alexis-s/2008/12/12/eyewitness-from-thessaloniki, accessed on 24 June 2009

SepiaMutiny (2008) The beginning of the end: Groundviews, 3 March. Available online at http://www.sepiamutiny.com/sepia/archives/005068.html, accessed on 24 June 2009

Sonwalkar, Prasun (2009) Byte by byte: Journalism's growing potential to reflect the idea of India, *Journalism*, Vol 10, No. 3 pp 374–6

Sunday Observer (Sri Lanka) (2009) BBC parrots Tiger propaganda without checking, 17 May. Available online at http://www.sundayobserver.lk/2009/05/17/new26.asp, accessed on 24 June 2009

Taylor, Lesley C. (2009) Bridging the divide: Covering Sri Lanka one story at a time, *Canadian Journalism Project*, 16 March. Available online at http://www.j-source.ca/english_new/detail.php?id=3507, accessed on 24 June 2009

Terzis, George and Smeets, Bert (2008) Online peace activism and journalism. Paper presented at symposium "Building sustainable futures: Enacting peace and development", Leeuwen, 15–19 July. Available online at http://soc.kuleuven.be/iieb/ipraweb/papers/Online%20Peace%20Activism%20and%20Journalism.pdf, accessed on 24 June 2009

Thussu, Daya, K. (2009) Turning terrorism into a soap opera, *British Journalism Review*, Vol. 20, No. 1 pp 13–8

Tomstechblog.com (2008) Oliver Wendell Holmes turning over in his grave, Tomstechblog.com, 26 November. Available online at http://www.tomstechblog.com/post/Oliver-Wendell-Holmes-Turning-Over-In-His-Grave.aspx, accessed 10 August 2009

Trager, Eric (2009) Joe the plumber: War correspondent? Commentary, 8 January. Available online at http://www.commentarymagazine.com/blogs/index.php/trager/49671, accessed on 27 June 2009

Tsimas, Pavlos (2008) Greek journalist: Media failed amid riots (transcript by Andrew Lam of speech at Global Forum for Media Development, Athens, 10 December), New America Media: Chez Andrew, 9 December. Available online at http:// blogs. newamericamedia.org/andrew-lam/1504/greek-journalist-discusses-role-of-media-amid-riots, accessed on 21 August 2009

Walsh, Nick Paton (2009) Grim scenes at Sri Lankan camps, Channel 4 News, 5 May. Available online at http://www.channel4.com/news/articles/politics/international_politics/grim+scenes+at+sri+lankan+camps+/3126257, accessed on 24 June 2009

Whitaker, Mark P. (2004) Tamilnet.com: Some reflections on popular anthropology, nationalism and the Internet, *Anthropological Quarterly*, Vol. 77, No. 3 pp 469–498. Also available online at http://www.tamilnation.org/digital/mark_whitaker.htm, accessed on 24 June 2009

Williams, Raymond (1982) Distance, *Raymond Williams on television*, O'Connor, Alan (ed.) London: Routledge

11

Building a peace journalists' network from the ground: The Philippine experience

JEAN LEE C. PATINDOL

Although not a new concept (see Galtung and Ruge 1965), peace journalism as a distinct field and discipline in itself only grew significantly in the 1990s, with articles, papers, training courses and books published and circulated internationally. Yet, as peace journalism continues to grow, one inevitably asks how those who have been trained can successfully practise it, as well as how can peace journalism become the mainstream journalism practised in a global society that has become increasingly complex and violent?

Since peace journalism as a discipline essentially challenges the main assumptions, paradigms and practices of traditional journalism, many of those who attempt to practise it are met with opposition, not just from individuals and groups but from the entire media system itself. For peace journalism to be sustainable, those who have been trained in the field need to band together and engage in mutually helpful exchanges, building solidarity as they jointly work towards implementing peace journalism in the mainstream.

This was the driving force that motivated a motley group of journalists and communication educators and professionals trained in basic peace journalism in Bacolod City, Philippines, in late 2004, to form the Peace and Conflict Journalism Network (PECOJON). Today, PECOJON has grown into a number of national and international networks, with around 250 members in the Philippines and 165 members from 15 countries worldwide.

Journalism in the Philippines

Perceived as having one of the "freest and least fettered" journalistic systems in all Asia (Florentino-Hofilena 1998: 77), the Philippines also ranks, after Iraq, as the most dangerous country for reporters to work and live in because of the number of journalists killed in the line of duty. Since the restoration of democracy after the removal of dictator Ferdinand Marcos in 1986 and up to 2006, eighty-one journalists were killed (International Federation of Journalists 2005). As generally understood, the concept of press freedom in the Philippines emphasises the creation and maintenance of an environment where media practitioners are able to function with relative freedom, though the protection of the people's right to know is less stressed (Rosario-Braid 1993: 1).

This has encouraged a proliferation of media in the country and even the tacit recognition of media as a power to reckon with, especially after the media played a key role in bringing about the People Power Revolution of 1986 (ibid: 1). By the early 1990s, media infrastructure was well-developed, with 303 radio stations nationwide, 77 television stations, 353 publications and 1,007 cinema houses in a country of around 80 million people. However, 66 per cent of all publications are currently in Metro Manila and in the English language while all five of the originating network television stations are based in Metro Manila. Some 72 television stations serve as relay stations with 95 per cent of their programmes sourced from Manila-based operations. There are also many community media and complementary media (blackboard newspapers, audio cassettes, theatre and puppet shows), especially in rural areas. But they are generally not able to reflect public opinion effectively due to their severe lack of financial, technical and adequately-trained human resources (ibid: 2). Radio still has the widest reach at 78 per cent of households, with television at around 40 per cent and newspapers reaching only 22 per cent (ibid).

Despite laws, regulations and published codes of ethics for the responsible conduct of the media, in actual practice, almost anybody can become a so-called "journalist" overnight, especially in the radio industry. There is a standing insider anecdote among radio practitioners, who refer to these overnight reporters as "vinegar journalists" – they were sent by their mothers to buy vinegar at the neighbourhood store but go back home as journalists, reporting to everyone who cares to hear the tidbits of information they heard on the way and back.

Koop (2006), currently PECOJON's international coordinator, points out that given the highly-developed media infrastructure in the Philippines, "the lack of access to high quality information might not be a result of a quantitative limitation but of the quality of information disseminated". She argues that there is a need to update the original peace journalism theory as developed by Galtung and Ruge (op cit) and Lynch and McGoldrick (2005), among others, to acknowledge the different working conditions and challenges faced by Filipino journalists, since the original theory was geared more for international media and from a European perspective. Citing an International Federation of Journalists' special report, *A dangerous profession: Press freedom under fire in the Philippines* (IFJ 2005), Koop further explains that in the Philippines, most journalists learn their skills on the job and have a disturbingly glaring lack of knowledge and background in media ethics. This view is supported by the ground-breaking study of journalists by journalists, *News for sale: The corruption of the Philippine media* (Florentino-Hofileña 1998), which shows that when offered money by their sources, one out of three beat reporters openly admitted to taking it due to any of the following reasons:

- the money was not asked for but offered;
- because of their paltry pay;
- or because they feared that refusing the money would jeopardise their chances of securing future interviews.

Salaried print news reporters who have college degrees earn an average of P10,000 a month before taxes (Koop op cit), a rate that is only a little above the official minimum poverty income of P6,195 for a family of five (National Statistics and Coordination Board 2007). The Center for Media Freedom and Responsibility (CMFR 2008), in a report on the state of employment in the Philippine media today, corroborates this finding while also highlighting the prevalence of short-term contracts and poor rates of pay. Dr Florangel Rosario-Braid, President and Dean of the Asian Institute of Journalism, in her book, *Social responsibility in communication media* (op cit), explains that low salaries have forced many journalists to "moonlight", resorting to self-censorship when news stories conflict with their vested interests. The Philippine Center for Investigative Journalism (PCIJ) explains that even if the country's press is considered one of the liveliest and freest in Asia, "deadline pressures, extreme competition and budgetary constraints make it difficult for many journalists to delve into the causes and broader meanings of news events" (PCIJ 2008).

In terms of academic preparation and training for the field, although there are about 200 journalism schools in the country, most graduates opt to go into the public relations and advertising fields because these pay better and are less dangerous. It is also difficult for teaching staff to find relevant and updated training and education materials, which are usually sourced from the West and are very expensive (Hume 2007).

Despite these constraints, journalists in the Philippines continue to do their work to the best of their knowledge and abilities, and they enjoy widespread public support for this, especially after the 1986 People Power Revolution (Rosario-Braid op cit: 1). Surveys of public opinion reflect positively on the continuing credibility of the press in the Philippines. Even those who are critical of the ways of the press, the sensationalism, the inaccuracies and lack of balance and fairness oppose government regulation of the media. According to Florentino-Hofilena (op cit):

> Public trust has...evolved a mindset of complacency, with disturbing lack of awareness about the news process and ignorance of journalistic rules that discipline the practice. People seem to turn to the media (now) as a source of entertaining distraction, not for knowledge and information that will help them understand the problems of daily life.

PECOJON: Birth and development

It is in this context that PECOJON was born. The first peace journalism training programme (PJ1) was led by Antonia Koop in October 2004 as part of the then-Peace Journalism Programme she ran for Pax Christi-Pilipinas (PCP) and the Niall O'Brien Center (NOBC) in Bacolod City, Philippines. Koop is a German journalist and documentary film maker whose experience is in covering conflict, mainly in Palestine. She has worked since 2006 as a development contract worker with the German AGEH (Arbeitsgemeinschaft fuer Entwicklungshilfe) for PECOJON.

Several months before this first programme, however, a group of media and communication professionals based in Bacolod regularly discussed with Koop the concept and issues in peace journalism. Among these volunteers and participants of the first training programme were Ledrolen Manriquez, who later became the international secretariat chief of operations, while I was also involved, later becoming the national coordinator in the Philippines until 31 March 2009. It was also from these meetings that the idea of a network "by journalists for journalists" was born. The group then decided to form an e-group to have an online venue for all volunteers, advocates and future training participants. The PECOJON e-group was created on 9 September 2004.

The next training sessions were held in Bacolod in May 2005 and in Subic (Luzon, northern Philippines) in the following month. It became clear that there was a need for advanced training for those who had finished the first peace journalism training (PJ1), and not just for journalists but for other communication professionals as well. Thus later sessions involved advanced (PJ2) training for journalists as well as "exchange deals" according to which inviting institutions such as a school or a civic organisation provided the audience and logistics while PECOJON provided the training for free. This strategy helped overcome financing problems and extended the training to groups other than just journalists. All this led to the creation of the Qualification Course for PECOJON Trainers (PJ3) to help interested members in becoming trainers.

It became clear during these sessions that specific funding arrangements needed to be established if PECOJON were to develop as a network, while the network also needed to create its distinct identity separate from but parallel to the peace movement. It was consistently stressed that the peace journalist chooses what and how to report in such a way that opens spaces for alternative solutions to conflict other than violence and war in the course of more truthful and responsible reporting, and is not a peace activist *per se*.

On 1 April 2006, PECOJON officially started as the Peace and Conflict Journalism Network under an approved, three-year development grant by Misereor. On 30 October 2006, the network was officially registered with the Philippine Securities and Exchange Commission (SEC) as a distinct non-profit, non-government corporate entity. With PECOJON's separate legal identity, trainings continued to be funded by InWent, but as a part of PECOJON now, and not as a programme of the Pax Christi-Pilipinas and Niall O'Brien Center. Additionally, the International Institute of Journalism (IIJ) based in Germany provided training funds for PECOJON via InWent in 2007, when InWent's budget for conflict management in the Philippines was channelled to other priority countries.

Misereor accounts for around 35 per cent of the total budget for PECOJON and covers mainly administrative and network-building programmes and activities while Pax Christi-Pilipinas (in 2004 only, 1 per cent), InWent (in 2005–6, 9 per cent) and IIJ (in 2007–8, 53 per cent) and private donations by the core team and voluntary contributions in kind by members account for the rest. Members in close geographical areas in the Philippines band together to form PECOJON chapters. For instance, in conflict-ridden Mindanao PECOJON grew quickly in membership, with three chapters formed in less than a year. For many members, there is always the constant struggle between attending to their profession and livelihood and helping build PECOJON's vision, given the constraints on their time and other resources.

To date, PECOJON in the Philippines has partnered with several colleges and universities, as well as civil society organisations in conducting introductory peace and conflict journalism presentations and/or trainings among campus newspaper staff and communications students. It is also formally linked with the Conflict and Reconciliation Studies MA programme of the Pax Christi Institute (PCI) and the University of St. La Salle, where it offers a special unit in Conflict-Sensitive Journalism.

Peace is a dangerous word in a dangerous world

When PECOJON started, it faced enormous challenges. It had a hard-to-pronounce name, in both its long and short versions (with the short name even drawing laughs if pronounced in the Spanish way). Its leaders were three women who were not full-time journalists (Koop put on hold her journalism career since she started with PECOJON) although they worked in film, local journalism and journalism and communications education, while its location was neither in Manila nor conflict-ridden Mindanao. Moreover, when PECOJON first approached organisations and journalists and invited them to its trainings, there were not many takers, even when the travel and trainings were fully subsidised by grants. "Who is PECOJON?" was the common response.

In a country where the word "peace" has not only been overused but also misused, people are wary and skeptical. "Is it another leftist media organisation fronting for the communists or a right-wing propaganda arm of the government?" "If PECOJON is just another peace organisation, what is it doing meddling with the independence of journalists then?" And then, the inevitable question: "What is peace, anyway?" In addition, questions would invariably arise on why PECOJON was including in the trainings and even accepting the applications for membership of a few journalists already known in the profession to be corrupt and unethical.

These were all hard questions which could not easily be answered by pat explanations nor even long lectures based on appropriate theory. Although its over-arching vision was to contribute to a more peaceful world (1st PECOJON national evaluation and planning workshop proceedings 2006), the network had to be weaned from its close association with the peace organisation that had "midwifed" it into existence by establishing itself as a separate legal entity. Moreover, in 2005, during a controversy over the arming of reporters amidst the increasing violence against journalists in the country, another organisation issued a public statement calling for tougher measures, using the name of PECOJON (without

PECOJON's knowledge and consent) to bolster its numbers and credibility. This led to the specific focus on drafting membership guidelines which emphasised only individual membership with voting rights while organisational membership could be considered only on specific project partnership arrangements and on a case-to-case affiliation basis.

A particular controversy emerged over the issue of whether to allow membership to people perceived to be "undesirables" in the profession. In response, the majority of PECOJON members looked to its vision and affirmed that if it was to contribute to a more peaceful world through the ethical, responsible, independent and professional exercise of journalism, then it had to be non-judgemental and non-discriminatory in its membership strategy.

Conflict-sensitive journalism instead of peace journalism

The trainings originally focused on "peace journalism" but participants often became confused. How could the notion of peace journalism involving the promotion of specific values be compatible with a belief in the ethical mandate of the journalist as an independent and objective reporter and interpreter of events and issues they cover? Although peace journalism theory (Lynch and McGoldrick op cit) systematically deconstructs this myth of independence and objectivity with an analysis of the news production system and processes, the myth is so well-entrenched in people's consciousness that even after repeated discussions and trainings on the same subject, it crops up again and again. Popular misconceptions about peace journalism are that it is:

- only reporting about peace, peace movements and peace initiatives (with no critical reporting on peace efforts);
- in effect, reporting for peace and thus best seen as peace propaganda, and
- peaceful reporting – thus concentrating on positive news, avoiding "bad" stories such as those involving violence.

This necessitated a gradual shift in naming the discipline and the trainings themselves from peace journalism to peace and conflict journalism to emphasise that the concept applies to the coverage of conflict and not its exclusion. Currently, the term conflict-sensitive journalism (CSJ) is being used by PECOJON in its trainings. It has been found that this term has significantly clarified the concept among participants and further focuses on the fact that:

- it is more accurate and appropriate to the real work of an ethical, responsible journalist;
- the concept applies to the reporting of conflict, not to avoiding it, and
- the emphasis is on the challenge for journalists in reporting conflict.

The term was adopted from the work of Ross Howard (2004), who emphasises that "professional journalists do not set out to reduce conflict. They seek to present accurate and impartial news. But, it is often through good reporting that the conflict is reduced".

Integrating theory and practice

The initial trainings (PJ1) involved the analysis of limitations and deficiencies of traditional journalism practice with regard to the task of providing reliable information, as well as an introduction to the concepts and principles of conflict-sensitive journalism (CSJ). However, the initial trainings could not provide a venue for the integration of the theories into practice. Feedback from the participants stressed that the training did not prepare journalists for dealing with the constraints of the media system. Thus, the training in PJ2 has been modified to take account of these criticisms. PJ2 trainings are more interactive and driven by members' focus group discussions and workshop outputs. They cover a review and deepening of the understanding of the concepts and principles introduced in the initial training as well as relate the theories to practice using the experiences and challenges encountered by the participants. Even so, the process is long and painstaking, particularly because conflict-sensitive content requires more time, research and careful thought – expensive resources in the context of the plight of the Philippine journalist faced with a system that demands more and more output in less and less time.

The need for long-term support

Journalists committed to practising conflict-sensitive journalism faced considerable professional barriers. They inevitably expressed the need for the support of peers who were similarly trained and committed to overcoming the institutional and ideological constraints (such as time pressures, editorial guidelines on what is newsworthy, market pressures). No matter how conflict sensitively an article is written, if an editor does not like it, it is cut or worse rejected. The editor will point to pressing publisher demands and advertiser constraints. PECOJON now has to face these challenges head on by engaging in top-level discussions on conflict-sensitive journalism with editors, publishers and even advertisers.

The reality of market forces

The strongest argument against the successful practice of conflict-sensitive journalism is that it contradicts the requirements of the market. Readers are perceived to require nothing but simple, attention-grabbing and entertaining news (Florentino-Hofilena op cit) and the entire media production system is designed to cater to this perceived type of readership. There is a need, then, to train and re-orient not only the journalists in the field, but also the other actors in the media system – the journalism and communication educators, editors, publishers, advertisers and especially the media consumers. So far, PECOJON has been developing media literacy training programmes for the academy and civil society-based organisations to help address this need, in addition to working on curriculum integration with partner universities. There is still the bigger challenge of reaching the editors, publishers, advertisers and the other sectors of the media system itself on a consistent, long-term basis.

The journey ahead

It is interesting to note that the Philippine experience highlights recurring issues in the field of peace journalism which are also raised at the international level. A key issue is the debate on preserving the journalist's "objectivity" in the practice of peace journalism. Lynch (op cit) points out that accepting the "objectivity" argument is, in effect, accepting and operating within the paradigms of traditional war journalism. Perhaps it is useful to conceive of a *journeying* in awareness and growth in consciousness from the *continuum of paradigms* ranging from traditional journalism to conflict-sensitive journalism and eventually to outright peace journalism, which Lynch (2008) describes as a "critical proposition, critical in the sense of owning its agenda and choosing to harness journalism for peace".

Lynch also points out the difference between seeing the journalist as a part of the "drama of intervention" (an observer of what is happening, temporarily intervening by reporting what is happening) or the "drama of complicity" (where the journalist, as well as the sources and readers, are all helping to construct "reality") is crucial in the debate. Until these elements are clarified in peace journalism discussion and education, the basic questions on the role of the journalist and its implications to journalism practice will never rest.

There must also be acute awareness of the true value of peace journalism – the provision for reflexivity, or a critical self-awareness; and anchorage, or using the principles and tools of conflict analysis and peace research in the application of good journalism (Lynch and McGoldrick op cit: xvii). It is also useful to note Hackett's (2006) three frameworks for assessing structure and agency in news media as a way of answering the question: "Is peace journalism possible (and sustainable)?" Hackett presents three models – Herman and Chomsky's propaganda model, Shoemaker and Reese's hierarchy of influences model and Bourdieu's journalism as a field model.

According to Hackett, the propaganda model is useful in highlighting the role of the state and capital in influencing journalism but risks being reductionist and functionalist, leaving no room nor hope for journalism to improve and transform itself to serve the highest ends of society. The hierarchy of influences model is useful in highlighting the pressures for and against journalism in the five levels identified – the media workers themselves, their daily work routines, the broader organisational imperatives, extra-media influences and ideology. However, the hierarchy of influences model, as well as the propaganda model, ignore "the specificity and coherence of journalism as a cultural practice and form of knowledge production in itself" (ibid: 1).

Hackett suggests the field model conceives of journalism as an autonomous institutional sphere interacting with other fields to a greater or lesser extent, "allowing conceptual space for both the structural influences of and on new media, as well as the potential agency and creativity of journalists". Three broad approaches for change are then suggested: reform the journalism field from within, intervene in adjacent fields and build a new field parallel to the currently existing field (ibid: 11). PECOJON's work so far appears to fall within the first two approaches: it is facilitating reform within the journalistic field through the trainings it conducts and the dialogue and activities among its members; and it is intervening in adjacent fields with its work on the academy and civil society in media literacy trainings and curriculum integration in journalism education.

On the matter of sustainability, Perlas (1998) posits a three-fold concept of sustainable development, as opposed to the single-fold (economy as driving force) and two-fold (economy and polity as driving forces) models. In the three-fold model, civil society holds the power to bestow legitimacy on the government and business, wanting "both to be transparent and accountable to the public interest, especially the poor and others who are marginalised". It is in this context of sustainability that the following recommendations for future action are proposed.

Networking and solidarity (continuing reform from within)

It is not enough to just train journalists any more. There have to be more regular and consistent forms of follow-up and support, as well as venues for mutual exchange and building solidarity among journalists and peace journalism practitioners, within countries and globally.

Reorienting the market: Producer and consumer literacy (intervening in adjacent fields)

Peace journalists must work with professionals in other fields, particularly to promote media literacy amongst consumers and curriculum integration in journalism education, especially in countries where a significant portion of the population are young (such as the Philippines, where half of the population is aged 35 and below), since investing in the social capital of the youth is, in effect, investing in the future. Peace journalists must also work with editors, publishers and advertisers and even government and non-government organisations, to raise awareness about how peace journalism can affect everyone. Later, they may even become involved in the establishment of a world media development bank as called for by Tehranian (2002), to reduce the inequalities of media production and access within and between nations.

Conclusions: Succeeding in a transformed market (building a parallel field)

Imagine a world where people demand from media not just entertainment but also intellectual, psychological and even psychic fulfilment, and reject the sensationalised reporting of war-journalism. Imagine a world where people demand news that truly helps inform them about the choices they have to make in their individual and social lives. Imagine a world where journalists compete not for the "scoop" but for the most useful and informative report for their audiences. Imagine a world where editors and publishers express a preference for excellent conflict-sensitive reporting content in their publications and broadcasts. Imagine a world where advertisers channel their huge budgets to supporting socially responsible media. Imagine a world where business and government focus on serving the authentic needs of people for full self-realisation and not in pandering to their superficial, material desires.

It can still be a free-market world: the landscape and requirements will just look, sound, smell, taste and feel different and transformed. This is the world that peace journalism can create, sustain and succeed in.

References

Center for Alternative Development Initiatives: Philippine Institute for Investigative Journalism (2008) *Journalism with an impact*. Available online at http://www.pcij. org/impact.html, accessed on 1 May 2008

Center for Media Freedom and Responsibility (CMFR) (2008) So you want to work in the media? *Philippine Journalism Review (PJR)*, May-June. Available online at http://www.cmfr.com.ph/_pjrreports/2008/may-june/0508_story04.html, accessed on 30 June 2008

Florentino-Hofileña, Chay (1998) *News for sale: The corruption of the Philippine media*, Quezon City, Philippines: the Philippine Center for Investigative Journalism (PCIJ) and the Center for Media Freedom and Responsibility (CMFR)

Galtung, Johann and Ruge, Mari (1965) The structure of foreign news: The presentation of the Congo, Cuba and Cyprus crises in four Norwegian newspapers, *Journal of International Peace Research*, Vol. 1 pp 64–91

Hackett, Robert A. (2006) Is peace journalism possible? Three frameworks for assessing structure and agency in news media, Conflict and Communication Online, Vol. 5, No. 2 pp 1–11. Available online at http://www.cco.regener-online.de/2006_2/pdf/hackett.pdf, accessed on 1 May 2008

Howard, Ross (2004) *Conflict-sensitive journalism: A handbook*, Denmark: International Media Support (IMS) and Institute for Media, Policy and Civil Society (IMPACS)

Hume, Ellen (2007) University journalism education: A global challenge, Center for International Media Assistance, August 1. Available online at http://www.ellenhume. com/articles/education.pdf, accessed on 15 June 2008

International Federation of Journalists (2005) *A dangerous profession: Press freedom under fire in the Philippines*. Available online at http://www.ifj.org/en/pdfs/Philippines.pdf, accessed on 1 May 2008

Koop, Antonia (2006) *Analysis of the work environment of Filipino journalists as basis for* the revision of the peace journalism theory and recommendations for its implementation. Unpublished Master's thesis for the Conflict and Reconciliation MA Studies Programme, Pax Christi Institute and the University of St. La Salle, Philippines

Lynch, Jake and McGoldrick, Annabel (2005) *Peace journalism,* Stroud: Hawthorn Press

Lynch, Jake (2008) The developmentalist and the critical: The emerging divide in journalist training as a form of media intervention in conflict. Paper presented at the International Peace Research Association (IPRA) conference in Leuven, Belgium, 15–19 July

National Statistics and Coordination Board (2007) *NSCB FAQ on poverty statistics.* Available online at http://www.nscb.gov.ph/poverty/2007/NSCB_FAQsOnPovertyStatistics.pdf, accessed on 15 June 2008

National Wage and Productivity Commission (2008) *Minimum wage rates.* Available online at http://www.nwpc.dole.gov.ph/rtwpb.html, accessed on 15 June 2008

PCIJ (2008) *Journalism and conflict in the Philippines*: Philippine Center for Investigative Journalism, 28 September. Available online at http://www.pcij.org/. accessed on 1 May 2009

PECOJON (2006) First national evaluation and planning workshop proceedings, National Secretariat, Bacolod City, Philippines

Perlas, Nicanor, Lynch, Damon, Sharman, Jim and Hey-Gonzales, Divina (1998) Three-fold image of society in PA2, *Philippine agenda 21 handbook*, Quezon City, Philippines

Rosario-Braid, Florangel (1993) *Social responsibility in communication media*, Quezon City, Philippines: Katha Publishing Co. Inc.

Tehranian, Majid (2002) Peace journalism: Negotiating global media ethics, *Harvard Journal of Press/Politics*, Vol. 7, No. 2, April pp 58–83

12

Peace journalism in practice – *Peace News:* For nonviolent revolution

MILAN RAI

Does *Peace News*, which has existed as a publication with that title since 6 June 1936, practise "peace journalism"? Putting it another way, to what extent does the specific form of media behaviour recently defined as "peace journalism" capture the actually-existing peace journalism of *Peace News*?

Editorial meetings of *Peace News* often involve fine judgements as to what forms of reporting and commentary are in the best interests of the peace movement, and in the best interests of peace and justice (assumed to be identical with the interests of the movement, though not necessarily the interests of a particular group within the movement). When we consider the peace journalism suggested by Jake Lynch and Annabel McGoldrick (2005), we find many points of convergence. They suggest: "Peace Journalism is when editors and reporters make choices – of what stories to report and how to report them – which create opportunities for society at large to consider and to value non-violent responses to conflict." Peace journalism "applies an awareness of non-violence and creativity to the practical job of everyday reporting" (ibid: 5).

The origins and early days

This is precisely the task that *Peace News* has set itself since its inception. In early 1936, North London's Wood Green Study Group (studying the implications of pacifism) found that existing peace publications could not successfully be sold on the street to the general public. The group decided that what was needed was a new "weekly newspaper serving all who are working for peace" (the magazine's first subtitle). The publication, soon harnessed to the also-new pacifist Peace Pledge Union (started in 1934 by Anglican priest Dick Sheppard), set itself the triple task of reporting contemporary affairs (the war in Spain, the Nazi annexation of Austria, the plight of Jewish refugees, the Japanese invasion of China, and so on); reporting the activism of people not often noticed in the mainstream press (people sacked from their jobs for wearing anti-militarist white poppies at work, war tax resisters prosecuted for not paying income tax on grounds of conscience, and others); and arguing for a just peace (the end of empire, a sharing society, international disarmament, and other major reforms) (Beale 1986: 9–10).

Nonviolence has always been at the core of *Peace News*, and the weekly was founded precisely to "create opportunities for society at large to consider and to value nonviolent responses to conflict" (in recent decades, *PN* has contracted the compound term non-violence to a single, more positive, "nonviolence").

The early history of *PN* is perhaps a cautionary tale in relation to peace journalism. Former *PN* co-editor (1971–1976) and long-time *PN* board member Howard Clark has offered some self-critical remarks in a historical overview of the period:

> Unfortunately, pacifism at that time – including the PPU and *PN* – could not anticipate the extremes of systematic destruction involved in modern totalitarianism. *PN* did report on the plight of Jews fleeing from the Nazis, but severely underestimated the menace of fascism, and lacked an immediate response other than appeasement as the wartime editor, the literary critic John Middleton Murry later admitted (Clark 2010).

Clark continues: "Some pacifists had been so intent on criticising the militarism and imperialism of their own government that they dismissed as 'hate propaganda' evidence about the character of 'enemy' states." Some pacifists were so determined to resist the demonisation of Hitler, to seek what Christians might call "that of God" even in the enemy, and to foster international understanding that "they neglected to denounce persecution" (ibid).

I'm sure this kind of error, or moral failing, is not at all what is intended within the peace journalism framework, but it is as well for overtly-committed journalists to acknowledge the dangers of their commitments, even as they point out the dangers inherent in the tacit political commitments of other (more respectable) journalists.

Interestingly, despite the analytical and political problems just referred to, *Peace News* recorded its best sales figures during the Second World War. Some 42,000 copies were sold in our best week. Sales stayed close to 20,000 copies a week throughout the war, via a network of committed volunteers. Wholesalers refused to stock *PN* in 1940, creating the need for a voluntary system of national distribution. Peace Pledge Union members cycled and walked miles each week to ensure that the *PN* message got through. Before the war, street sales were a critical part of the *PN* system, with nearly 1,000 street sellers at one time. A woman who had been a distributor of *PN* in Liverpool in the late 1930s near the central train station, told me in early 2009 of street selling while Oswald Mosley's Blackshirts sold their paper on the other side of the street (personal communication).

The political economy of peace journalism

In discussing peace journalism, it is perhaps worth referring to the political economy of journalism. Granted, peace journalism is a discipline aimed at practitioners in the mainstream mass media. For peace journalists outside the mainstream, however, a committed political base of the kind enjoyed by *PN* in its early years is crucial to economic survival and political effectiveness.

James Curran and Jean Seaton (2003: 33) note that, once the British press became dependent on advertising revenues in the mid-nineteenth century, "one of four things happened to national radical papers that failed to meet the requirements of advertisers": they "either closed down; accommodated to advertising pressure by moving up-market; stayed in a small audience ghetto with manageable losses; or accepted an alternative source of institutional patronage". *Peace News* has faltered from time to time – after separating from the Peace Pledge Union in 1961, *PN* was forced to become part of War Resisters International in 1990, becoming independent once again in 2004. However, despite temporary suspensions, the paper has not closed down – or sought advertising revenues by moving up-market. Institutional patronage from Peace News Trustees (PNT) has been essential throughout. (The main source of PNT revenue has been the rental on two buildings in London, one of them 5 Caledonian Road, given to *Peace News* in 1959.)

Curran and Seaton identify two turning points for the radical left-wing press. The abolition of the advertising tax in 1853 led to a surge in commercial advertising, which effectively subsidised mainstream middle-class newspapers, allowing them to invest in the most costly equipment with better-quality printing. This raising of expectations had a hugely damaging effect on radical newspapers, leading to the consequences identified above.

Earlier, the government had taken direct action against the unauthorised ("unstamped") working-class press (whose circulation exceeded that of the mainstream, respectable, stamped press). The government took on draconian powers of search and confiscation, increased the penalties for being in possession of an unstamped newspaper and reduced the stamp duty on newspapers by 75 per cent, all in order to "put down the unstamped papers", as the Chancellor of the Exchequer explained in 1836 (ibid: 8).

Before this, Curran and Seaton note, radical unstamped papers only needed a small circulation to become viable because they "paid no tax, relied heavily upon news reports filed by their readers on a voluntary basis, and had small newsprint costs because of their high readership per copy". In the early nineteenth-century,

> Unlike the institutionalised journalists of the later period, they [journalists working for the radical press] tended to see themselves as activists rather than as professionals...They sought to describe and expose the dynamics of power and inequality rather than to report "hard news" as a series of disconnected events. They saw themselves as class representatives rather than as disinterested intermediaries and attempted to establish a relationship of real reciprocity with their readers (ibid: 11).

Peace News journalists have tended to see themselves in a similar light, in the past four decades at least, though rarely with a working class perspective. The connection with peace journalism comes perhaps with the refusal to report events as "a series of disconnected events". Lynch and McGoldrick urge journalists to avoid "treating a conflict as if it is only going on in the place and at the time that violence is occurring", and instead "try to trace the links and consequences for people in other places now and in the future". They suggest that journalists avoid "only reporting the violent acts and describing 'the horror'", or "blaming someone for starting it".

They advocate, instead, "show[ing] how people have been blocked and frustrated or deprived in everyday life as a way of explaining the violence", and "looking at how shared problems and issues are leading to consequences that all the parties say they never intended" (ibid: 29). There is a difference between this no-blame approach, however, and setting out to "describe and expose the dynamics of power and inequality", the purpose ascribed by Curran and Seaton to Britain's eighteenth-century radical journalists. The latter mode of operation (actively contesting oppressive power) may perhaps be a subset of a family of approaches within peace journalism (trying to avoid complicity with oppressive power).

'A reflex of your minds'

Part of early British radical journalism (relying heavily on "news reports filed by their readers on a voluntary basis"), as noted above, was what we now call citizen journalism. This function is now very largely fulfilled by the internet, and by websites such as Indymedia in particular, which focus on self-publishing of activist news. At the same time, the rise of the internet, and the increasing power it gives to ordinary citizens to bypass the mainstream corporate media, has increased the participation permitted to ordinary citizens within the mainstream corporate media, within the web and in non-digital media both print and broadcast.

For *Peace News*, citizen journalism has meant activist journalism, with self-reporting by large numbers of social movement activists through the years. In its July-August 2009 issue, for example, *PN* carried the story of a peace activist acquitted of punching a police officer during an altercation in Brighton at an anti-arms trade demonstration (Bluemel 2009). In the previous issue, Tilly Giffin revealed the approach made to her by police officers seeking to turn her into an informant within the anti-climate change group Plane Stupid (Young 2009). Three issues before that, Nottingham University activist Tom Bennett reflected on the student occupation in his university, which had demanded an institutional response to the Israeli assault on Gaza (Bennett 2009). Such reflective reporting has been a key function of *Peace News* since its inception as a journal of a (broad and diverse) movement. For example, 2009 saw a string of articles by peace activists who had visited, or were at the time resident in, the Palestinian Occupied Territories (Cobham 2009; Kelly 2009; Linnell 2009a, 2009b, 2009c; Starhawk 2009).

Throughout the past thirty years, a staple of *PN* coverage has been self-documentation by members of various peace camps around Britain, most famously Greenham Common Women's Peace Camp in the 1980s, and now including Faslane nuclear submarine base in Scotland and the Atomic Weapons Establishment in Aldermaston, Berkshire. The number of *PN* street sellers may have shrunk over the years, but the number of journalist-activists has increased correspondingly.

Seaton and Curran quote the editor of the radical, independent working class newspaper *Northern Star*, writing in the paper's fifth anniversary issue in 1842:

> I have ever sought to make it [the paper] rather a reflex of your minds than a medium through which to exhibit any supposed talent or intelligence of my own. This is precisely my conception of what a people's organ should be (Curran and Seaton op cit: 12).

The Leeds-based *Northern Star* had, unusually, a large network of paid correspondents, and reached, at its peak, half a million readers, at a time when the population of England and Wales over the age of 14 was barely 10 million. While *Peace News* cannot claim to have ever had either the large network of paid correspondents or the reach of the *Northern Star*, the sentiments expressed by the editor of the latter have often been reflected in *Peace News*, producing, among other things, a sometimes startling devotion to anonymity that sought to work against egocentric exhibitionism.

In its early period, however, Albert Beale (op cit) notes that *Peace News* was part of Britain's intellectual elite culture, relying on the weightiness of the names that graced its pages. Vera Brittain, Eric Gill, Laurence Housman, Aldous Huxley, John Middleton Murry, Bertrand Russell, Donald Soper and Sybil Thorndike were among the intellectual luminaries who contributed to the paper and making it one of the leading journals of opinion (Murry was its wartime editor). In *PN*'s middle age, Adrian Mitchell, E. P. Thompson and Theodore Roszak (editor and later author of *The making of a counter-culture*) were just some of the significant figures who featured in its pages as the weekly participated in the ferment of the New Left and the growth of the "counter-culture". Features editor Tom McGrath went on to be the founding editor of the seminal London-based magazine *International Times* or *IT* (Fountain 1988: 30).

The conjunction of journalism and activism

Throughout its existence, *Peace News* has been not merely a journal but a focus for coordination and activism. *Peace News* trustee Andrew Rigby (1986) distinguishes between three pacifist positions during the Second World War: relief, resistance and reconstruction. Advocating "relief" were those such as Philip Mumford who urged that pacifists refrain from opposing government war measures such as civil defence and conscription, and confine themselves to humanitarian relief work. They should seek to soften the blows of war by helping to alleviate the suffering of its victims (*Peace News*, 1 January 1938). The Pacifist Service Corps (later Bureau) was established by the PPU to assist those pacifists and conscientious objectors who, in the words of Alex Wood, "are so sensitive to the claims of the community on their service, that they are eager to find some positive and constructive work to do which is not primarily war work" (*Peace News*, 2 December 1940). Rigby (op cit) continues:

> As opposed to this strand, the "resisters" advocated continued active opposition to war measures. Whilst not objecting to humanitarian relief work in itself, they urged that the prime duty of pacifists was to resist war rather than accept it and devote themselves to ambulance work. It was this element within the PPU that concentrated on political developments during the war and used the pages of *Peace News* to campaign for "Peace by Negotiation" and, later in the war, tried to launch an "Armistice Campaign" against the imposition of a vindictive peace

settlement. By contrast, the third group, the "reconstructionists", were those who eschewed engagement in such short-term protest campaigns, and emphasised the role of pacifists as a redemptive minority, bearing witness to a higher order of morality and pointing the way towards a new order of communal life.

At different times, *Peace News* has leaned more in one of these three directions than in others. Its peace journalism has had, at different times, different inflections, more directed to positive (non-war) relief, to active resistance or to the support of intentional communities engaged in social reconstruction in miniature.

Rigby traces one important strand of resistance that grew up around *Peace News* in the postwar period – perhaps its defining role, helping to create its defining political base in the 1970s and 1980s. A call by Roy Walker in 1945 for an "assertive pacifism", an "internationalism from below" that would deprive "all national governments of the mandate, the power and the means to threaten, prepare or wage war" (*Peace News*, 31 August 1945) helped to move the PPU to set up a "non-violence commission" in November 1949. This body began by studying nonviolence as a means of social change and resistance – the nonviolent resistance of the Danes and the Norwegians under Nazi occupation aroused particular interest. Rigby (1986: 13) records: "By the latter half of 1951, this group had begun to plan a number of nonviolent direct action projects of their own against the presence of US air bases in Britain and the manufacture of atomic weapons." Rigby continues (ibid):

> This was "Operation Gandhi", which was to help form the nucleus for the Emergency Committee for Direct Action against Nuclear War in April 1957, which in turn became the activist core of the Committee of 100. Strictly speaking, the Direct Action Committee (based in the *Peace News* offices in Blackstock Road, London) was formed from the Pacifist Youth Action Group, formed of voluntary workers at *Peace News*. ...A key figure in the development of this nonviolent action (resistance) wing of the peace movement was Hugh Brock, who had taken over the editorship of *Peace News* from Allen Skinner in 1955.

Operation Gandhi's second action (after a sit-down in Whitehall) was in April 1952 at the nuclear bomb factory known initially as Atomic Energy Research Establishment (AERE) Aldermaston, in Berkshire. (The site is now known as the Atomic Weapons Establishment or AWE Aldermaston.) In his detailed survey of *PN* history, Albert Beale notes (op cit: 20): "Jack Selkind, an enthusiast for rambler's rights on *PN*'s distribution staff, had chanced upon the secret establishment a year or more earlier, and first revealed its existence to the peace movement." In his own retrospective account, *PN* editor Hugh Brock (1962) recalled the way the British people learned of the location of their nuclear bomb production plant:

> We knew about the Atomic Energy Research Establishment at Harwell, the much boosted centre of research into the civilian uses of atomic energy, but had no clue to the bomb plant until someone suggested that there was another Atomic Energy Research Establishment in the Reading area which might be the place. It came from one of those types who are gluttons for bus timetables and seem to absorb every detail in them. He had noticed a bus stopping at "the AERE", and it certainly wasn't at Harwell. It was near a little village called Aldermaston. "Well, if it isn't where they're making the bomb, we can protest about all this atomic secrecy," we said. But we felt in our bones that this was the place. So with little more than a hunch to go on, I was sent down to Aldermaston in the early weeks of 1952 to survey the area and report back to "Operation Gandhi"...It was the vast stacks of bricks and piles of girders which most imprinted itself on my mind...Soon a fleet of buses and coaches left from a huge parking area, west of the Falcon and the present main entrance. They carried away a thousand or more builders and other workmen to hostels in neighbouring towns. Here was a "crash programme" being carried out of which almost everyone in Britain was ignorant.

There followed the 19 April 1952 march from the village to the gates of the construction site by 35 pacifists (who travelled to Aldermaston by coach). Brock recalls of the 1952 effort: "How silly we felt as an occasional farm-hand turned to wave at us. We had never paraded with posters in the country before, only in busy shopping centres." With only 35 demonstrators, the organisers decided not to attempt a sit-down at the entrance to the plant. This tiny demonstration laid the basis for the massive Aldermaston marches of the end of the decade that galvanised British society. The Direct Action Committee (DAC), based in the *Peace News* offices, as noted above, initiated the first march to Aldermaston in April 1958.

March organiser Pat Arrowsmith later recalled that the DAC would have been happy if 50 people had turned up for the four-day walk; instead 10,000 people crowded Trafalgar Square (Goff 2004). A considerable part of the massive impact of the march (apart from the film of the event, directed by Lindsay Anderson and narrated by Richard Burton!) derived from the dramatic design that dominated the protest, the mysterious new sign now universally known as the "peace symbol" or the "CND symbol".

The design was created by graphic designer Gerald Holtom, and presented for approval to *Peace News* and the DAC (CND 2008). With the approval of march organisers Hugh Brock (*PN* editor), Michael Randle (*PN* promotions worker), and Pat Arrowsmith (DAC volunteer, working in the *PN* office), briefed in the office by Holtom in February 1958, the new symbol became the dominant image of the 1958 march, carried on badges, banners and lollipop placards to communicate the message of unilateral nuclear disarmament. Holtom later remarked that the enthusiasm of the three committee members (especially Hugh Brock) was critical in overcoming his own later doubts about his innovative design (Miles 2008).

The Aldermaston march (thereafter reversed from Aldermaston to London) was, like Gerard Holtom's design, taken over by the Campaign for Nuclear Disarmament (CND), and both are now considered core elements of CND's identity. The key role of *Peace News* in bringing both into being has been almost entirely forgotten.

Peace News's role within British social movement

This is hardly the only time that *Peace News* has played an influential role within British social movements. Andrew Rigby notes:

> When it was proposed to construct a nuclear power plant at Torness in Scotland, *Peace News* was influential in shaping the nature of the campaign along the lines of autonomous affinity groups and alliances that had been developed at Seabrook, and performed a crucial role as a communication agency and discussion forum for the different local groups (Rigby op cit: 24).

The affinity group style of organising mass civil disobedience had been widely used in the United States in the campaign against the Seabrook nuclear power plant. It was enthusiastically promoted by *PN* in the late 1970s, and it remains a strand of thought and action that continues to be developed by the most active, radical (and disruptive) social movements of the day.

In another direction, the concept of "Greenpeace" was originated by *Peace News* co-editor Paul Wesley in a series of articles which inspired the development of the London Greenpeace Group, which predated the formation of the international campaigning group of the same name (Beale op cit: 38).

PN staff and volunteers have often been influential activists within different campaigns and movements. However, *PN*'s role in the discovery of Aldermaston, the early protest, the 1958 march, laying the basis for the Committee of 100, and the crystallisation of Gerard Holtom's symbol together illustrate perfectly the way in which the institutionalisation of peace journalism in a stable framework has provided a base for high-impact activism. *Peace News*, incidentally, provided a way of bringing together people of energy and determination, together with some of the resources needed for campaigning (office, telephone, duplicator and so on). This has continued to be the case, to varying degrees, over the years.

Counter-journalism

One of trials of being the journal of a social movement (or of several social movements) is the lack of resources this invariably brings. This is one cause of the recourse (to different degrees at different times) to commentary on the news and opinion pieces produced within the mainstream media. It has been a staple of the *Peace News* editorial position that nonviolent and/or radical perspectives, and critical information, have been denied access to the mainstream media, or at the very least have received insufficient attention.

In recent years, this perception has developed into a more searching critique of the mainstream mass media, along the lines of Noam Chomsky and Edward Herman's "propaganda model" of the media. According to Chomsky and Herman, the mainstream media in Western societies such as the United States and Britain are to a very considerable extent free from state interference, but nevertheless function as if they were part of a state propaganda machine; a phenomenon that Chomsky and Herman once described as "brainwashing under freedom". (Chomsky and Herman 1979: 66–79). Rather than serving the societal purposes of truth and justice and democracy, the media serve "the societal purpose served by state education as conceived by James Mill in the early days of the establishment of this system: to 'train the minds of the people to a virtuous attachment to their government', and to the arrangements of the social, economic, and political order more generally" (ibid: 67). The media serve power, not truth.

This is not the place to review the propaganda model, nor to evaluate the thousands of pages of evidence offered in its support. Suffice it to say that within the Chomsky-Herman model, there is considerable room for "leakiness", and for small fragments of disruptive information to bob up in the onrushing river of propaganda. They observe:

> That the media provide some information about an issue . . . proves absolutely nothing about the adequacy or accuracy of media coverage. The media do in fact suppress a great deal of information, but even more important is the way they present a particular fact – its placement, tone, and frequency of repetition – and the framework of analysis in which it is placed (Herman and Chomsky 1988: 15).

According to Chomsky, "the enormous amount of material that is produced in the media and books makes it possible for a really assiduous and committed researcher to gain a fair picture of the real world by cutting through the mass of misrepresentation and fraud to the nuggets hidden within" (Chomsky 1982: 14). Herman and Chomsky go on (op cit: 15):

> That a careful reader, looking for a fact can sometimes find it, with diligence and a skeptical eye, tells us nothing about whether that fact received the attention and context it deserved, whether it was intelligible to most readers, or whether it was effectively distorted or suppressed.

The purpose of journals such as *Peace News*, then, is precisely to search the output of the mass media with diligence and a sceptical eye, cutting through the mass of misrepresentation and fraud to discover nuggets that can help citizens to better understand – and to more effectively alter – the world in which we are living and acting. Part of the purpose of journals such as *Peace News* is precisely to give neglected facts the attention and context they deserve, with the appropriate placement, tone and frequency of repetition.

This could perhaps be incorporated into the framework that has been developed as "peace journalism". It is probably more accurate to describe it as counter-journalism (or "counter journalism"). One small recent example of this counter-journalism within *Peace News* concerns the reporting of mortality estimates in Iraq. In October 2007, *PN* carried a straightforward account of a new nationwide poll in Iraq that seemed to confirm earlier (high) estimates of the human cost of the war in Iraq. Gabriel Carlyle, the *PN* war news editor, wrote:

> British polling agency ORB, which has conducted polls for the BBC and the Financial Services Authority, asked randomly-selected adults in face-to-face interviews in mid-August how many members of their immediate households had "died as a result of the conflict (i.e. as a result of violence rather than a natural death such as old age)". 16 per cent said one family member, 5 per cent said two family members, and 1 per cent said three. The 2005 census counted a total of 4m households, leading ORB to suggest a total of 1,220,580 deaths since 2003 (Carlyle 2007).

In the following issue, a *Peace News* intern from New York State, Polina Aksamentova, described her attempts to investigate the reporting of this shocking statistic, which I reproduce in full:

> When the polling agency ORB's findings came out [see last issue], I was sure that the *Guardian, Independent, New York Times* and other major papers would

cry out in outrage and pronounce in thick, black ink across their respective front pages that 1.2 million Iraqis had died because of the Iraq war: a genocide revealed.

I expected fervent discussion, indignation and controversy across the entire world.

I was wrong: the poll was ignored.

Although it was hardly a surprise to my editor, Milan Rai, I was stunned. I could not believe that journalists of the free world would self-censor themselves. As a journalist student, I was taught that journalists served the public. My disillusionment was great.

34 seconds

The poll came out on 14 September and BBC's *Newsnight* carried the story that night – for 34 seconds. Host Gavin Esler said that the new number is significantly higher than the previous estimate of 650,000, published by the *Lancet* in October 2006 and that the Iraqi government puts the death toll at 75,000.

The following day the *Observer* reported the findings. The shocking 1.2m-dead figure was not given much prominence, however. The ORB story was paired with an article about Alan Greenspan's controversial memoir, and it came second. The headline read: "Greenspan admits Iraq was about oil, as deaths put at 1.2m."

And that was all the coverage the poll received from major media outlets. I couldn't believe it.

Outrage soon poured in from media watchdogs. *Newsnight* editor Peter Barron was one of the few to reply to a letter of complaint from MediaLens [the media monitoring website]. Barron was happy that the programme reported the findings – 34 seconds or not – and wrote that it was important to put them in "context".

My quest

In my own quest for answers, I called the editors of the *Guardian, Observer* and *Independent* (who did not answer), and emailed the writers of the *Observer* story (who did not respond). Hattie Garlick, news editor of *The Times*, told me she had never heard of the ORB poll and then never replied to my email with all the information. I had a rather rude and brisk conversation with a man (he did not identify himself) at the news desk of Channel 4, who abruptly transferred me to the messaging system when I explained my query. And, at the BBC, the advisor who dealt with my complaint, simply answered: "It's a news editor's personal choice what they choose to cover. I can't give you any more information."

To be rudely treated and ignored by journalists, who know exactly how vital and hard interviews can be, was surprising enough. But, to understand why the media was so hostile to the story was still harder.

Four reasons

To me, there could be only four reasons for not publishing the poll: the findings were not newsworthy, the media were ignorant, the polling agency was not credible or the editors were scared of the backlash.

The first two can be dismissed right away. The ORB findings put the death toll in Iraq higher than that of Rwandan genocide – what can be more newsworthy?

All media outlets also had to be aware of the poll. The BBC report and the *Observer*'s story would have alerted them.

Credibility could not have been the issue either. ORB is widely known and respected. Its clients include the Bank of Scotland, the Conservative Party and the BBC itself. The *Guardian* and the White House have quoted ORB surveys in the past.

And, to top it off, the ORB was awarded the international quality standard by SGS Systems and Services Certification, one of the world's leading certification agencies, this August.

Fear

That leaves the worst crime of all: fear. But, fear of what? It is an insult to the journalists of oppressed countries, like Russia and Burma, to even suggest this. What can UK or US media fear from the government? I contacted the editors of MediaLens, but their reply did not help me to understand how this happened.

So, after this unsatisfactory journey I concluded that the media were simply afraid of raising the dust. They were afraid to report such atrocious news; afraid of the number being wrong, maybe; afraid of the political consequences and, in essence, afraid of doing their jobs.

At least, *Newsnight*'s treatment of the poll indicated fear. The BBC was testing the waters. It announced the news briefly and waited for the others to make a move. Certainly, no one could accuse them of not covering the story; but no one could say they were blowing the whistle either. The last 34 seconds were just the thing. And, if there was an outcry they could have always picked it up at the top of the hour the next day with "as we reported yesterday...".

Something of that nature must have passed, because Esler recognised the importance of the findings during broadcast. He said: "The study's likely to fuel controversy over the true, human cost of the war".

But, of course, no controversy ensued, because the media failed at their job – the public remains uniformed.

I was always under the impression that the media – for the most part – helped decipher the lies of the government.

The media's treatment of the ORB poll proved me sadly wrong. It was a blow to my idealism and to my profession of choice (Aksamentova 2007).

A few months later, *PN* reported the apparent confirmation of the ORB findings in a follow-up national poll – a result that was met with a similar media silence (Aksamentova 2008). Yet this is but one of *PN*'s many efforts over the years to correct the systematic failures of mainstream reporting (and to expose the workings of the propaganda system).

Conclusion

The peace journalism practised by *Peace News* has largely followed Jake Lynch and Annabel McGoldrick's injunctions to illuminate "issues of structural and cultural violence, as they bear upon the lives of people in a conflict arena, as part of the explanation for violence"; to frame "conflicts as consisting of many parties, pursuing many goals"; to make "peace initiatives and images of solutions more visible, whoever suggests them"; and to equip citizens "to distinguish between stated positions, and real goals, when judging whether particular forms of intervention are necessary or desirable" (op cit 28–31). Making the peace initiatives of the Afghan Taliban and of the Iranian government "more visible" were particular priorities in *Peace News* in mid-2009.

At the same time, *Peace News* has functioned in many ways outside the framework of Lynch-McGoldrick-style peace journalism. To take one important area, *PN* has not always obeyed the injunction to look at "how shared problems and issues are leading to consequences that all the parties say they never intended", rather than assigning blame. In many conflict situations, *Peace News* has found it appropriate, and indeed necessary, to "assign blame", and to identify (and criticise) the hidden objectives that lie behind the rhetoric of "unintended consequences".

Perhaps more importantly, *Peace News* as an institution has been a vehicle for extra-journalistic activity that has sometimes been of larger historical significance. In recent decades, the merging of the "relief", "resistance" and "reconstruction" strands of nonviolent action within the peace movement has been reflected in the functioning of the newspaper itself. In the age of Indymedia, Blogger, Facebook and Twitter, print media face an uncertain future. It remains to be seen how a radical print journal long committed to functioning as the "reflex" of the minds of its readers and supporters will fare in this new digital and interactive environment. *Peace News* has a rich and inspiring past. It may also have a glorious future – if the movements that it serves grow and prosper, and if they find *PN*'s brand of peace journalism of use as they strive to build a new world in the ruins of the old.

References

Aksamentova, Polina (2007) Self-censored, *Peace News*, issue 2491, November

Aksamentova, Polina (2008) Censored again, *Peace News*, issue 2495, March

Beale, Albert (1986) *Fifty years of* Peace News, *1936–1986*, Nottingham: *Peace News*

Bennett, Tom (2009) Occupation!, *Peace News*, issue 2507, February

Bluemel, Chris (2009)…and the law lost!, *Peace News*, issue 2511, June

Brock, Hugh (1962) Marching to Aldermaston…ten years ago!, *Sanity*, 20 April

Carlyle, Gabriel (2007) 1.2m Iraqi war dead, says poll, *Peace News*, issue 2490, October

Chomsky, Noam and Herman, Edward S. (1979) *The Washington connection and Third World fascism*, Boston MA: South End Press

Chomsky, Noam (1982) *Towards a New Cold War: Essays on the current crisis and how we got there*, London: Sinclair Brown

Clark, Howard (2010) *Peace News*, Young, Nigel (ed.) *The Oxford international encyclopedia of peace*, Oxford: Oxford University Press

CND (2008) The disarmament symbol. Available online at http://www.cnduk.org/pages/ed/cnd_sym.html, accessed on 6 August 2009

Cobham, Sarah (2009) Annexing the Jordan, *Peace News*, issue 2507, February

Curran, James and Seaton, Jean (2003) *Power without responsibility: The press, broadcasting and new media in Britain*, London: Routledge

Fountain, Nigel (1988) *Underground: The London alternative press, 1966–74*, London: Taylor and Francis

Goff, Hannah (2004) Peace campaigners return to Aldermaston, BBC News Online, 7 April. Available online at http://news.bbc.co.uk/1/hi/uk/3575175.stm, accessed on 6 August 2009

Herman, Edward S. and Chomsky, Noam (1988) Propaganda mill: The media churn out the "official line", *Progressive*, June pp 14–5

Kelly, Kathy (2009) The strongest weapon of all, *Peace News*, issue 2506

Linnell, Jenny (2009a) Israel: A terrorist state, *Peace News*, issue 2506

Linnell, Jenny (2009b) Surviving Gaza, *Peace News*, issue 2508

Linnell, Jenny (2009c) In Gaza, the war goes on – against farmers, against fishermen, *Peace News*, issue 2510

Lynch, Jake and McGoldrick, Annabel (2005) *Peace journalism*, Stroud: Hawthorn Press

Miles, Barry (2008) *Peace: 50 years of protest*, Pleasantville NY: Readers Digest

Rigby, Andrew (1986) *Peace News*, 1936–1986: An overview, Chester, Gail and Rigby, Andrew (eds), *Articles of peace: Celebrating fifty years of* Peace News, Bridport, Dorset: Prism Press pp 7–26

Starhawk (2009) Starhawk on Gaza, *Peace News*, issue 2506

Young, Sarah (2009) Coming out of the Informer Closet? *Peace News*, issue 2510

13

Mediating peace? Military radio in the Balkans and Afghanistan

SARAH MALTBY

War is now fundamentally conducted with and through information. This is evident in the increasing military reliance on information and communication technologies and the use of intelligence, deception and perception management to pursue a competitive advantage over an adversary (Hirst 2001; Molander, Riddile and Wilson 1996; Webster 2003). Elsewhere I have argued that the media are of critical importance to the strategic organisation of military campaigns, where the practice of war is enacted through, and is dependent upon, the media's reporting of it (Maltby 2012). Here, I shift the focus from strategic military media management in war operations to tactically focused military influencing activities in peace-building campaigns.

Informed by ethnographic fieldwork with the military and drawing on case studies from Bosnia and Afghanistan, this chapter describes how the military use local radio in the conduct of peace building and conflict resolution operations. I consider how audiences are identified, what strategies are devised to appeal to and elicit responses from these audiences and how these strategies impact on other aspects of an operation, particularly counter insurgency. Utilising symbolic interactionism as a means through which we can understand this phenomenon, this chapter explains how military informants position the objectives of radio influencing activities in terms resonant with some of the key principles of peace journalism, namely: a commitment to providing a voice to the voiceless; a promotion of peace through open dialogue and an orientation to solution (and resolution) (see Galtung 1968; Kempf 2003 and 2007; Lynch and McGoldrick 2005; Keeble 2009; Carroll 1972). The extent to which we can consider these claims an adequate description of empirical reality is a question that needs further investigation and is not specifically addressed here. Neither is this chapter suggesting that the military's use of radio is a form of peace journalism; in many ways they are inimical. Instead, based upon claims made by the military, this is a descriptive account of an interesting phenomenon worthy of consideration due to the military positioning of their media activities as peace oriented.

Information warfare: Influencing activity in context

Information is now an integral part of *all* military warfare strategy as traditional boundaries between nations, governments, and public and private interests have become increasingly blurred. These conditions have not only accentuated the vulnerability of information systems to enemy attack but also emphasised the need for the military to maintain vital support through perception management and influence (Molander, Riddile and Wilson op cit; Hirst op cit). Both help facilitate the maintenance of civilian morale and support within the conflict zone; factors that are increasingly critical to success in the execution of aggressive and peace-building campaigns. This is especially true with the rise of insurgency and "new wars", where non-legitimised, guerrilla tactics are employed to destabilise an opponent and expose their vulnerabilities (see Laqueur 1977; Kaldor 2001). One such vulnerability is an opponent's information activities, used in part to influence the perceptions and actions of others within the battle space. Yet, information activities are not restricted to the domain of insurgents. As Western forces are experiencing, kinetic power and technological superiority no longer guarantee operational success. In the execution of insurgent asymmetric warfare there is symmetry in the need for *all* forces to influence others in their favour to achieve and give sustainability to operational objectives. It is within this scenario that military Information Operations can be situated.

Information Operations is one of a number of military information activities that attempts to harness the power of information to shape and influence the conflict environment. In British military doctrine it is defined as a set of "co-ordinated actions undertaken to influence an adversary or potential adversary in support of political and military objectives by undermining his will, cohesion and decision-making ability".[1] These coordinated activities include psychological operations, electronic warfare, computer network operations and deception; all of which seek to influence a course of action(s) that both civilians and the adversary may make.

One component of Information Operations is Influence Activity. This is the primary means through which the military attempt to influence and undermine the will[2] of the adversary to fight.[3] This is considered achievable by influencing the adversary's perceptions of their own actions (for example, by undermining both the legitimacy of the leadership or eroding the moral power base) *and* influencing the perceptions of civilians. By communicating messages of moral and physical support to those who oppose the adversary the military believe that they can potentially "affect" the battle space, enhancing opportunities to advance their own cause. Using influencing activity tools such as media, the military try to promote particular themes and messages that "seek to persuade, convince, deter, disrupt, compel or coerce audiences to take a particular course of action, or to assist, encourage and reassure those that are following a particular course of action".[4]

These tactically focused activities are defined as distinct from strategically focused media operations in a number of ways. In particular, whilst media operations disseminate information through the global media, information distributed with an Information Operations aim is editorially controlled, precisely selected and distributed through politically or military-owned media.[5] One such media is radio. Categorised by the military under the "psychological operations" banner, radio provides a key means through which the military can communicate to mass audiences, especially in regions where hostilities or limited technological capabilities prohibit more sophisticated means of contact.[6]

Radio influencing as impression management

In order to empirically ground military influencing radio in a symbolic interactionist framework, and to highlight the resonances with peace journalism in military accounts, the forthcoming discussion draws upon data about two military radio stations. The first is Oksigen, set up by NATO in 1999 in post-conflict Bosnia Herzegovina to unite audiences in the progression towards a peaceful, multicultural state. In an effort to encourage allegiance to particular presenters its programming was "personality led"[8] and based around popular dance music culture, particularly techno and electronic music from around Europe. Broadcasts included syndicated programmes from DJs such as Boy George, the British club scene featured prominently and DJs were regularly invited to host "sessions" or club events. In addition, Oksigen hosted a number of outside broadcasts and awareness campaigns, for instance at the Sarajevo Film Festival and the UK Brit Awards and a weapons amnesty. It ceased broadcasting in 2005.[7]

The second radio station is Rana[9] FM, launched by the Canadian military in 2007 in Afghanistan in support of NATO peace-building and counter insurgency operations. It broadcasts in the Pashtu language and is available via live stream on the internet. The format is currently 40 per cent speech and 60 per cent music but these proportions are likely to shift as news programming is gradually introduced. The music is based on a form of Afghan pop culture, incorporating the latest Pashtun music mixed with chart songs from Afghanistan, Iran, Pakistan and Bollywood hits.[10] Founded on the success of Oksigen, it also incorporates a similar "cult of celebrity" across its presenters and provides a section on women's issues and fashion. Rana continues to broadcast in the Kandahar region.[11]

There are clear differences between these two stations. While Oksigen was launched in post-conflict conditions, Rana FM broadcasts in a hostile environment where fighting continues between NATO forces and the Taliban. Influencing objectives in Afghanistan are, therefore, less clear-cut than in Bosnia Herzegovina in 1999. Primarily, intentions to establish a democratic regime in Afghanistan are complicated by ongoing counter insurgency activity against the Taliban, especially when the success of both is founded on the involvement of the civilian population. This is evident in the type of influence the military are attempting to exert through Rana FM and through the ways in which broadcasters articulate the objectives of the radio station:

> To generate a stable, secure Afghanistan that can develop to be a nation that Afghanis are comfortable with but that ties in neatly into the overall principles of the family of nations. So, in other words, to help build whatever form of democracy that they get; and it will never be anything that we have dreamed of because they are culturally very different. But where they are not harbouring terrorists, they have a nation that they are happy living in and where people don't get slaughtered everyday, where they have a modicum of human rights and where they are not a breeding ground for groups that will cause mass mayhem around the world. The broadcasting media is used to achieve that (Rana FM broadcaster, in an interview with the author).

In addition, Oksigen and Rana FM are aimed at quite different populations in terms of their experiences of conflict and their cultural backgrounds and thus require different forms of radio programming. Despite this, similarities exist in the objectives and organisation of both stations as an influencing activity tool. According to those broadcasters involved, both are oriented towards peace building and establishing a safe and secure environment for, and with the involvement of, civilians in the region. At a fundamental level, the achievability of these objectives is predicated on generating and maintaining favourable impressions of the military activity among target audiences, including impressions of the radio station itself through which they can encourage allegiance. It is through the generation of such impressions that the military believe they are able to attain influence, particularly in terms of empowering and mobilising civilians to unite in the cause for democratic peace.

To this end, we can understand radio influencing activity in accordance with Goffman's (1959) notion of impression management where the radio broadcast is a performance intended to influence the impressions that others come to formulate. Situated within Goffman's notion of the "interaction order", impression management is the act of managing one's identity during social interaction in a manner that attempts to influence and control the conduct of others:

> This control is achieved largely by influencing the definition of the situation which others come to formulate, and he can influence this definition by expressing himself in such as way as to give them the kind of impression that will lead them to act voluntarily in accordance with his own plan (ibid: 15).

Radio broadcasts are a collective team performance of impression management where broadcasters collaborate to project and sustain particular definitions of the station, their military and its activities in the region.

Target audiences: The voiceless

To manage impressions effectively, the military must develop a sense of the audience for whom radio performances are constructed, and among whom impressions will be manifest. They are able to identify their audience by considering the likely responses to their impressions of others. Those whose responses have a significant impact on tactical activities in the region are thereby identified as the audience for whom definitions are constructed. According to Schattschneider's model of conflict, direct partners to a feud are usually less interested in communicating with each and more interested in fortifying their relative position by attracting others to join them (1960 cited in Peleg 2007). To this end, whilst the military classify the adversary as one of their influencing activity audiences, the primary audience with whom they attempt to communicate are civilians in the region. Within the civilian category, a key target audience for the military are the "uncommitted".[12] The uncommitted are those who have not – or not yet – aligned themselves to a particular fighting force or ideology. Essentially they are the "swing voters" whom *all* forces will attempt to influence in their favour.

With this in mind, the "uncommitted" target audience for Oksigen radio in Bosnia Herzegovina was the young, specifically those aged between 15 and

25 years old. Given that the objective of Oksigen was to unite Serbians, Croats and Bosnians towards a multi-cultural, ethnically tolerant and cohesive state, the young were considered to be the best audience through which this could be achieved, as they constituted the next generation and their experiences and attitudes would impact upon the future of the region (Bailey 2008). Similarly, the main target audience for Rana FM in Kandahar is also the young. According to David Bailey, an Information Operations broadcaster, if the military are successful in their radio influencing attempts they believe it is the young who will form the "new Afghanistan in the image they want" (cited in Whisenhunt 2008). The targeting of young civilians is evident in the programming of both Oksigen and Rana FM that has been specifically designed to meet the perceived needs and desires of this audience group. Essentially, by identifying and incorporating into the performance what they believe will appeal to the target audience, broadcasters hope to generate favourable impressions through which they can engender loyalty to the station, and in turn, influence audiences.

In Afghanistan, however, within this category of the young uncommitted, Rana FM also attempts to reach specific sub groups. The first is young men of fighting age, especially those who are vulnerable to recruitment by the Taliban (Best 2009). These "vulnerables" are identified as young men who have low levels of subjective well-being due to a lack of economic and social prosperity and disillusionment with the current political climate in Afghanistan (Spencer 2009). They are the classic "swing voters" whose poor living conditions have the potential to engender a leaning towards insurgency as a form of empowerment or security. By attempting to influence and give voice to this group, the military hope that they can increase support for NATO activities that aim to provide security and economic prospects through legitimate means. The secondary – not unrelated – function of targeting this group is to prevent their conscription into Taliban activity (ibid). Ultimately, it is felt that attempts to address the concerns of these young men through radio broadcasts may encourage their engagement with legitimate political processes to bring about the new, peaceful Afghanistan.

In a similar vein, Rana FM is also targeted towards Afghani women (Best op cit). This is for a number of – not always cohesive – reasons that exemplify the ways in which broadcasters believe they are providing a voice to the voiceless. First, within the military community, Afghan culture is predominantly characterised as one that oppresses women in their day-to-day lives. A crucial aspect of this is the exclusion of women from the power building processes. Haugegaard (2009) argues that this is reflected in Taliban ideology where members' contact with women is equated with the weakening of strength and morale. Indeed, there is general agreement among military members that it is the women who stand to lose the most if the Taliban seize greater power. Consequently, NATO forces in Afghanistan (ISAF) have invested in attempts to empower women by providing access to knowledge of government policies (that they might otherwise be denied) and by offering forums in which they can network safely and debate their own rights (ibid). One such resource is Rana FM. Of course, there are clear problems with some of these intentions, not least that they are based upon Western assumptions about the role of women in Afghani culture. However, NATO forces hope that if their support for women is seen and recognised, "moderate" Afghani men may also be encouraged to empower women and, as a secondary consequence, offer active assistance to ISAF in the fight against the Taliban (ibid).

Second, drawing upon research into the role of women in counter insurgency activity, Haugegaard (ibid) identifies women as having a critical role in the management of the community in which insurgents may operate, particularly with regard to raising the next generation. It is the women who are identified as being key to the possibility of engendering a change in attitude towards the Taliban and ISAF by virtue of their power in the home. On the one hand, therefore, women are recognised as those who are at most need of empowerment due to their subjugated gendered position in Afghan culture. Radio influencing in this regard tends to be positioned as an essentially altruistic activity in military accounts. At the same time, the empowerment of women has a secondary function; by influencing women the military have the potential to influence others with whom the women interact, particularly potential or existing insurgents. However, the tensions that may arise from both these integrated objectives remains underexplored in military accounts, which raises ethical questions regarding the safety and future of audience members who may be persuaded to act in particular ways in a culture that is often quite different to Western interpretations of it. These questions are particularly important given that radio broadcasts are targeted at those whose age and status render them potentially the most susceptible to influence.

Despite this, there is some truth to the categorisation of these audience groups as those most neglected by the power structures that inform their daily lives and those who have the most to lose if peace processes are disabled by insurgent activities. In many ways they are the victims of others' power brokering, with little hope of affecting change without assistance from organisations such as NATO. As Carroll (op cit) argues, peace can be best advanced through the empowerment of non-state actors, particularly those who are otherwise isolated. This resonates with the military's identification of their target audiences as the vulnerable, the voiceless and those most in need of a platform for expression and action.

It is perhaps for these reasons – as much as their ability to assist with counter insurgency – that the "uncommitted" become the key target audience for Rana FM. Without them, traditional power struggles which have a definite impact upon the daily lives of these audiences, may continue and conflict may potentially erupt again. It is within this framework that the military attempt to cater for, and to, the voiceless as those most able to affect positive change and bring about peace and stability. This is particularly evident in their identification of Afghan women as a key target audience for Rana FM. By encouraging women to engage in power building processes they are attempting to ensure the place of women in the new, democratic Afghanistan. As one broadcaster stated:

> There was one woman who said: "I have learnt enough from listening to the radio to know that when I go into that ballot box it's between me and Allah" and we deem that to be an amazing success that a woman for the first time in her life had the right to be separated from her husband by a screen and to put her cross or her thumb print into a box (Rana FM broadcaster, in an interview with the author)

For the military, radio offers opportunities to provide audiences with information on which they can make their own decisions and choices. Similarly, it is through the same medium that they are able to gauge the needs and desires of these groups in order to progress their operations effectively.

Interaction and influence: Opening dialogue

A literal application of Goffman's notion of impression management has only limited relevance in this context because its analytical understanding of performance derives from direct, co-present interaction between performer and audience. In contrast, military radio broadcasting is predicated on a non co-present relationship with the audience, enacted through the medium of radio. This non co-present interaction enables communication with mass audiences simultaneously, especially in highly volatile conflict zones where face-to-face interaction is almost impossible. This is particularly true of regions such as Afghanistan where the military are at risk of attack from the "hidden" enemy – a classic insurgency tactic – and are thus forced to travel in armoured vehicles or wear body armour. Not only does this disable opportunities for meaningful interaction with civilians, but also undermines messages of reassurance about regional safety (Bailey 2008a).

Moreover, civilians are also at risk of attack from the Taliban if believed to be collaborating with military armed forces. Consequently, whilst the military express a reluctance to make their contact with civilians publicly visible, civilians tend to avoid engagement with the military for their own safety. Public, face-to-face interaction between military and civilians can therefore be extremely difficult. In contrast, the interaction through technologies such as radio is invisible (in the literal sense), anonymous and much safer for all parties involved.

Co-presence does not, therefore, mark the analytical boundary of radio influencing impression management. Instead, interaction between broadcasters and performers is essentially predicated on a "distanced" relationship. Through this relationship the military attempt to engender support for their activities. Yet, given the nature of the relationship, audience "support" is inherently difficult to determine. As one military member stated: "Just because you are transmitting does not mean that they are listening" (Morgan 2009). Hence, the degree to which the success of a broadcast performance can be measured is limited. For this reason, the generation of specific *actions* among specific audience groups is critical.

Actions are measurable in that they involve an expression of an act in response to broadcast performances. The generation of actions has a dual function. First, by virtue of their measurability, they offer some indication as to the success of the radio performance reach and influence.

> In the Influence Operations environment, we need to know if we have listeners, and what will those listeners do? . . . . The only way we can do that is by having audience interactivities (Bailey 2008a).

Actions are thus tangible through these "audience interactivities", which include radio phone-ins, music request slots, talk shows, SMS messaging and staged broadcast events. Opportunities for interaction via these means have been incorporated in to the programming of both Rana FM and Okisgen as key components of the performance in order to gauge who the audience are and why they are listening.

Secondly, these audience interactivities are used to facilitate an open dialogue with audiences in a manner that will help achieve military influencing aims. Open dialogue is apparent in two forms. First, broadcasters attempt to construct a channel of communication between themselves and the audience, either "on air" or "off air". As one Oksigen broadcaster stated: "We encouraged people to ring up and talk about things. If they wanted to do it off the air then we would." Through this direct interaction the military attempt to influence in their favour the responses of audiences, but also try to gain a sense of the realities of their audience groups. As one broadcaster stated:

> When you are running a radio station you get feedback from your audience in a way that nobody else can. There is no peer pressure: when you ring a radio station you can be anonymous, you don't have fear, you can say what you want (Rana FM broadcaster, in an interview with the author).

Hence, when young Taliban members ring up the radio station to ask questions about military activities – as the military state they do – this is taken as an indication that attempts to "open up dialogue" are working.[13] At times, success is measured as much by the act of initiating contact on behalf of the audience member as the content of the discussion.[14] Once contact has been established, the military may utilise this further to achieve their own operational objectives as one Oksigen broadcaster indicated:

> A lot of teenagers were asking questions about the future of their country. We were trying to put their minds at ease and to give them a message of hope.

The second form of open dialogue is the generation of a forum for dialogue *between* audiences that is safe and secure and where audience members – particularly those usually devoid of a voice – can express themselves openly with no perceived risk of reprisals. In this regard, the female audience of Rana FM are actively encouraged to express their "hopes, dreams and fears" through talk shows and phone-ins (Bailey 2008). By offering women a forum through which they can openly share their experiences and feelings, whilst also having the opportunity to challenge and express their frustrations, it is hoped that they may be encouraged to assert their power, especially in relation to men:

> We had one illiterate woman who wasn't able to write but she had made these wonderful poems up and she recited them, she read her two minute poem that she had put together about the rights of women ... and then we had phone calls in from a doctor who said: "The only way to lead this country forward is the Islamic way with the holy Koran and I want the male members of family to look to the Koran because it says that the women have the right to do this, don't turn your back on our religion, allow what the prophet Mohamed said." And we carried messages like that and it was successful because it was women supporting themselves in a way that their culture would know (Rana FM broadcaster, in an interview with the author).

Of course, accounts like the one above position the "opening of dialogue" in somewhat utopian terms. By emphasising the supportive nature of such forums, the elements dedicated to persuasion and influence are not adequately acknowledged. As such, they may reflect a self-legitimation of military practice more than a description of audience realities. Nonetheless the military's commitment to create these forums for dialogue *with* and *between* audiences is suggestive of how they understand broadcasts as a means through which to listen to, gauge and act upon audience accounts. In this way, communication via open dialogue becomes a critical determinant of peace building (and counter insurgency) as it raises consciousness of, and attentiveness to, potential solutions for empowerment, stability and peace.

Countering adversary influence: Orientation to solution

So far I have argued that in their construction of radio performances the military attempt to incorporate that which will both appeal to, and elicit action from, target audiences, particularly the young. It is through these performances that they attempt to achieve peace-building objectives such as uniting populations and empowering the vulnerable. From a symbolic interactionist perspective, these goals reflect the ways in which the military interpret and attribute meaning to their own actions, and the actions of others, in order to direct and guide the performance (see Blumer 1962).

In the same manner, military radio performances are also used to counter the adversary's influencing activities; particularly those that might further encourage conflict. Rana FM radio performances are particularly useful at demonstrating this point, not least because the Taliban are an identifiable adversary who also engage in information activities. It is here that the third element of influencing performances resonates with those of peace journalism in the orientation to "solution" (see Kempf 2003; 2007). Of course, what might be considered a solution for one is a not necessarily a solution for another. In this discussion, "solution" is understood in accordance with how it is interpreted by the military.

Given that the Taliban are perceived as the greatest threat to civilian safety and long-term social and economic prosperity, it is by identifying the weaknesses and strengths of Taliban influencing activities that the military devise their "orientations" to solutions. In the same manner that all other aspects of performances are built around the actions of others, Rana FM broadcasters consider the real and anticipated action of the Taliban (i.e. what they are doing, or about to do) and construct the performance according to what they take into account (see Goffman op cit: 47). With this in mind, one of the fundamental aims of Rana FM performances is to highlight to audiences that they have a choice with regard to the types of actions desired from NATO (Bains 2008). As one Rana FM broadcaster commented: "We target anyone that wants to question and give them the choice to make a decision, not forcing them."

This is in contrast to Taliban influencing activities that are argued by the military to be founded on the dissemination of threats. For example, Best (op cit) argues that the Taliban have shifted their messages from "join us" to those that threaten civilians and their families if they are seen to working with NATO forces. Consequently, Rana FM broadcast performances are deliberately constructed in a "friendly" manner to counter aggressive Taliban messages and instil confidence and trust in NATO activities (Morgan 2009). By focusing on audience empowerment, rather than the generation of fear, the military believe that they are offering choices to audiences.

In addition, Taliban messages are argued to be devoid of references to economic, social and political development in Afghanistan (Foxley 2009). Instead, they stress battle victories and body counts (particularly of NATO casualties), which may further generate impressions of unstable security among audiences (ibid). In part, this emphasis on body counts is identified as a weakness of Taliban Information Operations as it suggests a lack of wider strategic aims. By identifying this weakness, and in accordance with their own aims, the military consider it important to address the real concerns of the audience (ibid). These are identified as ranging from wider political and economic concerns including regional security and the rights of women, to everyday concerns such as lice prevention in children and the rise (or fall) of the local football team – sometimes within one broadcast. As a Rana FM Promotional broadcast details:

> One minute they'll [audiences] be listening to a short story about a soccer tournament in Kandahar, and the next a few tips about how to prevent your child from getting lice. That way, women and men get a glimpse into each others' interests, helping to close the gender gap. (Rana FM promotional broadcast for NATO members).

In this way, the military's attempts to offer solutions to issues that effect everyday life *and* peace-building processes is resonant with Kempf's (2003) notion of solution-oriented coverage. In particular, the military emphasise that peace building is unlikely to succeed unless the root causes of insurgency alliance are addressed (see also Kempf 2007). For Afghani audiences these are identified as economic and social insecurity, exclusion from political processes and the oppression of women. Thus, in the construction of their performances, military broadcasters attempt to address and offer potential solutions to these problems through audience engagement. In effect the military suggest they are attempting to enhance the lifestyles of audiences to progress peace processes (see also Galtung 1968). As suggested in the above quotation, wider, significant issues related to social and economic security are introduced through discussions about unremarkable, everyday, routine subjects. By focusing on, and attempting to solve, these problems the military believe they can stop the cycle of violence associated with insurgency. Ultimately, through these efforts the military attempt to influence audiences in their favour, whilst countering Taliban attempts to do the same.

Peace journalism and military radio: Inimical or aligned?

This chapter has been centrally concerned with describing how the military use tactical influencing activities in peace building campaigns. Using examples from radio in Bosnia Herzegovina and Afghanistan, and utilising symbolic interactionism as a theoretical framework, I have argued that radio-influencing activities can be understood as a form of impression management used to influence the impressions generated among, and the conduct of, target audiences. Moreover, drawing upon the military's own accounts of their radio influencing activities I have attempted to show how military informants position the objectives of radio influencing activities in terms resonant with some of the key principles of peace journalism. In particular, I highlight that the perceived empowerment of civilians, particularly the young and vulnerable, is situated as a military commitment to the voiceless. Similarly, their incorporation of "audience interactivities" is used – in part – to generate a safe, anonymous environment through which to open up dialogue. Lastly, in their counter-influencing activities they place an emphasis on solutions in order to achieve conflict resolution and peace.

Am I, therefore, suggesting that military radio influencing activity is a form of peace journalism? Definitely not. It is neither independent nor objective. As a military owned medium the necessary critical distance needed for peace journalism is unobtainable (see Kempf 2003). Indeed, even those working in radio influencing activity argue that despite their aspirations to instil peace in a region they are not peace journalists:

> I would really like to be identified with peace journalism but there is a hostile reaction to what we do because we do not apply the principles of British or Western journalism. If it's coming from us it's considered blatant propaganda.

I am not in a position to say that there are two sides to every story, I simply say to the target audience please trust me, I am providing a balance, I am talking peace, I am talking about non-violent confrontation. I would like to say that we are peace journalists but you need to prove objectivity and neutrality and you do that by bringing different views. In the environments that we are working in we can't always bring the "other view" (Rana FM broadcaster, in an interview with the author).

Thus, there is recognition among the military themselves that their influencing activities (in whatever medium) and peace journalism are to some extent inimical. Despite this, their self-proclaimed orientation to peace in radio stations such as Okisgen and Rana FM is worthy of note and raises some interesting questions. In particular, is the discourse of peace and empowerment used to legitimate military practices? At times the military's lack of real critical engagement and apparent cultural naivety (especially evident in attitudes towards the role of women) intimates this. At the same time, the descriptions provided here appear to show definite efforts to promote peace and open dialogue with civilians for *their* protection and *their* long term prosperity and it is these processes that need further critical evaluation if we are to better understand the use of influencing activities in modern peace building operations.

Notes

1 DTIO Policy Paper, 22 February 2001, cited *Joint Warfare Publication* 3–80, 2002: 2–1.
2 The other component is categorised as "Counter Command Activity" which seeks to attack an adversary's capabilities (*Joint Warfare Publication* 3–80, 2002: 2–2).
3 *JWP* 3–80, 2002: 2–4 [caps in original documentation].
4 *JWP* 3–80, 2002: 2–3.
5 See *JWP* 3–45, 2001.
6 In British military doctrine Psychological Operations (Psyops) is defined as "planned psychological activities designed to influence attitudes and behaviour affecting the achievement of political and military objectives" (*JWP* 3–80, 2002: Glossary-5). Psyops messages are delivered by various means such as print, radio, TV, loudspeaker, face to face, the internet or mobile communications (ibid: 2A-1).
7 For more information about Oksigen FM see: http://www.davidbaileymbe.com/oksigen_original/home.htm\.
8 Data obtained via interview with Okisgen FM broadcaster 2008.
9 In Arabic the word Rana means "light" so the strapline for the radio station means "light in your life". This is already suggestive of the positive image that the Canadian forces are attempting to communicate via the radio station.

10   From interview with Rana FM broadcaster 2008.
11   For more information about Rana FM see: http://www.ranafm.org/.
12   *JWP* 3–80, 2002: 2–1.
13   From interview with Rana FM broadcaster 2008.
14   From interview with Rana FM broadcaster 2008.

References

Bailey, David (2008) *Broadcasting in an operational environment: Results related radio.* Paper presented to Information Operations (IO) conference, Cranfield University, United Kingdom, 5–6 March

Bailey, David (2008a) A Voice for IO Broadcasting, Whisenhunt, John, An interview with David Bailey, *IO Sphere*, Fall

Bains, Paul (2008) *Evaluating the effect of the fear appeal in advertising, implications for information operations campaigns.* Paper presented to IO Conference at Cranfield University, United Kingdom, 5–6 March

Best, Allan (2009) *Afghanistan: A Canadian perspective.* Paper presented to IO and Influencing Activity symposium, Cranfield University, 4–5 March

Blumer, Herbert (1962) Society as symbolic interaction, *Human behaviour and social processes*, Rose, A. (ed.) London: Routledge pp 179–92

Carroll, Bernice (1972) Peace research: The cult of power. *The Journal of Conflict Resolution*, Vol. 16, No. 4 pp 585–616

Foxley, Tim (2009) *Where will Afghanistan be in 1, 5 and 10 years time?* Paper presented to IO and Influencing Activity symposium, Cranfield University, 4–5 March

Galtung, Johan (1968) Peace, Sills, D. (ed.) (1968) *International encyclopedia of the social sciences*, Vol. 2, New York: Macmillan pp 487–96

Goffman, Erving (1959) *The presentation of self in everyday life*, New York: Doubleday

Goffman, Erving (1969) *Strategic interaction*, Oxford: Basil Blackwell

Hirst, Paul (2001) *War and power in the 21st century*, Cambridge: Polity

Haugegaard, Rikke (2009) *Female power in Afghanistan: Local women's contribution to the fight against Taliban.* Paper presented to IO and Influencing Activity symposium, Cranfield University, 4–5 March

Joint Warfare Publication 3–80 (2002) Information Operations: Joint Doctrine and Concepts Centre: Available online at http://www.mod.uk/linked_files/jdcc/publications/jwp3_80.pdf, accessed August 2003

Joint Warfare Publication 0–01: British Defence Doctrine: Joint Doctrine and Concepts Centre second edition. Available online at http://www.mod.uk/DefenceInternet/AboutDefence/CorporatePublications/DoctrineOperationsandDiplomacyPublications/JWP/Jwp001BritishDefenceDoctrine.htm, accessed August 2003

Joint Warfare Publication 3–45 (2002) Media Operations: Joint Doctrine and Concepts Centre: http://www.mod.uk/DefenceInternet/AboutDefence/CorporatePublications/DoctrineOperationsandDiplomacyPublications/JWP/Jwp345MediaOperations.htm, accessed August 2003

Kaldor, Mary (2001) *New and old wars: Organised violence in a global era* Cambridge: Polity Press, second edition

Keeble, Richard (2009) *Ethics for journalists*, London: Routledge, second edition

Kempf, Wilhelm (2003) Constructive conflict coverage – A social-psychological research and development program, Conflict and Communication Online, Vol. 2, No. 2. Available online at http://www.cco.regener-online.de/2003_2/pdf_2003_2/kempf_engl.pdf, accessed January 2009

Kempf, Wilhelm (2007) Two experiments focusing on de-escalation oriented coverage of post-war conflicts, Shinar, Dov and Kempf, Wilhelm (eds) *Peace journalism: The state of the art*, Berlin: Verlag Irena Regena pp 136–57

Laqueur, Walter (1977) *Guerrilla: A historical and critical study*, London: Weidenfeld and Nicolson

Lawrence, Darren (2009) *The limits of information operations and military influence*. Paper presented to IO and Influencing Activity symposium, Cranfield University, 4–5 March

Lynch, Jake. and McGoldrick, Annabel (2005) *Peace journalism*, Stroud: Hawthorn Press

Maltby, Sarah (2012) *Media military management: Negotiating the frontline*, London: Routledge, forthcoming

Molander, Roger., Riddile, Andrew. and Wilson, Peter (1996) *Strategic information management: A new face of war*, RAND

Morgan, Chris (2009) *UK land forces in Helmand*. Paper presented to IO and Influencing Activity symposium, Cranfield University, 4–5 March

Peleg, Samuel (2007) Peace journalism through the lens of conflict theory: Analysis and Practice" in Conflict and Communication Online, 5 (2). Available at http://www.cco.regener-online.de, accessed January 2009

Schattschneider, Elmer (1960) *The semisovereign people: A realist's view of democracy in America*. New York: Holt, Rinehart and Winston

Spencer, Claire (2009) *Intel: Inside the challenges for research*. Paper presented to IO and Influencing Activity symposium, Cranfield University, 4–5 March

Webster, Frank (2003) Information warfare in an age of globalization. Daya Thussu, Daya Kishan and Freedman, Des (eds) *War and the media*, London: Sage pp 57–69

Whisenhunt, John (2008) An interview with David Bailey, *IO Sphere*, Fall

SECTION 3. PEACE JOURNALISM'S CRITIQUE: TRANSFORMING THE MAINSTREAM

14

Conflict gives us identity: Media and 'the Cyprus problem'

SUSAN DENTE ROSS AND SEVDA ALANKUS

The origins of contemporary conflicts around the globe are multiple, complex and shifting. Historical enmities, ethnic and cultural divides, conflicting nationalisms and territorial and resource claims – and more – come into play as (post) modern nation-states, sub-national groups, and supra-national formations struggle for autonomy, sovereignty and supremacy. Yet, consistently, the media play a significant part in the production, representation and legitimisation of violent conflict, militarisation and war as normal and efficient means for addressing contemporary problems.

Perhaps nowhere in the world are the multiple intersections of media and war more visible than on the island of Cyprus. Situated at the junction of three continents and populated for five centuries, Cyprus has always stood inside, outside and alongside the contested geography of Europe. Divided in two *de facto* in 1974, the island has been represented in the international arena for the past three decades only by the (Greek) Republic of Cyprus. The Republic joined the European Union in 2004, but the northern third of the island (the Turkish Republic of North Cyprus, TRNC) was excluded from EU membership (see Boedeltje et al 2007).

Earlier that year, the UN-led settlement referendum (the so-called Annan Plan) that would have re-unified the island was defeated for lack of majority support from Greek Cypriots, leading to the official exclusion of Turkish Cypriots from both the EU benefits and commitments and from being "European". Despite both Turkish and Greek Cypriots claiming "European-ness" within their imagined identities (thanks to British colonial rule of Cyprus from 1914 until 1960), only Greek Cypriots received the imprimatur of Europe. Turkish Cypriots' claim to European-ness was postponed at best, prompting a struggle for re-articulation of their identity that contributed to the ongoing, intractable conflict holding sway over the island (Calotychos 2000; Killoran 2000; Papadakis 1998; Yashin 2000). The conflict maintaining today's divided Cyprus is at once a struggle between two external [m]otherlands and an "internal" Cypriot struggle over territorial sovereignty, national self-definition and identity (Bhabba 1990: 301; Richmond 2002; Volkan 1979).

Given existing knowledge of the role news media play in exacerbating and perpetuating inter-communal conflicts, this study examines the press coverage of the 2008 election of a new president in the (Greek) Republic of Cyprus and the subsequent bilateral initiatives towards settlement of "the Cyprus problem" as a logical opportunity for the implementation of peace journalism by the media. The central question addressed here is whether and to what degree different organisations of the press altered their representation of "the internal others" across the divided island to reduce mutual demonisation during this period of potential peacemaking. More specifically, we examine Cypriot and international news content in 2008 related to the presidential elections in the Cyprus Republic, the initiation of bilateral "settlement" talks, and the highly symbolic opening of the Lokmacı crossing, which allowed passage between the two sides of the divided capital city, to explore the contributions of the print media in North Cyprus toward reconciliation of "the Cyprus problem" (Alankuş 2006; Bailie and Azgin 2000).

Recognising the strategic role of discourse, this study problematises the binary language embedded in war journalism and in Orientalist representations (Galtung 1971; Said 1978). The authors' contribution to the field of peace journalism is to highlight how Galtung's (op cit) dichotomy of war vs peace journalism as well as war journalism's focus on "two sides" to every conflict tie into the profoundly entrenched dualities of language and Western conceptualisations of reality. We argue that despite multiple, rich opportunities for the adoption of more open and inclusive coverage, more representation of chances for reconciliation and greater imaginings of a joint future, the press – both inside and outside Cyprus – did little to contribute to a constructive foundation for peace building on the island. Because the "Cyprus problem" (as it is broadly known) is an excellent surrogate for the broad array of seemingly intractable conflicts around the globe (e.g. Palestine/Israel, Pakistan/India), this study provides a window into the role of media discourses in the construction and polarisation of the East and the West, the Christian and the Muslim, the "civilised" and the "barbaric". As a consequence, the authors hope this work will shed new light on the ways in which media discourse continues to function as a site of post-colonial hegemony and fails to serve as a resource of reconciliation and peace making.

We examine the headlines and content of English and Turkish language print media circulated in Northern Cyprus (TRNC) as well as representatives of the international and Greek Cypriot press during a series of key events related to potential reconciliation of the "Cyprus problem" during the post-referendum period, starting with the presidential elections in the (Greek) Republic of Cyprus in February and continuing through the opening of the Lokmaci gate in April 2008. We argue that the press, singly and collectively, continued throughout this period of optimism and rapprochement to construct stark and fundamental differences between Turkish and Greek Cypriots, where each identity was grounded in and subject to the strictures of the culture of the respective "[m]otherland". This practice perpetuated animosities, undermined reconciliation and inhibited the emergence of a newly multiple, open and fluid transnational imagination. The entrenchment of a divided Cyprus works in and through the press in North Cyprus to perpetuate differences and to maintain strong connections to the [m]otherland that impede the emergence of an open, fluid and multiple pan-Cypriot, pan-European identity.

Identity as a media construction and site of conflict

The news media play a central role in producing, transmitting and maintaining the narratives from which national identity is discursively shaped. The press participates in the nationalistic project by creating, echoing and magnifying labels that signify membership and exclusion to mark the nation's boundaries and establish collective notions of belonging and commonality through identified difference (Altheide 2004). Through stories, structures and language that privilege the elite (nationalist) perspective and reinforce the status quo, the press shapes social assumptions and cultural norms about what is natural, what is taken for granted and who "we" are (Entman 2003). Shared national identity and collective well-being are reinforced through erasure of differences within and emphasis on narratives of threatening, dissonant outsiders (Schafer 1999).

National elites, with the collaboration and participation of media institutions, attempt to craft one singular, coherent and internally consistent national tale by "officially ignoring the hybrid and in-between" of all identities except that which is particularly significant to Turkish Cypriot identity, whose ambiguity is externally crafted and maintained (Constantinou 2006: 14). Simultaneously, recurrent juxtapositions of the morally upright "us" and the debauched and violent "other" increase fear and the likelihood of conflict with outsiders (Hackett 1989 and 2006; Ross 2003 and 2007: Triandafyllidou 1998).

Within nationalistic media discourse, geographic borders of nation-states take on "significance [that] goes far beyond geography" (Diez 2003). "The political practice of inscribing exclusive identities" into space and onto place occupies a "core position" in the construction of national identity and fuels contestations over land, homeland and habitus. While national identity is tied to place, it also is, as Anderson (1991) recognised, "imagined" in that it is discursively constructed around themes, ideas and ideals that are intangible and malleable, subject to the play of discourse (see also Lazar and Lazar 2004; Leuder, Marsland and Nekvapil 2004). Despite diverse critical challenges to the dominance and permanence of the nation-state as the primary site of identity attachment (e.g. Triandafyllidou op cit), the contemporary project of nations and the obsession with national histories in public discourses including the press perpetuates the primacy of national identity and the nation in opposition to those "outside" its borders (Constantinou op cit: 5).

In Cyprus, the narratives of colonialism, which "propagated the perception of a deeply divided society, comprising two antagonistic groups", undermine any claims of pan-Cypriot identity (Constantinou op cit: 13). The island's history of an always multiple, heterogeneous and divided population justifies dominant bi-communalism and undermines movement toward a conditional, inclusive and fluid pan-Cypriotness. Founding President of the TRNC Rauf Denktash captured this rejection of pan-Cypriot identity by Turkish Cypriots, quipping that only the donkeys in North Cyprus were "genuine Cypriots" (ibid: 2). In today's globalising world, Turkish Cypriots remain nation-less, occupying "an in-between", a nebulous "border region between 'East' and 'West,' between 'the Turk' or 'the Muslim'" (Yashin op cit: 1, 4 and 10) and straddling "the Muslim-Christian divide" (Constantinou op cit: 2). The insecurity of lives "written across the border", occupying "the periphery of 'mainland'" Turkey and "the outside/'other' side of Cyprus" (Yashin op cit: 5), forces Turkish Cypriots always to "translate themselves from one culture to another" (ibid: 3) and to defend their existence, struggle for identity and re-imagine their homeland.

Media and Cyprus

Journalism as an elite social institution consistently constructs a world of binary opposites, of linearity, and of ethnocentric, nationalistic pride (Tuchman 1978). Whether through aggressive government control, overt ideological practice, capitalistic objectives, over-dependency on elite sources and spokespeople, professional norms and strategies, and/or assimilation of dominant social values and perspectives, media serve primarily as tools of the hegemonic practice that fuels global capitalism and war (Galtung op cit; Hackett 2006; Lynch 2007a). The dominance of structural, social, and economic controls on and through media practice mitigates the potential for diverse media outlets to function as an open public sphere and leads to similarities in content despite differences of ownership and location.

The apparent abundance, diversity and distinct ideologies of the many print outlets in North Cyprus mask content that often does little more than rehash stories from previous editions or reprint verbatim excerpts from "competitors". Both the English and Turkish language newspapers in North Cyprus rely heavily on verbatim texts from TAK (Turkish Agency Cyprus, the official/national news agency controlled by the government), a fact that is openly acknowledged in the press. Among the six, dominant Turkish-language newspapers in North Cyprus, *Kıbrıs,* owned by the media group A-N Graphics Ltd, has the highest circulation in the North, and is generally considered the most influential and most professional.

The privately owned *Halkin Sesi*, the oldest remaining Turkish language newspaper, can be described as rightwing. *Afrika* is a left-wing, opposition paper that, unlike its competitors, includes the voices and commentaries of Greek Cypriots and its editor-in-chief Şener Levent has a column in a Greek Cypriot daily, *Politis*. *Yenidüzen* is an official press organ of the Republican Turkish Party, the ruling party of the TRNC at the time of this study. *Kıbrıslı* is a privately owned, right-centrist newspaper that changed its slogan at the onset of Annan Plan negotiations from "We are small Turkey" to a hopeful, progressive label: "patriot" which, when written together with "Kıbrıslı", means "patriot Cypriot", although this is not reflected in their discourse. *Volkan* is an extremist, nationalist paper connected with the militarist National People's Movement.

Of the six broadly circulated English-language newspapers in North Cyprus, *Cyprus Times* describes itself as "North Cyprus's first and only English daily". It focuses on local (even parochial) news, entertainment and arts. Its news coverage tends to rely on reprints/translations from other sources. *Cyprus Observer* (available online) is a rather staid, pro-government (at the time of the study) weekly published out of Turkey and targeted at the significant population of ex-patriate Brits in the North. The 17,000-circulation *Cyprus Today* belongs to the same media group that publishes *Kıbrıs* and bears the banner: "Your comprehensive North Cyprus weekly newspaper established in 1991." It covers news from the UK and emphasises hard news, with a penchant for gruesome photographs. *Dialog* is a trilingual weekly compendium of headlines and photographs from the island's media and serves as a primary conduit to the TRNC of Greek Cypriot media coverage.

Despite being prolific and highly political, the press in TRNC embodies many of the polarising practices and conflict-escalating tendencies noted in mainstream media worldwide. Bailie and Azgin (op cit: 34) summarised the situation:

> Rather than being witnesses to the "Cyprus conflict" itself, [readers] are rather witnessing carefully orchestrated "media wars" where media highlight and re-present social, cultural, political, and economic dynamics in and between the two Cypriot communities in selective and ideological forms.

Bailie and Azgin (ibid) found that the selective, strategic discourses of the media in Cyprus exemplified the characteristics of global war journalism (see also Galtung 1998; Kempf 2002; Lynch 2007a and 2007b). First, the "Cypriot media practise 'self-censorship' and the avoidance of speaking directly to the ideological construction of the official state positions" (Bailie and Azgin op cit: 29). Second, they "embrace a conflict-centered approach,... increased mystification of the conflict, and... a retrenching of divisive attitudes sympathetic to a cementing of division" (ibid: 2). And third, even during periods of optimism about peace initiatives and movement toward reunification of the island, the "Cypriot media... merely adopt [the] 'languages of unification' as techniques for furthering separatist agendas" (ibid: 3).

Cypriot media narratives in times of hope

The following analysis is based on a reading of both the press in North (Turkish) Cyprus and coverage of Cyprus in the *International Herald Tribune* and the (Greek) Cyprus News Agency Online. A major discursive project of Turkish Cypriot newspapers is the naming, definition and narrating of home, history and the future: "[m]other" Turkey is celebrated while the Greek Cypriot oppressor and the scornful, distant and two-faced European Union is demonised. The *International Herald Tribune* describes the two sides of the island as "rivals" and calls TRNC a "breakaway" region, but it is more likely to see the 1974 involvement of Turkey's military on the island as a "response" to the Greek-sponsored coup attempt than as a unilateral and unprovoked "invasion". In contrast, the Greek Cypriot media call the North the "illegal regime in the Turkish occupied North" and "the secessionist entity". They repeatedly evoke a history in which the "Turkish side" was cut off from the "common homeland" in "1974 when Turkey invaded and occupied [the island's] northern third". Constantly, Turkey – and the Turkish Cypriot infantile dependence on its [m]otherland – is the problem. Turkey is the puppeteer that manipulates North Cyprus and impedes the emergence of a truly Cypriot self-image.

While Greek Cypriot media construct an infantile image of Turkish Cypriots unable to separate from the parent, Turkey, the foreign press demeans both Greek and Turkish Cypriots and their governments, portraying them as temperamental children incapable of reasoned deliberation and progress. Irrational and reactionary fear – "of Turkey" on the Greek side and "of domination" by Greek Cypriots on the other – is represented as *the* force motivating voters and their leaders. A presupposition that Cypriots' narrow-minded, "sectarian" perspectives prevent them from thinking "in terms of the whole island" perpetuate a seemingly foolish and counterproductive division, and mires the island in pre-modern conflicts. The "Cyprus problem" is intractable not because of its inherent complexity but because of the essential stubbornness, petulance and emotionalism of the parties. According to the *International Herald Tribune* of 24 March 2008: "The history of attempts to overcome the division of Cyprus can be measured in false dawns. One or another leader could always be relied on to stand athwart the effort and yell 'No!'" At the same time, the *International Herald Tribune* conceded that "Cypriots aren't so immature that they need to be led by the hand" (19 March 2008). Orientalist and post-colonial paternalism and condescension towards Cypriots are pervasive but more overt with regard to Turkish Cypriots.

Research has shown that during negotiation of the Annan Plan, Turkish Cypriots experienced "an oedipal rebellion" against the [m]*other*(land) Turkey (İlter and Alankus 2001). The "This Land is Ours" movement generated pride and helped displace the hegemonic "[m]otherland-babyland" narrative of nationalist circles (ibid). After the referendum failed, Turkish Cypriot media slipped back into familiar discourses of failure and self-denigration under the continuing exclusion from the Europeanness that signifies Western civilisation and modernity. The narrative re-construction of the "oedipal rebellion" combined with post-referendum disillusionment helped slide the discourse of Turkish journalists from representing North Cyprus as a relatively secure "home" to an "enclave" (*Cyprus Times*) and "an anachronistic, backward, stale and antiquated…'abnormal' country" (*Cyprus Observer*).

Shifts in the discourse: From one Orientalist imagination to another

During the post-referendum period, the discourse of the Turkish Cypriot media demonstrated its usual indecisiveness as it shifted dramatically from one Orientalist imagination to another: from the image of "we are more European than the mainland Turks" to images of "we are more European than the Greek Cypriots" or "we are as European as Greek Cypriots" (Alankuş op cit). Turkish Cypriot media repeatedly reported that the (Greek) Republic of Cyprus "was hijacked by the Greek Cypriot majority in the early 1960s" (*Cyprus Observer*), and the North's exclusion from the modern world continues. Since their "rebellion" is unrecognised by Turkey and the modern world, the victimised and self-denying discourse of the Turkish Cypriot media returned through repeated reference to the immaturity and dependency of the North and its inhabitants, as it is captured in the former label of Cyprus as "the child country" (*Cyprus Observer*). Another example is this "humorous" comment in a news story about Greek Cypriots' reluctance to nego-tiate with Turkey for much-needed water: "Of course they have every right to be hesitant in taking anything from us Turks because we might have urinated in the water. We Turks are always so barbaric!" (*Cyprus Observer*).

Greek Cypriot political figure Glafkos Klerides's ironic statement that "the Cyprus flag is the best flag in the world because there is no-one willing to die for this flag" (*Kizilyurek* and *Cyprus Observer*) captures a recurrent strain of self-loathing that permeates the texts. Self-othering becomes a central force in Turkish Cypriot media discourse that re-presents and re-creates the liminal status of Turkish-Cypriot identity between the West and the East, the Christian culture and the Islamic culture, and the "less"ness of their "proper" Turkishness. Trapped in a persistent cycle of othering, Turkish Cypriots blame the Greek Cypriots – the "other" half, the complement and mirror image that completes "the people as one" – for their "less-developed", "less-European", "less-Cypriot" image. Thus, according to one *Cyprus Observer* report, "although the Turkish Cypriot commu-nity have lived through radical change, ... they have not been able to rid themselves of 'becoming the other'". Another report ran:

> English media continued to paint a bad picture of North Cyprus as a safe haven for fugitives and money-laundering. It was clear that it was not only the Geek Cypriots that were keen to continue putting down the TRNC (*Cyprus Today*).

The discursive self-distancing is eloquently captured in Greek Cypriot President Christofias's statement seeking to find or impose a Cypriot language (presumably Greek), as if a remembered "mother tongue" in which island residents once under-stood each other and communicated in their own voices without the distortions of external others and international power play.

> The first obligation, to solve the [Cyprus] problem, [is] to find a common language with our Turkish Cypriot compatriots. We knew this language before.... I hope that we both are going to speak the well-known Cypriot language, without any pressure from outside (Cyprus News Agency, 16 March 2008).

The wistful tone, the call to a dreamlike utopian history and the hope for a world free from global political pressure is part of an ongoing and overt reconstruction of history, of re-membering, erasure and forgetting. One significant piece of this project is accomplished through the strategic ambiguity of naming, the prevalent use of open signifiers that euphemise and de-locate "the Cyprus problem", "the Cyprus question", "the Cyprus issue", the "stalemate", the "political struggle" or, most pointedly, the "deadlock". The cause, the parties, the justifications, the victims, the perpetrators, the losses and the spoils remain undefined and outside history.

The constant mentions of "the Cyprus problem" as unspecified context and content is simultaneously hypnotic and provocative in its refusal to examine, address and move on. The deliberately open signification of "the problem" masks the hegemonic project, facilitates self-serving definitions, fuels misrepresentation and perpetuates misunderstanding through the absence of shared knowledge or common ground for settlement. Each reader, speaker, ethnic group, official and state group is freed to determine the size, significance, cause and solution to "one of the world's most intractable disputes". The substance of the problem remains the stuff of the imaginary, the shadow of constantly reinforced fears of the other and remembered pain.

Yet the problem is not entirely discursively open. Speakers continually define the problem in self-serving ways. The Turkish (Cypriot) discursive self-distancing requires a looking "constantly back to the past and to positions which are not constructive and productive" to provide obstacles to any contemporary knowing (Cyprus News Agency, 19 March 2008). Mutual demonisation and blaming is natural, normal, ubiquitous. In Turkish Cypriot papers, Greek Cypriots recurrently express dismay that "nowadays, outside of Greek Cyprus, nobody talks about the intervention of the Turkish army or the infringement on the refugees' human rights. Everyone now talks about the isolation of the Turkish Cypriots" (*Cyprus Times*). The dawning of a new Greek Cypriot administration brings new complaints that:

> ...the Cyprus issue has been turned from one of an invasion and occupation into the so-called Turkish Cypriot isolation, and this creates a lot of problems for us [Greek Cypriots]. We have to win back our friends (Cypress Online).

Self-dislocation, criticism and denial

The self-dislocation, criticism and denial evident in the outward and self-oppressive gaze of the Turkish Cypriot, post-colonial European fantasy plays out even in the midst of expressions of a hopeful future of self-determination, economic development and independence. The opening of crossings for the first time in April 2004 to allow Cypriots (though not Turks living in North Cyprus) to move more freely between the North and South represents the longed-for homecoming, the possible recapture of a lost vision of Cypriot identity, and the reconstruction of a united Cyprus with the return to occupied and abandoned homes, but it is also laden with the faint, sweet promise of a "change in the atmosphere" (Cyprus Online).

But for the Turkish Cypriots, openings of the border also meant facing their otherness, their in-between, ambiguous identity. In this complex and contested discursive space, the physical dismantling of the Lokmaci barricade in April 2008 to open Ledra Street, the focal point of the island's division at the commercial heart of the bifurcated capital city, was less a portal to increased economic and social exchange than it was the door through which Turkish Cypriots once again faced their otherness and their frightening and abandoned past. While Turkish dailies generally celebrated the opening by emphasising its economic benefits for TRNC, North Cyprus dailies that generally supported bi-lateral initiatives compared the backward, almost shameful scenes of the Turkish side of the street with the Greek side. One wrote: "Dirty buildings with their paint half gone, waiters who are raggedly dressed and one wonders whether they have work permits and health reports, plus disturbing Arabesque [musical] tones" (Başaran Düzgün, *Kıbrıs* 4 April 2008). Another reported: "Only a step ahead you feel like you are entering an entirely different country…People, ambiances, colors, sounds and tones are very different…"(Ahmet Tolgay, *Kıbrıs*, 9 April 2008).

Following the Lokmaci opening, the right-wing Turkish Cypriot press fueled distrust toward Greek Cypriots, referring to the opening as only "…a symbolic handshake between the leaders of Cyprus" (*Cyprus Today*). *Kibrisli* argued that if the Lokmaci gate – once a front for national resistance and now a potential symbolic step toward a fair and durable solution with political equality for the two people – were used to advance the dominating, chauvinistic politics of Greek Cypriots, "Christophias' Communist party will be responsible for the division of the island by its own hands" (3 April 2008).

The overall portrayal is bleak. Turkish journalists take the position of a Western voyeur, looking down on the Turkish side and its "backwardness" but blaming non-Cypriots (Turks, Kurds, Arab settlers and/or illegal immigrants from Turkey) for this state. Turkish Cypriot reporters employ the Lokmaci opening to reactivate the post-colonial fantasy of an "essentially" fixed Turkish Cypriotness within which the settlers, immigrants and workers from Turkey are treated as a blemish on the superior and "proper" European-ness of Turkish Cypriots. In short, the Turkish

Cypriot Orientalist imagination leaves little room for reconciliation. Dominant discourses in the Turkish Cypriot media undermine any possible peace-building process even when the media do not intend to (Alankuş op cit).

The deeply contested past

If new bilateral initiatives ushered in an era of "good intentions", they also prompted erasure, denial and an effort by "the other" to sweep away ongoing, substantive concerns "as if all of Cyprus's problems had been dealt with" (*Cyprus Today*). While acknowledging that "without closure, the pain remains" (Cyprus News Agency, 18 March 2008), neither side was willing to close the door to the deeply contested past that poisoned the present and impeded the future. Neither would be the first to walk away from the heavily coded discursive tug of war that gave both meaning and constructed memories of victimisation. From both sides of the Green Line that divides and buffers the two distinct peoples, readers differentially decoded statements such as "borders and states...must be safeguarded, and the sovereignty and the territorial integrity of the states must be respected" (Cyprus News Agency, 14 March 2008). "Security concerns" alternately recalled human, territorial and economic losses symbolised by empty, bullet-riddled buildings in the Green Line and the threat to face and political sovereignty presented by Turkish troops at crossing checkpoints. Distrust, dishonesty and manipulation were the taken-for-granted of bilateral communication, and putative steps toward reconciliation were seen as masked attempts at elimination of the other; the language of cooperation and destruction were indecipherable from each other.

Within these pervasive discourses of insecurity, fear, and distrust, initiation of bilateral talks about a solution to "the Cyprus problem" presented yet one more opportunity for demonisation and distancing between Greek and Turkish Cypriots, with each "side" marking its own turf and presenting the other as intransigent and untrustworthy. When newly elected Greek Cypriot leaders declared their unilateral "clear vision, a noble vision to reunite Cyprus, rid it of the occupation and unite all of its people" (*Cyprus Today*), how would Turkish Cypriots decode the statement's "real" political and on-the-ground meaning?

Actions represented outside Cyprus as positive steps toward reconciliation of "the problem" were interpreted by the Turkish Cypriot media as an "outright refus[al] to accept that there are Turkish Cypriots and Greek Cypriots on the island, and they are different from each other and they do in fact govern themselves" (*Cyprus Today*). Speeches promising a new dawn of cooperation and progress were decoded as harbingers of oppression, as "chauvinist policies aimed only at enslaving the Turkish Cypriot people and bringing them under Greek Cypriot sovereignty" (*Cyprus Times*). To talk in undertones was to speak guardedly or conspire, to engage in double talk, veiled lies, and coercive promises.

Thus, in covering comments by Christofias, *Kibrisli* (20 March 2008) ran two reports: one from Turkish Agency Cyprus (TAK) on page four under the title, "Greek leader tried to be positive: 'I will honor Papadapoulos' agreement'" and a column on page one titled "Christofias defended Greek sovereignty". Coded language in both suggested that the new president of the (Greek) Republic of Cyprus sought re-unification of the island through domination of Turkish Cypriots. In addition, a column by the owner and editor-in-chief, Doğan Harman, argued that the page-one article was intended to emphasise the "real" intention of the Greek leader and to contextualise the TAK report as Greek propaganda. He described media coverage as part of "an information war that is known as the most dangerous and its *bullets target the people's mind*" (*Kibrisli*, 21 March 2008) (emphasis in the original).

Little reduction in blaming and distrust

In this discursive space, the professed near euphoria of the initiation of talks did little to reduce blaming and distrust among the Cypriot negotiators. Amid proclamations of impending talks, the Turkish Cypriot foreign minister said: "Every action that makes the Greek Cypriots to feel uneasy, angry or annoyed is a right move" (*Cyprus Today*). At the same time, Turkish Cypriot leader and TRNC President Mehmet Ali Talat described the attitudes of North Cypriots "not [as] a question of trusting or not, it is further than that. We are firm on the political equality of the Turkish Cypriots and the creation of a new state" (*Cyprus Today*).

The inability of Turkish Cypriots to claim their own position is evident in the ongoing vacillation between fervent optimism that bilateral talks will transform their reality and breezy dismissals of talks as a "political trick" to "sell false hope" and avoid real change on the ground. Turkish Cypriots labeled the South "a spoiled child" but turned and re-turned to Greek Cypriots to make them whole. Rather than seize their own futures, they bemoaned Greek Cypriots for not "coming to terms with the plight of Turkish Cypriots" and for adopting "preventive policies to thwart opportunities for Turkish Cypriots" (*Cyprus Today*). Silent about their own role in "the problem", the Turkish Cypriot media argued that the problem rested with Greek Cypriots who "continue to fear and hate us … [and] use the same negative rhetoric to demonize the North and Turkey" (*Cyprus Today*).

In the opposition/left wing *Afrika*, comments were quite different, yet hardly supportive of the peace-building process. For example, one columnist devalued the Lokmaci opening as little more than illusory progress and a false hope. He concluded:

> I do not care if [Lokmaci] will be opened or not. I do not believe it may make any contribution to the solution process. If you like, open 10 more gates. All may only help the continuation of the division. It cannot be more than a little hole on the border that divides our island throughout (*Afrika*, 3 April 2008).

Conclusions

Throughout the 2008 period of elections in the (Greek) Republic of Cyprus, the opening of the Lokmaci gate and the initiation of bilateral talks, the press in Cyprus failed to provide a forum for true discussion or debate about "the Cyprus problem" as a foundation for real reconciliation. Rather it afforded the two "sides" highly public opportunities to posture and de-legitimised claims of "goodwill on both sides" as no more than a political game.

The period of news coverage examined in this study is particularly significant in the rhetorical construction of Cyprus because the electoral removal of Tassos Papadopoulos from the presidency of the (Greek) Republic of Cyprus was widely viewed as "a historic turning point" (Cyprus Online). Indeed, in the lead-up to the election, Turkish Cypriot newspapers repeatedly claimed "few elections in Cyprus have been so important" in offering new promise for a resolution of "one of the world's most intractable disputes" (*Cyprus Times*).

The press inside and outside Cyprus failed to seize the potential of European-ness, as a discursive platform and framework, to facilitate escape from dominant, hegemonic discourses of ethno-nationalisms and Orientalist imagination that mire both Turkish and Greek Cypriots in "the problem". Whereas the press might have acknowledged and represented the other, "the outside...as a constitutive part of the inside, and the other as a part of the self" (Howarth 2006: 11), the press represented rapprochement as veiled threat and cooperation as impending oppression in ways that reified and expanded the divide within "the people as one".

In place of the rote repetition of nationalistic imaginaries of bounded, "discrete, territorialised cultures", a more autonomous and critical press might have made visible the fluid porosity of identity and the highly strategic "intertwined processes of place-making and people-making in the complex cultural politics of the nation-state" (Gupta and Ferguson 1997: 4). Yet, rather than seize the opportunity for the practice of a new peace journalism that might enable both Turkish and Greek Cypriots to "rethink [their] relation to the outside and to the other" (ibid), the press re-inscribed and safeguarded the very identifies that constitute the discursive foundation of the Cyprus conflict (Diez 2002). The absence of press articulation of a more "radical democratic" pan-Cypriot/pan-European identity constituted a major obstacle to resolution of "the Cyprus problem" (Laclau and Mouffe 1985).

References

Alankuş, Sevda (2006) Writing for peace without the words for peace. Paper presented to Peace Journalism Conference, Famagusta, North Cyprus, 11 November

Altheide, David L. (2004) Consuming terror, *Symbolic Interaction,* Vol. 27, No. 3 pp 289–308

Anderson, Benedict (1991) *Imagined communities: Reflections on the origin and spread of nationalism,* New York: Verso

Azgın, Bekir (2000) Nationalism and the interest in the "Other Side's" Literature, *Step-Mothertongue: From nationalism to multiculturalism: Literatures of Cyprus, Greece and Turkey,* Yashin, Mehmet (ed.) London: Middlesex University Press pp 147–58

Bhabba, Homi (1990) *DissemiNation: Time, narrative, and the margins of the modern nation – nation and narration,* Bhabha, Homi (ed.) London and New York: Routledge pp 291–322

Bailie, Mashoed and Azgin, Bekir (2008) A barricade, a bridge and a wall: Cypriot journalism and the mediation of conflict in Cyprus, *The Cyprus Review,* Vol. 20, No. 1 Spring pp 57–92

Boedeltje, Freerk J., Kramsch, Olivier T., Van Houtum, Henk and Plug, Roald (2007) Outlook on Europe: The fallacious imperial geopolitics of EU enlargement – the case of Cyprus, *Tijdschrift voor Economische en Sociale Geografie,* Vol. 98, No. 1 pp 130–35

Calotychos, Vangelis (2000) (Pre)occupied Spaces: Hyphens, apostrophes, and over-sites in the literary imaginings of Cyprus, *Step-Mothertongue: From nationalism to multiculturalism: Literatures of Cyprus, Greece and Turkey,* Yashin, Mehmet (ed.) London: Middlesex University Press pp 49–69

Constantinou, Costas M. (2006) Aporias of identity and the "Cyprus problem". Draft paper presented at the ECRP Joint Sessions, Nicosia, Cyprus, 25–30 April

Diez, Thomas (2002) Why the EU can nonetheless be good for Cyprus, *Journal on Ethnopolitics and Minority Issues in Europe,* Vol. 2, No. 2. Available online at http://www.ecmi.de/jemie/download/Focus2–2002_Diez.pdf, accessed on 6 March 2009

Diez, Thomas (2003) "Roots" of conflict, conflict transformation and EU influence: Summary of initial comments. Paper presented at European Commission workshop,

Brussels, 14 February. Available online at http://euborderconf.bham.ac.uk/publications/files/brussels20030214.pdf, accessed on 10 March 2008

Entman, Robert M. (2003) Cascading activation: Contesting the White House's frame after 9/11, *Political Communication*, Vol. 20, No. 4 pp 415–32

Galtung, Johan (1971) A structural theory of imperialism, *Journal of Peace Research*, Vol. 8, No. 2 pp 81–117

Galtung, Johan (1998) Peace journalism: What, why, who, how, when, where. Paper presented in the workshop, What are journalists for? Transcend, Taplow Court, UK, September

Gupta, Akhil and Ferguson, James (1997) After "peoples and cultures", *Culture, power, place*, Gupta, Akhil. and Ferguson, James (eds) Durham, NC: Duke University Press pp 1–30

Hackett, Robert A. (1989) Coups, earthquakes and hostages? Foreign news on Canadian television, *Canadian Journal of Political Science*, Vol. 22 pp 809–25

Hackett, Robert A. (2006) Is peace journalism possible? Three frameworks for assessing structure and agency in news media, Conflict and Communication Online, Vol. 5, No. 2

Howarth, David (2006) Space, subjectivity, and politics, *Alternatives: Global, Local, Political*, April-June pp 1–24

İlter, Turgut and Alankus, Sevda (2001) Diaspora within: Reterritorialising practices of the Turkish Cypriot Community. Paper presented at Diasporic Communications Colloquium, University of Westminster, London, 5-7 September

Kempf, Wilhelm (2002) Conflict coverage and conflict escalation, *Journalism and the new world order. Volume II: Studying war and the media*, Kempf, Wilhelm and Luostarinen, Heikki. (eds) Gothenburg: Nordicom pp 59–72

Killoran, Moira (2000) Time, space and national identities in Cyprus, *Step-Mothertongue: From nationalism to multiculturalism: Literatures of Cyprus, Greece and Turkey*, Yashin, Mehmet (ed.) London: Middlesex University Press pp 129–46

Laclau, Ernesto and Mouffe, Chantal (1985) *Hegemony and socialist strategy: Towards a radical democratic politics*, London and New York: Verso

Lazar, Anita and Lazar, Michelle M. (2004) The discourse of the new world order: "Out-casting" the double face of threat, *Discourse and Society*, Vol. 15, Nos. 2–3 pp 223–42

Leuder, Ivan, Marsland, Victoria and Nekvapil, Jiri (2004) On membership categorization: "Us", "them" and "doing violence" in political discourse, *Discourse and Society*, Vol. 15, Nos. 2–3 pp 243–66

Lynch, Jake (2007a) Peace journalism and its discontents, Conflict and Communication Online, Vol. 6, No. 2. Available online at http://www.cco.regener-online.de/2007_2/pdf/lynch.pdf, accessed on 10 March 2008

Lynch, Jake (2007b) A reply to the replies – a counterplea, Conflict and Communication Online, Vol. 6, No. 2. Available online at http://www.cco.regener-online.de/2007_2/

pdf/lynch_reply.pdf, accessed on 10 March 2008

Papadakis, Yiannis (1998) Greek Cypriot narratives of history and collective identity: Nationalism as a contested process, *American Ethnologist*, Vol. 25, No. 2 pp 149–65

Richmond, Oliver P. (2002) The multiple dimensions of international peacemaking: UN and EU involvement in the Cyprus conflict, *The European Union and the Cyprus conflict: Modern conflict, postmodern union*, Diez, Thomas (ed.) Manchester and New York: Manchester University Press pp 117–36

Ross, Susan Dente (2003) Framing of the Palestinian/Israeli conflict in thirteen months of *New York Times* editorials surrounding the attacks of Sept. 11, 2001, Conflict and Communication Online, Vol. 2, No. 2. Available online at http://www.cco.regener-online.de/2003_2/pdf_2003_2/ross_engl.pdf, accessed on 10 March 2004

Ross, Susan Dente (2007) Peace journalism: Constructive media in a global community, *Global Media Journal, Mediterranean Edition*, Vol. 2, No. 2 pp 77–81. Available online at http://globalmedia.emu.edu.tr/fall2007/issues/9.%20Ross.pdf, accessed on 14 October 2007

Said, Edward W. (1978) *Orientalism*, New York: Vintage Books

Schafer, Mark (1999) Cooperative and conflictual policy preferences: The effect of identity, security, and the image of the other, *Political Psychology*, Vol. 20, No. 4 pp 829–44

Triandafyllidou, Anna (1998) National identity and the "other," *Ethnic and Racial Studies*, Vol. 21, No. 4 pp 593–612

Tuchman, Gaye (1978) *Making news: A study in the construction of reality*, New York: Free Press

Volkan, Vamik D. (1979) *Cyprus-war and adaptation: A psychoanalytic history of two ethnic groups in conflict*, Charlottesville: University Press of Virginia

Yashin, Mehmet (2000) Introducing Step-Mothertongue, *Step-Mothertongue: From nationalism to multiculturalism: Literatures of Cyprus, Greece, and Turkey*, Yashin, Mehmet (ed.) London: Middlesex University Press pp 1–21

15

The Peace Counts project: A promoter of real change or mere idealism?

MARLIS PRINZING

The German Peace Counts[1] project aims to discover role models for peacemaking around the world and to give them a high level of exposure by producing features and photographic essays. The project is interdisciplinary, combining the scientific know-how of conflict researchers with the media skills of experienced journalists. Its premise is "peace is possible!" (Gleich cited in Gerster 2005: 197–225).

Contrary to the mainstream public opinion and the mainstream media land-scape – both of which are overshadowed by the paradigm of war – Peace Counts maintains that "peace pays!" (ibid: 227–44) and that peace is imperative. The project adopts the "best practice" concept and aims to show the close relationship between stability and sustainable economic development. The project exploits multimedia to reach a large audience with content distributed through magazines, radio, television, books, and school curricular materials. Financial backing is provided by the Federal Foreign office in Berlin, by the foundation "Sonnenwiese" (Vaduz) and the "zivik programme", which is based in Berlin and forms part of the Institute for Foreign Cultural Relations (IFA).[2]

The project promotes the professionalisation of journalists as advocates for peace and not as impartial, neutral observers. To what extent does this project help find ways of overcoming the old paradigms of war reporting? Does it constitute an important critique of traditional definitions of professionalisation? Or is it nothing more than idealism?

These questions can be answered using material from conversations with journalists who have played a leading role in this project including Michael Gleich, Uli Reinhardt and Tilman Woertz. They were asked to what extent peace education, peace research and communication sciences provide them with sources and points of reference. Their answers were then set against the core positions of these research areas. Three aspects of the Peace Counts project are explored: To what extent does the aim of the project go against human nature? Does it fit into the existing categories of journalistic concepts? Does it put the findings from conflict research into practice? The answers to these questions will make it possible to assess how idealistic the concept is, and where it might be improved.

The project[3]

Peace Counts is basically a network of journalists operating worldwide to find and document examples and people who show that peace can work. The idea comes from Michael Gleich, a German journalist who has been to many war zones and who on many occasions felt it highly unacceptable that only failures and deaths of the combatants were reported. In 2002, he founded the Peace Counts project and shortly afterwards, as the head of the project, founded the non-profit Culture Counts Foundation which made it possible to apply for public funds – for example, from the Foreign Office or the Society for Technical Cooperation. He discovered a kindred spirit in photojournalist Uli Reinhardt. After decades working in war zones and disaster areas, Reinhardt founded a journalists' agency in the south of Germany called Zeitenspiegel[4] where he gathered together 40 photographers and reporters.

A second key partner was the Tuebingen Institute for Peace Education (Institut für Friedenspaedagogik, Tuebingen e.V.[5]). The educationalists got on board straight away as Peace Counts offered new stories, while much of their own material had become dated – stories about people like Mahatma Gandhi or Mother Teresa had little appeal, above all for the younger generation. The institute used the reports by Peace Counts journalists to produce brochures and multi-media CD-ROMs for schools and is working to show young people as early as possible how obstacles can be overcome.[6]

Peace Counts reporters and photographers do not focus on high-level politics: their approach is not "top-down" but "bottom-up". For this reason they show what peacebuilders achieve in their own – limited – area and who they are (Gerster op cit). They have introduced us to the Irish ex-terrorists Joe Doherty and Peter McGuire who offer young people ideas for their free time to keep them away from paramilitary groups. We hear from Victoria Maloka from South Africa who visits violent criminals in prison to encourage them to think about how to solve problems without breaking someone's neck. The project spotlights people with clear ideas on how to suppress violence in their specific environment and bring about harmonious co-existence, despite all the differences and conflicts of interest. Nobody has a fail-safe recipe for a rapid solution but everyone can contribute their experience to show how success can be achieved, even in long-drawn-out processes and seemingly dead end situations. Peace Counts reports and documents this work and passes on the impetus, showing how similar results could be achieved elsewhere.

Since the organisation was founded teams of Peace Counts reporters (generally teams of two: a writer and a photographer) have carried out research in more than 30 post-conflict regions including Afghanistan, the Balkans, Israel, Palestine, Rwanda, India and Brazil. The project uses examples of conflict to generate inductive findings on causes and escalation, and ways of transforming conflicts through human co-operation. Peace Counts is a multi-media project. It includes print publications in quality media[7], features on public television, a richly-illustrated book (Gerster op cit), forums where a broad audience can get to know, live in Germany, the peacebuilders shown in the reports from Sri Lanka or Colombia live in Germany, a homepage and the special sub-projects – the Peace Counts School and Peace Counts on Tour.

Peace educationalists from Tuebingen play a leading role in the Peace Counts School[8]. Their aim is to teach children and young people in Germany that peace is possible and demonstrate this with examples. To do this they prepare their reports to make it clear to children and young people which pattern of behaviour is required.

Peace Counts on Tour[9] works in conflict and crisis regions to sensitise people to the reasons for escalations in violent confrontations, using peace education resources and drawing on examples from journalism that focus on reconciliation. "Vivid examples of peacebuilders" aims to open people's eyes to possible paths to a solution. The tour converges on the multi-media exhibition, Peacebuilders around the World, and the accompanying programme with learning circles, workshops and lectures. The Institute for Peace Education has prepared examples of best practice and developed support material, and it organises workshops for teachers, teacher trainers, and members of security forces and NGOs in the area where the exhibition is taking place. The project achieves a high level of local media coverage.

In addition to the first two stages – bringing stories about peacebuilders around the world to Germany and bringing the stories behind pictures back to their countries – a third stage was introduced, working alongside journalists in these countries to write stories about peacebuilders there.

Tilman Woertz, who has worked frequently in the Ivory Coast reporting and training journalists, organised the first journalists' workshop of this type there together with Uli Reinhardt. The journalists who took part – five writers and five photographers – all came from the capital, Yamoussoukro, from neutral media groups, as well as others from different political positions. The workshop was financed by the Goethe Institute, the Swiss Embassy, GTZ and prize money from the Peter Becker Prize. Each participant could suggest people or initiatives that brought about solutions in the nation's trouble spots. Ten of the subjects were selected and assignments were distributed to determine who would write which report. The finished stories were discussed in detail during a second meeting.

Tilman Woertz talked of a "win-win situation": he learned a lot from the strong oral tradition of the Ivory Coast and some of the local participants got to know their own country better for the first time because they did not stay in the office for the research but drove out to the location; for the first time they had days to dedicate to this sort of research. "This experience was clearly quite unusual, as they kept on checking that it was really possible," explained Woertz. "In my opinion, there were no relevant cultural difficulties between us and them. Most of the differences were caused by the system." Thus, you had to know the characteristics of the political system and the media landscape, he said. This explains a lot. "The journalists there are used to reporting only on chiefs, leaders and leading politicians," he continued. "They are authority-oriented, wary of conflict and happy to leave out explanatory context because everyone knows how a soldier lives anyway."

The finished reports reached the publications where the participating journalists work. Government media and rebel broadcasters reported on the project. Traditional methods help to connect with the people whom the media cannot reach: a storyteller developed a programme jointly with Peace Counts and took it on tour in cities and villages with Woertz and Reinhardt. They now want to find buyers in Germany for a film and documentary about the project as well as for some of the reports. Their expectations are based on past experience: there is interest in stories about peace-building, but there are also some misgivings. However, there is no doubt that they will continue: the next workshops are planned for Guatemala and Sri Lanka.

Classifying the Peace Counts project

Can the journalistic concept, on which the Peace Counts reports build, show a way forward or is it simply an expression of idealism? Three aspects must be considered:

- is Peace Counts consistent with human nature or does it go against it?

- can Peace Counts be said to be using existing journalistic concepts and criteria? Is it a new concept? Or is it not a journalistic concept at all?
- is the key role of Peace Counts to put findings from peace education, and peace and conflict research into practice?

Between good and evil: Is Peace Counts consistent with human nature?

"Good news is good news" – the Peace Counts project overturns the old publicist's adage to show that "peace is possible", as Michael Gleich puts it. He criticises the emphasis on war and violence in journalistic reporting which mostly follows the opposite motto: "Good news, no news" or "If it bleeds, it leads."

Dieter Senghaas (2009: 2) argues that many historians regret the "loss of peace imagery in modernity" since works such as Picasso's Temple of Peace, installed in a chapel in Vallauris in South-East France, are the exceptions. Senghaas describes a radio broadcast in which the first movement of Gustav Holst's the Planets Suite "Mars: The Bringer of War" was played with trumpets, trombones and percussion, and then the final movement "Venus: The Bringer of Peace" was played in a bright and epic style with horns, harps and the glockenspiel. The presenter described the music of peace as boring and said that the composer had brought his full virtuosity to bear in his portrayal of battle and conflict. Similar comments are found on the internet: "Peace is boring" claimed editors to whom members of the Peace Counts team had offered their reports on peacebuilders.

The American psychologist, Leon Festinger (1957), developed his theory of cognitive dissonance half a century ago. According to this theory, information that does not fit into a person's own basic convictions is deflected, and increasingly so, the greater the distance from the dominant reality in a society. This would imply that journalism, as produced by the Peace Counts team, would not just be idealistic, but hopeless. Michael Gleich disagrees. People and society as a whole want to know how to progress and are looking for reasons to be optimistic. In his opinion the problem lies largely with the media and most of his colleagues there: denouncing failure is easier, because it makes an impact and attracts more attention. It also sells well because it satisfies a further need to warn people about dangers, even if it is only a warning against alleged dangers.

Michael Gleich sees himself as a sort of "entrepreneur" who wants to produce peace. He believes there are always only three options for dealing with reality: love it (acceptance and surrender), leave it (leaving the place, the company and so on), or change it (changing the conditions). In journalism a lot changes if you change your own perceptions and divert attention from failure to success.

Is Peace Counts a new concept?

The Gulf War in 1991 and the changes in war reporting that emerged in the coverage of the conflict contributed to the adoption of the concept of peace journalism (which really came from peace research) in the discourse of the communication sciences. The critical analysis of mainstream war reporting tended to highlight the distorting effects of conventional news values (negativism, personalisation, the emphasis on elite countries and elite people: see Galtung and Vincent 1992: 7; Schicha 1999: 12; Jaeger 2002) as well as the stress on winning and losing that was reminiscent of sports journalism (Albrecht and Becker 2002; Loeffelholz 2004).

In contrast, peace journalism is a "programme of journalistic reporting which contributes to peaceful conflict resolution through publications" (Hanitzsch 2004: 172). The journalist takes on the roles of information broker and critical inspector, performing central reporting functions such as informing, criticising and exposing (Weischenberg 2005). The Norwegian peace and conflict researcher, Johan Galtung, and the communication scientist, Richard C. Vincent, designed a practical concept for peace journalism. In essence it is a ten-point list (Galtung and Vincent op cit: 126). According to Galtung (1998), who summarises it in four core requirements, peace journalism should be:

1. peace- and conflict-oriented;
2. truth-oriented;
3. people-oriented; and
4. solution-oriented.

These requirements can be applied to the Peace Counts concept. The project focuses attention on solutions but also examines the conflict to make the context clear. This fully satisfies the first of Galtung's requirements. Requirement 2, truth-orientation, is satisfied by careful, critical research but the main concern of Peace Counts is not exposing the lies on both sides – nor is the priority that of exposing the phoneys among the peacebuilders. Requirement 3, however, is a clear focus for Peace Counts: it consciously aims to give initiatives a human face. Requirement 4, a focus on solutions, is a central point of Peace Counts. The ten-point list[10] is applied implicitly in many respects in the reports. The North-South divide, the arms race and problems in the media landscape are, however, a lower priority, since Peace

Counts wants to report on targeted examples for peacebuilding and does not (yet) cover the entire spectrum of crisis reporting. The Peace Counts team is, then, "part of the solution" as described by McGoldrick (2000: 19). Since reports are the main medium through which information is reported, the journalist becomes a "participating observer", as in the description of peace journalism by Lynch (2002).

The concept of peace journalism is controversial among journalists. Simone Richter (1999) interviewed a number of German foreign correspondents. All of them expressed the stereotypical view that journalists report primarily on the actions of the conflict. However, it is vastly preferable to show all sides – the military, the political and the human. Those responsible for Peace Counts do not rely on the concept of peace journalism either. "There is no such thing as peace journalism, it is a chimera," says Uli Reinhardt. "There is just good journalism or poor journalism." He much prefers the term "constructive journalism". Rather than investigative or research journalism, in the Anglo-Saxon style, which uncovers "bad" states of affairs, he does not just seek to expose a problem or corruption but also to offer a solution. This need not be only solutions to conflicts, which is the principal focus of peace journalism, but also ways out of very different crises. A report on the condition of the Alps would, under the premises of "constructive journalism", also show ways of fulfilling the ecological requirements. Offering solutions is not automatically precluded as a function of conventional investigative journalism but as a function of Peace Counts` way of "constructive journalism".

Communication sciences have long offered a term for such a concept – "solutions journalism". This refers to a still relatively minor trend, particularly in the USA, where mainstream reports tend to feature bad news rather than good news. Instead of pointing out what's wrong, "solutions journalism" points out what's right. It doesn't want to provide some kind of cheerleading in journalism but an example for a better world that people might imitate (Benesch 1998: 36–9).[11] Furthermore there is a relation to the concept of civic journalism (Rosen 1999). It considers journalists and the public as participants in community life and the media as a forum for civic conversation. Of course, to a certain extent the Peace Count team regards itself as a voice of the peacemakers and as a forum for conversation about a conflict. Indeed, the unique aspect of the Peace Counts approach is that stories should also be solution-oriented. A report about the far right, for example, would also show ways in which to stem the spread of the movement.

But what about when there are two conflicting solutions on offer? If, for example, party A wants solution A and party B wants solution B? What are the priorities of the Peace Counts journalist in this case? "He or she looks for people and examples of initiatives that mediate between the two sides to overcome the obstacles," explains

Reinhardt. People such as Elena Gulmadova, who mediated in the civil war between Christians and Muslims in Macedonia. The OSCE (Organisation for Security and Co-operation in Europe) supports the development of police forces there and wants to achieve a return to dialogue between the two conflicting parties. Elena Gulmadova plays a pivotal role in developing the dialogue between the cultures and this stems from her roots: she is Tajik, her father prays to Allah and her mother to Jesus. Her profession also helps: she is a doctor and diplomat.

However, such people are not so simple to find. "Michael Gleich and I just drove to Macedonia to observe how the OSCE works," explains Reinhardt. During their research they found Elena Gulmadova. The more they found out about her, the more they were convinced they had found in her a face of reconciliation. So they accompanied her in an armoured vehicle to meet village teachers and demonstrators, to talk to Macedonian soldiers and visit Albanian town halls. Words were among her strongest assets – face to face or on the phone. Her basic formula for peace grows out of this experience: "As long as people are talking to each other, they don't shoot" (Gerster op cit: 57).[12]

The core principles of peace journalism (McGoldrick 2006; Lee 2008) appear, then, to be practised by the Peace Counts team. But, intriguingly, they do not want to be described as practitioners of peace journalism. The term "peace journalism" is just a label, says Tilman Woertz. In their day-to-day work journalists should concentrate on what is most important. He finds Galtung's concept "stimulating" while the conflict analysis by peace and conflict researchers, such as Dieter Senghaas or Volker Rittbergern and Michael Zuern (1990), he considers "interesting" too. But Woertz argues that these theories do not help him with his work as a journalist. Nor does he believe that journalists need to develop a deep understanding of different media cultures – as stressed by a range of communications scholars (see Hafez 2002; Hepp 2006; Hahn et al 2008). A lot of experience abroad, empathy, openness and a basic knowledge of the media system in the country where you are working are essential – and sufficient, he maintains. But he stresses that theories are not a matter of great importance for him in his daily work. He says he wants to find out what lies at the heart of the issue and deal with it using journalistic methods.

Is the key role of Peace Counts to put the findings from peace and conflict research into practice?

Peace Counts is a practice-oriented project. There has been no scientific evaluation so far to see whether an audience that has read or heard stories that were produced in the framework of this project takes another position on conflicts, or whether interest in this type of approach is growing. However, this is essentially of secondary interest to Reinhardt, because he is focused on sustainable quality journalism with maximum levels of professionalism. He was delighted to receive the Peter Becker Prize,[13] awarded to the Journalists' Network, Peace Counts and the Institute for Peace Education in May 2009 by the Centre for Conflict Research[14] and the Philipps University in Marburg for the Peace Counts on Tour initiative.[15] This is not a journalism prize but, with prize money of 10,000 Euros, it is one of the major social sciences awards in Germany.[16] The award was given because the project has managed to apply findings from peace and conflict research and from peace education to the field of professional journalism..

To what extent is Peace Counts over-idealistic?

Showing what is good, presenting peacebuilders: that sounds like idealism. But if you look at the guiding reporting principles the picture changes. The journalistic approach adopted is hardly idealistic in that it is open to different results and ready to revise a theory. For example, the most recent project in the Ivory Coast presents a teacher who mediates in the conflict between two ethnic groups. Reports also explain that a monitoring system of an NGO was not as effective as promised. An observer wanting to idealise the situation would have left this out and simply praised the NGO.

Peace Counts is committed to professional and ethical standards in quality journalism, including balance, thoroughness, independence and critical research, stresses Gleich. "What differentiates us is that we have chosen peace processes as a subject in the same way that other journalists have specialised in the environment, development or sport." Moreover, "an idealistic element comes in sometimes when we directly support (even financially) peace projects that we have found to be exemplary," adds Gleich. There are also parallels here in the German mainstream media, for example, when a public broadcaster, such as ZDF, calls for donations, or a weekly magazine, such as *Stern*, collects for tsunami victims. Another "idealistic aspect" he describes is the desire to pass on his experience of "constructive journalism" by founding an Advanced Journalism Academy.[17]

One of the strong points of Peace Counts is that it handles the subjects of reports skilfully and with a high level of journalistic pragmatism and attentiveness. However, there has been a notable indifference, particularly towards some input from the communication sciences. Theory is useful in revealing practice, describing it and systematising it. Providing instructions is a matter of secondary concern, although this does sometimes happen specifically in journalism. An example is the concept of public journalism (Rosen op cit) where a journalist consciously intervenes to promote democracy. This concept was developed by a chief editor, David "Buzz" Merrit, of the *Wichita Eagle*, and by a professor of journalism in New York, Jay Rosen. Working on his peace journalism concept, Galtung started up the peace network, Transcend[18] and founded a university in Cluj, Romania. Lynch and McGoldrick also taught there while travelling as foreign correspondents for media including Sky News. They belong to another international network of journalists, Reporting the World, [19] which aims to exchange information on how journalists can continue to provide promote peace and understanding in an increasingly complex world.

"Constructive journalism" represented by Peace Counts could become a further positive example of this. This requires an interest among people working in the theoretical field of journalism studies and the practical world of journalism in dialogue (and research), covering effects as well as standards, roles and functions in journalism. For example, further research should be carried out into the example of the workshops in the Ivory Coast: What experiences did the journalists have there from their perspective? To what extent can these have a sustained influence on their day-to-day work? Did they pass them on to colleagues? All these questions have nothing to do with idealism.

Conclusion: Nothing to do with idealism – but real change

In the meantime almost every large German magazine has bought a Peace Counts story and it has become a brand, partly thanks to the Peter Becker Prize. But it is still a long way from achieving its aim – the attitude of "good news is good news" is spreading slowly but surely. This can be seen in new projects in the Ivory Coast, for example, and in other initiatives and individuals linked by a similar philosophy: The Fondation Hirondelle is one of the groups that is building up new media in crisis areas so that other voices can also be heard.[20]

Andreas Zumach, who has already put this approach into practice as a correspondent for the *Tageszeitung* in Berlin and for the BBC, was named as a representative independent journalist at the UN headquarters in Geneva. He was also recognised for his "services to the promotion of openness to peace", winning the Goettinger Peace Prize in 2009.[21] All of this involvement confirms an aphorism by Albert Einstein: "You cannot solve a problem using the same way of thinking that caused it in the first place." This also has nothing to do with idealism but, rather, with real change.

Notes

1 Peace Counts is part of the Advanced Journalism Academy (www.aja-online.org). This is the parent organisation for three Counts Projects (in addition to Peace Counts, Nature Counts deals with environment and sustainability, Culture Counts focuses on cultural diversity).

2 http://www.ifa.de/en/foerderprogramme/zivik/about-zivik/.

3 In addition to information from the websites mentioned, this study is based on interviews with Michael Gleich (Peace Counts), Uli Reinhardt (Peace Counts/Agentur Zeitenspiegel), Tilman Woertz (Peace Counts/Agentur Zeitenspiegel) and Guenther Gugel (Institute of Peace Education Tuebingen).

4 www.zeitenspiegel.de.

5 www.friedenspaedagogik.de (Institute of Peace Education, Tuebingen).

6 Further key partners are BICC (Bonn International Center for Conversion); the GTZ (Deutsche Gesellschaft für Technische Zusammenarbeit – German Society for Technical Co-operation), which assists with research, forums and exhibitions; UNESCO, which has recognised the project as a contribution to the "International Decade for a Culture of Peace"; WDR (Westdeutscher Rundfunk), a public broadcaster in Germany; and *zivil*, a magazine for peace and non-violence; the University of Oxford (where Anke Hoeffler evaluated findings on the economic significance of peace processes).

7 Amongst others: *Neue Zuercher Zeitung* (Switzerland), *Sueddeutsche Zeitung* (Germany), *Brand eins* (Germany), *Focus* (Germany).

8 www.peace-counts-school.org.

9 Project reports: www.friedenspaedagogik.de/projekte/peace_counts_on_tour

10 1) Report all sides; 2) clarify the frame of reference; 3) media ownership should not matter; 4) don't overemphasise certain views; 5) enhance the educational role of news; 6) understand the reality of the arms issue; 7) be attentive to arms race inner dynamism, 8) acknowledge the limitations of the media; 9) consider north-south dynamic; 10) portray clearly the benefits of peace.

11 http://solutionjournalism.com/, accessed on 24 April 2009.

12 In addition to "Elena mediates" there are ten other reports in Gerster (2005), as well as project descriptions.

13 http://www.uni-marburg.de/aktuelles/news/2009a/0218u, accessed on 22 June 2009.

14 www.uni-marburg.de/konfliktforschung, accessed on 22 June 2009.

15 The Peace Counts on Tour initiative is part of the Peace Counts project. Its reports are systematically evaluated.
16 http://www.uni-marburg.de/aktuelles/news/2009a/0218u, accessed on 22 June 2009.
17 http://aja-online.org/.
18 www.transcend.org.
19 www.reportingtheworld.org.
20 www.hirondelle.org; the foundation is based in Lausanne, Switzerland, and was founded in 1995 with support from the Direktion für Entwicklung und Zusammenarbeit (DEZA – Committee for Development and Co-operation).
21 www.goettinger-friedenspreis.de.

References

Albrecht, Ulrich and Becker, Jörg (eds) (2002) *Medien zwischen krieg und frieden*, Baden-Baden: Nomos

Benesch, Susan (1998) The rise of solutions journalism, *Columbia Journalism Review,* March/April pp 36–9

Festinger, Leon (1957) *A theory of cognitive dissonance*, Stanford, CA: Stanford University Press

Galtung, Johan and Vincent, Richard (1992) *Global glasnost*. Cresskill N.J.: Hampton Press

Galtung, Johan (1998) Friedensjournalismus: Was, warum, wer, wie, wann, wo? Kempf, Wilhelm et al. (eds) *Krieg, nationalismus, rassismus und die medien*, Muenster: Lit-Verlag, pp 3–20

Galtung, Johan and Vincent, Richard C. (2004) Krisenkommunikation morgen: Zehn vorschläge für eine andere kriegsberichterstattung, Loeffelholz, Martin (ed.) *Krieg als medienereignis: Grundlagen und perspektiven der krisenkommunikation*. Opladen: Westdeutscher Verlag pp 177–210

Gerster, Petra (2005) *Die friedensmacher*, Muenchen: Hanser

Gleich, Michael (2005) *Peace Counts: Wie man frieden macht*. Gerster, Petra Muenchen: Hanser pp 196–225

Hafez, Kai (2002) *Die politische dimension der Auslandsberichterstattung*, Two Vols, Baden-Baden: Nomos

Hahn, Oliver, Lönnendonker, Julia and Schröder, Roland (eds) (2008) *Deutsche Auslandskorrespondenten: Ein handbuch*, UVK: Konstanz

Hanitzsch, Thomas (2004) Journalisten zwischen friedensdienst und kampfeinsatz. Interventionismus im kriegsjournalismus aus kommunikationswissenschaftlicher perspektive, Löffelholz, Martin (ed.) *Krieg als medienereignis II. Krisenkommunikation im 21: Jahrhundert*, Wiesbaden: VS-Verlag pp 169–93

Hepp, Andreas (2006) *Transkulturelle kommunikation*, Konstanz: UVK

Jaeger, Susanne (2002) Mediale wahrnehmungsfilter: Nationalität, ethnie, Albrecht, Ulrich et al (eds.)*Medien zwischen krieg und frieden*, Baden-Baden: Nomos pp 194–204

Lee, Seow Ting (2009) Peace Journalism, *The handbook of mass media ethics,* Wilkins, Lee, and Christians, Clifford G. (eds) New York: Routledge pp 258–75

Löffelholz, Martin (ed.) (2004): *Krieg als Medienereignis. Grundlagen und Perspektiven der Krisenkommunikation*, Opladen: Westdeutscher Verlag

Lynch, Jake (2002) Impunity in journalism, *Media Development*, Vol. 2 pp 30–2

McGoldrick, Annabel (2000) Peace journalism: An introduction, Friedrich -Ebert-Stiftung (ed.) *Medien im konflik: Mittäter oder mediatoren? The media in conflicts: Accomplices or mediators?* Bonn: FES pp 19–24

McGoldrick, Annabel (2006) War Journalism and "objectivity". Available online at http://www.cco.regener-online.de/2006_2/pdf/mcgoldrick.pdf, accessed on 14 March 2009

Mikich, Sonia (2000) "Ueber die diskussion post festum", Friedrich-Ebert-Stiftung (ed.) *Medien im konflikt: Mittaeter oder mediatoren? The media in conflicts: Accomplices or mediators?* Bonn: FES pp 95–100

Richter, Simone (1999) *Journalisten zwischen den fronten: Kriegsberichterstattung am Beispiel Jugoslawien*, Opladen: Westdeutscher Verlag

Rittberger, Volker and Zuern, Michael (1990) *Forschung für neue friedensregeln: Rückblick auf zwei jahrzehnte friedensforschung*, Stuttgart: Akademie der Dioezese Rottenburg-Stuttgart

Rosen, Jay (1999) *What are journalists for?* New Haven: Yale University Press

Senghaas, Dieter (2009): Laudatio: Peter-Becker-Prize 2008/2009. Available online at http://friedenspaedagogik.de/institut/auszeichnungen_und_preise/peter_becker_preis_fuer_friedens_und_konfliktforschung_2008_2009, accessed on 21 June 2009

Schicha, Christian (1999): Kriegsberichterstattung zwischen anspruch und wirklichkeit: Kriterien für einen friedensjournalismus, *Zeitschrift für kommunikationsoekologie*, Vol 2 pp 10–14

Weischenberg, Siegfried et al (eds) *Handbuch journalismus und medien: Reihe praktischer journalismus Band 60*, Konstanz: UVK

16

Conscience and the press: Newspaper treatment of pacifists and conscientious objectors 1939–40

JOHN TULLOCH

This chapter explores the process by which a mass popular organisation of pacifists, the Peace Pledge Union (PPU), was marginalised under the impact of total war. Further, it explores the role of sections of the British press – in particular the *Daily Mirror*, the dominant popular newspaper of the time – in orchestrating this reformation of popular sentiment and change in the structure of national attitudes to pacifists. This process took place over the period from mid-1939 to early 1941. During that time, the PPU was increasingly harassed by the state, sales of its weekly newspaper *Peace News* were disrupted by the police and newspaper distributors and leading officials were prosecuted under the Defence Regulations. Finally, in February 1943 Stuart Morris, the general secretary and a former canon of the Church of England, was jailed for nine months under the Official Secrets Act and was forced to resign from his position (see Brittain 1989: 200–26).

The PPU had started out as the Sheppard Peace Movement, named after its charismatic founder Canon Dick Sheppard. His appeal to renounce war was made in 1934. Within a year more than 80, 000 men had signed pledge cards. He launched his peace movement in July 1935 at the Albert Hall and in May 1936 the PPU was established. Local branches were started in October and numbered more than 1,100 by 1939. The appeal to renounce war was widened to include women in 1936. According to the PPU, by September 1937 about 64,360 men and 18,670 women had signed pledge cards. Although Sheppard died suddenly in October 1937, by the summer of 1939 these figures had continued to grow to a mass movement of roughly 86,000 men and 43,000 women, with women making up a third of the membership (Overy 2009: 245; Peace Pledge Union 2009).

The mushrooming of the union, of course, represented a perfectly comprehensible reaction to a worsening international situation. But it also reflected a uniquely strong peace movement that had grown up between the wars. George Mosse (1990) argues that this was shaped by the fact that, despite severe economic dislocation, the transition between World War One and peace in Britain had been "relatively smooth" compared to other European countries.

> Moreover, the evangelical tradition gave pacifist movements a solid base that was missing in countries where religion and pacifism had not been linked. Protestantism in Germany, for example, had no such tradition, but in England pacifism could be practised as an act of faith (ibid: 197).

However, the pressure of events in 1940 that shaped the conflict into a war of national survival, and the powerful mythologising of this struggle, continued to rob the pacifist case of meaning.

Public anti-war opinion had forced the British Cabinet to set up a Defence Requirements Committee in secret in 1933 and only to begin talking about rearmament in public in July 1934. As Keith Middlemass observes, the Cabinet Committee on Disarmament only changed its name in July 1935 "although for eighteen months it had talked of nothing but rearmament" (Middlemass 1979: 343). This concealment was to do with the pressure exercised by anti-war sentiment and expressed through a network of pacifist societies – what Richard Overy (op cit: 221) calls a "broad church, though scarcely a united front". Although the impact of Nazi Germany, and the Spanish civil war, convinced many Labour supporters of the need for rearmament, a large section of British public remained sympathetic to pacifism into the late 1930s, if increasingly by the time of the Munich agreement membership of the organisation was becoming a "badge of dissent" (Middlemass op cit: 345).

Pacifist responses to the 'good war'

Popularly called the "good war" (Terkel 1984) in the United States and the "people's war" or "citizen's war" in the United Kingdom (Calder 1969: 163, Gardiner 2004b: ix, Rose 2003: 2), World War Two was a difficult conflict for pacifists to oppose, compared to World War One. For a start, this was plainly a war the nation had not wanted, as a former PPU member, J.B. Priestley, captured in a letter in October 1939:

the whole atmosphere is quite different from 1914 – no jingoism or flag-waving, no bands, none of that hysterical Holiday feeling, no romantic exaltation... It's just a damned nuisance, like having to tackle a huge raving drunk who threatens to set your house on fire (see Cook 1997: 178).

After the so-called "phoney war" of 1939 and early 1940, the conflict abruptly lurched into a struggle for national survival, in which the nation was under threat of invasion, facing defeat, and all civilians in the "firing line" of aerial bombing. Seventy years after the event, it still remains difficult to comprehend the speed and scale of the shocks to the national nervous system in 1940, subject to the "powerful tides of feeling [of] patriotism, rage against the Nazis, and the fear of invasion" (Addison 1975). Addison regards pure official panic as the best explanation for a series of repressive moves which saw aberrations such as the indiscriminate intern-ment of "enemy aliens", including many Jewish refugees from Hitler, widespread prosecutions for spreading "alarm and despondency", and "a grotesque campaign by the Ministry of Information for citizens to form a 'silent column' against rumour" (ibid: 104). The invasion of Norway and Denmark in April 1940, and then the German military breakthrough in May, constituted the "watershed" for British pacifism (Ceadel 1980: 296).

Under this pressure, many prominent and longstanding pacifists such as the philosopher Bertrand Russell left the PPU in the spring of 1940 (Monk 2000: 186; Clark 1975: 467), or laid low, adopting a form of quietism, overwhelmed by the scale of the crisis (for example, see Partridge 1978). Others, such as the novelist Aldous Huxley, based themselves in America (Murray 2003: 324). Or, like the composer Benjamin Britten, returned to the UK to declare himself a conscientious objector (CO) and convince a tribunal of his value to society as an artist rather than a war worker (Carpenter 1992: 174–77). Actors such as Sybil Thorndike, an international star and a leading PPU member, convinced themselves that, by throwing themselves into work (for example, Shakespeare for the miners via the Council for the Encouragement for Music and the Arts) they were helping to keep civilised values alive (Croall 2008: 292–3).

Quietism and getting on with one's work was barely an option. Virginia Woolf, with a Jewish husband, contemplated their planned mutual suicide by car exhaust fumes:

Sunday 9 June. I will continue – but can I? The pressure of this battle wipes out London very quick, A gritting day. As sample of my present mood, I reflect: capitulation will mean all Jews to be given up. Concentration camps. So to our garage (Woolf 1985: 292–3).

There was no way to escape the war and the burgeoning networks of what J.B. Priestley had termed in a celebrated phrase "the organised militant citizen" embodied in new networks of voluntary associations such as the Home Guard, the Observer Corps, the A.R.P. and fire-fighting services (Priestley 1940). Above all, there was no way to escape the hysterical myth-making and the media images of heroic fighters. Virginia Woolf observed with nervous distaste in the wake of the Dunkirk evacuation on Monday 3 June:

> We have now been hard at hero-making. The laughing, heroic, Tommy- how can we be worthy of such men? Every paper, every BBC rises to that dreary false cheery hero-making strain. Will they be grinding organs in the street in 6 months? It's the emotional falsity; not all false; yet inspired with some eye to the main chance. So the politicians mate guns and tanks. No. It's the myth-making stage of the war we're in (Woolf op cit: 292).

Transforming pacifists into pantomime eccentrics

Within this heroic myth pacifists and conscientious objectors were largely to figure as absent – an inconvenient truth – or pantomime eccentrics or shirkers. Nevertheless, they were too large a minority to ignore. Conscientious objectors – not all of whom of course were pacifists – were four times more numerous than in World War One and, as Arthur Marwick observes, "outright opposition to the war was numerically stronger than it had been in 1914–18, though it never seemed to attract as much attention" (Marwick 1976: 124). At the first provisional registration of objectors after the outbreak of war, in October 1939, 5,073 registered out of 230,009 – at 2.2 per cent the highest proportion for the entire conflict (Hayes 1949: 382). The PPU itself gained more than 4,700 members in September and October 1939 (Ceadel op cit: 295).

The proportion of objectors began to shrink as older age groups were called up. By the end of July 1940, 51,419 had registered as conscientious objectors (Hayes op cit: 13). Overall during World War Two around 58,000 men and 2,000 women applied to be registered as COs. Around 40,000 gained conditional exemption and 2,900 full exemption. About 5,000 were prosecuted and in many cases imprisoned (Taylor 1992: 457). Membership of the PPU continued to grow through the months of the "phoney war" and reached an all-time high of 136,000 in April 1940. It suffered its first net loss only in May 1940 (Ceadel op cit: 296). By the end of the war it still had more than 98,400 pledges in its live membership file (ibid: 312).

Hayes presents an analysis of conscientious objector applicants from March 1940–42 to one local tribunal – the South-western based in Bristol. Out of a total of 3,353 applicants the great majority are defined by Hayes as "religious" – 2,958 or 88 per cent, including 662 Methodists, 531 Church of England, 302 Quakers etc. He classifies a further 209 or 6 per cent as members of religious and ethical communities. The smallest group is "political" comprising 51 socialists, 11 communists, eight fascists and some others (Hayes op cit: 26–7). Hayes doubts that the proportion of religious is that high, and argues that many might have been described as Peace Pledge Union objectors – some no doubt devout but most formed within "a broadly humanitarian, broadly moral, broadly ethical" category (ibid: 28).

Rachel Barker, assessing the Fulham trbunal, identifies a very different cohort: of those applying for unconditional exemption, a considerable number were known as political objectors, mostly socialists or communists, who did not object to war as such, but who objected to a capitalist war. "Of all objectors it was perhaps this type that was most unpopular in and out of the tribunals" (Barker 1982: 20)

The historical consensus is that the treatment of COs was far better than in World War One. According to Taylor (op cit: 457): "The public looked on the conscientious objectors with tolerance, and they repaid this by dissenting from their fellow countrymen regretfully...Their objection was nearly always to war in general than this particular war." Certainly fewer went to prison. Juliet Gardiner (2004: 100) observes that "In the First World War approximately one in three Conscientious Objectors was imprisoned for their beliefs: in the Second it was around one in ten." However, "In 1939, 14 per cent of all objectors were granted unconditional exemption: as the war grew fiercer the tolerance grew less; those granted unconditional exemption fell to 5 per cent in 1940 and just 2 per cent in 1941."

The press, conscientious objectors and the emergence of the 'conchie'

In English, the term "conscientious objector" possesses an eloquent dignity with religious undertones. Quality newspapers such as *The Times* or the *Manchester Guardian* between 1939 and 1945 used the term extensively, sometimes shortened to "objectors" within a story and COs in a headline. Popular newspapers would employ both terms in the body text of stories but frequently utilised the term "conchie" in a headline, a contemptuous slang term first coined in World War One.

The collective memory of World War One was, of course, a major conditioning factor in framing the way preparations for war were presented – notably the brutal treatment of COs in 1916–18 and the fact that leading public figures had been gaoled for their beliefs. In the run-up to war, this memory was routinely invoked as an example of how *not* to behave, as in the *Daily Mirror* (1 June 1938: 13):

WHY THIS FUSS?

Why all this fuss about the suggestion that we should at once have conscription if we had a war? Did anybody suppose we could muddle on, as we did last time, coaxing and calling? Inciting silly girls to offer white feathers to boy friends? Getting up registration schemes of the willing to enlist, the not-so-willing, and the conchies?

No, no, we all know surely that next time there'll be no time for tomfoolery.

"Conchies" here is being invoked in a knowing, critical manner, as an example of "our" formerly stupid behaviour. "We" are older and wiser now. In fact, the *Mirror*'s coverage of COs in the run-up to war was respectful if disapproving. Papers broadly on the left tended to take a more supportive attitude to the rights of COs, reflecting the strong links that some sections of the Labour Party still retained with pacifism. These included the *Manchester Guardian* and the *Daily Herald* (one time official organ of the Trades Union Congress). On 30 March 1940, for example, a leader in the *Herald* referred to a London tribunal case where a young man had testified that he would like to go to Germany to preach pacifism and said he would welcome Germans to Britain "because I trust them as my fellow-men". A tribunal member commented: "It is quite obvious from your last answer that you have not got any conscience." In a comment that could just have easily have been in the *Mirror* (or, differently worded, in the *Manchester Guardian*) the paper argued :

The *Daily Herald* completely disagrees with the young man's attitude. But it claims he is entitled to hold that attitude. For Alderman Marshall's wisecrack it can find no justification whatever. Such superficial comments are a poor advertisement for the impartiality of the tribunals (*Daily Herald*, 30 March 1940).

In fact, most newspapers stated that allowing objectors the right to disagree was an expression of the democratic values which were being fought for. The *Daily Express*, which was to carry many "conchie"- baiting stories, carried a leader on COs on 4 May 1939:

There is a small number of people, a very small number, who oppose any form of national service for conscientious reasons. They will not fight, nor will they undertake work of national importance which would contribute to the nation's effort in war.

There is a certain amount of righteous anger against these people, and talk of putting pressure on them.

No persecution

It is suggested that they should be sent to prison for six months while the other lads of twenty are having their training. For conscientious objectors were sent to prison during the last war.

But bear in mind that prison corridors have often been paths that led to the House of Commons. In several Parliaments there have been men who went to prison for their principles.

Be patient, be enduring, and turn your backs on persecution. Judge not, that ye be not judged. For with what judgement ye judge, ye shall be judged: and with what measure you mete, it shall be measured to you again (*Daily Express*, 4 May 1939: 10).

The distinctive Old Testament preaching style of an *Express* leader, with the tone enjoining obedience to authority and revealed religion, differentiated it from the *Mirror*, with its labourist politics and attempts to ventriloquise the working class patois and slang of its readers (see Smith 1975: 53 and 65).

How the press delegitimised radical groups

James Curran (1978) observes that "challenges, or potential challenges, to the socio-political order tend to be characterised in the press as irrational, unrepresentative and a threat to the majority. Notwithstanding the political orientation of the press, there has been an extraordinary continuity in the symbols used in the popular press to de-legitimise radical or politically deviant groups". Leader writers might plume themselves on British freedom of speech and conscience, but conscientious objectors were speedily belittled. The revival of the "conchie" tag from World War One was accompanied by a mobilisation of jeering gender stereotypes (see Rose op cit: 175–6). In May 1939 a strip cartoon in the *Daily Mirror* cast aspersions on the masculinity of a pacifist with all the subtlety of a Charles Atlas advertisement. Headed "Was she right to jilt him?"

It told the heart-rending story of a girl who was "in love" with a pacifist and who, when the call to service came, found herself unable to stand up to her family's criticism of him, and left him. ("Suddenly I realised John was not a Man at all!") Then she met a man she "could be proud of" – a Territorial – and the last picture of the series showed her walking in the park with her uniformed gallant while in the background a pitiable figure – the pacifist of course – skulks by, books under arm, shoulders unhealthily bent (*Peace News*, 12 May 1939: 3).

However, in the early months of the war most routine press coverage of COs focused on the happenings at the local or appellate tribunals. These were a rich mine of material for local papers, who were "invariably present at hearings and quickly made public any sufficiently sensational exchanges" (Barker op cit: 36). Stories deriving from tribunals were frequently not exercises in straight court reporting but headlined or highlighted damaging details.

One attraction was the departure of these "Objectors' Courts" from the judicial norm. Performances varied greatly, with some conducted in a spirit of objectivity and others providing a stage for eccentric comments by objectors or tribunal members. These happenings could then be packaged by papers according to their editorial prejudices. One paper that specialised in extracting every ounce of ridicule from the tribunals was the *South London Advertiser*, which ran a series entitled "Stories from the Conchie Courts".

The art of packaging the story was to extract a quotation to hold up to ridicule or a "fancy that" reaction and put it in the headline or the opening section of the report (known in journalistic jargon as the "intro"). The report of 15 March 1940 is a good example:

> "USE GANDHI'S METHODS TO RESIST GERMANY", SAYS ARP WORKER
>
> A West Norwood conscientious objector, who said he believed that Britain should resist Germany by employing the principles of Mr Gandhi in India, was removed from the register at the Bloomsbury Tribunal on Tuesday.
>
> He is Peter Edward Martell, an ARP worker, of Glennie-Road, West Norwood. Judge Hargreaves (chairman of the Tribunal) said it was obvious that Martell's case was not a matter of conscience. Martell told the court that he would not assist a soldier wounded in this country by a German bomb. Soldiers who were not conscientious objectors ought to have been, he added.
>
> Sir Edmund B. Phipps, a member of the Tribunal: "That is the most extreme statement we have heard here since October 3."

Most stories presented COs in a poor light. But another genre presented Tribunal members abusing their powers. Both the *Mirror* and the *Daily Herald*, for example, criticised the administration of the Newcastle Tribunal under the notorious Judge Richardson. On 12 October 1939, the *Mirror* revealed:

CROWD HISS AT TRIBUNAL

"I am certain, as sure as I sit here, that if Christ appeared today he would approve of this war."

Hissing and booing by people in the court greeted this remark by Judge T. Richardson, a County Court Judge, at the conscientious objectors tribunal at Newcastle last night.

Twice the Tribunal adjourned because of disturbances (*Daily Mirror*, 12 October: 15).

The next day Cassandra, the *Mirror*'s principal columnist, took a page one slot to criticise the judge:

The movement for sanctifying this war rapidly increases.

God has been handed a gas mask and told to fight for Britain.

Easily the best recruiting sergeant so far in this unpleasant line of talk is Judge Richardson.

This legal (and presumably religious) gentleman has been acting as chairman at a tribunal for conscientious objectors.

His observation, made two days ago, will go down in history. Said he:

"I AM CERTAIN, AS SURE AS I SIT HERE, THAT IF CHRIST APPEARED TODAY HE WOULD APPROVE OF THIS WAR."

So the Almighty approves of the slaughter of countless German men, women and children, does He?

Let's hang up the machine gun, the poison gas cylinder and the bomb alongside the Cross as Holy symbols.

Listen, Judge Richardson!

God isn't on our side.

God isn't on Hitler's side.

Let's keep Him out of this dirty, hideous, mechanised campaign of bloodshed.

The whole thing adds up to the simple fact that we are out to save our necks by getting the other fellow first-and that's all. Also, it's less blasphemous.
(*Daily Mirror*, 13 October 1939: 1).

Yet positive reports about COs not infrequent

The following day the *Mirror* reported that education workers in Edmonton who were COs and ordered to do non-combatant service would get their pay made up to their normal salary. The chairman of the education committee, Alderman Harrington, was prominently quoted: "After all, why should they be penalised for their opinions? They will be treated just the same as others" (*Daily Mirror*, 14 October 1939: 3). In these early stages of the conflict, positive reports about objectors were not infrequent. A fascinating case occurred in the *Mirror* of 25 October:

READY TO DIE FOR HIS BROTHER

FROM OUR SPECIAL CORRESPONDENT

PORT GLASGOW, Renfrewshire, Tuesday

Tom Robinson, a twenty-seven-year-old driller, is ready to die for his brother.

He said so today, when he won for his younger brother exemption from military service by offering to go in his place.

Tonight, at their home in George-street here, his mother put her arm around Tom's shoulder and said: "Tom is a fine lad, and I am proud of him. He would sacrifice anything for his young brother, Joseph."

The brothers are the only children still living at home.

"Joseph has never been away from me," said the mother. "But all the same, I should hate to lose Tom..."

A few hours earlier twenty-year-old Joseph had applied to the Conscientious Objector Tribunal in Glasgow for exemption from military service on ethical grounds.

"I am willing"

During the hearing his older brother jumped to his feet in the court and said eagerly: "I am willing to volunteer if you will allow me to take his place.

"Our parents are much more attached to him than they are to me."

Members of the Tribunal leaned forward and listened in admiration as the shabbily dressed young man continued:

"I would like the chance to defend my home, and I want to spare my parents the shock of my young brother being taken away.

"I have had long talks with my brother and I know that he is sincere in his objections to war."

Tom's appeal was successful. It was announced later in the day – long after the brothers had left the court together – that the appeal had been granted (*Daily Mirror*, 25 October 1939: 11).

This adroit narrative works on a number of levels. A mini-fable of family solidarity, heroism and sacrifice is spun around the Tribunal. Primarily the report appears to celebrate family bonds, articulating powerful links between the brothers and their mother. It stages a sacrificial moment, with strong Christian undertones, as the Tribunal members "lean forward in admiration" of the "shabbily dressed young man" who wishes to "spare my parents". Whilst commemorating the younger brother's sincerity of conscience it foregrounds the older brother's desire to serve "to defend my home", which resonates not only as the familial home and Port Glasgow, but also the national home, Scotland. Later positive stories about COs – for instance as firefighters, merchant seamen, medical staff and bomb disposal workers – would also foreground the "sacrifice" theme.

Focusing on debates in local authorities

As tribunals gathered pace, another familiar story focused on the debates in local authorities about what to do about conscientious objectors in their employment. They were not legally obliged to do anything but numbers of local authorities began to fire COs, under pressure from their own electorates or local political magnates. Cassandra was again allowed to put the argument for civil liberties.

Open Mind

One of the toughest jobs of this war is to keep an open mind.

It is so easy to condemn those things with which we do not agree.

For instance – conscientious objectors.

The obvious target.

The easy jeer.

Howl "conchie" – one of the ugliest words in the language – and the mob roars in instant applause.

On the tail of this sorry shout you can pin most rotten rabble-rousing cries.

It is a corner-stone for jeers. It is the very foundation of scorn.

It is interesting to learn that an English Borough Council has decided to ask conscientious objectors in its employ to give notice.

Local government seems to be losing its grip.

I've no brief for conscientious objectors and I see no particular merit in grabbing a gun to combat those in other lands who are equally willing to pull the trigger.

BUT I DO THINK THAT IF WE ARE FIGHTING FOR LIBERTY, FREEDOM OF SPEECH AND EQUALITY, THOSE WHO DISAGREE WITH US SHOULD HAVE THEIR SAY WITHOUT BEING

THREATENED WITH THEIR LIVELIHOOD – OR WITH A TRUNCHEON, CLUB OR A GUN (*Daily Mirror*, February 1940: 10).

There is a paradox here. The tabloid use of slang, as Martin Conboy (2006: 23–24) puts it, is "an attempt to reinforce [the journalists'] relationship with their readers" and to demonstrate in their informal tone that they are "on the side of the people". Within Cassandra's rhetoric, "conchie" functions as an epithet of the "mob". At the heart of much popular media is, of course, a deep-seated contempt for the audience, the hydra-headed many. It is an axiom of successful popular journalism that such contempt should never become obvious in the ongoing "process of mutual confirmation", the "social transaction" (Hall 1975: 22) which maintains the performance. But elsewhere in the newspaper, "conchies" came in for a lot of abuse.

For instance, over in the *Mirror's* "Live-Letter Box", there was no objection to criticising "conchies". A reader wanting to know "whether the proportion [of men] registering as conscientious objectors has grown at all as older men, who are presumably able to think for themselves, are registering" was told:

> So far Scotsmen seem to be the most patriotic. They have an average of 1.8 per cent conchies, though England only has 1.9 per cent. Wales, however, has the highest rate…3.5 per cent…getting on for twice the English and Scottish figure. Tut-tut. Wales! (*Daily Mirror*, 21 February 1940).

"Live Letters" carried on a debate about the position of COs versus serving soldiers. Stories also emerged of people refusing to work with conscientious objectors or accept their services. In Cheshire people were reported to be walking miles to a council office rather than pay rent to a rent collector registered as an objector (*Daily Mirror*, 24 February: 2). And a strike at a Yeovil glove-making factory became a *cause célèbre* when strikers refused to work with a CO on the grounds that their sons in the forces were being paid a fraction of his wages (*Daily Mirror*, 29 February: 6). A number of major figures became involved in the debate, including Arthur Greenwood MP, deputy leader of the Opposition, who contributed a lengthy article in the *Daily Express* on March 8 portentously headed "Thus CONSCIENCE doth make COWARDS of us all. IS IT TRUE?"

> I suppose the experience of Norman Case, the young Yeovil glover, has done more than anything else in the war so far to make us re-examine in our own minds our reactions towards a conscientious objector….
>
> The glovers of Yeovil know what they feel about conscientious objectors. They refuse to work with a man who earns £4 or so a week while their own sons are in the Forces receiving 2s a day…

In the main public attitudes towards conscientious objectors is much more tolerant than it was in the last war.

My view is that the very deep conviction as to the freedom of speech and thought which forced us to go to war and the realisation that we must win to survive are allied to the reasons for our greater toleration towards conscientious objectors now (*Daily Express*, March 1940: 6).

Space for relaxed liberalism diminishing

But the space for this relaxed liberalism was diminishing. A succession of Conservative MPs raised questions about the favourable treatment of objectors. The security services were closely monitoring pacifist organisations and lumped them into the same "subversive" category as the British Union of Fascists and the Communist Party of Great Britain. The mood had begun to harden by March 1940, before the invasion of Norway and Denmark, the fall of France and the Dunkirk evacuation. Six PPU members were arrested at Marble Arch on 2 March – according to the *Daily Express* "following a scene...when a section of the crowd took objection to the leaflets being distributed" (*Daily Express*, 3 March 1940: 1). *Peace News* reported that police were using obstruction laws. The Ministry of Information began a drive to persuade regional newspapers to give less space to the reporting of objectors' arguments at tribunals, as was revealed in a letter by a regional information officer to local newspaper editors, leaked to *Peace News* (McLaine 1979: 57).

By the time of the invasion of Norway and Denmark, with its unnerving use of parachutists and Quisling elements, Cassandra's tone had shifted decisively:

Peace – It's Wonderful!

As long ago as November last I began to collect specimens of the leaflets that the pilots of our Royal Air Force were showering on German towns....Early in January we received a letter from the highest Government source requesting us, in the interests of national security, not to discuss the content of these pamphlets....but at the end of last week a pacifist publication plastered its front page with the whole story, together with translations.

This particular journal fiercely advocates coming to terms with Germany – an attitude which it still fervently professes in spite of the latest outrage in Scandinavia. Now, I claim that to allow this subversive sheet to flout a procedure which is considered by the Cabinet to be in the direct interest of the whole community is, to say the least, surprising.

We have it on an authority that we do not question that it is helpful to the enemy cause to publish these leaflets.

In spite of this, these misguided cranks, who feverishly believe in giving milk to sabre-toothed tigers and calling them kittens, cheerfully take action that we are assured will help Hitler's degraded cause.

Surely it is time to take a stand! Either it's right or it's wrong to print this stuff- and if it is wrong, then these eccentric olive branch experts should be made to pipe down. And stay piped down! (Daily Mirror, 15 April 1940: 6).

By the end of 1941 it was possible to insult COs with sarcastic abandon. For example, the answer to a "Live-Letter" question as to whether there were any conscientious objectors in Germany said "We are told that the German troops regard conchies, whether punished or not, more or less in the light of earth worms and cabbage slugs - like we do, in fact" (3 January 1941: 5). By 1944, the stereotype was well in place in the *Mirror*:

Conchies' rest home plan fails

Can you imagine a house of rest, inhabited entirely by vegetarians, teetotalers, pacifists, and conscientious objectors?

There was somebody who could, Mrs Jessie Winifred Norgate, of Earlham Green-lane, Norwich, and in her will she directed that her home at Cliff-drive, Cromer, had been used for this purpose.

In the Chancery Division yesterday, Mr Justice Uthwatt had to decide whether this constituted a "good charitable gift".

He decided that the supposed charity was not a practical proposition and there was no general charitable intention disclosed. The gift, therefore, faded and would fall into residue (*Daily Mirror*, 21 July 1944: 4).

Conclusion: The best deal COs were likely to get

The *Daily Mirror* was always going to be deeply equivocal about conscientious objectors. Although the *Mirror's* democratic credentials depended on being prepared to argue for some space for individual conscience, the reasonable voice of the leading article was but one of many distributed across the paper that created its identity (Tulloch 2007, Smith 1975).

The dominant *Mirror* take on the war from 1939 was the need for strong government, modernisation, new thinking, youthful energy and everyone pulling together. The men of Munich, bureaucrats and blimps stood in the way. Given this frame, COs could easily be identified as shirkers. Above all, the *Mirror* identified with the serving man and woman. Nearly a third of all service men and women read the *Mirror* at this stage. A loud trumpeting of human rights in leader columns, intertwined with jeering sarcasm in the letters page, was probably the best deal COs were likely to get.

References

Addison, Paul (1975) *The road to 1945*, London: Jonathan Cape

Barker, Rachel (1982) *Conscience, government and war: Conscientious objection in Great Britain 1939–45*, London: Routledge and Kegan Paul

Brittain, Vera (1989) *Diary 1939–1945: Wartime chronicle* (edited by Bishop, Alan and Bennett, Y. Aleksandra), London: Victor Gollancz

Calder, Angus (1969) *The people's war: Britain 1939–45*, London: Jonathan Cape

Carpenter, Humphrey (1992) *Benjamin Britten*, New York: Charles Scribner's Sons

Ceadel, Martin(1980) *Pacifism in Britain 1914–45: The Defining of a faith*, Oxford: Clarendon Press

Ceadel, Martin (2001) The opposition to war, Liddle, Peter, Bourne, John and Whitehad, Ian (eds) *The Great World War 1914 – 45 Vol. 2: The peoples' experience*, London: Harper Collins Publishers pp 435–49

Clark, Ronald (1975) *The life of Bertrand Russell*, London: Jonathan Cape and Weidenfeld and Nicolson

Conboy, Martin (2006) *Tabloid Britain: Constructing a community through language*, London: Routledge

Cook, Judith (1997) *Priestley*, London: Bloomsbury

Croall, Jonathan (2008) *Sybil Thorndike*, London: Haus Books

Curran, James (1978) The press as an agency of social control, Boyce, George, Curran, James and Wingate, Pauline (eds) *Newspaper History: from the 17*th *century to the present day*, London: Constable pp 51–75

Dekar, Paul (2007) The "Good War" and Baptists who refused to fight it, *Peace and Change*, Vol.32, No 2, April pp 186–202

Gardiner, Juliet (2004a) Prisoners of conscience, *History Today*, November, Vol. 54, No. 1 pp 32–39

Gardiner, Juliet (2004b) *Wartime. Britain 1939–45*, London: Headline Book Publishing

Hayes, Denis (1949) *Challenge of conscience*, London: George Allen and Unwin

Marwick, Arthur (1976) *The home front: The British and the Second World War*, London: Thames and Hudson

McLaine, Ian (1979) *Ministry of morale: Home front morale and the Ministry of Information in World War Two*, London: George Allen and Unwin

Middlemass, Keith (1979) *Politics in industrial society. The experience of the British system since 1911*, London: Andre Deutsch

Monk, Ray (2000) *Bertrand Russell: The ghost of madness*, London: Jonathan Cape

Mosse, George L. (1990) *Fallen soldiers: Reshaping the memory of the world wars*, Oxford:

Oxford University Press

Murray, Nicholas (2003) *Aldous Huxley: An English intellectual*, London: Abacus (previously published by Little, Brown 2002)

Overy, Richard (2009) *The morbid age: Britain between the wars*, London: Allen Lane

Partridge, Frances (1978) *A pacifist's war*, London: Hogarth Press

Peace Pledge Union (2009) Vera Brittain – women and peace. Available online at http://www.ppu.org.uk/e_publications/vera_women2.html, accessed on 15 June 2009

Priestley, J.B. (1940) *Britain speaks*, New York: Harper and Brothers. Extract available online at http://www.spartacus.schoolnet.co.uk/Jpriestley.htm, accessed on 18 June 2009

Rose, Sonya O. (2003) *Which people's war?: National identity and citizenship in Britain 1939–1945*, Oxford: Oxford University Press

Smith, Anthony C.H. (1975) *Paper voices: The popular press and social change* (with an introduction by Hall, Stuart) London: Chatto and Windus

Taylor, A. J. P. (1992) *English history 1914–1945* (paperback edition) Oxford: Oxford University Press

Terkel, Studs (1984) *The good war: An oral history of World War Two*, New York: Pantheon

Tulloch, John (2007) Tabloid citizenship: The *Daily Mirror* and the invasions of Egypt (1956) and Iraq (2003) *Journalism Studies*, Vol. 8, No 1, February pp 42–60

Woolf, Virginia (1985) *The diary of Virginia Woolf, Vol. 5 1936–41* (edited by Bell, Anne Oliver) London: Penguin Books

Websites

http://www.coproject.org.uk

http://www.ppu.org.uk

http://www.ppu.org.uk/learn/infodocs/people/pst_dick.html for information on Dick Sheppard

Newspaper resources

Friends House Library, London – cuttings archive of national and regional press for period 1939–41

Peace Pledge Union – archive, including bound copies of *Peace News*

British Newspaper Library electronic resources – digital *Daily Mirror* and *Daily Express*

Lincoln City Public Library – microfilm copies of *Lincolnshire Echo* (Thanks to *Lincolnshire Echo* for access to bound volumes 1939–41)

17

War as peace: The Canadian media in Afghanistan

JAMES WINTER

British author and journalist George Orwell warned in his classic novel *Nineteen Eighty-Four* (1949) that if citizens were not vigilant the state could come to control our actions and possibly even our thinking. Orwell described futuristic conditions under Big Brother, in which the official Newspeak language dictated that "war is peace". From a critical peace perspective, that time has long since arrived. As Noam Chomsky has observed (1991: 60): "Huge media campaigns wielding vacuous slogans to dispel the danger of thought are now a staple of the ideological system." For example, on the brink of the 1991 Gulf War, Canadian External Affairs Minister Joe Clark (1990: A18) told the House of Commons that: "What the world is doing in the Gulf... [is] returning to the notion that peace should not only be kept, but made."

If war is peace, then it is a very short hop to the notion that UN peacekeeping may become war, as it has in Haiti and elsewhere (Engler 2009; Engler and Fenton 2005). Indeed, if war can be sold as mere peacekeeping, then we are into the realm of what former *New York Times* correspondent Chris Hedges (2009) calls "the disease of permanent war".

International law, as established in the United Nations Charter, stipulates two scenarios under which war may be legally waged. Article 51 establishes that if a country is attacked and there is no peaceful remedy, there exists "the inherent right of individual or collective self-defence". The UN Security Council may also authorise war if international interests in peace and security are threatened. Post-9/11, there is also the "responsibility to protect", (R2P) the controversial measures adopted at the 2005 World Summit and ratified by the UN Security Council and General Assembly. A showpiece of Canadian Liberal Party philosophy, R2P was launched in 2000 through the International Commission on Intervention and State Sovereignty. R2P calls for collective action through the Security Council "should peaceful means be inadequate and national authorities manifestly fail to protect their populations from genocide, war crimes, ethnic cleansing and crimes against humanity". This was not the case either in Afghanistan or Iraq, but R2P has made many very nervous about the potential for serious abuse (Engler op cit: 22).

It is of paramount importance, then, to recognise that the US-led invasions of Afghanistan and Iraq are both illegal wars under international law (Mandel 2004), although they are portrayed as vehicles for bringing peace, freedom, democracy, and even "civilisation" itself to these countries. This simple, incontrovertible fact would be greeted with astonishment by the Canadian public, steeped as it is in mainstream news media mythology.

A peacekeeping nation

Canadians have long thought of themselves as international peacekeepers, at least since former Prime Minister Lester Pearson won a Nobel Peace Prize in 1957 for his role in the Suez Crisis. Polls over the years demonstrate that about 90 per cent of Canadians strongly endorse their country's UN peacekeeping role (McQuaig 2007: 76). Since the Vietnam War, Canadians have taken great delight in ridiculing US foreign policy, with an air of smugness and self-satisfaction. Canadians, who evolved seamlessly from a British colony to an American outpost, seemingly without a breath of independence in between, might be expected to side, reflexively, with other colonies. Imagine the surprise, then, as Canadians found themselves up to their necks in the service of imperialism.

Of course, beneath the thin veneer of Canadian social conscience lies the dirty little secret of armament manufacturing, gunboat diplomacy and far worse. In contrast to the altruistic imagery, Engler (op cit) details Canada's long-standing role as both a junior partner to imperial powers and an independent actor with its own distinct self interests, around the world. He writes: "Canadian internationalism has rarely been at odds with American belligerence" (ibid: 224). While Canadian soldiers were not officially participating in US invasions from the Vietnam debâcle onwards, the country's businesses were profiting handsomely. The veneer began to pull away in earnest, however, with Canadian troop participation in three US-led invasions of the 1990s, in the Persian Gulf, Somalia and the Balkans.

The Thatcher-Reagan-Mulroney years of the 1980s begat free trade agreements which saw Canada hitching its wagon ever more closely behind the American locomotive. As their economies became more closely entwined, Canada turned over its oil and water reserves to the Americans, and simultaneously began to further adapt its foreign policies. Prime Minister Trudeau's dalliance with Cuba's Fidel Castro in the 1970s became Brian Mulroney's tap dance with Ronald Reagan in the 1980s. The FTA of the 1980s became the NAFTA of the 1990s. By the time the World Trade Center in New York was struck in 2001, Liberal PM Jean Chrétien would rashly commit Canada to help defend the US against terrorism, leading to its partnership in the illegal invasion of Afghanistan.

Strong public opposition contributed to Canada's refusal to openly join the invasion of Iraq in 2003, despite strong tactical, supply, troop and leadership support (Engler op cit). But successive Canadian governments under Liberals Jean Chrétien and Paul Martin, and then Stephen Harper's Conservatives, have sent troops to join in the occupations of Afghanistan and Haiti. Canadian troops also helped to oust Haiti's former president Jean-Bertrand Aristide, in 2004, while the government supported the repressive and murderous client dictatorship of Gérard LaTortue, a former Miami talk show host.

By February 2006, newly-elected Conservative PM Stephen Harper was glad-handing the Canadian troops in Afghanistan, decked out in military fatigues, mimicking George Bush. Later in 2006, Harper's Minister of Defense Gordon O'Connor explained that the Canadian "mission" in Afghanistan was undertaken to deprive "Osama bin Laden's al-Qaeda of its base following the 9/11 attacks. The Taliban government gave shelter to al-Qaeda, forced women to wear burkas and kept them from working outside the home". Finally, he said: "Canada's focus in Afghanistan was on reconstruction and development" (Dougherty 2006).

Media salute war

The Canadian media have not simply reported O'Connor's stated rationale, but have adopted it as their own from the outset. Afghanistan, as the mainstream media proudly tell us, is "war: Canadian style". That is, when they are not disguising the war by calling it a "conflict" or a "mission". It is the first war with Canadian troops officially involved since Korea.

Mergers and takeovers in media industries over the past twenty years have led to huge conglomerates, with accompanying debt loads and a focus on payments and the bottom line. Cutting a swath through the ranks of journalists meant closing foreign bureaus and turning increasingly to international wire services for news. Gradually and covertly, then, Canada's news of the world has been increasingly written by the Associated Press or *The New York Times* News Service.

Today's mainstream coverage of Afghanistan almost entirely assumes that Canada's war efforts are noble and purely motivated. In this, we have adopted what American media critic Norman Solomon called "American exceptionalism" or "the belief that unlike other great powers, the United States is motivated not by the self-interest of some set of elites but by benevolence – which allows policy-makers to sell wars that are designed to extend and deepen US power as a kind of international community service" (Solomon 2005 cited in Jensen 2005).

On the (visible) "far left wing" of Canadian politics, New Democratic Party leader Jack Layton called in September 2006 for the immediate withdrawal of Canadian troops from Afghanistan, but apparently more because the war was unwinnable than because it was immoral and illegal. Layton wrote in the *Toronto Star* that the mission was "ill-defined, unbalanced" and with "no exit strategy". As Canadian progressive journalist Linda McQuaig (2006) wrote, in the con-text of the Iraq war, the problem is not the incompetence of the invading forces. "The real problem is that it is illegal for one country to invade another country." McQuaig's lone voice aside, this perspective is beyond the pale of Canadian jour-nalism, and even Jack Layton's protests were met with scorn by the press. The *Vancouver Sun*, for example, editorialised that when "Layton calls for Canada to pull out of Afghanistan, he is handing victory to these [drug] criminals and the Taliban" (Editorial 2006).

Below, we will conduct an detailed analysis of a case study in war coverage by Canada's largest daily newspaper. This analysis reveals the way in which Canada's mainstream media justify and promote the war, selling it to Canadians on behalf of the government, war-profiteers and the military. Beyond this, however, the media act to frame "Afghanistan" in a way that is consistent with a Canadian "rescue" or aid mission. The overall message is that Canada is coming to the rescue of Afghanistan: removing a despotic government, the Taliban, creating a "democratic" government led by President Hamid Karzai, improving the condi-tions of women, conducting reconstruction by building schools and other infra-structure. To accomplish this, the news media need to foreground some events, and background or omit others. For example, the efforts by troops to meet with elders and discuss reconstruction are foregrounded. President Karzai's office and some of his statements are also foregrounded, but how he came to office, his appoint-ment by the US, is omitted, as are his pleas for a stop to the bombing of Afghan civilians (Warnock 2009).

Serious shenanigans related to the postponed Afghan elections are completely omitted by the mainstream media. I was able to find only fleeting reference to these elections in April to June, 2009, a period when presidential candidates declared themselves and the elections themselves were postponed until late August. Ignoring the elections avoids having to explain why Karzai's running mate is Mohammad Qasum Fahim, one of the most notorious warlords in Afghan history (ibid). Similarly, it would be impossible to maintain the charade of a rescue mission if the (longstanding) plans for oil pipelines were to receive much coverage, so these are all-but-ignored. (Escobar 2009). Additionally, of course, there is no reference to the real role played by the US and its little buddy Canada in foreign affairs over the past century, from Mexico to Hawaii, Iran, Guatemala, Nicaragua and Chile (Blum 1998). It helps to undermine and downplay resistance to the war if these contradictions to the mantra of peace, liberty and reconstruction are conveniently omitted.

A close look at *Toronto Star*'s war journalism

Linda McQuaig has commented on the irony that the Canadian Journalism Foundation, a private organisation which describes itself as dedicated to promoting "excellence in Canadian journalism", held a public forum to address a question it saw as baffling in 2006: Why was there a lack of public support for the war effort? In a news release promoting the event, the foundation praised the media for "doing a credible job of reporting on the importance of Canada's role in the military operation". But McQuaig asked (2007: 8): "Shouldn't the media be expected to do a credible job of reporting the facts of the war, and let Canadians decide for themselves the importance and legitimacy of Canada's role?"

Just as it is difficult to distinguish Conservative PM Stephen Harper from his American counterpart, decked out in army fatigues, visiting the troops, so too has it been hard to discern a difference between Canadian news media cheerleading for the Afghanistan war effort and American media support for the invasions of Afghanistan and Iraq. In the spring of 2006, while the erstwhile progressive *Toronto Star* had columnist Rosie Dimanno abroad, drooling over the troops, I studied their special report news coverage, headlined, "Canada's war". Nowhere to be found was reference to the simple question of *why* Canadian troops were in Afghanistan.

Very briefly, let's return to the events of 2001. Allegedly, a group of terrorist hijackers brought down the World Trade Center's twin towers in New York, resulting in more than 2,900 deaths. Within two hours, the US administration identified the culprit as Osama bin Laden. Eventually, it was determined by the US that 15 of the 19 hijackers were from Saudi Arabia, with the others from the United Arab Emirates (2), Lebanon (1), and Egypt (1). However, George W. Bush immediately targeted the Taliban government of Afghanistan, as sheltering bin Laden, and threatened reprisals unless he was turned over immediately. The Taliban, while perhaps a despotic government, replied quite reasonably according to media reports that it would turn over bin Laden to an international court of law, in exchange for evidence of his involvement in 9/11. Bush responded that this was unreasonable, and as with Kosovo in 1999, using NATO as a vehicle, invaded Afghanistan, bombing that country's rubble into even smaller pieces and installing an interim government (Pilger 2001, 2003). Carried out without the approval of the United Nations, this was and is an illegal invasion under international law (McQuaig 2007: 89; Mandel op cit). According to Noam Chomsky (2001):

> A week after the bombing began, the President reiterated that US forces "would attack Afghanistan 'for as long as it takes' to destroy the al Qaeda terrorist network of Osama bin Laden", but he offered to reconsider the military assault on Afghanistan if the country's ruling Taliban would surrender Mr bin Laden, "If you cough him up and his people today, then we'll reconsider what we are doing to your country," the President declared. "You still have a second chance."

Despite all the vast resources at its disposal, the US has been unable to locate bin Laden as of 2009. Instead, the US government turned to its next target, Iraq. Failing to obtain UN sanction for an invasion of Iraq, the US acted unilaterally, and again illegally, with its "coalition of the willing", including Britain but this time not (officially) Canada. In the horror immediately following 9/11, Jean Chrétien's Canadian government offered whatever assistance it could, allowing American aircraft to land at Canadian airports, housing American passengers, and effectively offering to assist in any reprisals. This is how Canada became involved in Afghanistan, and eventually assumed a leadership role in the NATO "mission" there, in 2006.

War – Canadian style

I've chosen to examine some of the coverage of Afghanistan in Canada's largest and most "progressive" daily newspaper, the *Toronto Star*. The *Star* published a special report, an eight-part series in March 2006 written by journalist Mitch Potter. The report was carried at the time when Canada was assuming a more prominent role with the NATO forces in Afghanistan, and while Canadian soldiers were on a mission named "Operation Peacemaker". The series was captioned "War – Canadian style" and beneath this heading on the features page on the web, there was the brief explanation: "Canada's soldiers are fighting a battle in Afghanistan that few of their countrymen yet understand." This seemed to imply that the *Star* intended that its series would help to explain Canada's involvement in Afghanistan to its readers.

'Medieval religious dogma'

The first part of the series ("Bringing the war home: Drugs, dogma and insurgents") described how Canadian soldiers in Afghanistan were up against "Drugs and dogma". We're told the soldiers are well-trained, in readiness for Canada's first real combat mission since the Korean War. They were confronted by a "stone age" civilisation, with little more than poppies for opium, and mosques. Clearly, the implication is these people are in need of some form of intervention. We are told:

> Here, mud-walled homes stand in clustered communities that lack virtually everything one associates with modernity. They have no electricity, no teachers, no doctors, no roads worthy of the name, no means with which to rise from the ashes of a quarter century of conflict.

The article continued, juxtaposing calls to prayer at mosques and the crowing of roosters, (itself offensive) then, unbelievably dismissing Islam as "medieval religious dogma":

> What these villages do have are mosques, with calls to prayer five times a day the only sound that carries apart from the crowing of roosters. And...what will become a new poppy harvest...Drugs and medieval religious dogma, an unholy alliance...is what the Canadians find themselves up against.

Dismissing and de-humanising the enemy is a common tactic in war propaganda, and a means of justifying massive intervention in their lives. If they are medieval – if not stone aged – then they obviously need our help. As for their condition – mired in "a quarter century of conflict" – it is they who bear the responsibility, in a classic case of blaming the victims, who actually have long been pawns in a war of the superpowers (Potter 2006).

The second part in the series ("A fruitful meeting") describes how Canadian soldiers gain grudging acceptance from Kudalan villagers after making promises about building schools. The troops inform the villagers: "You must understand that these are not Canadian problems, these are Afghanistan's problems. We are only here temporarily to help get your government back on its feet." These military statements are presented by the reporter as factual, and there are no qualifications, contradictions nor alternative perspectives. It is a story about how helpful Canadian soldiers are to the locals, and how it is their role to help the people.

The third part of the series ("The birthplace of dust") describes the hardships suffered by the Canadian troops, living without running water or showers, in all the dust. The perspective on the enemy insurgents is revealing: in his own words the reporter describes how, in an earlier period under US infantry occupation. "The valleys were allowed to fester unchecked with an ever more emboldened insurgency, eager to test the will of the coalition forces." So here, Afghani resistance fighters are compared to infectious bacteria, which "fester unchecked".

Part Four in the series ("LAVs and Luck – the 'Ratpicker'") is one part advertisement, one part ode-to-technology. It is about the "LAV III", a Canadian-made light armoured troop carrier, a $3.5 million vehicle which we are told can withstand a direct hit from explosives beneath it. The reporter writes: "The LAV's top-mounted 24mm canon is the biggest gun – it fires a supersonic round whose shockwave alone can be fatal within one metre of its target." The effect here is to celebrate superior technology and accomplishments, and again, implicitly, to contrast these with the "stone age" inhabitants of Afghanistan.

Abandoning neutrality

Part Five of the series, ("Fathers and sons – true confessions"), is about family traditions, generations of soldiering, which gets into the blood. The story starts with the perspective of a 55-year-old soldier who describes soldiering as the hardest work, harder even than jackhammering, because when you're finished there's no hot tub or cold beer. We learn that he has a 25-year-old son in the same unit, whose grandfather also fought in World War I. This is, then, celebrating dedication to tradition and to your country. Another soldier says what they have is "not just a peacekeeping army, but a peacemaking army", reflecting the way in which the motto for the military operation has been internalised by the troops.

In part six of the series, ("Axe Attack – backup arrives – we're Okay") a Canadian lieutenant sitting in a circle with tribal elders is suddenly attacked by a 16-year-old youth with an axe, who delivers a head blow and then meets swift "justice": "Seconds later [he was] cut down by 14 bullets from three Canadian guns." For the embedded journalists, this brutal attack led them to openly abandon any principles of objectivity. No questions were asked about the propriety of putting 14 rounds in a teenager with an axe, in fact, these actions are justified by the reporter. That evening, the embedded journalists drew back, out of respect for the soldiers.

> Photographer Rick Madonik and I found a quiet corner far out of earshot as the 1st Platoon closed ranks to make sense of the incomprehensible. They huddled at the firepit, a private murmur of voices whose words will never be known. Eventually, they came to us. And came to realize that, *under the circumstances, their wound was in some way our wound as well*. This is dangerous terrain, we knew. The business of newspapering is built upon practiced detachment. But *there was no detachment on this night*, as Trevor Greene lay prone in the hospital at Kandahar Airfield. He was – he is – simply too likeable a man *to now revert back to the neutrality* with which we joined the Red Devils (emphasis added).

So, for the journalists, when a Canadian soldier was attacked and wounded in a war zone, his wounding was theirs as well, grounds for abandoning their "neutrality" and closing ranks. In part seven ("One soldier's week – a chance to fight"), one of the soldiers who shot the teenager is interviewed about his thoughts.

> What troubles him is that *killing was the only available option* in those fleeting moments after the axe came down. [Captain] Schamuhn saw the "pure poison hatred" in the young Afghan's eyes. It was *a look that sought death, for his victim, for himself.* And all the Canadians on the ground could do was oblige (emphasis added).

The journalist continues, regarding the Captain:

> The impulse to do more comes naturally to the soft-spoken Schamuhn, who commands his platoon with a maturity and nuance beyond his 26 years. On one hand, the Regina-born commander is a pastor's son, *spiritually committed to the humanitarian mission of changing lives for the better half-a-world away.* Another part of him is a warrior's son, dedicated to the belief that there is no greater honour than leading men into battle and getting everyone out alive (emphasis added).

So, here is a justification not just for this shooting itself, but for the military presence as a whole, seamlessly inserted into the story. The soldier's thoughts, the journalist's thoughts– what we all should think – is quite apparent. But of course, this is all heavily value-laden. First of all, the teenage insurgent's motives are as easily dismissed as his life. He was crazy. Possessed by irrational, "pure, poison hatred". The captain sees "honour" in the soldiers' killing of the teen. The boy wanted death for those around him and for himself. The soldier and the journalist know the intentions of the dead youth. All the Canadian soldiers were doing was obliging him. One wonders, would the Canadian account differ if this was a French teenager, during World War Two resistance, axing a German lieutenant, and being shot by German soldiers? Would Germans merely be obliging such a crazed youth by killing him? We next learn that the soldier is a pastor's son who is "spiritually committed to the humanitarian mission of changing lives for the better half-a world away". And so this, for the soldier, reporter and the *Toronto Star* itself, is what the invasion of Afghanistan is all about: changing lives for the better.

The next part of the story dismisses pacifists, those who object to the invasion, as being out of touch with reality. You have to be there, and to fight, to understand the "reality". Then, and only then, will your opinions have some merit.

> As a student of military history, the young captain also has something to say about the Canadian tendency to take its peace for granted. The sheer lack of fighting on our own soil, he says, has damaged the Canadian perception of what really goes on in the world and fostered a culture of blithe pacifism. It is one thing for someone to come back from seeing reality in a place like this and to say, "I'm a pacifist. I don't want Canada to have an army." "I can respect that, even if I don't agree," says Schamuhn. "But if you're born in Canada and that's all you've ever known, your words mean nothing to me. Because you haven't seen the other side of the world. You haven't seen the necessity of conflict. There are people who are fighting against peace, against stable government. And Canada, whether they want to know it or not, has a very strong warrior class. I guess that is what the front-line soldiers really want Canadians to understand. *We want Canadians to get on board*, to realize we are out here and to allow us to do what we are prepared to do" (emphasis added).

According to this view, the insurgents are irrational, "fighting against peace, against stable government". Nowhere to be found are the facts: their country was invaded, illegally, by a foreign occupational force, which deposed the government, bombed the countryside, and is now attempting to quash opposition, having imposed a client regime. The message is simple: "We want Canadians to get on board. Support our troops." It's not surprising that this message should come from the military; what's shocking is that it should come so forcefully from the news media.

Helping 'ungrateful locals'

In the final part of the series, ("Frustrations – back over the wire– small victories") we are told how Canadian soldiers give toys and gifts to the young children in the area near their encampment, but this ends after the attack on the lieutenant, for security reasons. "Helping ungrateful locals" could be the title of the series, it is certainly a theme running through it. The soldiers' challenge is fighting insurgents who are merely shadows, "shadows that hide behind a dirt-poor civilian population who must be brought onside if Afghanistan is to stand whole again". It is a common theme in imperialist propaganda: the ignorant, savage locals who stubbornly refuse help, and in so doing reject a better way of life. This is the story told by the French missionaries who came to Canada to convert native peoples to Christianity. It is the story told by American historians about the people of South Vietnam. And this paternalistic, bigoted language has been adopted by Canadian armed forces, and Canadian news media, in Afghanistan. Sergeant Scott Proctor is quoted:

> We were dealing with fairly educated populations in the past, he said. You could say to them: "Come on, you actually know better than this." And they would say: "Well, yeah. We do." That's not the case with Afghanistan, and that's part of what makes this such a big task. But it is doable, he said. And we're trying to go about it the right way with the support for the new Afghan government. We need to get them used to having a government and to get them to see that their police are actually police and not just another extortionist group. Right now, the people around here don't have anything Canadians would even consider a lifestyle. They live in a mud hut and have a little patch of dirt on which they grow a meager existence. Right now they probably just want us to leave, along with Taliban and other opposing military forces. But we can't leave until [the Taliban] leave and the government gets up and running.

Finally, the reporter sums up the series and the war effort. Again, we have the image of Afghanis as ignorant, helpless children, battered by (their own) warring factions.

> You may call the Afghan villagers of Gombad and places like it helpless. The lingering paradox now is that they may also be unhelpable, altogether too shredded by successive generations of conflict and decline to accept the hand within reach. It is a question Capt. Schamuhn has been pondering for months, even before he came to Kandahar. He went to his father, the pastor, for answers. "I was struggling with the problem that we can't help everybody. We could be here for the rest of our lives and we still won't be able to solve Afghanistan, it is such a complex and deeply rooted problem," he says. "But my dad's advice was: 'Don't worry about changing the world. Just change individual people's worlds, one at a time.' "There will always be war, there will always be bad guys," says Schamuhn. "It is the nature of humanity. But just to smile at the kids as we go through these villages, to see their faces light up, you are touching a life

on the other side of the planet. That's what we have to focus on: the individual victories."

Adopting American exceptionalism

Saving the world one country at a time. These are the same platitudes used by successive US administrations and foisted on their citizens and the world over the past century, to justify wholesale slaughter and exploitation. (Blum op cit). The reporter is explaining away any potential failures: these people may be beyond help, no matter how noble our intentions. It's all about benevolence, helping, educating, liberating, restoring (or introducing) democracy. There is no other way to look at this, other than through the crazed eyes of a teenager with a death wish, or the festering insurgents as a whole.

So, just as Canadian political leaders have adopted the US political economic mantra about "free trade", exporting jobs and manufacturing, so too has the Canadian state adopted the US mantra which portrays empire building as benevolent. It's apparent that the *Toronto Star*, as an effective arm of the Canadian state, is promoting Canadian exceptionalism. This is why John Pilger has called the media "weapons of war". The series I've examined is little more than public relations puffery, which couldn't have been more effectively written by the Canadian Armed Forces themselves. It is a value-laden narrative which has entirely adopted the army mantras about "peacemaking" and determination to "change lives for the better", no matter how unpopular these changes might be, in the invaded country. For their part, the embedded journalists are "sharing the wounds" suffered by the soldiers and openly abandoning any neutrality which might be called for by (easily discarded) professional standards. Events leading up to the invasion, and all historical context is omitted, such as the 1980s US support for Osama bin Laden and the Mujahadeen in their war against another imperialist aggressor – the Soviet Union. Censoring this information avoids having to ask messy questions such as: if the Soviets were invaders, why aren't we?

During wars, the media should question everything

Because of the huge stakes, and because truth is the first casualty, in a time of war the news media must be most skeptical, most adversarial: they should accept nothing and question everything. Instead, like their American counterparts, the mainstream Canadian media have adopted the role of stenographers to power, and cheerleaders for the war team. Although this performance has served the establishment well, it is a disservice to the public, the troops, and to the victims in Afghanistan. Canadian media, like our political leadership, have shamed us. By joining the US administration in its century-long campaign of privileging empire and profits over human rights and lives, this nexus of politics and pro-paganda has left Canadians with the blood of innocent victims on their hands. What's more, despite the government's contention that they are saving the world from terrorism, they have further endangered lives by exposing Canadians to retaliatory terrorist attacks.

References

Blum, William (1998) *Killing hope: US military and CIA interventions since World War II*, Montreal: Black Rose Books

Chomsky, Noam (1991) What we say goes: The Middle East in the new world order, *Z Magazine*, Vol. 4, No. 5, May

Chomsky, Noam (2001) The war in Afghanistan. Lakdawala lecture, New Delhi, 30 December. Available online at http://www.matrixmasters.com/wtc/chomsky/chomsky.html, accessed on 19 May 2009

Clark, Joseph (1990) Make peace by force, quoted in, Just what was said, *Globe and Mail*, 12 November

Dimanno, Rosie (2006) Taliban targets our troops, *Toronto Star*, 20 March

Dougherty, Kevin (2006) PR boost sought for Afghan mission, *Edmonton Journal*, 18 November

Editorial, (2006) Freeing Afghans from fanatics is a long-term, but necessary mission, *Vancouver Sun*, 27 September

Engler, Yves (2009) *The black book of Canadian foreign policy*, Nova Scotia: Fernwood Books

Engler, Yves and Fenton, Anthony (2005) *Canada in Haiti: Waging war on the poor*, Nova Scotia: Fernwood Books

Escobar, Pepe (2009) Pipelineistan goes Iran-Pak, *Asia Times*, 29 May

Hedges, Christopher (2009) The disease of permanent war, TruthDig.com: 18 May. Available online at http://www.truthdig.com/report/item/20090518_the_disease_of_permanent_war/, accessed on 19 May 2009

Jensen, Robert (2005) It's the empire, stupid, ZNet Commentary, 29 July

Mandel, Michael (2004) *How America gets away with murder*, Ann Arbor: Pluto Press

McQuaig, Linda (2006) The real problem is that it is illegal for one country to invade another country, *Toronto Star*, 29 October

McQuaig, Linda (2007) *Holding the bully's coat: Canada and the US empire*, Toronto: Doubleday

Orwell, George (1949) *Nineteen Eighty-Four*, London: Secker and Warburg

Pilger, John (2001) This war is a fraud, *Mirror*, 1 November

Pilger, John (2003) The betrayal of Afghanistan, *Guardian*, 20 September

Potter, Mitch (2006) War: Canadian-style Bringing the war home: A special report, *Toronto Star*, 12 March

Solomon, Norman (2005) *War made easy: How presidents and pundits keep spinning us to death*, New York: John Wiley and Sons

Warnock, John (2009) Crushing democracy in Afghanistan, GlobalResearch.ca, 14 May. Available online at http://www.globalresearch.ca/index.php?context=va&aid=13611, accessed on 18 May 2009

18

Normalising the unthinkable: The media's role in mass killing

DAVID EDWARDS

Turning our heads to see it

The American historian Howard Zinn has noted that all is not as it seems: "The truth is so often the reverse of what has been told us by our culture that we cannot turn our heads far enough around to see it" (Zinn 1997: 400).

Thus, our culture never tires of telling us that we live in a democratic society. We are free to make meaningful choices between political parties and leaders offering a range of fundamentally different policies. And we are free to choose from a wide media "spectrum", stretching from the liberal left out to the "Tory press" on the right. It requires a considerable feat of mental gymnastics to turn our heads far enough around to see the truth behind these claims.

Compare, for example, the conventional view of the US electoral system with the opinion expressed by three-time independent US presidential candidate, Ralph Nader: "We have a two-party dictatorship in this country. Let's face it. And it is a dictatorship in thraldom to these giant corporations who control every department agency in the federal government" (see Jay 2008). As for the corporate media, if our senior editors are to be believed, they function as fiercely independent watchdogs of power. In November 2008, editor Alan Rusbridger described the *Guardian*'s priorities (see Confino and Wright 2008): "... the papers should promote minority views as well as mainstream argument and should encourage dissent." In 2005, Simon Kelner, then editor-in-chief of the *Independent* and the *Independent on Sunday*, promised: "no retreat from the qualities that have underpinned the *Independent* since its launch... the role for an independent paper, one that is not driven by proprietorial agenda and that has no party allegiance, is as great as ever" (Kelner 2005).

The claims to uncompromising independence and progressive intent sit uneasily alongside the clear bottom-line priorities of media corporations. The fact is that newspapers such as the *Guardian* and the *Independent* are dependent on corporate advertisers for at least 75 per cent of their revenues (see Preston 2001). A newspaper's primary goal is not, as many people assume, to reach as many readers as possible; it is to sell wealthy audiences to advertisers. Journalists often loudly insist that advertising has no influence on content. But this is manifestly not the case. Media analyst James Twitchell explained how newspapers have evolved to serve the needs of advertisers:

> You name it: the appearance of ads throughout the pages, the "jump" or continuation of a story from page to page, the rise of sectionalisation (as with news, cartoons, sports, financial, living, real estate), common page size, halftone images, process engraving, the use of black-and-white photography, then colour, sweepstakes, and finally discounted subscriptions were all forced on publishers by advertisers hoping to find target audiences (cited in Beder 1997: 181).

An October 2001 BBC advertisement reminded the public: "Honesty, integrity – it's what the BBC stands for." Helen Boaden, the BBC's director of news, told one viewer: "People trust the BBC because they know it is an organisation independent of external influences. We do not take that trust lightly." (Helen Boaden, email forwarded to Media Lens, the media monitoring website I run with David Cromwell at www.medialens.org, on 2 December 2004). And yet the BBC's senior management are appointed by the government of the day. Steve Barnett (2001) noted in the *Observer*:

> Back in 1980, George Howard, the hunting, shooting and fishing aristocratic pal of Home Secretary Willie Whitelaw, was appointed [BBC chairman] because Margaret Thatcher couldn't abide the thought of distinguished Liberal Mark Bonham-Carter being promoted from vice-chairman. Then there was Stuart Young, accountant and brother of one of Thatcher's staunchest cabinet allies, who succeeded Howard in 1983. He was followed in 1986 by Marmaduke Hussey, brother-in-law of another Cabinet Minister who was plucked from the obscurity of a directorship at Rupert Murdoch's *Times* Newspapers. According to Norman Tebbit, then Tory party chairman, Hussey was appointed "to get in there and sort the place out, and in days not months".

The machinations of Tony's cronies

The same machinations continue to this day. At the time of the 2003 invasion of Iraq, both the BBC chairman, Gavyn Davies and his director-general, Greg Dyke, were supporters of, and donors to, the Labour Party. Davies's wife ran Gordon Brown's office; his children served as pageboy and bridesmaid at the Brown wedding. Tony Blair had stayed at Davies's holiday home. "In other words," columnist Richard Ingrams noted (2001), "it would be hard to find a better example of a Tony crony."

BBC journalists claim to be scrupulously impartial. In January 2000, Andrew Marr, the BBC's (then) recently appointed political editor, declared to the press: "When I joined the BBC, my organs of opinion were formally removed" (Marr 2000). Three years after undergoing this procedure, Marr stunned his ideological surgeons in reporting the rapid fall of Baghdad to US tanks on 9 April 2003. His comments are worth quoting at length:

> Well, I think this does one thing – it draws a line under what, before the war, had been a period of… well, a faint air of pointlessness, almost, was hanging over Downing Street. There were all these slightly tawdry arguments and scandals. That is now history. Mr Blair is well aware that all his critics out there in the party and beyond aren't going to thank him, because they're only human, for being right when they've been wrong. And he knows that there might be trouble ahead, as I said. But I think this is very, very important for him. It gives him a new freedom and a new self-confidence. He confronted many critics.
>
> I don't think anybody after this is going to be able to say of Tony Blair that he's somebody who is driven by the drift of public opinion, or focus groups, or opinion polls. He took all of those on. He said that they would be able to take Baghdad without a bloodbath, and that in the end the Iraqis would be celebrating. And on both of those points he has been proved conclusively right. And it would be entirely ungracious, even for his critics, not to acknowledge that tonight he stands as a larger man and a stronger prime minister as a result (Marr, BBC1, 22:00 News, 9 April 2003).

This was as appalling as it was unexceptional. On the same day, the BBC's Nicholas Witchell declared of the fall of Baghdad: "It is absolutely, without a doubt, a vindication of the strategy" (BBC News at Six, 9 April 2003). BBC news reader and dance show celebrity Natasha Kaplinsky beamed as she described how Blair "has become, again, Teflon Tony". The BBC's Mark Mardell agreed with her: "It *has* been a vindication for him" (BBC1, Breakfast News, 10 April 2003). Over on ITN, Tom Bradby exulted: "This war has been a major success" (ITN, Evening News, 10 April 2003). ITN's John Irvine commented: "A war of three weeks has brought an end to decades of Iraqi misery" (ITN Evening News, 9 April 2003).

On Channel 4, foreign secretary Jack Straw told Jon Snow that he had met with the fiercely anti-war French foreign minister that day: "Did he look chastened?" Snow asked wryly (Channel 4, 9 April 2003). On the same programme, reporter

David Smith pointedly chose to end his report from Washington with a quotation from "a leading Republican senator": "I'm just glad we had a commander-in-chief who didn't listen to Hollywood, or *The New York Times*, or the French." And yet Marr commented the following year (2004: 279):

> Gavin Hewitt, John Simpson, Andrew Marr and the rest are employed to be studiously neutral, expressing little emotion and certainly no opinion; millions of people would say that news is the conveying of fact, and nothing more.

Rationalising the unthinkable: The division of labour

As the above sample from a veritable mountain of evidence suggests, the corporate media system does not in fact operate as an independent watchdog. On issue after issue, year in year out, it functions as a propaganda system for power. One of the media's most important roles was described by Edward Herman (1991):

> There is usually a division of labour in doing and rationalising the unthinkable, with the direct brutalising and killing done by one set of individuals; others keeping the machinery of death (sanitation, food supply) in order; still others producing the implements of killing, or working on improving technology (a better crematory gas, a longer burning and more adhesive napalm, bomb fragments that penetrate flesh in hard-to-trace patterns). It is the function of defence intellectuals and other experts, and the mainstream media, to normalise the unthinkable for the general public.

The unthinkable is normalised as a result of the media presenting Western actions within a highly supportive ideological framework. British historian Mark Curtis commented:

> Fundamentally the assertion, or assumption, is that the world role of Britain and the West, despite occasional deviations, is at root benign, both in motivation and in effect. Little is seen to be basically wrong with the basic policy priorities and the major institutions and domestic structures of society that shape them (Curtis 1995: 4).

Thus, the chairman and the deputy director of one of Britain's leading academic institutes wrote in their study of foreign policy:

> The promotion of democratic values through foreign policy is most directly demonstrated by government attitudes to human rights outside Britain. In the nineteenth century the Royal Navy extended the anti-slavery campaign from Britain to the Atlantic and Indian Oceans, enforcing basic standards of civilised

behaviour... Human rights issues are no less controversial or difficult today, though British governments have far less capability to intervene in the affairs of other countries (ibid: 2).

The human rights myth

Similarly, *Guardian* journalists have written of "Britain's reputation as both a respecter and champion of human rights". In their book on New Labour, two *Guardian* writers referred to Tony Blair as "a high minded champion of human rights" (see Curtis 2009). The same pattern is found across the media. On the 12 April 2005 edition of the BBC's flagship Newsnight programme, diplomatic editor Mark Urban discussed the significance of a reduction in Iraqi attacks on US forces since January of that year: "It is indeed the first real evidence that President Bush's grand design of toppling a dictator and forcing a democracy into the heart of the Middle East could work" (Urban, Newsnight, BBC2, 12 April 2005). Was it journalism or propaganda to suggest that democracy was the motivating goal behind the Bush-Blair attack on Iraq?

In April 2009, Urban wrote on the BBC website of Iraq: "...protest had a righteous place in trying to prevent what many considered an unjust and illegal war. But once British troops were engaged, the success of their mission should have become an issue of broad national consensus" (Urban 2009). I wrote to Urban asking him: "Are you proposing this as a general principle? If so, you are advocating that 'once [Russian] troops were engaged [in Afghanistan], the success of their mission should have become an issue of broad national consensus'. Or are you proposing a principle for your own government and its allies? If so, this is standard jingoism" (Edwards email to Urban, 24 April 2009). I received no reply. In January 2006, as Iraq collapsed under the violence and chaos of military occupation, Jeremy Bowen, the BBC's Middle East correspondent, commented:

> Thanks to the Americans, Iraq had elections in December 2005. Voting in itself is not a magic formula to make people's lives better. Just because they cast their ballots the violence won't stop and the electricity won't run all day. But voting is the way to create a fairer system, so something better might have started. Under American protection, Iraq's newly elected politicians now have to show they can build a democracy (Bowen 2006).

He added:

> All this does not mean that the dreams that the Bush administration has for the region are coming true... The Americans are discovering that the problem

with democracy is that it can produce results that you don't like. That's just the way it is.

Bowen is one of the BBC's most respected reporters. The *Independent* has described his work as "scrupulously unbiased" (*Independent* 2009). But was it "scrupulously unbiased" to suggest that post-invasion Iraq under superpower occupation was free to seek genuine democracy under "American protection"? Correspondent Jonathan Rugman declared on Channel 4 News: "Yes, the Americans want democracy here [Iraq], but they don't want to die for it" (12 November 2003). We are to assume, then, that the Americans wanted Iraqis to have the right to have nothing whatever to do with America, perhaps preferring to forge a Shi'ite alliance with Iran. What did it matter to America if, in securing that noble end, it paid the price in thousands of dead and injured troops, and trillions of dollars spent? Helen Boaden, the BBC's director of news, wrote to us at Media Lens:

> To deal first with your suggestion that it is factually incorrect to say that an aim of the British and American coalition was to bring democracy and human rights, this was indeed one of the stated aims before and at the start of the Iraq war and I attach a number of quotes at the bottom of this reply (Boaden, email to Media Lens, 20 January 2006).

Remarkably, in making her point Boaden supplied no less than 2,700 words filling six pages of A4 paper of quotations from George Bush and Tony Blair. In March 2009, a Media Lens reader asked BBC reporter Reeta Chakrabarti why she had claimed that Blair had "passionately believed" that Iraq had weapons of mass destruction. After all, an alternative interpretation might be that Blair had been lying through his teeth. Chakrabarti responded: "I said Mr Blair passionately believed Iraq had WMD because he has consistently said so" (forwarded to Media Lens, 2 March 2009).

In our eight years of work on Media Lens, we have collected numerous examples of this kind of propaganda. The pattern is consistent and heavily biased towards powerful interests. Rare indeed are the journalists who will dare suggest that Britain and America had more ruthless, cynical and self-serving motives in Iraq. In his memoir, the economist Alan Greenspan, former chairman of the US Board of Governors of the Federal Reserve, offered a point of view that is essentially taboo right across the mainstream media: "I am saddened that it is politically inconvenient to acknowledge what everyone knows: the Iraq war is largely about oil" (*Sunday Times* 2007).

Kosovo: The fictional genocide

The unthinkable is also normalised by consistent media support for British and American state violence. In the crucial periods when the "allies" are urgently seeking public backing for war, the media is almost always on-side. The liberal press, particularly the *Guardian* and *Independent*, strongly supported Nato's 78-day assault on Serbia from 24 March until 10 June 1999. Jonathan Freedland wrote in the *Guardian*: "The prize is not turf or treasure but the frustration of a plan to empty a land of its people." It was, Freedland said, "a noble goal" (Freedland 1999). A *Guardian* editorial on 26 March described the war as nothing less than "a test for our generation".

The attack was intended to stop "something approaching genocide", Timothy Garton Ash declared (Garton Ash 2002). The *Mirror* referred to "Echoes of the Holocaust" (see Pilger 2004a). The *Sun* urged Britons to "Clobba Slobba" and "Bomb, Bomb, Bomb" (see Hammond 1999). As British bombs fell on Serbia, Andrew Marr's organs of opinion became inflamed with war fever. He supported Blair's call for a ground offensive and wrote articles in the *Observer* with titles such as: "Brave, bold, visionary. Whatever became of Blair the ultra-cautious cynic?" (*Observer*, 4 April 1999) and "Hail to the chief. Sorry, Bill, but this time we're talking about Tony" (*Observer*, 16 May 1999). Marr declared himself in awe of Blair's "moral courage", adding: "I am constantly impressed, but also mildly alarmed, by his utter lack of cynicism."

A 2002 BBC documentary on the alleged Serbian genocide, "Exposed" (BBC2, 27 January), was billed as a programme marking Holocaust Memorial Day. A LexisNexis database search showed that in the two years from 1998–1999, the *Los Angeles Times*, *New York Times*, *Washington Post*, *Newsweek* and *Time* used the term "genocide" 220 times to describe the actions of Serbia in Kosovo. In the ten years from 1990–1999, the same media used the same word just 33 times to describe the actions of Indonesia in East Timor. And yet, following Indonesia's December 1975 invasion, some 200,000 East Timorese, or one-third of the population, are estimated to have been killed in one of history's premier bloodbaths (Pilger 1994).

So what is the truth of the Serbian "genocide" in Kosovo? In February 1999, one month before the start of Nato bombing, a report released by the German Foreign Office noted that "the often feared humanitarian catastrophe threatening the Albanian population has been averted". In the larger cities "public life has since returned to relative normality" (Curtis 2003: 136). A second German report, exactly one month before the bombing, refered to the CIA-backed Kosovo Liberation Army (KLA) seeking independence for Kosovo from Serbia:

> Events since February and March 1998 do not evidence a persecution program based on Albanian ethnicity. The measures taken by the [Serbian] armed forces are in the first instance directed towards combating the KLA and its supposed adherents and supporters (ibid: 136).

Following the war, Nato sources reported that 2,000 people had been killed in Kosovo on all sides in the year prior to bombing. George Robertson MP testified before the House of Commons that until mid-January 1999, "the Kosovo Liberation Army was responsible for more deaths in Kosovo than the Serbian authorities had been" (see Chomsky 2003: 56).

Cause and effect were reversed by the media – rather than preventing a humanitarian crisis, Nato bombing caused a massive escalation of killings and expulsions. The outpouring of refugees from Kosovo began immediately *after* Nato launched its attack. Before the bombing, and for the following two days, the United Nations Commissioner for Refugees (UNHCR) reported no data on refugees. On 27 March, three days into the bombing, UNHCR reported that 4,000 had fled Kosovo to the neighbouring countries of Albania and Macedonia. By 5 April, *The New York Times* reported "more than 350,000 have left Kosovo since March 24" (Gall 1999).

A study by the Organisation for Security and Cooperation in Europe (OSCE) recorded "a pattern of expulsions and the vast increase in lootings, killings, rape, kidnappings and pillage once the Nato air war began on March 24" and that "the most visible change in the events was *after* Nato launched its first air strikes" (Curtis 2003: 137, my emphasis).

Journalists were happy to acknowledge their role in the conflict. Responding to British government press spokesman Alastair Campbell's accusation of press negativity over the Kosovo intervention, Channel 4 correspondent Alex Thomson declared: "If you want to know why the public supported the war, thank a journalist, not the present government's propagandist-in-chief (see Glass 1999). The *Guardian's* Maggie O'Kane agreed: "But Campbell should acknowledge that it was the press reporting of the Bosnian war and the Kosovar refugee crisis that gave his boss the public support and sympathy he needed to fight the good fight against Milosevic" (ibid). As did John Simpson of the BBC: "Why did British, American, German, and French public opinion stay rock-solid for the bombing, in spite of Nato's mistakes? Because they knew the war was right. Who gave them the information? The media" (ibid).

Iraq – boosting Blair and burying the dead

In the run up to the invasion of Iraq, George Bush and Tony Blair claimed that Iraq had refused to cooperate with UN (Unscom) weapons inspectors between 1991–98. Therefore, Iraq retained deadly stockpiles of weapons of mass destruction (WMD) that represented a "serious and current threat" to Western interests, including British military bases on Cyprus. And yet, before the invasion, in 2001 and 2002, former chief UN weapons inspector Scott Ritter insisted that Iraq had been "fundamentally disarmed", with 90 to 95 per cent of its weapons of mass destruction "verifiably eliminated" by the time he and the other inspectors left the country in December 1998 (Ritter and Rivers Pitt 2002: 23). Of the missing 5 to 10 per cent, Ritter said: "It doesn't even constitute a weapons programme. It constitutes bits and pieces of a weapons programme which in its totality doesn't amount to much, but which is still prohibited" (ibid: 24). Ritter added of Iraq's alleged nuclear threat:

> When I left Iraq in 1998…the infrastructure and facilities had been 100 per cent eliminated. There's no doubt about that. All of their instruments and facilities had been destroyed. The weapons design facility had been destroyed. The production equipment had been hunted down and destroyed. And we had in place means to monitor - both from vehicles and from the air – the gamma rays that accompany attempts to enrich uranium or plutonium. We never found anything (ibid: 26).

A Media Lens media database search on 26 November 2002 found that the *Guardian/Observer* had mentioned Iraq in 2,955 articles that year – just 49 of these contained a mention of Scott Ritter. This constituted a shocking suppression of serious and credible dissident views (soon to be entirely vindicated) by the country's "leading liberal newspaper". A 30 April 2003 media database search found that Ritter had been mentioned in 12 articles in the *Guardian/Observer* so far that year out of 5,767 articles mentioning Iraq. This covered the crucial weeks leading up to the 20 March attack and invasion.

In the autumn of 2002, Ed Vulliamy, one of the *Observer*'s most senior reporters, received testimony from Mel Goodman, a former senior CIA analyst. Goodman, who retained his high security clearance and remained in communication with senior former colleagues, told Vulliamy that the CIA were reporting that Saddam Hussein had *no* weapons of mass destruction. Over the next four months, Vulliamy submitted seven versions of his article for publication by the pro-war *Observer* –all were rejected (Davies 2008: 329). Ray McGovern, a former high-ranking CIA analyst, told John Pilger: "It was 95 per cent charade. And they all knew it: Bush, Blair, Howard" (see Pilger 2004b).

But the charade was never exposed by the mainstream press. In the endless mentions of Iraqi WMD there was almost zero serious analysis of the likely condition of any retained Iraqi biological and chemical agents. Bush, Blair and others were thus allowed to spread scare stories without significant opposition from mainstream journalists. In a BBC interview with the much vaunted Jeremy Paxman, for example, Blair was able to declare, without challenge: "We still don't know, for example, what has happened to the thousands of litres of botulism and anthrax that were unaccounted for when the inspectors left in 1999" (Blair on Iraq: A Newsnight Special, BBC2, 6 February 2003). But Iraq was known only to have produced liquid bulk anthrax, which had a shelf-life of just three years. The last batch of liquid anthrax had been produced in 1991 at a state-owned factory that was subsequently demolished by UN weapons inspectors in 1996. Any remaining anthrax would therefore long since have become useless sludge.

Covering up catastrophe in Iraq: The *Lancet* controversy

The media has been equally adept at burying the true scale of the catastrophe unleashed by the US/UK occupation of Iraq. In November 2004, a report in the leading medical journal, the *Lancet*, estimated almost 100,000 excess Iraqi civilian deaths as a result of the invasion. The media response was overwhelmingly sceptical and subdued (a pattern repeated in 2006, when a second *Lancet* study reported 655,000 excess deaths as a result of the invasion). The 2004 report was produced by some of the world's leading research organisations: the Johns Hopkins Bloomberg School of Public Health in Baltimore, Columbia University, and Baghdad's Al-Mustansiriya University. Gilbert Burnham, one of the report co-authors told Media Lens:

> Our data have been back and forth between many reviewers at the *Lancet* and here in the school (chair of Biostatistics Department), so we have the scientific strength to say what we have said with great certainty. I doubt any *Lancet* paper has gotten as much close inspection in recent years as this one has! (Dr. Gilbert Burnham, email to David Edwards, 30 October 2004).

Nevertheless, the British government cynically exploited public and media ignorance of epidemiology in rubbishing the report. A 29 October 2004 Downing Street press release invented "a number of concerns and doubts about the methodology that had been used". The media happily swallowed the "dodgy methodology" thesis. A 20 July 2005 *Independent* editorial claimed the *Lancet* findings had been reached "by extrapolating from a small sample... While never completely discredited, those figures were widely doubted". The *Guardian's* Patrick Wintour and Richard Norton-Taylor commented (2004):

> The controversy about the study largely turns on whether the sample size of 7,800 people used by the team of US and Iraqi academics was sufficiently large, and whether the 33 neighbourhoods chosen were representative of the rest of the country.

This was nonsense, as any number of senior epidemiologists were willing to testify. Michael J. Toole, head of the Center for International Health at the Burnet Institute, an Australian research organisation, said of the *Lancet's* methodology: "That's a classical sample size." Toole noted that researchers typically conduct surveys in 30 neighbourhoods, so the Iraq study's total of 33 strengthened its conclusions. He concluded: "I just don't see any evidence of significant exaggeration" (Guterman 2005).

The pro-war *Observer* sank even lower in promoting a smear that was then popular in the right-wing US press. This noted that the *Lancet* study "was published soon before the US election, bringing accusations that the respected journal had become politicised. Journalist Michael Fumenton, of the US-based TCS (Tech Central Station) website called it 'Al-Jazeera on the Thames' ". Roger Alton, editor of the *Observer* at the time, gave Media Lens his considered view of the *Lancet* report: "I find the methodology a bit doubtful..." (email to Media Lens, 1 November 2004). Columnist David Aaronovitch, then of the *Guardian*, probably spoke from a comparable level of understanding: "I have a feeling (and I could be wrong) that the report may be a dud" (email to Media Lens, 30 October 2004).

Congo: A study in contrasts

In 2000, the lead author of the 2004 *Lancet* report, Les Roberts, had used the same methodology in researching the death toll in Congo for the International Rescue Committee (IRC). Roberts' first survey estimated that an astonishing 1.7 million people had died in Congo over 22 months of armed conflict – an average of 2,600 deaths per day. The IRC's president, Reynold Levy, put the figures in perspective: "It's as if the entire population of Houston was wiped off the face of the earth in a matter of months" (Hranjski and Brittain 2000).

As Roberts commented in 2005, the political and press reaction to these findings could hardly have been more different: "Tony Blair and Colin Powell quoted those results time and time again without any question as to the precision or validity" (see Guterman op. cit). Even though the estimates of death in Congo surprised experienced observers of the conflict, the media reported the figures without concerns about the validity of either the numbers or the methodology. Roberts pointed out the contradiction to journalists at the *Independent* in 2005:

> It is odd that the logic of epidemiology embraced by the press every day regarding new drugs or health risks somehow changes when the mechanism of death is their armed forces (Roberts, email to Media Lens for forwarding to the *Independent*, 22 August 2005).

In response to a second *Lancet* study in 2006 reporting 655,000 excess deaths as a result of the invasion, foreign office minister Lord Triesman told the press: "The way in which data are extrapolated from samples to a general outcome is a matter of deep concern" (Bennett-Jones 2007). And yet, six days earlier, the Ministry of Defence's chief scientific adviser, Sir Roy Anderson, had reported: "The study design is robust and employs methods that are regarded as close to 'best practice' in this area, given the difficulties of data collection and verification in the present circumstances in Iraq" (ibid).

A Foreign Office official was forced to conclude that the government "should not be rubbishing the *Lancet*". The editor of the *Lancet*, Richard Horton, commented on Tony Blair's "shameful and cowardly dissembling" in rejecting the study when he had been told it was robust. Horton added:

> This Labour government, which includes Gordon Brown as much as it does Tony Blair, is party to a war crime of monstrous proportions. Yet our political consensus prevents any judicial or civil society response. Britain is paralysed by its own indifference (Horton 2007).

Denying discussion and choice

As Horton's comments suggest, the unthinkable is also normalised by the media's failure to expose the public's inability to oppose British and American mass killing. Lawrence Jacobs and Benjamin Page (2005) found that the major influence on US foreign policy was "internationally oriented business corporations".

The authors found that public opinion had "little or no significant effect on government officials".

So much for democracy! British state violence has similar roots and is similarly insulated from democratic pressures. Mark Curtis said of British foreign policy: "Virtually its *raison d'être* for several centuries" has been "to aid British companies in getting their hands on other countries' resources" (Curtis 2003: 210). An unthinkable thought for the liberal press.

Elite interests are naturally unwilling to allow the public to interfere in this profit-making by other means. Thus, at election time, the leading political parties and mainstream media typically do not even discuss foreign policy and defence issues. Peter Golding, of the communications research centre at Loughborough University, found that in the first three weeks of campaigning for the 2001 general election, there had been "little sign of real issues" in media election coverage, where "few issues make the news" (Golding 2001). Issues such as the environment, foreign policy, poverty and defence were "all but invisible" (Golding, email to David Edwards, 10 June 2001). Loughborough University reported that this media performance closely followed the pattern of the 1997 and 1992 elections. Golding's report was mentioned in a small article in the *Guardian*'s media section and quickly forgotten.

In similar vein, the Media Tenor website reported that in the first few weeks of the 2005 UK election campaign – just two years after the catastrophic invasion of Iraq – the Labour and Conservative parties had almost nothing to say about foreign policy issues, including Iraq. The media were correspondingly silent. Media Tenor reported (2005) that between April 1–15 foreign politics accounted for a little over 1 per cent of all information on ITN news, BBC1 news and ITV news.

Loughborough University confirmed that Iraq made up just 8 per cent of topics coded in all media reporting over the 2005 campaigning period. This compares to 44 per cent devoted to the most popular topic, the election process itself (i.e. the actions, strategies and prospects of the participants). But even this does not tell the whole story. The researchers reported that discussion of Iraq was very low in the first two weeks of campaigning. Coverage rose dramatically half way through week three to half way through week four as the Conservatives tried to make political capital out of New Labour's "political improprieties" in misleading the public over Iraq.

Discussion of Iraq then fell away sharply to the end of the campaign as the Conservatives detected that their efforts were back-firing (they, after all, had supported the war). (Deacon et al 2005: 29). During the campaign, as usual, foreign policy (aside from the attempt to suggest the government had deceived the public over Iraq) accounted for just 0.4 per cent of coverage.

Conclusions: The world wide web – saviour or snare?

In 1993, a young internet pioneer, Michael Hauben, predicted the imminent future:

> Welcome to the 21st Century. You are a Netizen (a Net Citizen), and you exist as a citizen of the world thanks to the global connectivity that the Net makes possible. You consider everyone as your compatriot. You physically live in one country but you are in contact with much of the world via the global computer network. Virtually you live next door to every other single Netizen in the world. Geographical separation is replaced by existence in the same virtual space (Hauben 1993).

As Hauben noted, the corporate mass media were facing a very real challenge:

> The top-down model of information being distributed by a few for mass-consumption is no longer the only news. Netnews brings the power of the reporter to the Netizen. People now have the ability to broadcast their observations or questions around the world and have other people respond. The computer networks form a new grassroots connection that allows the excluded sections of society to have a voice (ibid).

In 2002 and early 2003, regular and massive anti-Iraq war protests took place in capital cities the world over. 15 February 2003 saw the largest protest march of any kind in London's history, with some estimates placing the number of marchers at 2 million. Historically, this level of pre-war opposition was entirely unprecedented. Ordinarily, opposition only builds, if at all, long after a war has got under way.

In 2009, after the BBC refused to broadcast a charity appeal for the victims of Israel's Operation Cast Lead massacre of civilians in Gaza from December 2008 to January 2009, the corporation received 22,000 complaints. Many of these were emails, many prompted by analysis appearing on numerous independent websites. We at Media Lens received hundreds of complaints to the BBC copied to us by readers of our media alerts on the subject. There is little doubt that this increased level of public dissent is related to the rise of unfiltered dissident opinion made possible by the internet. In South Korea, which has the world's highest broadband access per capita, enormous anti-government protests, known as Candlelight 2008, packed the centre of the capital, Seoul. South Korea's leading Netizen news service, Ohmynews, described the role of the internet:

> The impetus for the demonstrations was the agreement the new President Lee Myung-bak made when he visited George Bush in the US in April to end the restrictions on beef imports from the US into South Korea. The underlying

demand of the demonstrators, however, was that the programme of Lee and his Conservative Party not be allowed to take South Korea back to the days of autocratic rule...The earliest of the 2008 candlelight protests were inspired and supported by middle and high school students using the internet and cell phones to discuss the issues and to spread word about demonstrations (cited in Hauben 2009).

France 24 reported: "In these gatherings, laptops are a must have. Some people carrying computers film the crowd with their webcam and broadcast live videos thanks to high-speed wifi connections" (Touret 2008).

During the 2002 South Korean presidential election campaign, Ohmynews had played a decisive role in securing the election of progressive candidate Roh Moo-hyun. Elite interests quickly clamped down on internet freedom. In 2007, laws were implemented preventing websites from expressing their opinions on public forums or websites. Candidates could only be recommended on private blogs. Ohmynews editor-in-chief, Lee Han-ki, commented: "It was officially forbidden to voice support for one candidate. People who wrote such articles were arrested by the police and this stopped people from voicing their opinions on the internet" (cited in ibid). It was only after the election, that Netizens were once again able to freely express their opinions.

It is clear that the internet currently provides an unprecedented, and perhaps short-lived, opportunity to escape the "brainwashing under freedom" provided by our "free press". The world wide web may yet become a giant shopping service offering superficial, filtered state-corporate propaganda. Or it can become a means for creating a far more rational and compassionate society, one that no longer subordinates people and planet to profit. The results are not pre-ordained by destiny nor God – they are open, up for grabs and up to us.

References

Barnett, Steve (2001)Right man, right time, for all the right reasons, *Observer*, 23 September

Beder, Sharon (1997) *Global spin: The corporate assault on environmentalism*, Devon, UK: Green Books

Bennett-Jones, Owen (2007) Iraqi deaths survey "was robust", BBC Online, 26 March. Available online at http://news.bbc.co.uk/1/hi/uk_politics/6495753.stm, accessed on 29 June 2009

Bowen, Jeremy (2006) Middle East on the road to change, 2 January . Available online at http://news.bbc.co.uk/1/hi/world/middle_east/4551726.stm, accessed on 29 June 2009

Chomsky, Noam (2003) *Hegemony or survival*, London: Routledge

Confino, Jo and Wright, Emma (eds) (2008) *Living our values: Sustainability report*, Guardian News and Media, 17 November. Available online at http://image.guardian. co.uk/sys-files/Guardian/documents/2008/11/14/report2008.pdf, accessed on 29 June 2009

Curtis, Mark (1995) *The ambiguities of power*, London: Zed Books

Curtis, Mark (2003) *Web of deceit*, London: Vintage

Curtis, Mark (2009) Basic benevolence: An extract from *Web of deceit*. Media Lens Media Alert, 3 June 2009. Available online at http://www.medialens.org/alerts/03/030603_ Basic_Benevolence.html, accessed 29 June 2009

Deacon, David, and Wring, Dominic, and Billig, Michael, and Downey, John, and Golding, Peter and Davidson, Scott (2005) *Reporting the UK 2005 General Election*, Loughborough: Loughborough University

Davies, Nick (2008) *Flat earth news*, London: Chatto and Windus

Freedland, Jonathan (1999) No way to spin a war, *Guardian*, 21 April

Garton Ash, Timothy (2002) Imagine no America, *Guardian*, 19 September

Gall, Carlotta (1999) Misery and disease sweep Macedonian camp, *New York Times*, 5 April

Glass, Charles (1999) Hacks versus flacks, *Z Magazine*, August

Golding, Peter (2001) When what is unsaid is the news, *Guardian*, 28 May

Guterman, Lila (2005) Researchers who rushed into print a study of Iraqi civilian deaths: now wonder why it was ignored, *Chronicle of Higher Education*, 27 January. Available online at http://chronicle.com/free/2005/01/2005012701n.htm, accessed on 29 June 2009

Hammond, Philip (1999) The unasked questions: Reporting of the war in Yugoslavia has been strong on rhetoric and short on genuine attempts to get at the truth, FAIR, 4 September. Available online at http://www.fair.org/index.php?page=2449, accessed on 29 June 2009

Hauben, Michael (1993) The net and netizens, Spring. Available online at http://www. columbia.edu/~rh120/ch106.x01, accessed on 29 June 2009

Hauben, Ronda (2009) Netizen journalism as watchdog journalism, Ohmynews, 1 May Available online at http://english.ohmynews.com/articleview/article_view.asp?article_ class=2&no=385169&rel_no=1, accessed on 29 June 2009

Herman, Edward (1991) The banality of evil. Available online at http://www.information-clearinghouse.info/article7278.htm, accessed on 29 June 2009

Horton, Richard (2007) A monstrous war crime, *Guardian*, 28 March. Available online at http://www.guardian.co.uk/comment/story/0,,2044157,00.html, accessed on 29 June 2009

Hranjski, Hrvoje and Brittain, Victoria (2000) 2,600 a day dying in Congolese war, *Guardian*, 10 June

Independent (2009) Leader: Bad judgement, 16 April. Available online at http://www. independent.co.uk/opinion/leading-articles/leading-article-bad-judgement-1669307. html, accessed on 29 June 2009

Ingrams, Richard (2001) We don't need Tony's cronies at the BBC, *Observer*, 23 September

Jacobs, Larence R. and Page, Benjamin I (2005) Who influences US foreign policy, *American Political Science Review*, February pp 107–23

Jay, Paul (2008) Interview with Ralph Nader, Realnews.com, 5 November. Available online at http://therealnews.com/t/index.php?option=com_content&task=view&id=31&Ite mid=74&jumival=2717, accessed on 29 June 2009

Kelner, Simon (2005) The *Independent*: A new look for the original quality compact newspaper, *Independent*, 12 April

Marr, Andrew (1999) Brave, bold, visionary: Whatever became of Blair the ultra -cautious cynic? *Observer*, 4 April

Marr, Andrew (2000) Politicians aren't as loathsome as we think: discuss, *Daily Telegraph*, 10 January

Marr, Andrew (2004) *My trade: A short history of British journalism*, London: Macmillan

Media Tenor (2005) Economy dominates news while Iraq coverage slows down. Available online at www.mediatenor.com, 22 April

Pilger, John (1994) Land of the dead; journey to East Timor, *Nation*, 25 April. Available online at http://www.geocities.com/CapitolHill/Senate/7112/essay_02.htm, accessed on 1 May 2009

Pilger, John (2004a) Reminders of Kosovo, 13 December. Available online at http://www. johnpilger.com/page.asp?partid=376, accessed on 29 June 2009

Pilger, John (2004b) Universal justice is not a dream, ZNet, 23 March

Preston, Peter (2001) War, what is it good for? *Observer*, 7 October

Ritter, Scott and Rivers Pitt, William (2002) *War on Iraq*, London: Profile Books

Sunday Times (2007) Leader: Power, not oil, Mr Greenspan, 16 September

Touret, Nathalie (2008) South Korean "netizens" take to the streets, 18 June. Available online at http://www.france24.com/en/20080618-south-korea-internet-netizen-demonstration-democracy-broadcasting%20&navi=ASIE-PACIFIQUE), accessed on 29 June 2009

Urban, Mark (2009) The price of division, BBC website, 14 April. Available online at http://www.bbc.co.uk/blogs/newsnight/markurban/2009/04/the_price_of_division. html, accessed on 29 June 2009

Wintour, Patrick and Norton-Taylor, Richard (2004) No 10 challenges civilian death toll, *Guardian*, 30 October

Zinn, Howard (1997) *The Zinn reader: Writings on disobedience and democracy*, New York: Seven Stories Press

19

US coverage of conflict and the media attention cycle

STEPHAN RUSS-MOHL

The following study will summarise the latest research about the US coverage of terrorism and the Iraq War of 2003 and consequent occupation, showing how an economic theory of journalism can provide a clearer understanding of its complexities simply by viewing a familiar subject of investigation from a new angle. Modern warfare takes place in two interrelated realms. Generally, in an "attention economy", besides the customary circulation area where goods and services are exchanged for money, a secondary area of circulation appears where information is exchanged for attention (Franck 1998; Davenport and Beck 2001; Fengler and Russ-Mohl 2005).

As a result, during a war, a media conflict appears in tandem with the military conflict. "The media are missiles," says Matthias Karmasin (2009). Media outlets serve as artillery and their messages become bullets. In a globalised world linked by media networks, this becomes even more decisive in determining the outcome of a war, particularly in situations in which the warring parties depend upon the approval of a democratic public. Essentially, journalists are "embedded" at all times – not necessarily with military troops, to be sure, but definitely within their societies or "hemispheres". The personal interests of war reporters, bureau chiefs, editors and publishers (and other ideological factors) ensure that most of them follow herd behaviour.

The problems posed by information asymmetries in "principal-agent" relationships have real consequences for journalism (Höhne and Russ-Mohl 2004; Fengler and Russ-Mohl 2005 and 2008). When two actors are involved in a market transaction and both are interested in making a "deal", usually they are not equally well informed about the conditions of the "sale". The "agent", in most cases the subordinate or seller – possesses more information about the goods or service to be provided than the "principal", mostly the boss or the client. This imbalance may lead to distrust.

Similar information asymmetries characterise many transactions in the media, though there exists no formal contract relationship between journalists and their sources. When starting an investigation, journalists can be seen as "principals" depending on information, which is made accessible to them by PR "agents" or other sources. At the same time, journalists act in reversed roles as "agents" for their publics. The twofold role as principals and agents makes it difficult for journalists – if not virtually impossible – to admit to their audience that they themselves are, in fact, *not* the well-informed "information and news professionals" they like to appear.

Many more principal-agent-relationships influence the process of news production – some of them working in a cascade-like fashion one behind the other. Each of them may contribute to the partial distortion of news content, to under- and over-reporting as well as to the non-disclosure of facts. The "blind spots" of media coverage are not merely accidental. They are, most frequently, the result of self-interested behaviour.

During the Iraq invasion of 2003, the majority of American correspondents were placed alongside the troops, and this "embedding" tended to shape their perception of events (Cooke 2007; Lewis 2003; Wells 2003) – their very location forcing war reporters into the principals' roles being fed selectively with information by their "agents", the military. In the patriotic upsurge prompted by the initial phase of the invasion, bureau chiefs and in-house editors (now the "principals" of war reporters) stuck unpleasant news reported by their own correspondents ("agents") in the back pages of their newspapers. They responded to the national mood, oriented their coverage to what their competitors were reporting, and reserved the front pages for Bush administration spin (Broder 2008).

This has another effect, one that is probably as old as war reporting itself: both warring parties (now in the role of publics, and thus "principals" of the media) perceive reports by media outlets beyond their direct control as hostile. Robert P. Vallone, Lee Ross and Mark R. Lepper (1985) identified this "hostile media phenomenon", using the example of a massacre that occurred in Beirut.

The three major phases of an issue attention cycle

During the Iraq invasion of 2003, the Bush administration had unprecedented success in controlling the flow of information via a highly professional system of news management (Robertson 2005). The administration claimed that the Iraq War was part of the struggle against terrorism, and in doing so became "victims of group-think" (Janis 1972), not even realising that its own policies boosted the recruiting efforts of the Al Qaeda terror network (Bennett et al. 2007: ix). The debâcle has been subject to much analysis, but mostly published in books, scholarly articles, and the back pages of elite publications rather than in the mass-media outlets that reach the majority of Americans (cf. Kamalipour and Snow 2004; Rich 2006; Isikoff and Corn 2006; Bennett et al. op cit; Cooke op cit).

There are three distinguishing elements of the Iraq War coverage. First, an exceptionally long process of framing and thematisation, which should in retrospect be seen unquestionably as a phase of herd behaviour and of a collective failure of journalistic professionalism. After 11 September 2001, the media largely promoted the propaganda of the Bush administration. Later, there was a brief period of backpedaling, self-criticism, and an examination of errors, but it focused on renouncing past mistakes rather than charting a new direction. Since mid-2007, the media's attention has shifted elsewhere.

Phase One: The government's exploitation of the American media

In the first phase, the American government perpetuated the idea that Saddam Hussein possessed weapons of mass destruction and was also closely allied with the Al Qaeda terror network. There were few influential journalists who questioned the administration's propaganda-style presentations and provided in-depth analysis of their veracity. The terrorist threat induced a kind of paralysis which resulted in near *de facto* cooperation between the government and mainstream media (Seib 2009). The few who questioned the prevailing wisdom were quickly branded as "unpatriotic" and bowed to the climate of opinion, insuring that there was little chance of a critical viewpoint taking hold.

Despite the freedom of press principle, anti-war voices are rarely heard in a nation involved in conflict. An investigation shows that in India and China, anti-war coverage constituted 35 and 40 per cent, respectively, of total coverage of the Iraq War in 2003, the first year of the war – despite vastly different media systems (one characterised by censorship, the other by freedom of the press), while in the US only 8 per cent of the coverage was anti-war (Yang 2008). But why is this so? As media analyst and political scientist Robert Entman (2009) argues, in democratic societies, a necessary condition for war is the development of a "patriotic consensus" among the public that becomes a part of reality and reduces the war into a single, compelling plot: the defence of national values. In the initial phase of a military confrontation, there is an elite consensus – or at least the effect of a "spiral of silence" – among the elites to stifle those who oppose the war.

Researchers identified more than 900 instances in which President Bush and his government lied to the public, especially regarding Iraq's possession of weapons of mass destruction, his regime's alleged links to Al Qaeda, and Iraq's attempt to procure uranium supplies from Africa (Center for Public Integrity 2008). Philip Taubman (2008), senior editor of *The New York Times* and former head of the paper's Washington, DC bureau, confirmed from a journalist's perspective what had already been disclosed by former Bush spokesman and administration insider Scott McClellan (2008): the White House and the Pentagon engaged in brazen manipulation of the media. To mention just one more example, Vice-President Dick Cheney hoodwinked *The New York Times* by having his minions make "off the record" leaks to the paper asserting that intelligence reports indicated that Iraq had acquired the necessary equipment for uranium enrichment.

On the day when this "exclusive" was published, Cheney and National Security Advisor Condoleezza Rice referred explicitly to *The Times* article – even though it had been planted by Cheney's own staff (McManus 2009). This reminds cynics of Karl Kraus's famous saying: "How is the world ruled and how do wars start? Diplomats tell lies to journalists, and then believe what they read"(see Isikoff and Corn op cit).

During the first days of the invasion, reporters embedded with the US Army provided reports of fighting at close quarters. However, the television reports were subject to all the advantages and disadvantages of the embedding system, in which correspondents limited themselves to reporting only what they had seen themselves. Some 94 per cent of contributions were primarily geared to present facts, without interpretation of events; 60 per cent of the reports were broadcast live and 80 percent of the contributions consisted of just the reporters, without any quotation of other sources – not even soldiers (Seib op cit).

As the political scientist Brigitte Nacos (2009) notes, right-wing media also allayed public concerns about the use of torture by the Bush administration. Ultra-conservative talk radio shows and Rupert Murdoch's Fox TV channel (home of the series *24*, which featured the anti-terrorist agent Jack Bauer as its hero) were flanked by intellectuals such as Mark Robert Bowden, Jonathan Alter, and law professor Alan Dershowitz. Television networks willingly granted them repeated appearances on talk shows, while opponents of the use of torture, such as Dershowitz's Harvard colleague Philip B. Heymann, were rarely seen on screen.

There is some comfort in knowing that the leaders of two main publications focusing on journalism and the media have formulated a different standard of what constitutes a "patriotic" journalist. *AJR* managing editor Rem Rieder (2003) recalled the invaluable role played by journalists at the end of the Vietnam War. "Some of the best journalism in my memory was the work of the young reporters in Vietnam," he says, citing the work of David Halberstam, Neil Sheehan, Malcolm Browne and Peter Arnett. Rieder's colleague at *Editor and Publisher*, Greg Mitchell, faults newsroom leaders for shortchanging "the biggest political and moral issue of our time" (cited in Ricchiardi 2008).

Phase Two: Self-reflection and explanation

Later there was a period of self-flagellating clarification as to how the mass media was systematically misled by the Bush administration (Massing 2004; Isikoff and Corn op cit; Rich op cit; Bennett et al. op cit; Mitchell 2008). This marked a turning point in the coverage of the war and occupation of Iraq. It is surely no coincidence that the beginning of this period of self-reflection in 2004 coincided with the publication of images of the torture scandal at Abu Ghraib, which were broadcast around the world and further discredited the American military engagement in Iraq. Seymour Hersh, who had exposed the My Lai massacre during the Vietnam War, once again played a key role in uncovering the scandal. He contributed an in-depth investigative article to the *New Yorker* (Hersh 2004), thus providing background and giving sense to the images of torture scenes that had circulated widely on television before, particularly on the Arabic, Qatar-based television station *Al Jazeera* (Hallin 2009).

Daniel Hallin (ibid), comparing the media coverage of Vietnam and the Iraq War, found "striking similarities to the reporting pattern" between this stage in the Iraq conflict and the period in which public opinion gradually turned against the war in Vietnam. In both cases, the turning point came about two years into the conflict. Both *The New York Times* and the *Washington Post* issued apologies to their readers for their failings. *The Times* published an extensive editor's note, which included between the lines an acknowledgement of how difficult it is for newsroom leaders to admit failure in cases as sensitive as this (*New York Times* 2004), a point reiterated by the *Times*'s Ombudsman (Okrent 2004). The *Post* published a lengthy piece by their media critic, Howard Kurtz, which the paper's chief editor, Downie, did not get to read in advance (Mitchell 2004; Strupp 2004).

However, to the best of our knowledge, none of the leading media outlets ever discussed the extent to which they were – like it or not – economic beneficiaries of both war and terrorism. The idea that the media has a "symbiotic" relationship with both belligerent governments and with terrorists (Frey 2004; Rohner and Frey 2007), is understandably taboo, but it is nevertheless difficult to deny. Among the early critics of the coverage of the Iraq war in the mainstream media was Michael Getler (2008). As ombudsman of the *Washington Post*, he documented around 25 times lapses of journalistic professionalism in his Sunday column. One must look closely, he argues, because the editors had in different ways failed to meet their own standards. In the case of the *Washington Post*, the problem was that they had "buried" many important stories in their back pages. *The New York Times*, on the other hand, published misleading front page articles, placing trust in reporter Judith Miller, who faithfully reproduced the propaganda of the Bush administration and Iraqi spin doctors. This view is confirmed by David Broder (op cit), a veteran reporter and a prominent foreign policy expert at the *Washington Post*.

The most notable scoop in the reassessment of the Iraq debacle was contributed by *The New York Times*'s David Barstow (2008). Barstow explained how the Pentagon controlled coverage of war and terrorism on American television through dozens of commentators who appeared repeatedly on different TV channels as "independent" military experts, including 10 retired generals. In fact, they were consulting contractors linked to the military-industrial complex, including lobbyists and managers from a total of 150 Pentagon affiliates. They were also regularly briefed and provided with information to assist in their television appearances.

However, even as self-criticism prevailed in the second phase of the Iraq War coverage, the Bush administration managed to spin the issue of torture, keeping it low key and maintaining that the problem was confined to a few individual cases. Instead of using the term "torture", officials strategically opted to speak of "abuse" – a term adopted by most of the media as well (Nacos 2009).

Phase 3: Slipping from the media's radar

In early 2007, the attention given to the incipient presidential campaign and the race for the nomination absorbed coverage of the war. Reporting on events in Iraq and the political debate about the local military involvement constituted only around 12 per cent of the news coverage. The media – and with them most likely the majority of Americans – simply lost interest in the Iraq war.

The media had allowed "the third-longest war in American history to slip off the radar screen" according to Sherry Ricchiardi (op cit), writing in the *American Journalism Review*. Armando Acuna, ombudsman of the *Sacramento Bee*, pointed out that the conflict, which costs taxpayers about $12.5 billion a month (nearly $5,000 a second), had all but disappeared from front page news. Acuna calculated a 70 per cent decline in Iraq-related articles on the front page of the *Bee*. The AP news agency, which has asked researchers to chart the daily reporting from 65 US newspapers, found similar results. In September 2007 there were 457 front-page reports on Iraq, but in the months that followed the number dwindled to less than 50 (ibid).

The Project for Excellence in Journalism (2008) revealed that by 2008 the Iraq war had vanished essentially from evening television news. During the first 10 weeks of 2007, Iraq remained a hot topic, claiming 23 per cent of news broadcasts. One year later, Iraq-themed stories constituted only 3 per cent of total broadcasts. Cable channels showed the figure drop from 24 per cent to a meager 1 per cent. During the first half of 2008, three main networks (CBS, ABC and NBC) combined devoted a total of 181 minutes to Iraq, compared with 1,157 minutes for the entire previous year. Mainstream media collectively turned away from the war. CBS no longer maintained a single correspondent in Iraq, where 150,000 US soldiers remained deployed in 2008. In Afghanistan, not a single US broadcaster employed a permanent correspondent (Stelter 2008).

It was becoming increasingly difficult for foreign correspondents – particularly those based in the war zones of Afghanistan and Iraq – to have stories featured on the evening news. Lara Logan, chief correspondent for CBS News, mischievously described strategies used to negotiate with news headquarters. "Generally what I say is: 'I'm holding the armor-piercing RPG,'" referring to the acronym for *rocket propelled grenade*. "'It's aimed at the bureau chief, and if you do not put my story on the air, I'm going to pull the trigger'"(ibid). Logan's dark anecdote is amusing, though the issue it confronts is no laughing matter. The displacement of the war from the nation's front pages is not solely the fault of the media: According to Terry McCarthy, ABC's Iraq correspondent, bringing up Baghdad at a dinner party "is like a conversation killer" (ibid). Bill Keller, the editor-in-chief of *The New York Times*, offers another variation on the theme:

> There is a cold and sad calculation that readers and viewers are not that interested in the war, whether because they are preoccupied with paying four dollars for a gallon of gas and avoiding foreclosure, or because they have Iraq fatigue (quoted in Carr 2008).

Yet to assume a society might engage with an unreported crisis is simply absurd. The local orientation of American mass media is working against in-depth war coverage. Even on Memorial Day (on the last Monday of May of each year), an occasion calling for the war to return to front pages, luring the conflict's many consequences back to the spotlight, the main focus remained a local one. The *Los Angeles Times* dedicated its front page to soldiers from California who died in Afghanistan and Iraq, and the *Washington Post* personalised the war with a series called "Faces of the fallen" (ibid).

In the spring of 2008 – the fifth anniversary of the war's onset – the media commemorated the 4,000 US deaths. Apart from that, according to Andrew F. Hayes and Teresa Myers (2008), of Ohio State University, war casualties became victims of hyper-local reporting, as media attention was primarily bestowed upon coffins buried in local cemeteries. When Lt. Col. Billy Hall – one of the highest-ranking officers killed in Iraq – was buried in Arlington Cemetery, his family agreed to grant media access to the ceremony. The military, however, took pains to ensure journalists were kept away from the funeral. According to Dana Milbank, of the *Washington Post,* the *de facto* ban on media at Arlington funerals fits neatly with White House efforts to sanitise the war in Iraq (Ricchiardi op cit).

Local audiences intermittently respond to the coverage with calls for withdrawal from Iraq. This, in turn, may also be seen a consequence of the "feminisation of journalism", says Daniel Hallin (op cit). According to Hallin, female journalists view the war differently, and tend to take on personalised home stories in order to cover the grief of affected families. Otherwise, however, the war is far away and much less present in the collective consciousness than the Vietnam War was to the earlier generation. The old formula – in which an increasing number of casualties diminishes public support of a war – no longer seems to apply. In Vietnam, however, three times as many soldiers were in action than in Iraq (ibid). By July 2009 there had been more than 4,200 American soldiers killed in Iraq, against 58,000 in Vietnam. Above all, the military acted on a commitment to avoid the mistakes associated with the Vietnam quagmire. As the draft is no longer a requirement in the US, the army can now avoid the public spotlight more effectively (Getler op cit).

The costs of war reporting

The previously discussed developments are not simply due to the particular dynamics of issue-attention cycles (Downs 1972), they can also be attributed to changes in the media's own policies governing its operations. Safety risks and economic factors are more likely to explain the withdrawal of reporters from Iraq. Under the present circumstances, correspondents jet and parachute from crisis to crisis. Maintaining a long-term presence of reporters is no longer affordable, beginning with insurance costs for operations in war and disaster areas. "They are prohibitive," says Matthew Stannard (2008), an experienced foreign reporter with the *San Francisco Chronicle*. This leads to outsourcing.

Increasingly more freelance journalists – either inexperienced 25-year-olds or native stringers – are on the front lines. Some of them provide excellent work, others may fall short of providing reliable levels of professionalism (ibid; Mabry 2008). In any case, concerns about insurance costs are significantly reduced. The notion that the life of an Iraqi is not worth as much as the life of an American outrages moralists and human rights activists, but in economic terms, it's true. In plain figures expressed as insurance risks, a human life in Third World countries is worth just a few thousand dollars, while in the US a life may be worth 10 million dollars – a figure in line with rising premiums.[1]

Even more shocking is the fact that *The New York Times* spends three million dollars a year to maintain its office in Iraq. And the number excludes the salaries of journalists, rather covering fees for rent, guards and electric generators! Disclosed in the *Columbia Journalism Review* (2007), the figures raise questions of how we are to be informed about war and terror, and to what extent it is reasonable to expect private media companies to inherit the cost. The journal's editorial celebrates maintaining this level of coverage as an act of commitment to democracy. Less euphorically put, it shows at least a high degree of corporate social responsibility which is rarely found among private media companies, and frequently not even in government-funded media.

Most competitors will make a different assessment, partially because of the influence of their investors on Wall Street. Already a few months earlier, the *American Journalism Review* (Ricchiardi 2007) reported that many media companies were ordering their correspondents back from the front in light of escalating threats to foreigners in Iraq and the astronomical cost of security. Paul Friedman, Senior Vice-President of CBS, said that attempts to share the immense costs and security risks with other broadcasters failed due to logistical issues (Stelter op cit).

High risks for journalists remaining in Iraq

Reporters on the ground "struggle mightily to cut through the fog and spin", reports Sherry Ricchiardi (2007), but the correspondents' mobility is extremely limited. When they attempt to gather material to verify statements made by the military or the Pentagon, reporters place themselves into life-threatening situations. In Fallujah (a city 43 miles west of Baghdad, the site of two major assaults by the Americans in 2004), or in certain neighbourhoods of Baghdad, they may not venture out at all. According to Ricchiardi (ibid):

> Before they go out on assignments, correspondents work through a litany of questions: Where is it? What time is it? How can I get there? How can I get back? Who can I talk to? Who controls the neighborhood? Who guards the checkpoints? Is there enough fuel in the car and plenty of air in the tires? Is this story worth the risk?...To blend in, female journalists often don an *abaya*, a long robe worn by Muslim women, and a head scarf. Some male reporters with dark features grow mustaches and beards and try to emulate the attire of Iraqi men. Some blondes dye their hair black. Many operate on the 15-minute rule: they never stay longer in any one place for fear that someone with a cell phone will alert assassins of the soft target. Even the smallest of details can be giveaways, for instance wearing a seatbelt in a car, as Iraqis rarely use them.

Iraq differs from other wars in another respect: in the fight for media attention, journalists themselves have become targets. Samantha Appleton, a photographer who worked for *Time* and the *New Yorker* in Iraq, said that in 2003 it was still possible to move about with relative freedom. Four years later it was customary to travel with at least two cars and three to five armed bodyguards (ibid). Moreover, for the few remaining reporters, the military makes their work more difficult (Carr op cit).

Of the 123 journalists detained for their work in 2007, only three were based in Iraq. However, according to Reporters without Borders (2007), 46 (more than half) of the 83 journalists who died while working in 2007 perished in Iraq. Yet these 46 murders undoubtedly received much more media attention than most other casualties in the war. This raises again a question posed years ago by the economist Bruno S. Frey (2004): to what extent does the media become an accomplice of the terrorists by reporting on their attacks – in this case, writing about and overexposing the murders of their colleagues?

The social costs of insufficient war and terror coverage

What are the social costs if the media lacks sufficient capacity to effectively monitor the most powerful government and to adequately inform the public about what is going on in the world? (McManus 2009). The war in Iraq provides some preliminary answers. American journalism is in a state of crisis because it has lost not only much of its resource base but also much of its moral authority.

The near-perfect control of the news cycle by the military and the US government explains also the American public's ignorance regarding the amateurish manner with which the Bush administration's Coalition Provisional Authority arranged a transitional government after the invasion. As Rajiv Chandrasekaran (2007 and 2008), former head of the *Washington Post*'s bureau in Baghdad, documented, "expert" personnel sent to the country proved to be clueless Republican Party hacks who had never worked outside of the United States and had little to no linguistic, political and cultural knowledge to contribute to efforts to ensure peace, democracy, and reconstruction. The author also points out that not a single American Congressman had anything but rudimentary knowledge of what was actually going on in Iraq (ibid).

Conclusions: Endangering progress to a more peaceful world

Given the above argument, it is possible to conclude the following:

- Wars have become media wars, and such "mediatised" wars tend to become subject of one or even several issue-attention cycles with an upturn, a turnaround, and a downturn phase.
- Government spin and efforts by official sources (military, government, industry, political parties and non profit organisations involved) to control the media agenda are increasing. Institutions spend a great amount of resources to shape public attention.
- The resource base to finance investigative war and terror reporting is shrinking. The public's willingness to pay for journalism, and thus for news and adequate information, is decreasing, and it becomes less likely that journalism can be financed adequately by advertising.
- War reporting in itself seems to have become more dangerous, as reporters become more frequently targets of the warring parties. Media outlets are paying perhaps too much attention to this aspect of war coverage, and thus encourage terrorist attacks on journalists because of the media attention guaranteed.
- However, the mainstream media's overall introspective and self-critical analysis of war coverage was insufficient and all too brief – which may have

been partially compensated by new forms of media criticism, particularly in the "blogosphere".

- Rational decisions of individual media users, spin doctors, war reporters, editors and publishers collectively produce the lies, half-truths and disinformation which promote war and endanger any political progress towards conflict resolution – and, thus, towards a more peaceful world.

References

Barstow, David (2008) Behind TV Analysts: Pentagon's hidden hand, *New York Times*, 20 April. Available online at http://www.nytimes.com/2008/04/20/washington/20generals.html, accessed on 1 May 2009

Bennett, Lance, Lawrence, Regina G. and Livingston, Steven (2007) *When the press fails: Political power and the news media from Iraq to Katrina*, Chicago/London: University of Chicago Press

Broder, David (2008) The US presidential race 2008. Presentation at Stanford University, 3 April

Carr, David (2008) The war we choose to ignore, *New York Times*, 26 May. Available online at http://www.nytimes.com/2008/04/20/washington/20generals.html, accessed on 1 May 2009

Center for Public Integrity (2008): Center documents 935 false statements by top administration officials to justify Iraq War. Press release, 23 January. Available online at http://www.publicintegrity.org/news/entry/189/, accessed on 1 May 2009

Chandrasekaran, Rajiv (2007) *Imperial life in the Emerald City*, New York: Vintage

Chandrasekaran, Rajiv (2008) Presentation, Stanford University, 19 May

Cooke, John Byrne (2007) *Reporting the war: Freedom of the press from the American Revolution to the war on terrorism*, Houndsmills/New York: Palgrave Macmillan

Entman, Robert (2009) Surging beyond realism: How the US media promote war again and again. Presentation at the symposium "War, media, and the public sphere", Austrian Academy of Sciences and the University of Klagenfurt, Vienna, 6 and 7 March

Davenport, Thomas H. and Beck, John C. (2001) *The attention economy. Understanding the new currency of business*, Boston: Harvard Business School Press

Downs, Anthony (1972) Up and down with ecology – the "issue-attention cycle", *Public Interest*, Vol. 28 pp 38–50. Available online at http://www.anthonydowns.com/upand-down.htm, accessed on 1 May 2009

Fengler, Susanne and Russ-Mohl, Stephan (2005) *Der Journalist "homo oeconomicus"*, Konstanz: UVK

Fengler, Susanne and Russ-Mohl, Stephan (2008) The crumbling hidden wall: Towards an economic theory of journalism, *Kyklos*, Vol. 61, No. 4 pp 520–42

Franck, Georg (1998) *Ökonomie der Aufmerksamkeit: Ein Entwurf,* München/Wien: Edition Hanser

Frey, Bruno S. (2004) *Dealing with terrorism: Stick or carrot?* Northampton: Edward Elgar Publishing

Getler, Michael (2008) Interview with the author in Washington DC, 13 April

Hallin, Daniel (2009) Between reporting and propaganda: Power, culture, and war reporting. Presentation at the symposion "War, media, and the public sphere", the Austrian Academy of Sciences and the University of Klagenfurt, Vienna, 6 and 7 March

Hayes, Andrew and Myers, Teresa A. (2008) Testing the "proximate casualties" hypothesis: Local troop loss, attention to news, and support for military intervention. Presentation at the annual ICA conference "Communicating for social impact", 22–6 May, Montreal

Hersh, Seymour (2004) Torture at Abu Ghraib, *New Yorker*, May. Available online at http://www.newyorker.com/archive/2004/05/10/040510fa_fact, accessed on 1 May 2009

Höhne, Andrea and Russ-Mohl, Stephan (2004) Zur Ökonomik und Ethik der Kriegsberichterstattung, *Zeitschrift für Kommunikationsökologie*, Vol. 1 pp 11–23

Isikoff, Michael and Corn, David (2006) *Hubris. The inside story of spin, scandal, and the selling of the Iraq War,* New York: Three Rivers Press

Janis, Irving Lester (1972) *Victims of groupthink*, Houghton Mifflin: Boston

Kamalipour, Yaha R. and Snow, Nancy (2004) *War, media, and propaganda: A global perspective*, Lanham: Rowman and Littlefield

Karmasin, Matthias (2009) Wars and public spheres. Keynote presentation at symposium "War, media, and the public sphere", Austrian Academy of Sciences and the University of Klagenfurt, Vienna, 6 and 7 March

Lewis, Justin (2003) Facts in the line of fire, *Guardian*, 6 November. Available online at http://www.guardian.co.uk/media/2003/nov/06/broadcasting.politicsandthemedia, accessed on 1 May 2009

Mabry, Marcus (2008) Presentation, Stanford University, 22 April

Massing, Michael (2004) Now they tell us, *New York Review of Books*, Vol. 51, 26. February. Available online at http://www.nybooks.com/articles/16922, accessed on 1 May 2009

McClellan, Scott (2008) *What happened: Inside the Bush White House and Washington's culture of deception*, New York: Public Affairs

McManus, John (2009) *Detecting bull: How to identify bias and junk journalism in print, broadcast, and on the wild web*, Available online at: http://www.detectingbull.com/buy%20page.htm, accessed on 1 May 2009

Mitchell, Greg (2004) Washington Post says Iraq coverage was flawed, *Editor & Publisher*, 12 August

Mitchell, Greg (2008) *So wrong for so long: How the press, the pundits – and the President – failed on Iraq*, New York NY: Union Square Press

Nacos, Brigitte (2009) Mass mediated debate on torture in post-9/11 America. Presentation at the symposium "War, media and the public sphere", Austrian Academy of Sciences and the University of Klagenfurt, Vienna, 6 and 7 March

New York Times (2004) From the editors: *The Times* and Iraq, Editors' Note, 26. May. Available one at http://www.nytimes.com/2004/05/26/international/middleeast/26FTE_NOTE.html?ex=1400990400&en=94c17fcffad92ca9&ei=5007&partner=USERLAND, accessed on 1 May 2009

Okrent, Daniel (2004) The public editor: Weapons of mass destruction or mass distraction? *New York Times*, 30 May. Available online at http://query.nytimes.com/gst/fullpage.html?res=9C06E7DC1E3EF933A05756C0A9629C8B63, accessed on 1 May 2009

Project for Excellence in Journalism (2008) The state of the news media 2008: An annual report on American journalism. Available online at http://www.stateofthenewsmedia.org/2008/, accessed on 1 May 2009

Reporters without Borders (2007) Worldwide press freedom index. Available online at http://www.rsf.org/article.php3?id_article=24025, accessed on 1 May 2009

Ricchiardi, Sherry (2007) Obstructed view, *American Journalism Review*, April/May. Available online at http://www.ajr.org/Article.asp?id=4301, accessed on 1 May 2009

Ricchiardi, Sherry (2008) Whatever happened to Iraq? *American Journalism Review*, June/July. Available online at http://www.ajr.org/Article.asp?id=4515, accessed on 1 May 2009

Rich, Frank (2006) *The greatest story ever sold: The decline and fall of truth in Bush's America*, New York: Penguin

Rieder, Rem (2003) In the zone: the Pentagon's embedding plan was a winner for journalists and their audiences, *American Journalism Review*, Vol. 25, May

Robertson, Lori (2005) In control, *American Journalism Review*, February/March. Available online at http://www.ajr.org/Article.asp?id=3812, accessed on 1 May 2009

Rohner, Dominic/Frey, Bruno (2007) Blood and ink! The common-interest-game between terrorists and the media, *Public Choice*, Vol. 133 pp 129–45

Seib, Philip (2009) Delivering war to the public. Presentation at the symposium "War, media and the public sphere", Austrian Academy of Sciences and the University of Klagenfurt, Vienna, 6 and 7 March

Stannard, Matthew B. (2008) Interview with the author, Stanford University, 6 May

Stelter, Brian (2008) Reporters say networks put wars on the back burner, *New York Times*, 23 June. Available online at http://www.nytimes.com/2008/06/23/business/media/23logan.html?hp, accessed on 1 May 2009

Strupp, Joe (2004) Kurtz explains his critique of *Washington Post* Iraq coverage, *Editor & Publisher*, 12 August

Taubman, Phillip (2008) Presentation at the Center for International Security and Cooperation, Stanford University, 19 May

Vallone, Robert P., Ross, Lee and Pepper, Mark R. (1985) The hostile media phenomenon: Biased perception and perceptions of media bias in coverage of the Beirut massacre, *Journal of Personality and Social Psychology*, Vol. 49, No. 3 pp 577–85

Wells, Matt (2003) Embedded reporters "sanitised" Iraq war, *Guardian*, 6 November. Available online at http://www.guardian.co.uk/media/2003/nov/06/broadcasting. Iraqandthemedia, accessed on 1 May 2009

Yang, Jin (2008) One war, three pictures: A cross-country analysis of the 2003 Iraq War. Presentation at the ICA annual convention "Communicating for Social Impact", Montreal, 22–26 May

20

Perspectives on conflict resolution and journalistic training

RUKHSANA ASLAM

"...since wars begin in the minds of men, it is in the minds of men that the defences of peace must be constructed."

Preamble to UNESCO Constitution (1945)

Introduction

Following the spectacular "terrorist" 9/11 attacks in New York and Washington, the United States declared an unending "war on terror" and conflicts spread across the globe. PR (and the battle for the hearts and minds of the peoples of the world) has been central to the military and political strategies of all sides. As a result, the news media today have become central arenas where political and ideological conflicts are conducted; not surprisingly the role of news media in either promoting or even possibly resolving conflict has become one of the most significant and pressing issues of the day (Wolsfeld 1997: 2).

The coverage and framing that media provides to issues of conflict can have an immense effect on the outcome of any conflict situation. Liberal theorists since John Stuart Mill (1806–1873) have argued that an independent press can serve as an instrument to bridge differences and promote peace and harmony, if information disseminated respects human rights and reflects diversity of opinion. However, the press can also serve the interests of the warmongers when it propagates messages of intolerance or disinformation that manipulates public sentiment.

Role of media in conflict situations

Upholding the principles of truth and justice are the ultimate goals that every journalist strives to achieve. Yet history tells us it is not always the case. After the Gulf War of 1991, many Western journalists claimed they had been "duped" by the US-led forces. Several reporters who covered the war for their channels and newspapers later described how Western journalists – despite their ideals of professional objectivity and social responsibility – became obsessed with the military jargon surrounding the "precise" and "clean" weaponry. Iraqi civilians were reduced to "targets" and the night air raids were described as "fireworks". The horror of the mass slaughter of Iraqi soldiers and citizens lay hidden behind claims of "heroic victory". According to McCombs (1992, cited in Brosius and Weimann 1996):

> Audiences not only learn about public issues and other matters through the media, they also learn how much importance is attached to an issue or topic from the emphasis the mass media place upon it.

This ability to effect cognitive change among individuals is one of the most important aspects of the power of mass communication, which is intensified by the process of framing news. Entman (1993; cited in Norris, Kern and Just 2003: 329) argues that framing occurs when the media make some aspects of a particular issue more prominent to promote "a certain problem definition, causal interpretation, moral evaluation, and/or treatment recommendation". Thus it follows that if the agenda of the media is for peace and the framing is done in a manner that aims to promote rapprochement, then it can influence public opinion towards the resolution of conflict.

A logical question at this juncture would be that if framing and agenda setting by the media affects the process of the making of public opinion then what role do the personal perception and prejudices of journalists play in interpreting the conflict situations? As Wilbur Schramm argues (1993): "News exists in the minds of men. It is not an event; it is something perceived *after* the event... it is an attempt to reconstruct the essential framework of the event which is calculated to make the event meaningful to the reader." After going through the various stages of observing, collating, writing, editing and publishing, the end product is the combination of "witness accounts, second hand accounts, tertiary comments and explanations and the reporter's own knowledge and predispositions".

Najam Sethi (1999), a Pakistani journalist, touched on this issue in his talk on the decades-long India-Pakistan conflict when he argued that "the role the press plays in both countries in reinforcing prejudices and old enmities" makes "the press part of the problem rather than part of the solution". Thibeault (2000), in his detailed analysis of the reporting of the India-Pakistan Kashmiri conflict, found that many editorials in both India and Pakistan "manifested the deep skepticism, and often hostility, with which journalists in India and Pakistan view the actions and pronouncements of their neighbour and rival".

Another study by Subarno Chattarji (2006) suggested that Hindi and Urdu news media in India and Pakistan have the tendency to report negatively on each other, with news reports and editorials reflecting skepticism and mistrust in the peace process. However, he also points out that the negative reportage is not monolithic: rather, there are exceptions where writers try to provide a positive perspective. Clearly the personal biases of the Pakistani and Indian journalists against each has its roots in the bloody partition of the Indian sub-continent in 1947 that resulted in displacement of hundreds of thousands of families and in the long-standing rivalry between Hindus and Muslims.

Shubha Singh (2007), in her study, stresses the "obsession of Indian media to cover Pakistan" and writes: "The turmoil in Pakistan has been a constant windfall for the new business here. The action unfolds there and analysis unfolds here." In another study Sevanti Ninan (2007) observed that the coverage of a controversy involving the chief justice in both print and electronic media of India was highly coloured by the personal opinions and influenced by the nationality of Indian editors, carrying a patronising tone in their coverage: "O you poor things living under dictatorship! None of this could have happened here."

The peace journalism option

It is clear that the media have a role to play in conflict situations. The nature of that role – as a perpetuator of a conflict or agent for peace – largely depends on the framing and agenda setting of the media. It also follows that the agenda setting may be affected by the biases and prejudices of journalists at the individual level which can be reflected in the interpretation of the events. This realisation has extended the debate from "what is" to "what should be" the role of media in conflict situations and new concepts have emerged such as "civic journalism", "peace journalism", "citizen journalism", "reliable journalism" and "innovative journalism". All of them are essentially drawn from notions which stress the social responsibility of the media and advocate a proactive role for the media in resolving conflicts.

Jake Lynch, a freelance British television reporter and academic, is one of the chief proponents of what he calls the "peace journalism option" (2008). He believes that mainstream coverage of conflicts concentrates on highlighting events and generally represents war as a simple "them versus us" struggle in which one side wins and the other loses. Martin Bell, a former BBC correspondent and later Independent MP, seriously questioned the Western coverage of Bosnian ethnic cleansing in 1994–95. He called for a journalism of attachment "that cares as well as knows ... that will not stand neutrally between good and evil, right and wrong, the victim and the oppressor" (Bell 1998: 16). The BBC's guidelines required reporters to be objective and dispassionate. Bell continued:

> I am no longer sure what "objective" means: I see nothing object-like in the rela-
> tionship between the reporter and the event, but rather a human and dynamic
> interaction between them. As for "dispassionate", it is not only impossible but
> inappropriate to be thus neutralised – I would say even *neutered* – at the scene of
> an atrocity or massacre, or most man-made calamities (ibid: 18).

In a similar vein, Ross Howard (2003) points out the need for a more reliable journalism.

> Reliable journalism means journalism practices which meet the international
> standards of accuracy, impartiality and social responsibility. There is also support
> for creating diversity within the media industry to reflect competing opinions
> and to ensure the industry enjoys independence.

Howard also mentions another kind of initiative called "intended outcome programming" which sees entertainment, street theatre, dramas and posters as means to communicate attitudes towards conflict resolution.

> The media becomes a facilitator of positive social change rather than a
> professional disinterested observer. This kind of initiative...is not journalism
> as we know it, although it adheres to values such as accuracy, fairness and
> responsibility. It is attracting audiences and donor support (ibid).

Stuart Allan (2007) sees the rise of "citizen journalism and mass-self communi-cation" (through email, blogs SMS and such like) as a direct alternative to "jour-nalism's traditional role or mission, its public responsibilities". He quotes Lewis D'Vorkin, editor in chief of AOL News: "The world is turning to the fastest growing news team – citizen journalists – to get a human perspective through the eyes of those who lived or experienced the news as it unfolds" (ibid).

Re-examining role of media, conflict resolution and objectivity

While the debate revolves around the media, all these suggested solutions focus too much on "journalism" and not enough on the *journalist as an individual*. At the time of reporting it is journalist-the-individual whose words are being read or heard, whose images are being seen and whose interpretation of the events forms the "first draft of history". In this moment, the political economy of the media system is pushed into the background.

Secondly, while the media can clearly promote "conflict resolution" the job of the journalist is not to organise the peace settlement itself. Journalists can at best offer a platform to the conflicting parties and even interpret events for the audience. In doing so they provide what Jannie Botes (2000) describes as "an essential requisite of conflict resolution which is communication".

Thirdly, one of the crucial tasks of the war journalist is to record its impact on human lives. But does the concept of objectivity help or hinder this process? Rosen, an American journalist cited by Howard (op cit) says no:

> We make an error if we assume that the price of an interest in conflict resolution is giving up commitment to truth and professional objectivity. It is in fact quite the opposite: conflict sensitivity is a journalist's pass into a deeper understanding of what it means to seek the truth in journalism (ibid).

Over the past few years, the principle of objectivity has been re-examined by those working in conflict resolution. Jake Lynch and Annabel McGoldrick (2001) are particularly critical of the traditional defence of journalists: "We are here to report the truth objectively, we don't get involved." For Lynch and McGoldrick, journalists are involved whether they like it or not. Nor can they be wholly objective – they only see a fraction of the action especially in battle, they don't know the whole picture. For the same reason they question how the reporter can claim to be reporting the truth. A small slice of truth, perhaps, not the whole picture. And a partial reporting of the truth often distorts the overall picture.

Lynch and McGoldrick (2005: 210) charge that "objective journalism" is biased and favours official sources and event over process. Confining reports of conflict to violent events can leave violence to appear as the only solution. They assert that "dualism" is the key part of objectivity which "prepares the ground of escalation". It may be a safe way for a reporter to "hear both sides" but each side might end up viewing the report as a victory.

The challenge, therefore, is not whether the journalist should be objective or not but whether journalists and committed academics are willing to shun this ideal in favour of a more "involved role". The Pulitzer Prize-winner and author of *The making of the atomic bomb* (1987), Richard Rhodes, talks about it in terms of "deeper investigation" (2008). This means a journalism that is more assertive in the pursuit of a story, more sceptical towards the mighty and more sympathetic towards the weak. The challenge is to strike a balance. In a similar vein, the veteran war correspondent Chris Hedges comments (2008): "I didn't go to the war to be objective. I wanted to be the champion of the weaker side."

Integrating conflict resolution in journalistic training

There is clearly a great need in professional journalistic education to promote knowledge about conflict analysis, resolution and prevention as well as an awareness of the "social responsibility" role of the reporter. The potential of the media to educate, inform, correct misperceptions, enable consensus-building, build confidence and offer plausible solutions needs always to be stressed. As Howard argues (op cit):

> As a profession, journalists are in constant search of conflict as news, and they have rudimentary to highly sophisticated skills in reporting it in conventional terms. But world-wide, journalism training and development contains almost no reference to the discipline of conflict analysis. Little of the wisdom of nearly five decades of academic and professional study of conflict is included in journalism training, and certainly not at the basic level. This is unfortunate because such knowledge can better inform journalists in their work, especially in their analysis of conflict, its sources and its alternative responses and in their reporting of efforts to diffuse conflict.

There are two aspects to this kind of journalistic education: theoretical knowledge and practical exposure. The first can give the contextual and conceptual understanding of what constitutes conflict, peace and violence while the second can provide the skills and tools required to report on conflict situations.

Journalistic training in field: Trends and practices

Journalistic training in the field is meant for journalists already working in the profession. It may be conducted by non-profit organisations, media companies or by a self-motivated group of media workers and aims towards skills enhancement and capacity-building of journalists in the form of training workshops and seminars. There are several examples of such field training projects around the world which target various aspects of journalistic training in conflict resolution ranging from developing reporting skills in the conflict areas to employing safety and survival techniques and post-conflict trauma awareness programmes.

One example of an organisation promoting research and guidance for journalists in conflict situations is the Network of Conflict Resolution in Canada (www. nicr.ca). One of the tools it offers is the Alternative 5 Ws for conflict reporting:

Who: Who is affected by this conflict; who has a distinct stake in its outcome? What is their relationship to one another, including relative power, influence and affluence?

What: What triggered the dispute; what drew it to your attention at this time? What issues do the parties need to resolve?

When: When did this conflict begin; how often have the circumstances existed that gave rise to this dispute?

Where: What geographical or political jurisdictions are affected by the dispute? How has this issue been handled in other places?

Why: Why do the involved parties hold the positions they do; what needs, interests, fears and concerns need to be addressed?

How: How are they going to resolve this e.g. negotiation, mediation, arbitration, administrative hearing, court, armed warfare; what are the costs/benefits of the chosen method?

Options: What options have the parties explored, how do the various options relate to the interests identified?

Another such organisation is the non-profit *Medios Para La Paz* (Media for Peace) (www.mediosparalapaz.org) which was created in Colombia in 1997 by a group of journalists who wanted to find a way to contribute to peace-building. Since then, *Medios Para La Paz* has delivered workshops, round-tables, publications and created a network of journalists. They promote what they describe as the "disarmament of language" used by journalists so that words may become instruments of understanding and reconciliation. A dictionary entitled *Para desarmar la palabra*

(*Disarming words*) was published in 1999, followed by *Traps of war journalism and conflict* in July 2001 which records the peace process negotiations in Colombia since the 19ᵗʰ century. It analyses the current peace efforts and recommends actions for an approach to journalism which can serve the current peace process. So far, *Medios Para La Paz* has offered 37 workshops to 990 journalists from around Colombia. Topics covered include conflict resolution, Colombian and international law, humanitarian law and journalistic efforts to contribute to peace.

Another effort in professional journalistic training is the Crimes of War Project which was set up following the publication of *The crimes of war: What the public should know* in 1999 by Roy Gutman, the Pulitzer Prize-winning journalist who exposed the Serbian concentration camps during the Bosnian war (1992–5). The project is a collaboration between journalists, lawyers and scholars dedicated to raising public awareness of the laws of war and their application to situations of conflict among journalists, policy makers and the general public. They hope that a wider knowledge of legal framework governing armed conflict will lead to greater pressure to prevent breaches of the law and to punish those who commit them. Through its website www.crimesofwar.org, educational programmes and seminars, the project also hopes to promote consultation among journalists, legal experts and humanitarian agencies about how to increase compliance with international humanitarian law.

The Asia-Pacific Institute for Broadcasting Development (AIBD) has initiated a number of projects to train journalists in conflict resolution. They have conducted a number of workshops in Nepal, Sri Lanka, Pakistan India, Philippines, Bangladesh and Indonesia. Their latest project is a joint television project by two producers, one from Pakistan and one from India, on the children of Kashmir entitled "Children growing up in a conflict situation". Broadcasting such joint programmes, they hope will reduce the tensions between the two countries by highlighting the stories of children through entertainment (see Mottaghi 2008).

The UK-based Dart Centre Europe is a global network (www. dartcenter.org/europe) of journalists and mental health professionals, working to improve the coverage of violence, trauma and tragedy. It works with the BBC on helping them to develop a trauma awareness curriculum for their foreign news teams. They have also worked with ABC in Australia, the *Washington Post*, Al Jazeera, NBC, WDR in Germany and other international news organisations as well as some major journalism schools in the US and UK. They help journalists cope with post-conflict trauma and provide them with much needed space to think about these issues and to discuss them with their peers. "We believe that this is the best way of boosting their resilience and the quality and accuracy of what they write when covering issues which arouse public emotion," says Dr Gavin Rees (2008). He continues:

> Our work is very much journalism-led. We present concrete information on evidence-based research into traumatic stress, but the Dart method relies on drawing on the previous experience of the group. Rather than imposing a set of solutions on people we work with, we ask the group to develop their own set of proposals for self-care and best practice that reflects their own needs and working methods. We shape the direction of these conversations by feeding into them our own knowledge and experience.

The International Institute for Journalism (IIJ) at InWENT-Capacity Building International, Germany (www.inwent.org/iij/index.php.en), has been offering advanced training courses for mid-career journalists from developing and transitional countries since 1964 with special focus on print and online media in Sub-Saharan, Africa, Asia and the Middle East. The emphasis is placed on political reporting, economic and financial reporting, online journalism and media ethics in the light of conflict transformation and peace building.

Improving the journalism curriculum

The argument remains whether journalistic training in conflict resolution should be conducted in the classrooms or left to be learned in the field. The first choice might reap more benefits for various reasons. First, the curricula in most universities in the developed world that offer degrees in journalism are already designed to provide the skills required in the field: reporting, editing, news gathering, publishing, production, broadcasting and even specialised reporting. Making such subjects as conflict analysis and resolution part of their scheme of studies can more easily develop the students' sense of social responsibility and also help prepare them to face challenges in the field.

Secondly, it will help initiate more research on the impact of peace initiatives on people's lives. At present, universities offering degrees in mass communication or communication studies focus more on the theoretical subjects such media and society, social change, communication theories, and development support communication but little in the area of conflict resolution. However, in recent years some universities have launched peace and conflict studies. More research into the actual and potential role of media in conflict resolution is desperately needed. Howard (op cit) argues that despite the media playing significant roles in conflict situations, the effect of media interventions' on peace processes is not well documented. And as Gordon Adam and Lina Holguin point out (2003):

> Bearing in mind the proliferation of local and regional conflicts since the end of the Cold War, along with the emergence of new communications technologies, the interaction of media and conflict is likely to be a growth activity. What is needed is an academic institution to monitor this field and publish action research. There also needs to be much more research into an evaluation methodology which can help determine the media's impact in the peace-building process. This would need to be an innovative, participatory methodology that could be used by production teams as well as specialist evaluators.

Thirdly, journalists need to be aware of their own weaknesses and biases. They are a product of society and hence not free from their own biases and misperceptions which are ingrained in their minds from childhood. These biases might not be prominent in conflicts where they can act as "outside observers" but when faced in conflicts which challenge their own ideologies and beliefs as individuals or citizens these biases are reflected in their language and approach to the issue. Moreover, journalists who are able to shed their biases and develop sensitivity towards conflict situations do so after years of working in actual conflict situations and have started questioning the role of media in it. The sensitivity towards social conflicts and situations along with the knowledge about concepts such as *resolution* and *prevention* need to be developed among journalism students within the classroom along with other journalistic values.

And finally it is in classroom that the basic journalistic professional values and practices are ingrained in the students. What makes the news? Or who makes the news? Most of the text books on journalism would answer "conflict" to the first question and "important people" to the second. Can such an approach, which judges the value of a news item in terms of the numbers of deaths or the position of a person speaking, make room for the slow process of peace building or be a voice of the people at grass root level against the high profile politicians or officials? John Paul Lederach (1997: 94), a noted peace researcher, says that mainstream media tends to marginalise "people at grass root from the conflict simply by giving more emphasis to the 'official sources' ":

> I have not experienced any situation of conflict...where there have not been people who had a vision for peace, emerging often from their own experience of pain. Far too often, however, these same people are overlooked and disempowered either because they do not represent "official" power, whether on the side of government or the various militias, or because they are written off as biased and too personally affected by the conflict.

Journalists Lynch and McGoldrick (2005) believe that such "conceptual reforms" are "necessary to modernise the study of journalism, as taught to journalism students; a contribution to problematising elements of journalistic practice which pass unexamined in many current courses". Their course on peace journalism is taught in many universities of the world including Australia, UK and USA as part of peace and conflict studies. It is designed mainly to provide a theoretical understanding of violence, peace and conflict in societies along with the media dynamics for the students of journalism, peace studies and international relations.

> If there is one real skill in peace journalism it lies in tracing connections between the stories of people…and the big issues and eye catching events of the day – showing how the actions and concerns of individuals bear indirectly on the personal fortunes of every reader, listener or viewer. To do that journalists need to be able to draw upon a deep understanding of how conflicts develop and how people can respond to them in ways likely to reduce the risk of violence (ibid).

Hence the course delves deep into Galtung's ideas relating to cultural and "structural violence", Noam Chomsky's propaganda model and the role of the media as a social agent for peace (ibid).

The model curricula for journalism education prepared by UNESCO in 2007 is another important initiative. Available at http://unesdoc.unesco.org/images/0015/001512/151209E.pdf, these curricula for undergraduate and postgraduate programmes were designed by some of the top journalism educators in the world "to be adaptable to just about any situation". The curricula have three categories: professional practice, journalism studies and arts and science. They advance the concept that a democracy is based on the free flow of information which represents the full spectrum of the community. These model curricula have been translated into French, Spanish Arabic, Russian and several other languages and widely distributed among journalism schools in both developing countries and countries in transition. UNESCO has also developed a Freedom of Expression Toolkit for secondary school students in post-conflict societies.

A somewhat different initiative which is partly academic in nature is the Deutsche Welle's series of Global Media Forum. Starting in 2008, the symposium takes place regularly in Bonn. The main agenda items change but the event always addresses ways to cope with the professionalisation of journalists. At the first forum, with the theme of "Journalistic training in conflict situations", experts and scholars in journalism were brought together along with the media representatives and internationally experienced trainers from all over the world. The forum provided a central platform for those present to share their experiences and discuss the central theme of what qualifications and know-how journalists need in order to contribute to peace and conflict de-escalation. In 2009, the topic was "Bridging the digital divide – how to prepare your staff".

Challenges and dangers

Journalistic training in conflict resolution is urgently needed, but there are clearly many challenges and dangers to be faced. The first is the digital revolution. Several factors affect the training of journalists in the digital world making it a more complicated and complex phenomenon. The digital revolution and advances in satellite technology have given people unprecedented access to global events, with immediate and detailed reporting of war now possible. And while new media technologies do not alter the fundamental tenets of journalism, they do change user behaviour and hence news room paradigms, discussions and decisions. Today, speed and user participation share the same media priorities: authenticity, balance and accuracy.

The nature of information has also changed being more entertaining, interactive and instantaneous: for instance, blogs, vlogs, SMS and now Twitters. It transcends the conventional geographical boundaries and hence has the capacity to absorb audiences at a global level. Therefore, the ability to view issues from a global perspective while connecting to local sources and understanding the local context, would be a critical aspect of any future journalism education. This includes mixing with people of different cultures, living in different countries, learning various languages and understanding local sensitivities.

The second challenge is more theoretical in nature. Dr Vladimir Bratic and Dr Lisa Schirch (2008) argue that despite an "optimistic shift" of media in conflict, the debate about the media's role in peace-making leaves many questions unanswered: "The theoretical argument for the media's impact on peace is underdeveloped, the practical projects are vastly scattered and a systematic analysis of the practice is missing." While they acknowledge the "positive media engagement" in conflict prevention and peace-building, they argue:

> A central question in the discussion about those principles revolves around the question of how far journalists should go in advocating peace, but these discussions do little but reiterate old debates about the role of social responsibility model of the press....While this discussion has its place, its universal and philosophical nature tends to *divert and dilute the discussion* and it rarely leads

toward a broader and more comprehensive understanding of the media (ibid, emphasis added).

Bratic and Schirch acknowledge that the media impact on conflict and peace increases "when a greater number of media strategies are employed". This could be done by "peace and conflict-sensitive *journalism*; peace promoting *entertainment media*; *advertising or social marketing* for conflict prevention and peace building; and *media regulation* to prevent the incitement of violence" (2008, emphasis added). Many organisations are already working on one or more of these strategies such as:

- documentaries competitions (UNESCO, NICR Canada);
- joint television productions (between India and Pakistan by Asia-Pacific Institute for Broadcasting Development);
- community radio programmes and dramas (BBC Radio's *New home: New life* in Afghanistan and Pakistan, Oxfam Quebec's *Radio Galkayo* in Somalia, *The new neighbours* in Columbia, and USAID-funded *Our neighbours, ourselves* in Rwanda, *Song of peace* in Angola to mention just a few).

The important factor in all these initiatives is that they are pro-active, reconciliatory and designed to counter the "hate media".

Other problems related to the journalistic training in conflict affected areas particularly in the war affected countries include lack of resources, non availability of local expertise plus infrastructure and severe security threat to journalists' lives. For instance, all the training of Iraqi journalists is conducted either in the neighbouring countries or in Europe due to the daily risk to life which makes such training ventures not only extremely expensive but also condensed in time and content. There is also the danger of heavy reliance on foreign expertise which further pulls the training out of its cultural context.

A unique case in the analysis of journalistic training in conflict resolution emerges from the "war on terror" being fought in Pakistan's tribal areas. These areas lie in the remote region of the North West of Pakistan bordering Afghanistan. Despite being the epicentre of the conflict, there is no access for Pakistani or foreign journalists to cover the conflict. The local journalists not only face death everyday but are also looked upon with mistrust by the government. On 16 June 2006, journalist Hayatullah Khan, who was kidnapped by gunmen six months previously, was shot in North Waziristan. A reporter for the English language daily *The Nation* and the Urdu newspaper, *Ausaf,* he was also the general secretary of the Tribal Union of Journalists (TUJ) and had been covering the war in Waziristan since the beginning. His family and many others believe he was kidnapped and detained by the security agencies for his reporting on US military action in tribal areas. On the other hand, the local Taliban's approach towards the media is even worse. They are hostile to the presence of any outside media person considering them all "Western spies" (Dietz 2006).

Suba Chandran (2006) reported that, while the murder of Daniel Pearl (South Asia bureau chief of the *Wall Street Journal*) in February 2002 attracted much attention and occupied the headlines, the Taliban ban on media in the region had gone largely unnoticed. For instance, two journalists working for the *Frontier Post* and Khyber TV, Amir Nawab Khan and Allah Noor Wazir, were killed in Wana town by militants in February 2005. Others were luckier: Dilawar Khan Wazir, a Wana-based journalist working with BBC World Service, was warned with a bomb in his compound after he participated in a Voice of America show in December 2005. "Militants have repeatedly issued threats against any adverse reports, both in the electronic and print media" (ibid).

Other media-related NGOs such as Internews Pakistan reported in June 2006 that at least 20 journalists in the tribal areas were killed, kidnapped, arrested, tortured or threatened by the local administration, the law enforcement agencies and Taliban all during the first six months of the conflict. The Pakistan Press Freedom Report (2007) concluded that "most journalists in tribal areas have either been forced to give up their profession or leave their home town. The few that remain, limit their coverage to innocuous topics such as school functions and activities of administration officers".

Since then, the only source of information left in these tribal areas is provided by the Inter Services Public Relations (ISPR) which is the army's official agency. Its news credibility remains questionable as most of it is written in and disseminated not from the conflicted areas but its offices in Islamabad. ISPR has claimed dozens of Taliban leaders have been killed yet not a single photograph has been released to the press. It has claimed the tribal area of Swat has been cleared of all Taliban elements yet the Radio News Network reported on 21 July 2009 the Taliban were running an FM radio station – just days after the internally displaced people (IDPs) from the valley were allowed to go back to their homes. (Before the military operation in Swat began in April 2009, an estimated 88 FM radio stations were estimated to be operating illegally in the area, mostly by the Taliban.)

Clearly the problems facing a media aiming to promote peace in this situation are vast: when its engagement in the conflict is nil; when there is no information available about the human suffering and when no images are captured to evoke audience emotions. Moreover, how can journalists play a positive role in the tribal areas such as Waziristan when the community, the Taliban and security forces are violently opposed to their very presence?

Conclusion

The world today is faced with many political, economic and ideological conflicts. There is no denying that the media has been playing a significant role in conflict situations. Yet, as identified here, there is a wide range of journalistic training projects taking place in the world that are aiming to develop the media's role in conflict resolution. At present, there is a great disparity in the various parts of the world regarding the media's access to conflict. While the developed world is talking about training journalists in a complex digital world, the simple task of the media gaining access to conflict in war-ridden countries such as Iraq and Pakistan is daunting.

Most of the peace-building initiatives in other parts of the world (such as Colombia, Rwanda and Serbia) started when conflict had crossed its peak point and the local communities were ready to start life anew. This does raise questions regarding the ability of the media to engage in peace-building efforts without any community support as in the tribal areas of Pakistan where none of the three fighting parties – the Taliban, the locals and the security forces – are willing to work with journalists. The support, readiness and will of the people in local communities might very well be the major factor in determining the effectiveness of the media's role in conflict resolution and peace building. As Javed Mottaghi (2008) concludes:

> I do not believe that we change anything in the globe until we first change ourselves. I certainly feel that the most important challenge of the day for us as journalists is how to bring about a revolution in our hearts and minds, a revolution which has to start with each one of us. Could this be done by training? Perhaps. But it has to come from our hearts and minds.

References

Adam, Gordon and Holguin, Lina (2003) *The media's role in peace building: Asset or liability?* Paper presented to the Our Media 3 conference, Barranquilla, Colombia

Allan, Stuart (2007) Citizen journalism and the rise of "mass-self communication": Reporting the London bombings, *Global Media Journal*, Australian edition, Vol. 1, No. 1. Available online at http://stc.uws.edu.au/gmjau/iss1_2007/pdf/HC_FINAL_Stuart%20Allan.pdf, accessed on 17 June 2009

Bell, Martin (1998), The journalism of attachment, Kieran, Matthew (ed.) *Media ethics*, London: Routledge pp 15–22

Botes, Jannie (2000) *Regional media in conflict*. Paper presented at the Institute for War and Peace Reporting, London

Bratic, Vladimir and Schirch, Lisa (2008) *The role of media in peace building: Theory and practice*. Paper presented at symposium on journalistic training in conflict relation situations, DW-AKADEMIE, Bonn, 3 June 2008. Available online at http://www. kubatana.net/docs/media/dw_journalistsic_training_symposium_2008.pdf, accessed on 21 July 2009

Brosius, Hans-Bernd and Weimann, Gabriel (1996) Who sets the agenda? Agenda-setting as a two-step flow, *Communication Research*, Vol. 23, No.5 pp 561–580

Chandran, Suba (2006) *Waziristan: Taliban, state and media*, Institute of Peace and Conflict Studies, 23 June 2006. Available online at http://www.ipcs.org/articledetails. php?articleNo=2048, accessed on 23 July 2009

Chattarji, Subarno (2006) *Negative reportage in Indo-Pak media*. Available online at http:// www.thehoot.org/web/home/story.php?storyid=1985&pg=1&mod=1&sectionId= 38&sectionname=INDO%20PAK%20MONITORING&valid=true, accessed on 27 March 2007

Dietz, Bob (2006) The last story: Hayatullah Khan, Committee to Protest Journalists. Available online at http://cpj.org/reports/2006/09/khan.php; accessed on 1 May 2009-11-27

Entman, Robert M. (1993) Framing: Toward clarification of a fractured paradigm, *Journal of Communication*, Vol. 43, No. 4 pp 51–8

Hedges, Chris (2002) *War is a force that gives us meaning*, New York: Public Affairs

Hedges, Chris (2008) *Ault keynote speaker*, International conference on media, war and conflict, Bowling Green State University, Bowling Green, Ohio, 18 September

Howard, Ross (2003) *The media's role in war and peace building*. Paper presented to conference on the role of media in public scrutiny and democratic oversight of the security sector, Budapest

Internews, Pakistan (2006) *Half yearly report on attacks on media*. *Available online at* www. internews.org.pk/HalfYearly%20reportabout%20attackson%20media.doc accessed on 23 July 2009-11-27

Lederach, John Paul (1997) *Building peace–sustainable reconciliation in divided societies*, United States Institute of Peace Press, Washington

Lynch, Jake and McGoldrick, Annabel (2001) *Reporting the world*, London: Conflict and Peace Forum

Lynch, Jake and McGoldrick, Annabel (2005) *Peace journalism*, Stroud: Hawthorn Press

Lynch, Jake (2008) *Debates in peace journalism*, Sydney: Sydney University Press

Mottaghi, Javed (2008) *Media diversity: Training for a digital world*. Paper presented at symposium on journalistic training in conflict situations, DW-AKADEMIE, Bonn, 3 June 2008. Available online at http://www.kubatana.net/docs/media/

dw_journalistsic_training_symposium_2008.pdf, accessed on 21 July 2009

Ninan, Sevanti (2007) *Those barbarians in Pakistan.* Available online at http://www.thehoot. org/web/home/searchdetail.php?sid=2510&bg=1, accessed on 10 April 2008

Pakistan Press Foundation (2007) Pakistan press freedom report. Available online at http://www.pakistanpressfoundation.org/userRAndDDetails.asp?uid=248, accessed on 23 July 2009

Rhodes, Richard (2008) *Florence and Jesse Currier keynote address,* International conference on media, war and conflict, Bowling Green State University, Bowling Green, Ohio, 18 September

Schramm, Wilbur (1993) *Mass communication readings: The nature of news,* Illinois: University of Illinois Press

Sethi, Najam (1999) *Media at the millennium; India.* A talk at the India Media Forum. Available online at http://www.freedomforum.org/publications/international/ MediaForum/1999/asia/indiaforum.pdf, accessed on 29 March 2007

Singh, Shubha (2007) *The Indian media's Pakistan obsession.* Available online at http:// www.thehoot.org/web/home/story.php?storyid=2517&pg=1&mod=1&sectionId=3 8&valid=true, accessed on 10 April 2008

Thibeault, Stephen (2000) *Kashmir: Aborted cease-fire provides fodder for Indo-Pak media war.* Available online at http://www.fas.org/news/india/2000/war-000818-kashmir_ comment.htm, accessed on 29 March 2007

UNESCO (2007) Model curricula for journalism education. Available online at http:// unesdoc.unesco.org/images/0015/001512/151209E.pdf, accessed on 23 July 2009

Wolsfeld, Gadi (1997) *Media and political conflict: News from the Middle-East,* Cambridge: Cambridge University Press

Web sources

Asia-Pacific Institute for Broadcasting Development. Available online at http://www.aibd. org.my, accessed on 21 July 2009

Crimes of War Project. Available online at www.crimesofwar.org, accessed on 18 July 2009

Dart Centre Europe. Available online at http://www. dartcenter.org/europe, *accessed on 21 July 2009*

DW: *Report on symposium on journalistic training in conflict situations,* DW-AKADEMIE, Bonn, 3 June 2008. Available online at http://www.kubatana.net/docs/media/dw_ journalistsic_training_symposium_2008.pdf, accessed on 21 July 2009

International Institute for Journalism. Available online at http://www.inwent.org/iij/index. php.en, accessed on 23 July 2009

Internews: Pakistan. Available online at http://www.internews.org.pk, *accessed on 23 July 2009*

InWENT – Capacity Building International, Germany. Available online at http://www.inwent.org/portal/internationale_zusammenarbeit/frieden/friedensentwicklung/index.php.en, accessed on 23 July 2009

Medios Para La Paz (Media for Peace). Available at http://www.mediosparalapaz.org/index.php?idcategoria=2240, accessed on 18 July 2009

Preamble to UNESCO Constitution: Available online at http://typo38.unesco.org/pt/unesco-home/organization/about-unesco-srtct/constitution.html, accessed on 23 July 200

Afterword

JEFFERY KLAEHN

The essays presented in this volume are authored by leading international writers, journalists, theorists and campaigners working within the fields of peace journalism and communication studies. These highly-regarded international contributors not only provide a definitive, up-to-date, critical overview of central issues concerning theory, international practice, and critiques of mainstream media performance from a peace perspective: by creating and then opening new windows, and by mapping new crossroads, the contributors have (collectively) created what is, in essence, a benchmark collection that offers new understandings of what peace journalism fundamentally is while concurrently affording new opportunities for renewed critical engagement and debate.

The chapters in the first section explore how media and journalism practice are understood and theorised within academic discourses. Clifford G. Christians explores non-violence as an ethical principle in relation to journalism and media practice. Oliver Boyd-Barrett's chapter offers a wonderful historical overview, charting how different schools of thought have advanced competing ways of understanding media. This chapter also provides empirical analysis of media coverage of the "war on terror" and makes a valuable contribution to the range of existing scholarship on the "propaganda model" of media operations developed and advanced by Edward S. Herman and Noam Chomsky (1988) in their classic work, *Manufacturing consent: The political economy of the mass media.* Richard Lance Keeble's chapter critically engages with the intellectual history of media and communication studies, highlighting its multiplicity of focus and interdisciplinary origins, while investigating the concept of journalistic neutrality in relation to both political context and political practice. The chapter by Jake Lynch, which closes this section of the book, deploys critical discourse analysis to highlight how media and power connect with various circuits of the communicative process. This chapter illuminates the dialectic between power and ideology and explores ways in which media and political discourses intersect. Theoretically-rich, lively and engaging, these opening chapters explore theoretical, epistemological and political issues that are of central importance towards developing new perspectives on peace journalism, while also enabling new insights into how social communication, cultural politics and public pedagogy intersect. Beyond this, they set out the foundations for the chapters that follow.

This collection is notable and important in the first instance for three reasons:

1. the strength of the theoretical and original empirical analysis presented above in the various chapters of the book is exemplary and will afford new opportunities for students and scholars alike to pursue new areas of scholarly investigation in the future;
2. peace journalism as a distinct field of study is growing and this collection represents an essential roadmap of the discipline;
3. the collection is international in scope and the individual chapters enable new understandings of how mainstream media work, how discourse phenomena play out in specific time/place contexts, and how communicative power links with political and material (economic) power, cultural politics and basic democratic principles.

Recall a key point made by John Pilger in his thought-provoking introduction to the book: that mainstream media are "committed almost exclusively to the interests of power, not people". The contributors demonstrate how social communication and journalism intersect with power, explore ways in which power meets meaning within media discourses, and investigate how communicative power plays out into various circuits of the communicative process, directly and indirectly interfacing with political and economic power. The contributors also highlight how political-economic elements influence overall patterns of media performance, consistent with the interests of power.

In addition to offering new theoretical insights and valuable empirical analysis, the contributors have detailed ways in which ideology and communicative power connect with social class and social inequalities in both domestic and global contexts. In addition to analysing the realities and perceptions of peace journalism, the contributors highlight ways in which media connect with hegemonic and social control, cultural politics and the broader issue of public education. The collection as a whole enables critical literacy and creates necessary pathways that future scholarship will now be able to explore.

To engage with even the most basic questions about the contemporary social order, it is necessary to understand how ideological power connects with political-economic dimensions of power. What makes this collection so very notable and important in the final instance is its international focus and the range of the scholarship presented. The editors deserve much praise for bringing together such a diverse range of outstanding international contributors, and for organising the book as they have. They have succeeded in creating a book that is outstanding, and I've no doubt that this collection will be widely influential. More importantly, though, the editors and contributors have created a book that for many different reasons is also very necessary.

List of Contributors

Sevda Alankus is Professor and Dean of the Faculty of Communication at Izmir University of Economics. As former Dean of the Faculty of Communication and Media Studies at Eastern Mediterranean University, she set up the Center of Peace and Communication Research. A project initiator, researcher and project coordinator on a variety of media monitoring and training initiatives, she also promotes human, women's and children's rights-focused reporting.

Valerie Alia is Adjunct Professor in the Doctor of Social Sciences programme at Royal Roads University, Victoria, BC (Canada) and Visiting Professor in the Centre for Research into Diversity in the Professions and former Professor of Ethics and Identity at Leeds Metropolitan University. She is known internationally for defining the discipline of political onomastics (politics of naming) and for her work in media ethics, Arctic and Indigenous communications. She has a PhD in social and political thought from York University (Canada); was the inaugural Distinguished Professor of Canadian Culture at Western Washington University; a Senior Associate of the Scott Polar Research Institute, Cambridge; and a journalist in the US and Canada. She is Media Topics series editor for Edinburgh University Press and author of *The new media nation: Indigenous peoples and global communication* (2009), *Names and Nunavut: Culture and identity in Arctic Canada* (2007), *Media ethics and social change* (2005) and *Un/Covering the North: News, media and Aboriginal people* (1999).

Stuart Allan is Professor of Journalism in the Media School at Bournemouth University, UK. He has a longstanding interest in the news reporting of war, conflict and crises. Related books include *Journalism after September 11* (with Barbie Zelizer,

2002), *Reporting war: Journalism in wartime* (with Zelizer, 2004), *Online news: Journalism and the internet* (2006), *Digital war reporting* (with Donald Matheson, 2009) and *Citizen journalism: Global perspectives* (with Einar Thorsen, 2009).

Rukhsana Aslam, a graduate from City University (UK), has more than ten years' experience in the mainstream media and eight years' in higher education in Pakistan. From 1991 to 2000 she was a staff correspondent of the national daily, the *News*, and a freelance for the BBC's Urdu Service, Bush House London, Pakistan Television and GEO TV. From 2000 she has been a media academic at the Fatima Jinnah Women's University, Rawalpindi, and at Hamdard University, Islamabad. Currently she is the Chair at the Centre for Media and Communication Studies, International Islamic University, Women's Campus, Islamabad. In August 2006, she set up the university's FM radio station, Voice of Women, in collaboration with USAID and Internews. She is one of the founding members and former information secretary of the Britannia Alumni Association of Pakistan (BAAP) which networks the Pakistan scholars who studied in the UK on awards and scholarships. She is currently pursuing her PhD in media and conflict resolution at Auckland University of Technology (AUT), NewZealand.

Oliver Boyd-Barrett graduated from Exeter University (UK) and acquired his PhD from the Open University (UK). He has published extensively on international communication, particularly concerning the operations of the international and national news agencies. In recent years he has turned his attention to media coverage of the "war on terror". Boyd-Barrett was founding director of the graduate distance learning programme of the Centre for Mass Communication Research at the University of Leicester (UK). He is currently Professor of Journalism at Bowling Green State University, Ohio.

Clifford G. Christians is Professor of Communications at University of Illinois-Urbana, the current Director of the Institute of Communications Research and Chair of the doctoral programme in communications, a position he also held from 1987 to 2001. He has been a visiting scholar in philosophical ethics at Princeton University, in social ethics at the University of Chicago, and a PEW fellow in ethics at Oxford University. On the faculty at Illinois since 1974, Christians has won five teaching awards. His teaching interests are in the philosophy of technology, dialogic communication theory, and media ethics. He has published essays on various aspects of mass communication (including professional ethics) in *Journalism Monographs*, *Journal of Broadcasting*, *Journalism History*, *Ethical Perspectives: Journal of the European Ethics Network*, *Ethical Space: The International Journal of*

Communication Ethics, Journal of Communication, Journal of Mass Media Ethics, Media Development, Communication, Qualitative Inquiry, European Journal of Communication and the *International Journal of Mass Communication Research*. He is a member of the Society for Philosophy and Technology and has authored several essays on communications technology for its publications. He serves on the editorial boards of a dozen academic journals, is the former editor of *Critical Studies in Media Communication*, and currently edits *The Ellul Forum*. He has lectured or given academic papers in such countries as Belgium, Norway, Russia, Finland, Taiwan, Germany, France, Italy, Netherlands, Switzerland, Belgium, England, Singapore, Korea, Scotland, Philippines, Slovenia, Canada, Brazil, Mexico, Puerto Rico, Spain, and Sweden.

David Edwards is co-editor of Media Lens (www.medialens.org). He is the author of *Free to be human* (Green Books, 1995) and *The compassionate revolution* (Green Books, 1998). He is also co-author with David Cromwell of *Guardians of power* (Pluto Press, 2006) and *Newspeak in the 21st century* (Pluto Press, 2009).

Agneta Söderberg Jacobson is a journalist, media trainer and consultant media activist with the Kvinna till Kvinna Foundation, a peace and women's rights organisation that supports women's peace initiatives and works for women's human rights in conflict-affected areas. She is currently working for Fojo Media Development Institute, a media-training institute based in Sweden. Her publications include *Russian voices* (1999), *Rethink! – a handbook for sustainable peace* (2003), *Security – on whose terms?* (2005) and *Reporting on women in war and conflict* (2006).

Richard Lance Keeble is Professor of Journalism at the University of Lincoln. He previously taught in the journalism department at City University, London, for 19 years. He has written and edited 14 publications including *Secret state, silent press: New militarism, the Gulf and the modern image of warfare* (John Libbey, 1997), *The newspapers handbook* (Oxon, Routledge 2005, fourth edition) and *Ethics for journalists* (Oxon, Routledge 2008, second edition). He edited *Print journalism: A critical introduction* (Routledge 2005), co-edited *The journalistic imagination: Literary journalists from Defoe to Capote and Carter* (Routledge 2007) and *Communicating war: Memory, media and military* (Arima 2007). He is also the joint editor of *Ethical Space: The International Journal of Communication Ethics*.

Jeffery Klaehn is a widely published author and cultural commentator. His scholarly writings have been published in international peer-reviewed journals, including the *European Journal of Communication, International Communication Gazette, Journalism Studies* and the *Westminster Papers in Communication and culture* (WPCC). He holds a PhD from the University of Amsterdam (2007) and is currently completing a second PhD from the University of Stathcylde. He has compiled, edited and contributed to several books that are centrally concerned to explore ways in which media and hegemonic power interface with politics and strucutural inequalities, including *Filtering the news: Essays on Herman and Chomsky's propaganda model* (2005), Bound by *power: Intended consequences* (2006), *Roadblocks to equality: women challenging boundaries* (2008) and *The politocal economy of media and power* (2010). His research interests include pop culture, media, political economy, power, social inequality, education, and human rights. His current research explores the dialectic between communicative power, social class and cultural politics. He is a member of the editorial boards for the *Journal of Global Mass communication, ImageText: Interdisciplinary Comics Studies and Fifth-Estate-Online: The International Journal of Media Criticism*. He has published widely online and has contributed pieces to *Publishers Weekly*, the Graphic Novel Reporter, and Swans Commentary. He lives and works out of Kitchener, Ontorio, Canada, and he maintains a personal blog that includes links to his online publications.

Jake Lynch is Associate Professor, Director of the Centre for Peace and Conflict Studies at the University of Sydney, and co-author, with Annabel McGoldrick, of *Peace journalism* (Hawthorn Press, 2005). He has also written numerous book chapters and scholarly articles and two educational documentaries, *News from the Holy Land* (Hawthorn Press and Films for the Humanities, 2004) and *Peace journalism in the Philippines* (2007). Previously he was a professional journalist. He worked as a presenter and reporter for BBC World, a political correspondent for Sky News and as Sydney correspondent for the *Independent* newspaper. He is co-convenor of the Peace Journalism Commission of the International Peace Research Association, a member of the Advisory Panel of the Sydney Peace Foundation and of the International Advisory Council of the Toda Institute for Global Peace and Policy Research. He has led training workshops for editors and reporters in many countries including the UK, Indonesia, the Philippines, Norway, Nepal, Armenia and Georgia. He and Annabel McGoldrick are investigating prospects for a global standard for reporting conflict for the Australian Research Council, in partnership with the International Federation of Journalists and Act for Peace. He is chair of the Organising committee for the 2010 conference of the International Peace Research Association, an executive member of the Sydney Peace Foundation and serves on the International Advisory council of the Toda Institute for Global Peace and Policy Research.

Donald Matheson is Senior Lecturer in Media and Communication at the University of Canterbury, New Zealand. Among his publications are *Media discourses* (2005) and *Digital war reporting* (with Stuart Allan, 2009). He co-edits the journal *Ethical Space* (with Richard Lance Keeble). He writes on journalism practices, with particular emphasis on news discourse and the communicative ethics of the news, interests that have led him to study weblogs and other digital media. He previously worked at Cardiff and Strathclyde universities in the UK and as a journalist in New Zealand.

Sarah Maltby is a lecturer in Sociology at City University, London. Her research agenda focuses on the intersection of media, war and terrorism with particular regard to contemporary military and media practice. This includes the tactical and strategic role of mediated information in the implementation of security provision, institutional information management in conflict, and the impact of mediated information on social behaviour in conflict scenarios. Dr Maltby is the founder and co-ordinator of the War and Media Network (ww.warandmedia.org) which is an online resource and networking forum that promotes productive dialogue between academics and practitioners interested in the intersection between war, terrorism and the media. She co-edited *Communicating war: Memory, military and media* (Arima, 2008) with Richard Lance Keeble which locates the emergence of recent wars and terrorist activity in a wide frame of global socio-political change.

Annabel McGoldrick is a television reporter, currently for World News Australia on SBS. She is co-author, with Jake Lynch, of *Peace journalism* (Hawthorn Press, 2005), and a part time lecturer at the Centre for Peace and Conflict Studies at the University of Sydney. She has led peace journalism training workshops for professional editors and reporters in many countries. She is also a qualified psychotherapist working with families to help resolve their conflicts.

Jean Lee C. Patindol was the National Coordinator of the Peace and Conflict Journalism Network (PECOJON) in the Philippines from 1 April 2006 to 31 March 2009, where she was also a founding member and volunteer since 2004. She works full-time as an Assistant Professor at the University of St. La Salle in Bacolod City, Philippines, where she teaches economics, communications, journalism and popular culture courses. She is a member of the World Futures Studies Federation, Pax Christi Pilipinas, Pax Christi International and the International Peace Research Association (IPRA). She is also a multi-awarded children's book author in the Philippines.

John Pilger is the most acclaimed journalist of his generation. As well as campaigning print journalism, he has produced many award-winning television documentaries and written and edited a range of important books (for full details see www.johnpilger.com). He also has a regular column in the *New Statesman*.

Marlis Prinzing is Professor of Journalism at the Macromedia University of Applied Studies in Cologne, Germany, and lecturer at the University of Fribourg, Switzerland. She was project director at the European Journalism Observatory and then web-editor. Prinzing studied Political Science, History and Mathematics at the universities of Regensburg and Tuebingen, all this time working as professional journalist.

Milan Rai is the author of *Chomsky's politics* (Verso, 1995), *War plan Iraq* (Verso, 2002), *Regime unchanged* (Pluto, 2003) and *7/7: The London bombings, Islam and the Iraq War* (Pluto, 2006). He became a co-editor of *Peace News* in March 2007 – 25 years after becoming a *Peace News* seller at his English secondary school. Arrested more than twenty times for peace activism, once for breaking sanctions on Iraq (by attempting to take children's medicines on a peace delegation), he has served four brief prison sentences, the last of them in August 2007, in HMP Wandsworth, south London.

Susan Dente Ross holds a PhD in mass communication and serves as Professor of English at Washington State University. An expert in media representation, peace journalism and press freedom, she trains journalists around the world and publishes widely on issues of media, identity, and inter-communal and international conflict. A Fulbright Scholar and author/ editor of three books, her scholarship appears in a wide variety of communication and law journals. Dr. Ross has been a Faculty Fellow at the University of the Aegean in Greece, at Netanya Academic College in Israel, at Eastern Mediterranean University in North Cyprus, and at the University of Calgary's Consortium for Peace Studies. She is a principal investigator in several peace journalism research groups, including PAXIM.

Pratap Rughani is an award-winning documentary film-maker with thirty broadcast credits for BBC TV, Channel 4 and the British Council, including *New model army*, Channel 4 (1999, RIMA award 2000 and shortlisted for the Grierson Contemporary Documentary Award) and *Glass houses* (2004). His work includes gallery collaborations such as *The botanist* (Museum of Modern Art, Oxford, May 2009). He is Course Director for Documentary Film MA at the London College of Communication (University of the Arts, London) and has a particular interest in how documentary film can evolve as a tool for mediation.

Stephan Russ-Mohl has been Professor of Journalism and Media Management at the Facolt di Scienze della Comunicazione, Universite della Svizzera italiana, Lugano; since October 2003, Director of the European Journalism Observatory from 1985 to 2001, and Professor of Journalism and Media Management at the Institut fur Publizistik und Kommunikationswissenschaften, Freie Universitet Berlin. Since 1986 he has been Director of the Continuing Education Programme for Journalists at the Freie Universitet Berlin. Since 1989 he has taken up a number of Visiting Fellowships, for instance at Stanford University, the European University Institute, Florence, Italy; and at the University of Wisconsin, Madison, USA.

John Tulloch is Professor of Journalism and Head of the School of Journalism, University of Lincoln. Previously he was chair of the Department of Journalism and Mass Communication at the University of Westminster. Recent work includes jointly editing, with Colin Sparks, *Tabloid tales* (Maryland: Rowman and Littlefield 2000) to which he contributed the essay "The eternal recurrence of the New Journalism". He has written on press regulation, official news management, popular television and the press's coverage of the "war on terror". He has also had a chapter on the journalism of Charles Dickens in *The journalistic imagination: Literary journalists from Defoe to Capote and Carter* (edited by Richard Lance Keeble and Sharon Wheeler, Routledge, 2007).

James Winter, PhD., is Professor in the Department of Communication, Media and Film, at the University of Windsor, Ontario, Canada. He has published extensively on the role played by the mainstream media in a social construction of reality which supports hegemony, inequality and elite power relations. His recent books include *Lies the media tell us* (2007) and *MediaThink* (2002), both published by Black Rose Books of Montreal.

Florian Zollmann is studying for a PhD at Lincoln University's School of Journalism. In his dissertation he analyses how the mainstream press represents US/UK warfare in Iraq. His main research interests are press coverage of Western foreign policy in the Middle East and propaganda studies. He has recently written for *Ethical Space: The International Journal of Communication Ethics*, and is also a contributor to the German independent magazine *Publik-Forum* where he is a blogger as well as a regular writer and internet editor for its young adult supplement *Provo*.

Index